A Constellation of Courts
The Courts and Households of Habsburg Europe, 1555-1665

A Constellation of Courts

The Courts and Households of Habsburg Europe, 1555-1665

Edited by
René Vermeir, Dries Raeymaekers,
and José Eloy Hortal Muñoz

LEUVEN UNIVERSITY PRESS

ISBN 978 90 5867 990 1
e-ISBN 978 94 6166 132 6
D / 2014 / 1869 / 47
NUR: 685, 697

Cover illustration: Lucas I van Valckenborgh, "Frühlingslandschaft (Mai)",
(inv. Nr. GG 1065), Kunsthistorisches Museum Vienna
Typesetting: Friedemann BVBA

GPRC
Guaranteed
Peer Reviewed
Content
www.gprc.be

Contents

Courts and households of the Habsburg dynasty: history and historiography

The cultural movements, political doctrines and ideologies that emerged in Europe starting in the thirteenth century shared particular features and structures because they arose from a common court culture, and the courts of European monarchs achieved unquestionable political pre-eminence amongst the different forces that both characterised and shaped the social configurations found in the *Ancien Régime*[1]. However, this culture was gradually eroded during the nineteenth century, when the rise of the nation-state increasingly called the court's political relevance into question. The bourgeois elites who gained power tried to legitimize this new political structure through the creation of anachronistic national histories, which posited that not only did the origins of individual nations lie in the remote past, but that they were more or less unchanged in the present. As a result, the image of the court became deformed in this ideologically motivated literature, turning into a grotesque caricature of itself: a setting for palace intrigues, sumptuous extravagance, immoral behaviour and the exercise of absolute power.

The historiography did not begin to reprise this interpretation of the court and its role in history until a number of researchers working both inside and outside Europe began studying aspects of the early modern era through the lens of the court, rather than the nation-state. First came *The Court Society*, the pioneering study of Norbert Elias, published in 1969[2]. Then, in 1977, Arthur G. Dickens edited an ambitious volume whose novelty consisted in making a thorough comparative study in order to define the phenomenon of the court in space and time. The courts analysed were chosen "not simply because these courts typified these periods, but also in order to display the rich contrast of styles which could mark near-contemporaries"[3]. The historiographical genre of 'Court Studies' was born, and one year later, Carlo Ossola concluded

[1] Regarding the concept of the court as a political organisation, see: José Martínez Millán, "La corte de la Monarquía hispánica," *Studia Histórica, Historia Moderna*, 28 (2006), 17-61.

[2] Norbert Elias, *The Court Society* (Oxford, 1984 English version, original in German 1969).

[3] Artur G. Dickens (ed.), *The Courts of Europe. Politics, Patronage and Royalty, 1400-1800* (London, 1977), 7.

that understanding this institution was essential for understanding the early modern period[4].

After 1985, when Cesare Mozzarelli characterized the court as a political institution that had defined a large chunk of European history[5], 'the court' became an unavoidable topic in any research into early modern governance. A series of investigations were initiated that took the court as a starting point for analysing government relations and the informal organization of power, as well as the anthropological and the cultural aspects of court etiquette and ritual[6]. The year 1994 marked the complete reversal of the nation-state distortion in the literature. In a publication that resulted from a conference on the origins of the modern state, Marcello Fantoni made it clear that the concept of court could not be anachronistically approached from the perspective of the nation state because it was an authoritative institution with its own unique characteristics[7]. And its inclusion at such a symposium was, as Trevor Dean stated in the same volume, "the clearest demonstration of the long route undertaken by the Court Studies during the last twenty years"[8].

Another step was made in 1988 with the publication of a volume edited by Maurice Aymard and Marzio A. Romani that focused on the economic aspects of the court[9]. Until that point the court had been the object of numerous cultural studies, but now more general historical analyses were contending with the issue. As John Adamson has stated, the court's significance was not limited to affairs of state, "almost invariably, it was the principal cultural and social centre of the realm"[10]. Indeed, Carlos Javier de Carlos Morales' chapter in this

[4] Carlo Ossola, "Il 'luogo' della Corte," in Marzio A. Romani (ed.), *Le Corti farnesiane di Parma e Piacenza, 1545-1622* (Rome, 1978), 39-40.

[5] Cesare Mozzarelli, "Principe, corte e governo tra '500 e '700," in *Culture et idéologie dans la gènese de l'État Moderne* (Rome, 1985), 370.

[6] Amongst others, David Starkey e.a., *The English Court from the Wars of the Roses to the Civil War* (London, 1987); Antoni Mączak (ed.), *Klientelsysteme im Europa der Frühen Neuzeit* (Munich, 1988) or Ronald G. Asch and Adolf M. Birke (eds.), *Princes, Patronage and the Nobility. The Court at the Beginning of the Modern Age* (Oxford, 1991).

[7] Marcello Fantoni, "Corte e Stato nell'Italia dei secoli XIV-XVI," in Giorgio Chittolini e.a. (eds.), *Origini dello stato. Processi di formazione statale in Italia fra medioevo ed età moderna* (Bologna, 1994), 449-466.

[8] "Le corti: Un problema storiografico," in Chittolini e.a. (eds.), *Origini dello stato*, 458.

[9] Maurice Aymard and Marzio A. Romani, *La Cour comme institution économique* (Paris, 1998).

[10] John Adamson (ed.), *The Princely Courts of Europe 1500-1750* (London, 1999), 7.

volume demonstrates that the courts and households of the Spanish monarchy were also important economic institutions.

From the year 2000 onwards, a steady stream of scientific meetings, symposia and international conferences brought together an increasing number of specialists from different backgrounds. Currently, Court Studies attracts a great deal of interest, and there exist several centres dedicated to the subject in Europe and the United States, including *Europa delle Corti* (Italy), the *Residenzen-Kommission* of Göttingen (Germany), the *Society for Court Studies* (Great Britain), the *Centre de recherche du château de Versailles* (France) and the *Instituto Universitario La Corte en Europa – IULCE* (Spain), all of which are characterised by their interdisciplinary approach.

Inspired by this renewed interest in the court, René Vermeir of Ghent University and Luc Duerloo of the University of Antwerp, aided by José Eloy Hortal Muñoz of the Universidad Autónoma of Madrid at the time, convened an international round table titled "A Constellation of Courts. The Habsburg Courts and Households in Europe (1555-1665)". This two-day conference (November 3-4, 2006) at the Palace of the Academies of Brussels, centred on the study of the various Habsburg courts and households among the two branches of the dynasty that arose following the division of the territories originally held by Charles V: first, the Spanish branch that began with Philip II, the heart of which was located in Madrid, and secondly, the Austrian branch that originated with Ferdinand I, and which centred on Prague until 1612, when it shifted to Vienna.

This round table not only helped further the attendees' ongoing research by providing a forum for mutual communication and assessment, but it also sought to address a long-standing debate on terminology. For the purposes of the discussion, a working definition was adopted for the terms 'court' and 'household'. The latter term only denotes the personal entourages of the dynasty's non-ruling members. The former, however, was defined as the various departments and individuals that directly aided the ruler or his *alter nos*, the viceroys and governors, in some aspect of governance, as well as their personal entourages. Such courts were located in the various capitals of the composite Habsburg monarchies, and each represented princely authority. While subject to debate, these working definitions are employed in this collection in order to create a typology, which, however imperfect, will allow for comparative research.

Between the sixteenth and seventeenth centuries, the Habsburg dynasty steered the course of European history. Its two branches controlled the Hispanic kingdoms and the Holy Roman Empire, as well as the Netherlands, northern Italy, and everything from central Europe to the borders of the Ottoman Empire. During the sixteenth century, the Spanish Monarchy took the lead, and was responsible for spearheading a partnership founded on dynastic loyalty and dedicated to defending the Catholic faith. This state of affairs was somewhat altered by the Thirty Years War (1618-1648), which saw both the pinnacle of the collaboration between the two branches of the House of Habsburg, and the start of its decline. The Spanish line became extinct following the death of Charles II in 1700, and the resultant War of the Spanish Succession and Treaty of Utrecht heralded a definitive change in the balance of European power.

Without doubt, this evolution affected the influence that the Hispanic court had on its Austrian counterpart, not only with regard to how its component parts were organized, but its etiquette as well. According to Ludwig Pfandl[11], Philip II largely modelled the Spanish court after that of the Burgundians, and this model was then carried throughout Europe by the infantas dispatched from Spain in service to the family's marriage politics. In each case, certain adaptations were made to meet local requirements and expectations, just as they had been in Spain with the addition of Castilian elements to the court. During the sixteenth century, this method of expansion was quite successful; such was certainly the case with infanta Catherine Michelle's marriage to Charles Emmanuel of Savoy[12]. Furthermore, the *dinasticismo* promoted by Philip II also resulted in long-term ties between the Spanish and Austrian branches, which in turn consolidated a growing network of allied territories under the House of Habsburg, and promoted peace and stability. The archdukes Albert and Ernest were instrumental in these plans, which ultimately led to the cession of the Netherlands in 1598[13].

[11] Ludwig Pfandl, "Philipp II und die Einführung des burgundischen Hofzeremoniells in Spanien," *Historisches Jahrbuch*, LVIII (1938), 1-33.

[12] María José Del Río Barredo, "De Madrid a Turín: el ceremonial de las reinas españolas en la corte ducal de Catalina Micaela de Saboya," *Cuadernos de Historia Moderna*, Anejo II (2003), 97-122; José Martínez Millán, "La Casa de Catalina Micaela y sus hijos," in José Martínez Millán and Maria Antonietta Visceglia (eds.), *La monarquía de Felipe III* (Madrid, 2008), I, 1064-72.

[13] José Martínez Millán and Carlos Javier de Carlos Morales (eds.), *La configuración de la Monarquía hispánica* (Valladolid, 1998), 257-61.

This situation changed during the course of the seventeenth century. The decrease in the Hispanic Monarchy's political prestige strongly affected the ability of its members to implement its court structure, etiquette and rituals, which came under fire by Spain's enemies in an effort to contest Madrid's apparent dominance of the continent. The first such political attack came with the expulsion of the Hispanic household of the infanta Anne of Austria[14], who Louis XIII forced to adapt French clothing[15] and submit to the etiquette of the Parisian court. Despite this, the princess maintained some aspects of her culture, as Olivier Chaline's analysis of Val-de-Grâce Abbey in this volume demonstrates. At the same time, the imperial court also began to resist Castilian influences over the course of the seventeenth century, as demonstrated by the cases of empresses Maria Anna and Margaret Theresa[16].

It is important to note that authors such as Werner Paravicini[17] and Christina Hofmann have called into question Pfandl's thesis regarding the origins, construction and dispersal of the Spanish model. For example, Hofmann argues in her *Spanische Hofzeremoniell* that the reforms of Ferdinand I, despite his Castilian upbringing, show little in the way of Burgundian influences, and goes on to suggest that the *Spanisches Hofzeremoniell* was not extensively implemented at the Viennese court[18]. Jeroen Duindam believes that Pfandl's views need nuanced at the very least. For example, he questions whether the decrees regarding etiquette issued by Ferdinand I in 1527 and 1537 were Burgundian in

[14] María José del Río Barredo and Jean-François Dubost, "La présence étrangère autour d'Anne d'Autriche (1615-1666)," in Chantal Grell (ed.), *Anne d'Autriche. Infante d'Espagne et Reine de France* (Paris, 2009), 111-52; Laura Oliván Santaliestra, "Retour souhaité ou expulsion réfléchie? La Maison espagnole d'Anne d'Autriche quitte Paris (1616-1622)," in Giulia Calvi and Isabelle Chabot (eds.), *Moving Elites: Women and Cultural Transfers in the European Court System, Working Papers* (Florence, 2010), 21-31.

[15] Regarding these clashes, see María del Carmen Simón Palmer, "Notas sobre la vida de las mujeres en el Real Alcázar," *Cuadernos de Historia Moderna*, 19 (1997), 21-38, especially 32.

[16] See Laura Oliván Santaliestra in "La influencia del modelo borgoñón en la Casa de las emperatrices hispanas (1629-73)," in José Eloy Hortal Muñoz and Félix Labrador Arroyo (eds.), *La Casa de Borgoña: la Casa del rey de España* (Louvain, 2014), 547-573. The last section of the collection deals exclusively with the households of the various Hispanic infantas and their role in exporting the Spanish court model.

[17] Werner Paravicini, "The Court of the Dukes of Burgundy. A Model for Europe?," in Ronald G. Asch and Adolf M. Birke (eds.), *Princes, Patronage, and the Nobility*, especially 98-9 and 102.

[18] Christina Hofmann, *Das Spanische Hofzeremoniell von 1500-1700* (Frankfurt-am-Main, 1985), 294-6, especially 296.

style, given the distance that the rules imposed between the emperor and the court. He believes that this reflects a more Castilian way of doing things, and was probably the result of the future emperor's education on the Iberian Peninsula[19]. Furthermore, Duindam argues that the Austrian Habsburgs employed the term 'Burgundian' as a way of claiming historical legitimacy, and that it does not actually indicate that the Viennese court was Burgundian in some essential way. Frank Huss[20] and John Spielman, however, disagree and think that the Viennese court was heavily influenced by Spain's preference for the Burgundian style. According to Spielman, Ferdinand I granted the Burgundian office of *Oberhofmeister* a central role at court, while his son, the archduke Charles then adapted Burgundian dining rituals in his decree of September 10, 1550[21].

In light of the above, we must consider the debate regarding the exact nature of the Austrian court still open. Indeed, it is, as Duindam has pointed out[22], difficult to delineate what elements were Burgundian, particularly after successive reforms and reinterpretations of etiquette and ceremony, not to mention the possible influence of other courts, whether Aragonese, Papal, or even Native American. In particular, more research is required into the courts of those infantas that later became empresses. These institutions were formed according to the Castilian model and included elements that were obviously Burgundian in origin, but those portions of the court most inspired by the Burgundian tradition returned to Madrid after delivering the infanta to Vienna. And yet, distinctly Burgundian ceremonial usages – albeit with Castilian modifications – did become incorporated into the courts of the empresses. With regard to the retinues of those who made the reverse journey during the sixteenth and seventeenth centuries – Anne of Austria[23],

[19] Jeroen Duindam, "El legado borgoñón en la vida cortesana de los Habsburgo austriacos", in Krista De Jonge, Bernardo J. García García and Alicia Esteban Estríngana (eds.), *El legado de Borgoña. Fiesta y ceremonia cortesana en la Europa de los Austrias 1454-1648* (Madrid, 2010), 35-58, especially 49.

[20] Frank Huss, *Der Wiener Kaiserhof. Eine Kulturgeschichte von Leopold I. bis Leopold II* (Grensbach, 2008), 214-9.

[21] John P. Spielman, *The City and the Crown: Vienna and the Imperial Court 1600-1740* (Purdue, 1993), 54.

[22] Duindam, "El legado borgoñón", 49.

[23] José Martínez Millán, "La corte de Felipe II: la Casa de la reina Ana", in Luis Ribot García (ed.), *La Monarquía de Felipe II a debate* (Madrid, 2000), 159-84. For the structure of the household, José Eloy Hortal Muñoz, "Organización de una Casa. El Libro de Veeduría de la reina Ana de Austria", in José Martínez Millán and Maria Paula Marçal Lourenço (eds.), *Las Relaciones Discretas entre las monarquías Hispana y*

Margaret of Austria[24], Mariana of Austria[25], and the archdukes Rudolph, Ernest, Albert and Wenceslas[26] – they were severely curtailed in number, and very few attendants were allowed to keep their positions. The emperors occasionally lent their assistance here, such as when Maximilian II insisted that Anne of Austria's servants remain in Castile, as outlined by José Hortal Eloy Muñoz's chapter in this volume. The preceding paragraphs demonstrate, however briefly, that the two branches of the House of Habsburg had a close, on-going relationship. Yet until quite recently, we have only had detailed analyses on their separate evolutions[27], none of which take into account the dynastic logic and cooperation that helped shape these changes. Similarly, their respective courts have been intensively, but separately, investigated in the last few decades[28]. Fortunately, however, we now have more

Portuguesa: las Casas de las Reinas (siglos XV-XIX). Arte, música, espiritualidad y literatura (Madrid, 2008), I, 275-309.

[24] Félix Labrador Arroyo, "La Casa de la reina Margarita", in José Martínez Millán and Maria Antonietta Visceglia (eds.), *La Monarquía de Felipe III*, I, 1125-68.

[25] See José Rufino Novo Zaballos, "La Casa de la reina Mariana de Austria durante el reinado de Felipe IV y el período de regencia", and Diego Crespí de Valldaura, "La Casa de la reina Mariana de Austria durante su Regencia (1665-1675)", both in the second volume of José Martínez Millán and José Eloy Hortal Muñoz (eds.), *La Monarquía de Felipe IV: la Casa del rey* (Madrid, 2014).

[26] See the contribution of José Eloy Hortal Muñoz in this volume.

[27] The first scientific work devoted to the political evolution of the Austrian Habsburg branch, for example, is also the most comprehensive reconstruction of it for the period between 1494 and 1848: the 6 volumes of Eduard Vehse's *Geschichte des österreichischen Hofs und Adels und der österreichischen Diplomatie* (Hamburg, 1851). The historiography improved in the mid-20th century as a result of the work carried out by influential Czech historians such as Bohdan Chudoba, whose bilateral history of Habsburg Spain and the Holy Roman Empire has yet to be revised (*Spain and the Empire, 1519-1643*, Chicago, 1952). Robert Evans and Karl Vocelka were involved in renewing interest in the Habsburgs during in the 1970s, while a prominent school has recently been established in Vienna under the leadership of Alfred Kohler, Thomas Winkelbauer and Friedrich Edelmayer.

[28] With regard to Spain, see among others, José Martínez Millán (ed.), *La corte de Carlos V* (Madrid, 2000), 5 vols.; José Martínez Millán and Santiago Fernández Conti (eds.), *La Monarquía de Felipe II*; José Martínez Millán and María Antonietta Visceglia (eds.), *La Monarquía de Felipe III*; and José Martínez Millán and José Eloy Hortal Muñoz (eds.), *La Monarquía de Felipe IV*. With regard to Austria, see Jeroen Duindam, *Vienna and Versailles: The Courts of Europe's Dynastic Rivals, 1550-1780* (Cambridge, 2003) and Karin J. MacHardy, *War, Religion and Court Patronage in Habsburg Austria* (Houndmills, 2003) in particular. Nevertheless, much remains to be done on this subject.

comprehensive studies[29], like that of Alejandro López Álvarez, whose contribution to this collection examines the ceremonies employed by the Habsburg monarchs of both branches.

This divide must be crossed in order to truly comprehend the relationship between the European courts under Habsburg rule. As José Martínez Millán ably explains in his contribution to this volume, Philip II inherited a political entity lacking overarching structures, and whose constituent territories felt the physical absence of their prince quite keenly[30]. In order to keep his inheritance intact, Philip II initially decided to employ his father's proven model for uniting these disparate regions: incorporating their elites into his service via the court. However, this plan proved short-lived, since the Castilian elites advocated Castilian hegemony throughout the Monarchy, and at court[31]. Both the process of Confessionalization[32] and the decision to permanently locate the court at Madrid – accompanied by measures designed, as far as possible, to make the sovereign omnipresent – undoubtedly reinforced this trend[33]. Philip II was well aware that he needed an organizational structure, and he decided that the harmony of the body politic could best be guaranteed via hierarchy and inequality. Castile would head up his territories, and its councils would form the basis of the political entity to which they belonged.

This change, in the words of Lope de Vega, turned Madrid into an 'archive of nations' enabling the non-Castilians who resided at court to live there just as if they were in their countries of origin, under their own jurisdictions. However, the majority of the non-Castilians active

[29] José Martínez Millán and Rubén González Cuerva (eds.), *La dinastía de los Austria: las relaciones entre la Monarquía Católica y el Imperio* (Madrid, 2011), 3 vols.

[30] With regard to this process, see José Martínez Millán, "La integración de las élites ciudadanas castellanas en la Monarquía a través de la Casa Real", in José Martínez Millán and Santiago Fernández Conti (eds.), *La monarquía de Felipe II*, I, 645–85.

[31] For the ongoing rivalry between those elites who fought for the hegemony of Castile and those who supported the greater involvement of other kingdoms, see José Martínez Millán, "La articulación de la Monarquía hispana: Auge y ocaso de la Casa Real de Castilla", in *Plus ultra. Die Welt der Neuzeit. Festschrift für Alfred Kohler zum 65. Geburtstag*, ed. by Friedrich Edelmayer, Martina Fuchs, Georg Heilingsetzer and Peter Rauscher (Münster 2007), 407–52.

[32] An account of the historical development of this concept can be found in Ulrich Lotz-Heumann, "The Concept of "Confessionalization": A Historiographical Paradigm in Dispute", *Memoria y Civilización: Anuario de Historia*, 4 (2001), 93–114.

[33] With regard to this process, see Manuel Rivero Rodríguez, "El Consejo de Italia y la territorialización de la monarquía (1554–1600)", in Ernest Belenguer Cebrià (ed.), *Felipe II y el Mediterráneo* (Madrid, 1998), III, 97–113.

in the Madrilene court no longer belonged to the upper aristocracy and the various royal courts and households had ceased to welcome them into their service. Thus it was necessary to seek new ways of ensuring that the crown's munificence filtered throughout Spain's vast holdings, as Manuel Rivero Rodríguez discusses in his contribution to this volume[34]. The crown's viceroys and governors, semi-autonomous in the regions they governed, gradually began to incorporate local elites into their own service, a process that was consolidated under Philip III. Their households evolved into large courts that mirrored the royal court in Spain. The local elites, both the titled and the untitled, decided, therefore, to seek positions in their native lands rather than Madrid. At the very most, they sent their offspring to Castile to be brought up as pages, *meninos*, companions for the royal children in other words, ladies-in-waiting or *coustilliers*, those who accompanied the king to worship or on journeys. This led to the revival of some vice-regal courts, such as those located in Naples, Sicily and Portugal, as well as the erection of new, larger courts in the Americas.

With regard to the Habsburg Netherlands, the leading members of the nobility were, at best, only marginally associated with the Madrilene court during the second half of the sixteenth century onwards. They remained in the north, and as a result, created a court of some significance in Brussels, one that flourished culturally in much the same way as other analogous courts in the Spanish Monarchy. This was certainly the case during the archducal period, when Albert and Isabella ruled the Habsburg Netherlands as sovereigns[35]. The Brussels court lost some of its prominence after Albert's death in 1621 and the subsequent return of the Netherlands to the Spanish crown, but remained an important court, especially following the creation of the *Maison Royale de Bruxelles* in the mid-seventeenth century[36].

[34] See also Manuel Rivero Rodríguez, "Una monarquía de casas reales y cortes virreinales", in José Martínez Millán and Maria Antonietta Visceglia (eds.), *La Monarquía de Felipe III*, IV, 31–60, and chapter 4, 'La Edad de Oro', in *La edad de oro de los virreyes. El virreinato en la Monarquía Hispánica durante los siglos XVI y XVII* (Madrid, 2011), 133–74.

[35] There has been extensive research on the subject, see the comprehensive overview in Alejandro Vergara (ed.), *El Arte en la Corte de los Archiduques Alberto de Austria e Isabel Clara Eugenia (1598–1633). Un Reino Imaginado* (Madrid, 1999).

[36] See José Eloy Hortal Muñoz and Koldo Trápaga Monchet, "The Royal Households in the Habsburg Netherlands after the Departure of the Household of Burgundy: From the Entourages of the Governors-General to the *Maison Royale de Bruxelles*", *Dutch Crossing* (forthcoming).

Until recently, few historians paid any attention to the Brussels court of the sixteenth and seventeenth centuries outside of the archducal period, and those who did – J. Proost[37], S. Clercx[38], and V. Coremans[39] among them – took an institutional approach. Yet understanding this court's history is key to unravelling the evolution of the relationship between both branches of the family during the sixteenth and seventeenth centuries, since no less then three Austrian archdukes – Ernest (1593-5)[40], Albert (1595-8)[41] and Leopold-Wilhelm (1647-56)[42] – were governors-general of the Habsburg Netherlands, and Albert was its sovereign from 1598 to 1621. Fortunately, interest has increased since the 1990s. The fourth centenary of the cession of the Habsburg Netherlands to the archdukes in 1998 spurred further research into Albert and Isabella's court[43], and many historians began applying Court Studies' new methodologies to their research on the region.

The project funded by the Research Foundation Flanders (FWO) and directed by René Vermeir and Luc Duerloo from 2005 to 2009 was particularly important in this respect. The goal was to encourage research into the entire history of the Brussels court in the hopes that this would further our understanding of how the Spanish Monarchy was governed, as well as the evolution of the relationship between both branches of the House of Habsburg over the course of the sixteenth and seventeenth centuries. The project culminated in the conference

[37] Jean Joseph Eugène Proost, "Le prévôt général de l´Hôtel, ses attributions et ses prérogatives", *Annales de l´Académie d´archéologie de Belgique*, 33 (1876), 141-64.

[38] Suzanne Clercx, "La chapelle royale de Bruxelles sous l´ancien régime", *Annuaire du Conservatoire de musique de Bruxelles*, 65 (1941), 159-79.

[39] Victor Coremans, "L´archiduc Ernest, sa cour, ses dépenses (1593-1595)", *Compte rendu des séances de la Commision royale d´histoire ou recueil de ses bulletins*, 13 (1847), 85-147.

[40] For his period as general-governor, see Victor Coremans, "L'archiduc Ernest" and José Eloy Hortal Muñoz, "La casa del archiduque Ernesto durante su gobierno en los Países Bajos (1593-1595)" in Antonio Álvarez-Ossorio Alvariño and Bernardo J. García García (eds.), *La Monarquía de las Naciones. Patria, nación y naturaleza en la Monarquía de España* (Madrid, 2004), 193-213.

[41] See the bibliography of José Eloy Hortal Muñoz's chapter in this volume.

[42] See René Vermeir, "Un austriaco en Flandes. El archiduque Leopoldo Guillermo, gobernador general de los Países Bajos meridionales (1647-1656)", in José Martínez Millán and Rubén González Cuerva (eds.), *La Dinastía de los Austria*, I, 583-608 and the bibliography, as well as Sophie Aspeslagh, *Het leven in het paleis op de Coudenberg te Brussel onder landvoogd Leopold Willem van Oostenrijk (1647-1656)* (Master's thesis, Catholic University of Louvain, 2007).

[43] Principally compiled in Werner Thomas and Luc Duerloo (eds.), *Albert & Isabella, 1598-1621. Essays* (Turnhout, 1998).

that ultimately led to this collection of articles, as well as two doctoral theses: one by Dries Raeymaekers regarding aspects of the archdukes' court (1598-1621)[44], and one by Birgit Houben, which focused on the governorships of both Isabella Clara Eugenia (1621-33) and Cardinal-Infant Ferdinand (1634-41)[45]. The renewed interest that the project generated also led to several masters' theses[46], as well as studies carried out by specialists such as Werner Thomas, Krista De Jonge, Alicia Esteban, and Violet Soen.

An updated and comprehensive study on the dynamics of the imperial court is also lacking[47]. However, thanks to the results of the University of Vienna's recent project titled "Zu Diensten Ihrer Majestät. Geschichte der Organisation des Wiener Hofes in der Frühen Neuzeit", progress has been made on several fronts[48]. Further research in this area is of paramount importance because for a considerable part of the period under consideration in this collection, the responsibility of governing Austria's hereditary lands was divided among several members of the family, and as a result, distinct archducal courts came into being at Innsbruck (1564–1665) and Graz (1564–1619). These constituted a discernable, second level of princely courts within the Austrian Habsburg territories, one step below the imperial court in

[44] Published by Leuven University Press in 2013 as *One foot in the palace. The Habsburg Court of Brussels and the Politics of Access in the Reign of Albert and Isabella, 1598–1621.*

[45] *Wisselende gedaanten. Het hof en de hofhouding van de landvoogden Isabella Clara Eugenia (1621–1633) en de kardinaal-infant don Fernando van Oostenrijk (1634–1641) te Brussel* (unpublished doctoral thesis, Ghent University). Portions of this thesis were published as articles, see, among others, Birgit Houben, "Les dignitaires bourguignons de la cour comme agents de la Franche-Comté: du courtage provincial à la cour bruxelloise (1621-1641)," *Revue du Nord*, 90 (2008), 747-773 and Birgit Houben and Dries Raeymaekers, "Women and the Politics of Access at the Court of Brussels: The Infanta Isabella's Camareras Mayores (1598-1633)," in Nadine Akkerman and Birgit Houben (eds.), *The politics of female households. Ladies-in-waiting across Early Modern Europe* (Leiden, 2013), 123-45.

[46] Among them: Ellen Roegis, *Het hof van don Juan José de Austria, landvoogd in de Habsburgse Nederlanden (1656-1658)* (Master's thesis, Ghent University, 2006) and Sophie Aspeslagh, *Het leven in het paleis op de Coudenberg* [see n. 42].

[47] Indeed, when compared with the extensive bibliography on court factions and their political roles available for other contemporary centres of power, the Austrian court appears sorely neglected. However, this has been somewhat rectified with regard to the reigns of Ferdinand II (1619-1637) and Ferdinand III (1637-1657) as a result of the University of Vienna's wide-ranging 2000 project titled "Patronage- und Klientelsysteme am Wiener Hof" (http://www.univie.ac.at/Geschichte/wienerhof/).

[48] See http://www.fwf.ac.at/de/abstracts/abstract.asp?L=D&PROJ=P20157 (consulted October 13, 2013).

Prague and Vienna. The Spanish Monarchy on the other hand consisted of various formerly independent entities. Some of these continued to be governed from their former capitals, as was the case in Naples or in the Spanish Netherlands. These cities remained seats of royal sovereignty in a number of ways, and the entourages of the resident viceroys or governors should therefore to be considered a third level of court. The court of Brussels under the reign of the archdukes Albert and Isabella (1598–1621) however, falls into the same category as Innsbruck and Graz.

The Austrian branch of the dynasty underwent a rapid expansion in numbers. At its highpoint in 1613, there were no fewer than 14 archdukes and 13 archduchesses, and regardless of their seniority, all of them had to be provided for in a *Standesgemäß* fashion. If they reached adulthood, they received a household of their own. In quite a few cases they were allowed their own residence, and some went on to become the governors of provinces, or, as in the case of the aforementioned archduke Albert, rulers in their own right. Others were provided with ecclesiastical benefices, which gave them access to important revenues and sometimes allowed them to act as independent rulers, as was the case with prince-bishoprics, or grandmasterships of the Teutonic Order. As for the archduchesses, they mainly wed, although a few took monsastic vows. And as widows, some chose to reside in or nearby a convent.

Alongside the various levels of Habsburg courts, were the households established for the non-ruling members of the family. There were of course huge differences in size between, on the one hand, the courts of Madrid or Vienna, and of the households of the younger members of the family, on the other. Being a Poor Clare, Sor Margarita de la Cruz had only a minute household serving her in the *Descalzas Reales*, but she had a household nevertheless. These households were spread out across Europe, but together they comprised a crucial power-base for the dynasty, and offered an important source of employment to the extensive network of aristocrats and lesser men and women who spent their lives serving the House of Austria.

The ultimate goal of this volume is to trace the connections between the various Habsburg courts and private households, regardless of their standing or composition, in order to begin outlining the network they created. Cutting across the traditional division in the historiography between the two branches of the House of Habsburg outlined above, and seeking to examine the roles played by the courts and households of lesser known members of the dynasty, will help to determine to what degree their organization followed a particular model, to what extent individuals were able to move between them in pursuit of career opportunities and advancement, and whether this increased their cosmopolitanism. In this fashion, we hope to help establish the impact that a single dynasty and the evolving relationship between its constituent parts had on the development of its related courts.

José Eloy Hortal Muñoz, Dries Raeymaekers and René Vermeir

The political configuration of the Spanish Monarchy: the court and royal households[1]

José Martínez Millán
Instituto Universitario "La Corte en Europa" – Universidad Autónoma de Madrid

Theoretical schemas that historians have constructed to explain the development of the modern state, based on the premise of the progressive and uninterrupted rationalization of state power, have proved incapable of providing a systematic account of the intricate socio-political reality of the early modern age. The reason is that, behind that monolithic power, which researchers have tried to convince us is there, the projected image of the interplay of multiple powers swiftly appears, refuting any claim to total abstraction and impersonality on the part of the State.[2] In the last few years, this view of history has changed. What has proved decisive, in this respect, has been research into concepts that do not obviously correspond to the categories of "modernity"; on the contrary, it sends us down a plurality of theoretical and disciplinary pathways characterizing the ethical and political culture of the *Ancien Régime*. The point is that the dynastic state, Bonney's term for the European monarchies

[1] This work has been carried out as part of a project funded by the Spanish Ministry of Education, HUM, 2006-12779-C-1.

[2] Hegel regarded historical phenomena as essentially political since history unfolds in the State. "It is necessary to accept that a historical account, and the acts and events that take place in history, appear simultaneously: a common internal foundation gives rise to them together [...]. Only the State provides a content which corresponds to the prose of history, and which it also engenders," see *Sämtliche Werke*, ed. Hermann Glockner, 12 vols. (Stuttgart: Frommann Verlag, 1927–1930), 2: 97–98. Cited by Bernard Bourgeois, *El pensamiento político de Hegel* (Buenos Aires, 1972), 11. Because of the sense of the universal which it demands and objectifies, the State encourages individuals to carry out universal acts and, through the narration of the past, to retain this universal efficiently in the memory; the universal cannot be presented as such, in all its permanence, in the intuition of the present moment, because this is always particular.

between the fifteenth and eighteenth centuries[3] – and despite the fact that it may, at times, have behaved in an impersonal and bureaucratic fashion – was orientated towards the person of the king, who was the single source of different forms of power, and of material and symbolic resources (money, honours, titles, indulgences, monopolies, and so on). Monarchs were able to use the selective redistribution of favours to maintain relationships of dependence (client networks) or, perhaps it would be better to say, personal recognition, and so perpetuate themselves in power, while at the same time keeping their kingdoms united.

The philosophical foundation of the political system in the Early Modern Age

In recent years, the important role of Aristotelian "practical philosophy"[4] has been recognized as a fundamental characteristic of the ethical and political knowledge of the Early Modern Age, as opposed to the interpretation of the modern state as process, one culminating in a rational entity, the seat of power, situated over and above society. Of course, the Aristotelian model should not be understood as being reproduced in a fixed form down the centuries, but as a framework of essential reference points from the late Middle Ages to the eighteenth century. It should be emphasized that the origins of medieval moral discipline lay in the Peripatetic tradition, which branched, from Boethius onwards, into ethics, paying attention to the individual in the *res familiaris,* and politics, whose focus was the *res publica.*[5] This subdivision did not imply defining different disciplines to guide different subjects; it was concerned above all else with specifying the boundaries and particular techniques of any single area of ethical knowledge referring to the formation of the individual at the point

[3] Both the title and the structure of the study by Richard J. Bonney, *The European Dynastic States, 1494–1660* (Oxford, 1991), express much the same as what I affirm here. He expresses the idea in idem, "Guerre, fiscalité et activité d'Etat en France (1500–1650): Quelques remarques préliminaires sur les possibilités de recherche," in Jean-Philippe Genet and Michel Le Mené (eds.), *Genèse de l'État moderne: Prélèvement et redistribution* (Paris, 1987), 194–195.
[4] For a synthesis, see Franco Volpi, "La rinascita della filosofia pratica in Germania," in Claudio Pacchiani (ed.), *Filosofia pratica e scienza politica* (Abano Terme, 1980).
[5] Roberto Lambertini, "Per una storia dell'oeconomica tra alto e basso Medievo," *Cheiron* 2 (1985), 46.

where he has to administer justice in the various spheres of social life, or translate *virtus* into behaviours, actions and practices. In this sense, not just politics, but all practical philosophy took "man in community" as its reference point.[6]

Typical of the Aristotelian model and the way it was reworked during the sixteenth and seventeenth centuries was the view of the political sphere as a necessary outlet to channel the tendency of the individual to express a sociability which, for historical and functional reasons, was spreading outwards from the family into increasingly broader forms of social and political coexistence. If the family was the original community created to cater for everyday needs, the organization of the state arose to satisfy other, more sophisticated, vital needs that living in society involved. This division implied, on the one hand, recognizing the obvious priority of the domestic sphere and the economic discipline needed to regulate it; on the other, it pointed to the moral superiority of civil and political life as the realm of the common good and justice. The aim of practical philosophy was to subordinate human relations to the ethical principles and virtues that the father, citizen or prince, each in his respective area, was called upon to embody. The different areas of practical philosophy set out, therefore, to link functional knowledge to the establishment of various other models of action and behaviour as they affected the individual subject in the various spheres of human activity.[7] It is important to point out the way in which the establishment of this model in the medieval period was followed later, in the Renaissance, by the attempt to articulate that tradition in relation to very different social actors: the prince, the cardinal, the gentleman, and so forth. The widespread production of treatises in the sixteenth century is an indication of the theoretical effort that was being made to put forward, once more, the claims of practical philosophy in response to the modification and organization of an increasingly complex and stratified society.[8]

It was personal relationships, rather than the institutions, that provided the political foundation for shaping power relations in the European monarchies from the late Middle Ages until the eighteenth

[6] Alasdair MacIntyre, *Dopo la virtù: Saggio di teoria morale* (Milan, 1988), 225–226.

[7] Diego Quaglioni, '*Civilis sapientia*': *Dottrine giuridiche e dottrine politiche tra Medievo ed Età Moderna* (Rimini, 1990), 107ff.

[8] Amadeo Quondam, "La virtù dipinta: Noterelle (e divagazioni) guazziane intorno a Classicismo e Institutio in Antico Regime," in Giorgio Patrizi (ed.), *Stefano Guazzo e la Civil conversazione* (Rome, 1990), 268.

century, given that the organizational model was based on the domestic economy (government and administration). Coupling these principles of classical philosophy onto the monarchies as a political formation had its contradictions, but made gradual progress during the Early Modern Age: in matters that had nothing to do with justice, the prince was recognized as possessing powers beyond the scope of *iurisdictio* and whose appropriate model was the "natural" authority of the father in the domestic sphere.[9] The analogy between the power of the father and that of the prince, between household and city, between family and state, which set out to draw attention to the way the domestic dimension functioned in the aristocratic management of the life of the citizens,[10] or the legitimization of public power deriving from an original authority figure, found here immediate political and legal application: it enabled the sovereign to intervene in some of these spheres, while dissociating his actions from the limits imposed by jurisdictional forms. Love and personal loyalty had a central role in this model of political relations; at the same time, the model for distributing functions was valid for domestic offices and monarchy alike; each depended on the final decision of the *pater familias* (the prince), based on criteria (of loyalty and merit especially) which were quite different from those of today, since the domestic model maintained an intimate relationship with the clientelist model.[11]

This political foundation did not lead to the *Ancien Régime* being organized in Europe as states; instead the monarchies made the court their power base, that is, a powerful centre of authority where the monarch resided with his household, councils and tribunals, and

[9] For this reason, the image of "household" was always present as the government of the Monarchy took shape. Crespí de Valldaura said that, along with the *iurisdictio*: "residet tamen in Principe alia oeconomica et politica potestas, quae ei, tamquam Reipublicae capiti et parenti, ut cuilibet patri familias in propia domo competit," Cristóbal Crespí de Valdaura, *Observationes illustratae decisionibus Sacri Supremi Regni Aragonum Consilii* (Lugduni, 1662), 72.

[10] Daniela Frigo, "Governo della casa, nobiltà e "republica": l'"economia" in Italia tra Cinque e Settecento," *Cheiron* 2 (1985), 75–79.

[11] Daniela Frigo, "L'affermazione della sovranità: famiglia e corte dei Savoia tra cinque e settecento," in Cesare Mozzarelli (ed.), *"Familia" del Príncipe e Famiglia aristocratica* (Rome, 1988), 1: 306–307. This, according to Colin M. MacLachlan, was how the Spanish monarch governed the Indies, "Los fundamentos filosóficos del imperio español de América: la Monarquía de los Habsburgo," in Alfredo Castillero Calvo (ed.), *Historia General de América Latina: Consolidación del orden colonial*, vol. 3, bk. 2 (Paris, 2001), 693–694.

from which he not only ruled the kingdom but also transmitted a model of social, cultural and artistic behaviour. This model of political organization is particularly appropriate when referring to the Spanish Monarchy from the sixteenth to the eighteenth centuries, since it is difficult to explain in any other way the creation of such a long-lasting consensus established within it, both among the political elites and within the kingdoms as a whole.[12] What seems to be clear is that the Monarchy opted for the court formula as the number of kingdoms increased through inheritance, annexation or conquest. In some cases it reinforced courtly spaces that already existed (as in Valencia, Barcelona, Saragossa, Naples, Palermo, Milan, Brussels or Lisbon), whilst in others it created viceregal courts of a new stamp (Lima and Mexico City) on top of the centres of the pre-Columbian empires. This wealth and variety of courtly realities, covering such a long period (from the fifteenth to the eighteenth century) and such very different spaces (Europe and America), have not only not been studied in global terms within Spanish historiography, but still, in large measure, lack specific studies using the methodologies that have arisen in our field to analyse the phenomenon.[13] This situation seems even more paradoxical if we consider that the court in Madrid and the viceregal courts of the Monarchy served as a model for the courts of Europe throughout the sixteenth and seventeenth centuries, only being replaced as a reference point, from the end of the seventeenth until the nineteenth century, by the court of Versailles and the Prussian court.

[12] Antonio Álvarez-Ossorio Alvariño, "La Corte: un espacio abierto para la historia social," in Santiago Castillo (ed.), *La Historia Social en España: Actualidad y perspectivas* (Madrid, 1991), 255–256.

[13] The line of research I propose has been clearly marked out by Carlos José Hernando Sánchez, "Estar en nuestro lugar, representando nuestra propia persona: El gobierno virreinal en Italia y en la Corona de Aragón bajo Felipe II," in Ernest Belenguer (ed.), *Felipe II y el Mediterráneo* (Madrid, 1999), 3: 215–238; Josep María Torras i Ribé, "El entorno clientelar de los virreyes de Cataluña durante el reinado de Felipe II," in *ibid.*, 359–376. For the Indies, the same methodological approach is followed by Pedro Pérez Herrero, "La Corte como simbología del poder en las Indias (siglos XVI y XVII)," *Reales sitios* 39 (2003), 28–42. A very full bibliography on studies of the viceroys of Peru is to be found in P. Latasa, "La corte virreinal peruana: perspectivas de análisis (siglos XVI y XVII)," in Feliciano Barrios (ed.), *El gobierno de un mundo: virreinatos y audiencias en la América hispánica* (Cuenca, 2004), 341–373.

The royal households of the Spanish Monarchy

In dynastic monarchies, the royal household not only constituted the founding element of all those that made up the court, but also gave substance to the dynasty and legitimized dominion over the kingdom.[14] From the late Middle Ages, each prince established his own household (his own form of service) and, though all of them sought originality to lend prestige to their monarchy, most had the same departments and structures by means of which the elites of the realm were taken into their service. The chroniclers and treatise writers of the time coincided in pointing out that the royal household was the essential element of the court, which has led certain present-day historians to erroneously regard the two organisms as the same.[15]

The Spanish Monarchy opted to use the court to bring together the additional territories gained through inheritance, annexation or conquest, meaning that none of the structures of any of the kingdoms was eliminated. This pattern of political configuration favoured a series of features that have not always been taken into account. Firstly, incorporating new kingdoms alongside the existing ones entailed the proliferation of royal households; in view of the fact that the royal households were the elements that had given the kingdoms their political shape, keeping their autonomy also meant that their respective households had to be retained even when the king was not in residence. In the second place, it can be deduced that any change made to the political structure of the Monarchy inevitably affected the organization of the royal households, which, during the sixteenth and seventeenth centuries, were gradually reduced to the household of Burgundy, with the others being eliminated. We will now see how this evolution came about.

The origins of the royal household of Aragon

The organization of the household of Aragon took place between the thirteenth and fourteenth centuries, attaining its most complete form in the reign of Peter IV, whose *Ordinacions de Cort* [Court Ordinances], issued between 1338 and 1355, fixed the offices and the order of the household, and whose basic structures endured until the seventeenth

[14] For the development of the court, see José Martínez Millán, "La corte en la Monarquía hispana," *Studia Historica. Edad Moderna* 28 (2006), 17–61.
[15] David Starkey, *The Reign of Henry VIII* (London, 1991), 17.

century.[16] In the *Ordinacions fetes per lo molt alt senyor en Pere terc, rey d'Aragó* [Ordinances made by the most high lord Peter III, king of Aragon], there were four main offices in the household: *mayordomo* [≈steward or seneschal], *camarlengo* [≈lord high chamberlain], *canciller* [≈chancellor] and *maestre racional* [≈chancellor of the exchequer].[17] According to the *Ordinacions* of Peter IV, slightly more than two hundred officers served in the royal household. The complex administration of expenditure remained in the hands of the *maestre racional*, the administrator of the royal wealth and revenues. The *Ordinacions* had a much greater reach than the private space of the monarch since they sought to describe the relationships of all existing powers in the kingdom, beginning with the monarch; that is, they tried to outline the composition of the royal household and court and the integrating role it played in his relationship with the world around him: the kingdom. On this basis, it is apparent that it was only political government that was structured from the court, because in the various kingdoms that made up the Crown of Aragon, the viceroys, lieutenants or ministers were the ones who reserved full jurisdictional powers for themselves during the king's absence.[18]

The lengthy description of offices, courtesies, styles and ceremonial expressed in the *Ordinacions* is, in effect, a classification showing the hierarchical structure in rank order, starting with the person of the king. Even when the distribution of this order seems merely symbolic, it is filtered through the imaginary construct of the Monarchy, which takes

[16] Próspero Bofarull y Mascaró, *Ordenamiento de Corte de Pedro IV, año 1384; Colección de Documentos Inéditos (CODOIN), vol. 5 (Barcelona, 1850);* Francisco A. Roca Traver, "Un manuscrito de ordenaciones de la casa del rey en la Corona de Aragón," *Anuario de Historia del Derecho Español*, no. 18 (1948), 515–530; Olivetta Schena, *Le leggi palatine di Pietro IV d'Aragona* (Cagliari, 1983); Manuel Rivero Rodríguez, "Las otras Casas Reales: Aragón y Portugal," in José Martínez Millán and Santiago Fernández Conti (eds.), *La Monarquía de Felipe II: la casa del rey*, [hereafter *La Monarquía de Felipe II*], 2 vols. (Madrid, 2005), 1: 802–810.

[17] Francisco Carreras Candi, "Ordenanzas para la casa y corte de los reyes de Aragón," *Cultura española*, 2 (1906), 327–338; Josep Trench, *Casa, Corte y Cancillería de Pedro el Grande, 1276–1285* (Rome, 1991); José Ernesto Martínez Ferrando, "Super officiis Aragonum," *Hispania* IV (1944), 499–535; Francisco Sevillano Colom, "Apuntes para el estudio de la cancillería de Pedro IV el Ceremonioso," *Anuario de Historia del Derecho Español*, no. 20 (1950), 137–241; Ana Isabel Sánchez Casabón, "Los cargos de mayordomo, senescal y dapifer en el reinado de Alfonso II de Aragón," *Aragón en la Edad Media* 8 (1989), 599–610.

[18] Jesús Lalinde Abadía, *Los fueros de Aragón* (Zaragoza, 1976), 93–120; Teresa Canet Aparisi, "Derecho y administración de justicia en la formación del reino de Valencia," *Estudis: Revista de Historia Moderna* 10 (1983), 7–31.

on coherence as a body. The court-dominions nexus was established in a field foreign to institutions, by means of hierarchical bonds that were much more solid than the actual administrative or institutional ones. This link enabled two ostensibly opposing tendencies to be sustained: the strengthening of the centre by means of the household and the "forced decentralization" of royal authority through the institutional autonomy of the kingdoms, ruled by the lieutenants. As these were prominent members of the royal family, each of their residences was a replica of the royal household in the particular kingdom being governed, so that the *alter ego* had its corresponding *alter domus*.[19]

In this set of othernesses, the "inorganic courts" of the lieutenants[20] were juxtaposed with the king's so that, when the sovereign was present in the territory, they were absorbed into his household and court without any problem, recovering their autonomy once the monarch had left the kingdom. The cohesion and solidity of the Crown of Aragon was based on the interplay of presence-absence and the splitting of the royal majesty and his household into two. In this way, we realize that the royal household was the only institution common to the Crown as a whole, and also that, with the arrival of the Habsburg dynasty, the same offices of the royal household of Aragon were added to those of Castile and Burgundy, by being integrated into the unity of the new (Spanish) Monarchy in the domestic sphere.[21]

The royal household of Castile

In order to explain the evolution of the household of Castile, it must be stressed that union with Aragon was carried out in the kingdom of Castile, which meant in practice the adoption of the less institutionally evolved household of Castile as the mode of service for the new political entity that came into being.[22] As a matter of fact, information about the

[19] The expression is taken from Manuel Rivero Rodríguez, "La Casa y Corte de Aragón," in José Martínez Millán (ed.), *La Corte de Carlos V* (hereafter, *Corte de Carlos V*), 5 vols. (Madrid, 2000), 1, 84.

[20] This felicitous expression is from Teresa Canet Aparisi, *La audiencia valenciana en la época foral moderna* (Valencia, 1986),16.

[21] The structure of the household of Aragon in the time of Ferdinand the Catholic can be found in Jaime Vicens Vives, *Historia crítica de Fernando II de Aragón* (Zaragoza, 1962).

[22] For the background, see Claudio Sánchez-Albornoz, "El *Palatium Regis* astur-leonés," *Cuadernos de Historia de España* no. 59–60 (1976), 5–104; José Ángel García de Cortázar and Esther Peña Bocos, "El *Palatium*, símbolo y centro de poder en los reinos de Navarra y Castilla en los siglos X al XII," *Mayurqa* 22, no.1 (1989), 281–296.

composition, officers and structure of the Castilian royal household has existed since ancient times: Alfonso X, the Wise, described the main offices in the *Segunda Partida* [Second Part of the Seven-Part Code] and numerous references appear later in chronicles, in the Castilian *Cortes* and in documents about Crown property;[23] however, until 1496, the date when the Catholic Monarchs set up a household for their son, prince John, in the Castilian style, which was essentially the same as his mother queen Isabella's and his grandfather John II's,[24] there is no complete description of the composition of that household. The household of Castile, which had no ordinances, consisted of a series of modules or sections, according to Fernández de Oviedo's description,[25] and at the head of each, there was a designated member of the Castilian high nobility who had direct access to the king. Domínguez Casas has produced a

[23] Jaime Salazar y Acha, *La casa del Rey de Castilla y León en la Edad Media* (Madrid, 2000). For the queen's household, see Angela Muñoz Fernández, "La casa delle regine: Uno spazio politico nella Castiglia del Quatrocento," *Génesis* 1, no. 2 (2002), 71–95; for the royal princes' households, see Isabel Beceiro Pita, "Los dominios de la familia real castellana (1250–1350)," *Génesis Medieval del Estado Moderna: Castilla y Navarra, 1250–1370* (Valladolid, 1987), 79–106; Josep Trenchs Odena, "La Comitiva de Alfonso XI: notas para su estudio," *Saitabi* 30 (1980), 11–19. To understand the structure of the royal household, see Betsabé Caunedo, "Un importante papel de los mercaderes de Toledo en el siglo XV: abastecedores de la Casa Real," *Anales Toledanos* 16 (1983), 139–150; Hilda Grassotti, "El repostero en León y Castilla (siglos XII–XIV)," *Cuadernos de Historia de España* 69 (1987), 41–75.

[24] María Concepción Solana Villamor, *Cargos de la Casa y Corte de los Reyes Católicos: Los modestos colaboradores de los Reyes Católicos* (Valladolid, 1962); Álvaro Fernández de Córdova y Miralles, *La Corte de Isabel I* (Madrid, 2002); Miguel Ángel Ladero Quesada, "La Casa Real en la Baja Edad Media," *Historia, Instituciones y Documentos* 25 (1998), 327–350; Miguel Ángel Ladero Quesado, "L'Hôtel du Roi et la Cour comme institutions économiques au temps des Rois Catholiques (1480–1504)," in Maurice Aymard and Marzio A. Romani (eds.), *La Cour comme institution économique* (Paris, 1998), 43–49; Alicia Gómez Izquierdo, *Cargos de la Casa de Juan II de Castilla* (Valladolid, 1968); Amalia Prieto Cantero, *Casa y Descargos de los Reyes Católicos* (Valladolid, 1969). The following deal indirectly with the topic of the composition of the household: Rafael Domínguez Casas, *Arte y etiqueta de los Reyes Católicos* (Madrid, 1993); Higinio Anglés, *La música en la Corte de los Reyes Católicos* (Barcelona, 1941).

[25] Gonzalo Fernández de Oviedo, *Libro de la Cámara del Príncipe Don Juan* (Madrid, 1870). The description of the modules and offices that made up the household of prince John has been interpreted by historians as if they were ordinances of the household of Castile, although it never had any. The description was simply an old man's reminiscences about the kind of service he had been a part of in his youth. Jeanne Allard, "La naissance de l'étiquette: les règles de vie à la Cour de Castille à la fin du Moyen Âge," in Nilda Guglielmi and Adeline Rucquoi (eds.), *El discurso político en la Edad Media* (Buenos Aires, 1995), 11–28.

clear, precise study of the structure of the household, showing that the Chapel was run in accordance with thirty-four rules written to prevent defects and vices in the behaviour of its officers, although his description of the rest of the departments is based on Fernández de Oviedo.[26] There is no doubt whatsoever that the lord high steward and the lord high chamberlain were the offices of greatest responsibility and standing in the household, given that the steward had jurisdiction over all the servants in the household, whilst the chamberlain controlled the chamber; that is, he watched over the most private redoubt of the king and, therefore, enjoyed the confidences of the king himself, gave him advice and monitored the people who wanted to have closer contact with the king.

The premature death of the young prince in 1497 meant that his household was dissolved so that his servants had to look for posts in the households of other members of the royal family; the result was that the only established household in the kingdom of Castile was queen Isabella's. After the death, in 1500, of the grandson of the Catholic Monarchs, prince don Miguel, the Castilian throne passed to Joanna who came to Castile, with her husband, Philip the Handsome, to be sworn in as heir to the throne at the *Cortes* in Toledo in 1502.[27] For the first time, the style of the household of Burgundy was introduced to Castile, as the archduke brought this service with him to attend his person, whereas his wife kept the Castilian style service from the time when, in 1496, she had been given a household to go to Flanders to contract marriage with Philip the Handsome.[28]

The twin services and duality of the royal households were repeated once more after the death of Isabella the Catholic in 1504, when Joanna

[26] Domínguez Casas, *Arte y etiqueta,* 213–233. The regulations for the royal chapel are found in Archivo General de Simancas (AGS), *Patronato Real* (PR), leg. 25, fol. 83r.

[27] The description of the household of Burgundy that Philip the Handsome brought with him can be found in Louis Prosper Gachard, *Collection des voyages des souverains des Pays-Bas*, 4 vols. (Brussels, 1876), 1: 345–375. On the formation of the household of Burgundy and the functions it fulfilled, see Charles A.J. Armstrong, "The Golden Age of Burgundy: Dukes that Outdid Kings," in Arthur G. Dickens (ed.), *The Courts of Europe: Politics, Patronage and Royalty 1400–1800,* (London, 1978), 55–75; Werner Paravicini, "The Court of the Dukes of Burgundy: A Model for Europe?" in Richard G. Asch and Adolf M. Birke *Princes, Patronage and the Nobility: The Court at the Beginning of the Modern Age* (Oxford, 1991), 69–102. The ideology that dominated in the creation of the small duchy has been the subject of study in Jonathan Boulton and Jan R. Veenstra (eds.), *The Ideology of Burgundy: The Promotion of National Consciousness, 1364–1565* (Leiden, 2006).

[28] Lorenzo de Padilla, *Crónica de Felipe I llamado el Hermoso, CODOIN*, 8: 35–36; Domínguez Casas, *Arte y etiqueta de los Reyes Católicos*, 621.

took the oath as queen of Castile at the *Cortes* of Valladolid in 1506. In view of the fits of madness that Joanna began to suffer, her husband took charge of the government. In order to win the political support of the Castilian elites, Philip decided to include them in his household. The sudden death of Philip, however, meant that the Burgundy household disappeared from Castile, leaving Joanna with her service;[29] but, given the delicate state of her mental health, her father assumed the government of Castile in 1507. King Ferdinand the Catholic very soon realized that ruling Castile peacefully meant having to use his own political structure, in other words, from within his own household, using it as the organizing mechanism for such a powerful kingdom. So, he divided up the servants that formed the household of Castile: half of them were left with his daughter Joanna, whom he shut away in Tordesillas, whilst the rest of the officers were taken away with him so that they could serve him together with his own household of Aragon.[30] This decision had profound and lasting consequences on the way the Spanish Monarchy was organized, both in the "central government" and in each of the kingdoms.

A king with as many royal households as kingdoms: a model of integration

This was the situation that prince Charles found when he arrived in Castile in September 1517 to take possession of the kingdoms his grandparents had bequeathed to him. However, archduke Charles, son of Philip the Handsome and Joanna the Mad, had been brought up in Flanders under the protection of his aunt Margaret and it was she who, on October 25, 1515, had proclaimed the new regulations governing the palace domestic service of the young Charles.[31]

When Charles arrived in Castile, he found himself with another two completely organized royal households, Castile and Aragon, just

[29] See Miguel Ángel Zalama, *Vida cotidiana y arte en el palacio de la reina Juana I en Tordesillas* (Valladolid, 2000), especially, chap. 3; Bethany Aram, *La reina Juana: Gobierno, piedad y dinastía* (Madrid, 2001), 49ff.

[30] AGS, *Casas y Sitios Reales* (CSR), leg. 96, nos.1–2.

[31] For a study of what the household of Burgundy signified, see Paravicini, "The Court of the Dukes of Burgundy," 73–90. Older, but more important, documents are to be found in Frédéric-Auguste F.T. de Reiffenberg, *Particularités inédites sur Charles-Quint et sa Cour* (Brussels, 1833); Alfred De Ridder, *La Cour de Charles-Quint* (Bruges, 1889). The ordinances of the household of Burgundy of 1515 are transcribed in Martínez Millán, *Corte de Carlos V*, 5: 137–168.

as they had been left on the death of his grandfather. The Castilians who had occupied the principal posts in the kingdom and the Castilian household during the regency of Ferdinand the Catholic hastened to meet him and to offer to serve him; Charles, however, sent them on to Valladolid where the *Cortes* were to be held and he was to take the oath as heir to Castile, and these problems could be discussed. Indeed, at the *Cortes* of Valladolid in 1518, the Castilian procurators showed their disquiet at the fact that it was not possible to serve him because he had brought his own household with him, already set up and full of foreigners.[32] Once the complaints had been heard, Charles I hinted that affairs in the royal households were, in fact, less than harmonious and that it would be necessary to make adjustments. Now, when he made this remark, he was referring only to the household of Castile (divided between his mother and his late grandfather), since in his own mind there was no doubt that his service should be provided by the household of Burgundy and Burgundians of rank; so, after promulgating ordinances that amended the household of Castile serving queen Joanna in Tordesillas in a way that would dignify it, Charles himself added the other half of the household of Castile to his Burgundian retinue, just as Ferdinand the Catholic had done. Nevertheless, whereas under the former Aragonese king, this service and its officers had played a leading role in political decision-making, under the young Charles, the officers of the Castile household played a merely secondary role to those of Burgundy. This decision turned out to be unwise since the Castilians found themselves ousted from the central government of the kingdom. They had to watch as their own interests were administered by Flemings, and, moreover, the servants of the household of Burgundy were paid out of revenues raised in the kingdom of Castile. This generated such malaise that, together with the growing climate of social discontent in Castile, it provided the spark for the rebellion known as the Revolt of the *Comuneros* (1520–21), which broke out when Charles was absent from the kingdom at his coronation as emperor.

After the defeat of the *comunero* movement, and the return of Charles to Castile as Charles V, there was speculation about the political organization that should be implemented in the collection of kingdoms and territories that the young emperor was going to govern, and about the reform of the royal households.[33] In January 1523, Charles V sent

[32] Cortes de los Antiguos Reinos de León y Castilla, 4: 262–282. The topic has been covered in depth by Carlos Morales, in *Corte de Carlos V* [see n. 19], 1: 166–168.
[33] Real Academia de la Historia (RAH), *C-71*, fol. 29v.

a memorandum to the Council of Castile in which he submitted the concerns he had about such matters for their consideration. During the summer of the same year he proceeded to reform the household of Castile. Not only had the expenses and stipends of its servants increased, but Charles also recognized the political significance of the household and its role as an integrating mechanism for the Castilian elites; for this reason, he actively absorbed certain modules into his Burgundy household. Furthermore, he committed himself to introducing high-ranking Castilians into the service of the household of Burgundy, with the result that it gradually took on a more Spanish flavour during the time he spent in the peninsula (1523–1529). At the *Cortes* of Valladolid, held in 1523, Charles V presented his plan, which reflected the reforms he intended to implement both in the way the kingdoms were to be governed in general, and the royal household, in particular. It was all embodied in the political philosophy that he put to the procurators:

> To this we respond to you that, as it is not advisable to separate members that God wished to be joined in one body, we have the authority, as is right, to use together all the nations of our kingdoms and dominions, allowing each one to keep its laws and customs; and holding these kingdoms [Castile] as the head of all the others, we have the authority to prefer them to all the others, receiving into our royal household a greater number of nationals from them than from any other kingdom or dominion.[34]

The impact caused by this political reform was recorded by Martín de Salinas,[35] who, in his correspondence, confirmed the many Castilian nobles that had been appointed to posts in the household of Burgundy. This process took place gradually over the course of his reign; meanwhile, the remaining households in the other kingdoms continued to be kept up and fully organized.[36] In this way, the Castilian elites, to the exclusion of those of other kingdoms, began to influence the monarch in the government of the extensive territories that he had inherited.

[34] *Cortes de los Antiguos Reinos de León y Castilla*, 4: 366–367. A draft can be found in AGS, *Consejo y Juntas de Hacienda* (CJH), leg. 7, no. 203; it is identified as a holograph of Francisco de los Cobos. The evolution of this process has been traced in: José Martínez Millán, "La Corte de Carlos V: la configuración de la casa del Emperador, 1517–1525," in Alfred Kohler (ed.), *Carlos V/Karl V* (Madrid, 2001), 398–408.

[35] RAH, *C-71*, fols. 76v–87r.

[36] See Martínez Millán, *Corte de Carlos V* [see n. 19], 5: 169–175, for the list of Charles V's Burgundy household in 1534, where the process can be observed.

So, during the reign of Charles V, the various departments and servants of the households of Castile and Burgundy coexisted, although they retained their independence, associated with each other in the palace system; this slow process of convergence and juxtaposition became institutionalized during the reign of Philip II. Meanwhile, the Burgundian, Castilian and, to a lesser extent, Aragonese court structures were gradually combined to provide political and personal services, generating ordinances and etiquettes that corresponded to the activities of attendance and service that the king and his family demanded.

The imposition of the household of Burgundy as the model of service of the Spanish Monarchy during the reign of Philip II: 1555–1598

Given the strength of the kingdom of Castile among the territories of the Empire and the influence in government of its social elites, a service based on the Castilian model was imposed on Charles V's son and heir to the throne, prince Philip, from the age of seven. On March 1, 1535, Juan de Zúñiga y Avellaneda, Knight Commander of Castile, received the title of tutor to the prince. This appointment established the initial nucleus of the household of Castile and the rest was completed by June of the same year. On the organization of the household, Zúñiga held talks with Gonzalo Fernández de Oviedo, (a servant of prince John, the son of the Catholic Monarchs), who informed him how to serve the prince. The people chosen to serve him belonged to the Castilian elites.[37] After the death of the empress Isabella, discussions were held with Charles V about the composition of the prince's household: its former condition, the heterogeneous provenance of the officers and the kind of agreements to be reached were all outlined; the obligatory reference was the queen's household of Tordesillas or, failing that, the list of offices in prince John's household.[38] Around June 1539, various decisions were taken, but shortly after, a second series of appointments was made, increasing the number of some offices.[39]

[37] See the officers' payroll in: AGS, CSR, leg. 59.

[38] "Lo que agora se ha de consultar para lo que toca al servicio del príncipe," AGS, CSR, leg. 35, no. 28; this document, together with others referring to the individual petitions of the various servants, have been used by José Luis Gonzalo Sánchez-Molero, "El príncipe Juan de Trastamara, un "exemplum vitae" para Felipe II en su infancia y juventud," *Hispania* 59, no. 203 (1999), 890ff.

[39] For this, see the proposal in AGS, *Estado* (E), leg. 45, no. 282. Thus, a list in 1540 is headed as follows: "Sumario de todos los oficiales de la Casa del príncipe nuestro señor que están asentados en sus libros e que sirven a su alteza, *asy de los que se asentaron por el*

The result of this was that, while the Castilians looked forward to a rosy future bringing up the heir according to their own ideals and instilling in him the defence of their interests in this vast Monarchy, the elites in the other kingdoms were not quite so happy. Charles V himself was of a similar opinion and, in the summer of 1548 (thinking now about his succession), he gave orders for the household of Burgundy to be established for prince Philip, ahead of his imminent journey around Europe to visit the kingdoms and territories that he would soon inherit.[40] The duke of Alba was given responsibility for organizing the Burgundy household, on the understanding that the household of Castile, which had been serving the prince up till then, was not to disappear; in other words, Charles V prolonged the same complicated system of service that he had inherited and that had provided such good results in keeping his heterogeneous collection of kingdoms together.

The precise structure of the Burgundy household, as set out in its ordinances, and the variety of models for serving both the monarch and members of his family, enabled Philip II to integrate the elites of all the kingdoms and territories, united for the first time, and in such a way that they felt committed to the objectives of a new monarchy (the Spanish Monarchy) taking shape as a political entity under Philip. Nevertheless, on close inspection, it is clear that the two most important households on which his service was based were those of Burgundy and Castile and that, given the wide range of functions that the various sections of each household fulfilled, a degree of symbiosis arose between some duplicated positions and functions.[41] So, in the chamber, the offices peculiar to the household of Castile, such as *camarero mayor* [≈lord chamberlain] and *escribano* [≈notary] were eliminated and their holders, Antonio de Rojas and Francisco de España, transferred to the household of Burgundy as *sumiller de corps* and *grefier*, respectively. Other grooms, who were carrying out tasks in the chamber of Castile, went on to occupy different offices in the household of Burgundy under the jurisdiction of the *sumiller de corps* and which had not existed in the Castilian service. The offices of the table (sewer, *reposteros de*

asyento primero como de los otros que agora se *han asentado...*"

[40] Juan C. Calvete de Estrella, *Viaje del felicísimo del muy alto y muy poderoso Príncipe don Phelipe,* 1549 (reissue Madrid, 2001).

[41] The process has been carefully studied by Santiago Fernández Conti, "La proyección del príncipe Felipe: Viajes y regencias en la corte hispana," in *Corte de Carlos V*, 2: 209–225.

estrado, carvers, and so on) disappeared completely to the benefit of the Burgundy household. In addition, the pages in the Castile household were replaced by those from Burgundy, although many of them simply changed households. The chapel also underwent important changes, although at a later date:[42] the most important post in the chapel of the household of Castile, the *capellán mayor* [≈dean of the chapel], merged with the post of *limosnero mayor* [≈lord almoner], who ran the chapel in the household of Burgundy; the office of *repostero de capilla* [≈ chapel supervisor] disappeared, whereas the number of *cantores* [cantors], an office characteristic of the Burgundy household, increased slightly.[43] The chaplains and preachers were, essentially, those of the household of Castile.[44] To complete the process, the guards were brought together so that the Spanish guard was joined by the Bodyguard of the *Archeros*.

Finally, the household of Burgundy, which was imposed on the heir and which was destined to continue as the ordinary service of the dynasty, was charged exclusively with serving the prince directly in the significant areas of the stable, the table and providing company and private attendance, while the offices of the household of Castile that remained, such as the harbingers, were of lower rank and did not have direct contact with the royal person.[45] As a result, in the process of reorganizing the prince's service to bring in Burgundian etiquette, the household of Castile suffered severe depletion, its two hundred and forty servants dropping to fewer than a hundred.[46]

At the *Cortes* of Toledo in 1560, prince Carlos took the oath as heir and the new queen, Isabella of Valois, Philip II's third wife, was presented, as were their respective households. They were not the only members of the royal family with their own service: the monarch's brother and sister, don John of Austria and doña Joanna of Austria also had a large number of servants at their disposal. Shortly afterwards, the archdukes of Austria, who came to Spain to be brought up by their uncle, joined the list of those with households. This proliferation of

[42] On the adaptation of the different chapels (Burgundy, Castile, Aragon), see Véronique Gérard, "Los sitios de devoción en el alcázar de Madrid: capilla y oratorios," *Archivo Español del Arte*, no. 223 (1983), 278–279.
[43] Anglés, *La música*, 102ff.
[44] Henar Pizarro Llorente, "La capilla real," in *La Monarquía de Felipe II*, 1: 181–225.
[45] María José Rodríguez-Salgado, "Honour and profit in the Court of Philip II of Spain," in *La Cour comme institution économique*, 69–73.
[46] AGS, CSR, leg. 64, no. 843.

households meant that the many demands by important personages to be admitted to the royal service could be met.

Once the court was finally settled in Madrid, the power groups who dominated during the reign of Philip II were formed; it quickly became clear that the Castilian elites were going to occupy a pre-eminent role, prevailing over those factions – even when some of their members were Castilians by birth – whose political ideas supported foreign interests and positions. Indeed, the distribution of the representatives of the social elites in the service of the royal family was not heterogeneous, but obeyed very precise criteria that prevailed as a result of factional infighting at court. So, in the king's household, the major posts soon finished up in the hands of the Castilian elite, whose political ideals defended, at least implicitly, the pre-eminence of Castile over the other kingdoms, the imposition of ideological intransigence, an "intellectual" spirituality and, consequently, the practice of a formal religiosity. The Castilian factions, as well as those from other kingdoms who had not managed to connect with the previous elites because of disagreements with their political ideals or their social and economic interests, were found posts in the households of the other members of the royal family.

With this group of Castilian lawyers and theologians, Philip II began the process of turning all his inherited kingdoms into confessional states. The result was to bring into being a new political entity known as the Spanish Monarchy.[47] One of the essential parts of the process was to organize the respective courts and households as fundamental political entities for channelling royal power in each kingdom. In the case of Spain, Philip II commanded ordinances for the queen's household to be drawn up along Castilian lines, whereas he ordered Jean Sigonney, in 1575, to recoup the ordinances of the household of Burgundy that had served his father.[48] In this way, the Prudent King respected the Castilian model of service (the household of Castile), but took the household of Burgundy, which was that of the dynasty, as the official model for the Monarchy. The Castilian faction had no problem accepting this as long as important members of its elites occupied the main posts in that household, which was foreign to the kingdom. Accordingly, Philip II constructed the Spanish Monarchy as a separate entity, although paradoxically, the official model for the household was not that of the

[47] This process has been studied in José Martínez Millán and Carlos Javier de Carlos Morales (eds.), *Felipe II (1527–1598): La configuración de la Monarquía hispana* (Valladolid, 1998).

[48] These ordinances have been published in *Corte de Carlos V*, 5: 179–211.

kingdom (Castile), which had helped to to shape it, but that of the dynasty (the household of Burgundy). In recognition of the original importance of Castile, the Prudent King agreed to maintain the Castilian service, but amalgamated many posts with those of the household of Burgundy. The most significant changes related to the chapel and the chamber, departments of the royal household in which the Burgundian structure prevailed.[49] Along with this reform, Philip II structured the administrative organization of the government of his Monarchy.

Now, the political actions of the Castilian party aroused resentment among the elites of all the kingdoms and, by the end of the reign, the ruling faction had taken on all the appearance of a real coalition. Rome was not indifferent to this uneasy atmosphere. The pontiffs, as temporal lords, felt similarly subjected to and, even, threatened by the Spanish monarchs because of the decisive influence that they had been bringing to bear in the conclaves at the time of electing pontiffs. This was done by using the temporal power that they had built up in their client network of cardinals,[50] and through Philip II's interference in matters of church jurisdiction and religious reform, when the monarch was wont to apply the decrees of Trent in pursuit of his interests and interpret the Catholic doctrine that derived from them for his own ends.[51] By the end of his reign, there were sufficient symptoms to demonstrate that the Castilian faction had been ousted from power and supplanted by others.[52]

The attempt to restore the household of Castile as the model of service of the Spanish Monarchy during the reign of Philip III: 1598–1621

By the time of Philip II's death, the Spanish Monarchy had been constructed as an entity in its own right, although, paradoxically, the official household model was that of the dynasty, the household of

[49] I refer the reader to the study by Henar Pizarro Llorente in the two volume series of *La Monarquía de Felipe II* and to the study by Rubén Mayoral López in José Martínez Millán and Maria Antonietta Visceglia (eds.), *La Monarquía de Felipe III: La Casa del Rey*, 4 vols. (Madrid, 2007).

[50] Ricardo Hinojosa, *Los despachos de la diplomacia pontificia en España* (Madrid, 1896), 399–405.

[51] Luciano Serrano, "El papa Pío IV y dos embajadores de Felipe II," *Cuadernos de Trabajo de la Escuela Española de Arqueología e Historia en Roma* 5 (1924), 1–65; Ignasi Fernández Terricabras, *Felipe II y el clero secular: La aplicación del concilio de Trento* (Madrid, 2000), especially 361–381.

[52] For context, see the introduction to volume 1 of *La Corte de Felipe III*.

Burgundy, rather than that of the original kingdom that had given it shape. The contradictions, latent in the earlier reign, of making the dynasty and hence the specific etiquette of its household coincide with kingdoms foreign to it, came to the surface with Philip III's accession to the throne. The members of the Castilian faction, removed from power during the final years of Philip II's reign, began to criticize the situation openly and show their disagreement with the direction that the Monarchy was taking, the composition of the court and the royal household. At the *Cortes* in 1598, they made it abundantly clear to the new monarch, Philip III that:

> The grandeur and antiquity of the royal household of Castile is widely known to everyone, and although, through the union with the most serene house of Austria on the occasion of the marriage of the Most Serene Queen Doña Juana to the lord don Philip, count of Flanders, the style and form of the household of Burgundy were introduced into the royal household in the names and offices and service, the Kingdom, in 1579, beseeched His Majesty King Philip, our lord, may he be in glory, to restore the service of his royal household to the customs, office and names of old Castile and which at that time ceased to be provided. Now, through the just causes that moved His Majesty in the marriage of the Most Serene Infanta Doña Isabella Clara Eugenia to the Most Serene Archduke Albert, the States of Flanders have left the crown of Castile; however, since they have retained direct control over it [the crown], it appears that what was once beseeched as advisable, has now come down to necessity. With this in mind, we beseech Your Majesty to kindly consider that it is right that, since this kingdom carries the burden of so many obligations, and at the crown of it Our Lord has seen fit to increase such a great Monarchy, its former name of the household of Castile be restored, as well as its customary offices and names; it not being fitting that this province, being the head of this Monarchy, should be governed by a name and titles foreign to it and not its own.[53]

[53] *Actas de las Cortes de Castilla*, 16, 639–640, cited by Carlos María Gómez-Centurión Jiménez, "La herencia de Borgoña: el ceremonial real y las casas reales en la España de los Austrias (1548–1700)," in Luis Antonio Ribot García and Ernest Belenguer (eds.), *Las Sociedades Ibéricas y el mar a finales del siglo XVI: La Corte, centro e imagen del poder* (Madrid, 1998), 15, where the Spanish original can be found.

As Helen Nader has appositely remarked, during the reign of Philip III the Burgundian service began to be referred to in contemptuous terms as barbarous and foreign; more specifically, she quotes the chronicler, Fray Prudencio de Sandoval, who, describing the establishment of the household of Burgundy for prince Philip in 1548, confined himself to the laconic comment: "And likewise, don Fernando Álvarez, duke of Alba, lord steward to the Emperor and his captain general, was brought in on his orders to organize the prince's journey and set up the government of his household according to the custom of the household of Burgundy,"[54] without mentioning or reporting anything else. However, his contempt for the Burgundian style becomes patently obvious a little further on when he states: "He set up the Prince's household in the Burgundian style, depriving the Castilian household of authority, which should be kept, if only for its antiquity, and more so as the Kings of Castile have nothing of Burgundy in them."[55] The same xenophobia towards all things Burgundian can also be perceived in the chronicler Luis Cabrera de Córdoba, a contemporary of Philip III's, who simply reported the same fact: "He went to Valladolid, and formed his household according to the custom of Burgundy, against the wishes and hopes of Castile."[56]

Criticism of the household of Burgundy became more pointed whenever the policies deployed by the Monarchy – and which the elites excluded from power disagreed with – required an increased tax burden, which seriously damaged the economy of the kingdom, precisely when the Castilian elites had been removed from positions close to the monarch, making it impossible for their voice to be heard in policy decisions. During the reign of Philip III, there was a positive mania for regulating the ordinances and etiquette of the offices, practices and ceremonies of the household of Burgundy in an attempt to cut down on expenses and avoid the criticisms of the tax system that rained down on the government. When the process is looked at more closely, we find that the copious legislation was confined to meticulously regulating the obligations of each and every office with the aim of avoiding waste, rather than changing the structure of the

[54] P. de Sandoval, *Historia de la vida y hechos del Emperador Carlos V* (Madrid, 1956); (*Biblioteca de Autores Españoles*, vol. 82), 318.

[55] *Ibidem*, 337.

[56] Luis Cabrera de Córdoba, *Historia de Felipe II, rey de España*, ed. J. Martínez Millán and C. J. Carlos Morales (Valladolid, 1998), 1: 15.

household or making major modifications to the Burgundian style,[57] whilst the household of Castile was left untouched. The *Cortes* of 1617 joined in the general chorus of those who wanted reforms carried out. Baltasar de Córdoba, procurator for Cordoba, presented a list of ills that were afflicting Castile, among which the most important were: the doubling of the number of servants in the royal households since the death of Philip II, the substantial outlay in grace and favour payments, and imports of foreign goods to the detriment of Castilian ones. Before his fall, Lerma sent an official note to the president of the Council of Castile asking him to free Castile from collapse.[58] On February 1, 1619, the Council of Castile responded with its famous proposal for reform, outlined by don Diego Corral de Arellano.[59] The reform of the royal household and cutting back on expenditure were ever present, so it seemed impossible to avoid drawing up new ordinances which – without touching the household of Castile – would make savings to the budget in the Burgundy household; however, Philip III died before he could implement them.

The household of Burgundy is finally imposed as the model for the Spanish Monarchy: reforms carried out during the reign of Philip IV

A week after Philip IV succeeded to the throne, he was presented with a written document entitled: "What His Majesty should execute as soon as possible and the main causes of the destruction of the Monarchy,"[60] in which corruption was declared one of the major evils afflicting the

[57] The scholar with the best understanding of the evolution of the royal households in the Spanish Monarchy is Luis Robledo Estaire, "La música en la corte madrileña de los Austrias: Antecedentes: las casas reales hasta 1556," *Revista de musicología* 10 (1987), cuadro 5 [summary sheet 5]. In addition, in the aforementioned summary sheet, he points out that the household of Aragon, which had existed in parallel with Castile's since the time of Ferdinand the Catholic, disappeared in 1618.

[58] *La Junta de Reformación: Documentos procedentes del Archivo Histórico Nacional y del General de Simancas*, 1618–1625 (Valladolid, 1932), 379–408, doc. 4, transcribed by Ángel González Palencia; Michael Weisser, "The Decline of Castile Revisited: the Case of Toledo," *The Journal of European Economic History* 2 (1973), 614–640.

[59] Corral's authorship is confirmed by P. Fernández Navarrete, *Conservación de Monarquías y Discursos Políticos* (Madrid, 1982), 21. For the person himself, see León Corral y Maestro, *Don Diego Corral y Arellano y los Corrales de Valladolid* (Valladolid, 1905), 40; *Junta de Reformación*, 29.

[60] Archivo Histórico Nacional (AHN), *Estado* (E), Estado, lib. 832.

Monarchy and, if he did not want a recurrence of what had happened in his father's time, he ought to act immediately by removing from government those who formed the nucleus of all this evil. To solve the problem, the new government set up a *Junta de Reformación* [Reform Board] with the mission of raising the standard of public morality.[61] The Board of ten members, which was supposed to meet every sunday in the home of the president of the Council of Castile, Fernando de Acevedo,[62] issued one or two proposals, but was eventually wound up; even so, it instilled a good deal of fear when it ordered all those who had held office from 1603 onwards to present an inventory of their goods to see if they had enriched themselves fraudulently at the cost of the Crown. The most pressing problems, however, remained: reducing the Monarchy's expenditure on wars, and cutting back the budget of the royal household.

The 1624 ordinances for the household of Burgundy

To solve the first problem, that is, find income with which to boost the royal exchequer, the count of Olivares proposed a series of reforms set out in a lengthy letter, dated October 20, 1622,[63] which he sent to the cities with representation in the *Cortes*. In it, he requested, on the one hand, maintenance for thirty thousand soldiers for six years at the rate of six ducats per month per soldier and, on the other, a network of treasuries and savings banks to be established, following a different scheme from the one agreed in the *Cortes* held in Madrid from 1598 to 1603.[64] The representatives of the cities were not persuaded, however, so that when it came to the final vote on October 4, 1623, the procurators had already resorted to the traditional means of raising money: the *millones* and a variety of fiscal measures left to the discretion of the *Cortes*. Nevertheless, the sum of money voted was unprecedented (sixty

[61] Gonzalo Céspedes y Meneses, *Historia de don Felipe IV, Rey de España* (Barcelona, 1634), fol. 35; Biblioteca Nacional de España (BNE), MS. 18670, cédula real de creación [royal letters patent].

[62] Ángel González Palencia, "Quevedo, Tirso y las comedias ante la Junta de Reformación," *Boletín de la Real Academia española* 25 (1946), 43–86.

[63] The letter, transcribed by Ángel González Palencia, can be found in *La Junta de Reformación*, 379-408.

[64] For the context, see Antonio Domínguez Ortiz, *Política y Hacienda de Felipe IV* (Madrid: 1983), 19–33; also by Domínguez Ortiz, *Política fiscal y cambio social en la España del siglo XVII* (Madrid, 1984), 41–43; Felipe Ruiz Martín, *Las finanzas de la Monarquía hispánica en tiempos de Felipe IV, 1621–1665* (Madrid, 1990), 37–41.

million ducats payable over twelve years, as well as twelve million due from the previous award). To convince the procurators about the plans to be implemented, the amount to be assigned under each heading was specified: 1,200,000 ducats for the prisons; 1,300,000 for the navy; 300,000 for the salaries of ministers and officers; 610,000 for the royal households. To demonstrate the veracity of these items, Olivares announced to the *Cortes*, on February 8, 1623, that they would save 67,000 ducats a year on the king's household expenses and 80,000 on the queen's.

As for the second problem, the reform of the royal household, a solution was sought through the promulgation of new ordinances. To this end, on September 14, 1622, Philip IV ordered the Board of Stewards, consisting of the count of Arcos, the marquis of las Navas and the count of la Puebla, to convene a meeting to make changes in the expenditure of the Burgundy household. The conclusions were presented to the monarch on October 17, 1622. Despite the fact that they had seen papers concerning costs and procedures from the time of Philip III, the introduction to their conclusions stated that the household of Burgundy in the time of Philip II had been their reference and model for making changes to the above-mentioned household, that being the model they wished to impose, both in terms of the number of servants and expenditure.[65]

The following year, the same Board of Stewards met to discuss "the way the offices were to be governed." The agreements were presented to the king on December 6, 1623, and provide a clear insight into the alarming state of the royal coffers. The account began with a statement by the stewards that "the steward's office involves responsibility for reforming and supervising the offices of the table and expenditure on provisions," but they also took the liberty of advising his Majesty "what it is best to do in each office for the good government of it." Having said that, they stated their general rule that "for the good government of the offices of the table of Your Majesty's royal household, it would appear advisable for the stewards to draw lots on the first day of the year for the supervision of each office so that they can order anything they deem necessary to be carried out." This demonstration of centralization and control of economic resources by those with authority became

[65] "And whenever we refer to that agreed yesterday in the meeting about the number of servants, stipends and bouche of court in the past, it is understood to mean at the time of His Majesty the King Don Philip the Second, may he be in heaven" (Archivo General de Palacio (AGP), *Administrativa*, leg. 928).

obvious in the warnings that were sent out to each of the specific offices with regard to what it did: "the *sumiller de la panadería* [≈serjeant of the bakehouse] must not, solely on his own authority, order provision to be made for wheat, which is a necessary cost, but it should be done under the supervision of the appropriate steward." "In the fruitery, the steward on duty should take care to make provision by buying in units of *arrobas* in the morning at the same price as those selling it in the market place, and that it should be accounted to Your Majesty at this same price." "More is spent in the larder than in any other office of the table and, therefore, it will be necessary for the duty steward to keep a particularly careful eye on its management, ordering that everything which comes in, whether it be by number, weight or measure, should go out in the same way, and ensuring that the *veedor de viandas* [≈food supervisor] is present in this office when the officers are there and checks the amount and provision received," and so on. In short, it was a question of saving through cutbacks in the officers' bouche of court. At the same time, they pointed out the little tricks that some offices employed to pilfer provisions to the detriment of the royal household: "The purveyor of this office earns a lot of money from it and it seems it would be advisable not to buy at fixed prices, but to purchase, on his Majesty's behalf, the hens, pullets, pigeons and other fowl that are brought in from different places and sold in the market square every morning." "Large numbers of eggs are consumed every day and the buyer's price is fixed at five *maravedís*, whereas the ordinary purchase price is four and a half," ... "the cellar should not just be stocked in Esquivias, but in Valdemoro and other places nearby, because the quality of the wine will be sufficient for bouche of court and, being a fixed contract, let the pack animals from the mule stable bring it, for it will save a lot." The reform was accompanied by changes in the main posts in the exchequer of the royal household so that the decisions taken could be implemented quickly and accurately.[66]

[66] "His Majesty sent D. Lorenzo de Cárdenas, count of la Puebla del Maestre, to visit Francisco Guillamás Velázquez, and inspect the office he held as treasurer of the chamber, and this office was given to D. Manuel de Hinojosa, the former *guarda mayor* of D. Rodrigo Calderón; and since he did not accept it, it was given to captain Tomás de Carona, servant of the count of Olivares; and the aforementioned Francisco Guillamás was given the title of councillor of the Exchequer when the inspection visit was over"; Andrés de Almansa y Mendoza, *Cartas* (Madrid, 1886), 181–182.

In view of both memoranda, and after consulting some of the nobles, Philip IV announced the ordinances of his household in 1624. Philip IV made no secret of his intentions when he introduced the new general *ordinances*:

> The sorry state in which I found the finances of my kingdoms when I acceded to them and the great occasions for spending which have arisen here subsequently through the need to enlarge my navies because of the many enemies roaming the seas, and to go to Italy and Germany and other necessary parts, and the lack of funds for so many things has obliged me to employ every possible means to obtain them [funds] and one of them being to reduce non-essential expenditure so as to make better provision, I have considered it advisable to begin with my household and so I have resolved that it should be reformed in the following way.[67]

And yet, when it came to reforming the offices of his households, the monarch gave notice that "the servants of the household of Castile cannot be extinguished, because there is a need for fowlers, hunters, doctors following the court and who have to be in residence, harbingers for the same reason, and they have fewer stipends than those of Burgundy, foot squires, doorkeepers of the chamber serving in the palace, the Councils and Chancelleries and other servants that there have not been in the household of Burgundy and having to give them stipends irrespective of the cost." The reason was explained in the first point of the ordinances:

> 1. The households of Castile and Aragon are the foundation of the greatness of the Spanish royalty and their wealth, blood, lives and loyalty preserve and sustain the other states that have joined them. There are no words, nor is there head of any subject that wants the Royal Households of the kingdoms of Castile and Aragon to disappear and if the kingdoms knew what was being attempted, they would be very angry, since it is more just that the name of the households of Castile and Aragon prevail than to reduce everything to a foreign household. Until now, the progenitors of His Majesty have kept servants with the name of those households; the countrymen of both kingdoms want

[67] Madrid, February 7, 1624, see BNE, MS. 18716/43: "Reformación de la Casa Real hecha en el año de 1624" p. 2ª, (nos. 63–70 struck out and replaced by fols. 17–24).

> favours and stipends in them so as to serve their natural king as they have done in the other states. [68]

The promulgation of the ordinances in 1624 was followed by a series of meetings at the residence of the Count-Duke of Olivares with the aim of finding a way to apply them rigorously. This reform, like others in matters of the exchequer, enjoyed strong support from the men of letters, at least in the early years.[69] However, from 1626, there was a sudden deterioration, both in the general economic situation of the kingdom, and in the crisis of the royal exchequer.[70] The suspension of payments in 1627 heralded the first bankruptcy of the kingdom. The price and wage rates dictated by the Council of Castile had no effect, given the rise in inflation, so that, on August 7, 1628, a devaluation edict was issued by means of which the *vellón* coinage was reduced to half its value, at the same time as the pragmatic sanction fixing rates (proclaimed to prevent price increases) was abolished on the grounds of ineffectiveness.[71]

In view of the economic situation, it is hardly surprising that the royal household budget should come up constantly as an area for cost cutting. In fact, this practice served more as an example for the urban elites, who were repeatedly asked to increase the *servicios* [type of tax] that they paid, than for raising substantial sums of money; of course, the reduction in costs and elimination of offices in the royal service went hand-in-hand with complaints and a feeling of unease among the nobles and other elites in the kingdom who saw their chances of being part of the court disappearing. They referred to the court of the Monarchy when the Count-Duke of Olivares was the royal favourite as "a court of petty nobles."[72] The fact is that what the monarch needed to maintain his estates and territories and implement his foreign policy led him to adopt a series of measures that destroyed the model of

[68] He added: "2. The number of servants depends on the will of His Majesty which is always to honour and extend favour to his vassals according to the quality of each one to make use of them." (Copy of the proposal made to his Majesty by the lord steward, duke of the Infantado, on September 26, 1623, concerning the reform of October 17, 1622: "Casa-reformas," AGP, *Administrativa*, leg. 928). These are reforms, particularly from the beginning of the reign of Philip IV.

[69] Charles Vincent Aubrun, *La Comédie Espagnole,1600–1680* (Paris, 1966), 48.

[70] Domínguez Ortiz, *Política fiscal y cambio social*, 46–47.

[71] On this topic, see Felipe Ruiz Martín, "La banca en España hasta 1782," *El banco de España: Una historia económica* (Madrid, 1970), 104–106.

[72] The peculiarities of the Spanish court with respect to other European courts are highlighted by Carl Justi, *Velázquez y su siglo* (Madrid, 1999), 178–181.

political organization that had underpinned the Spanish Monarchy since Charles V and Philip II, that is, one based on integrating the elites of the different kingdoms into his service.[73] In spite of everything, the Count-Duke of Olivares embarked on a policy of cost cutting in the royal households that led him to monitor the effectiveness of the 1624 ordinances. To this end, he set up a new Board, which met periodically, to examine how far they had been complied with. The Board met a total of nine times, and in every session, discussion centred on the immediately superior office-holder tightly controlling the activities of those beneath him; this vigilance, it was thought, would stop economic resources being squandered and bring about substantial savings.

The resolutions taken by the Board at the nine meetings, held in the Count-Duke's rooms, were formalized in fifty-nine points which restricted the ordinances of 1624 even further,[74] at the same time as another twenty-six articles were drawn up, laying down norms for the quantities of food corresponding to each office, with the aim of reducing expenditure as much as possible. However, the savings made with these measures were negligible. As a result, Philip IV issued a proclamation on January 29, 1627, in which he expressed his intention to implement the measures agreed the previous year; to confirm the savings made as a consequence of those ordinances, the expense accounts of the king's households were presented: a total of 101,703,574 *maravedís*. The report ended by warning that "during this year of 1628, costs will rise because the prices of many items in His Majesty's household have increased, such as wheat, which last year cost eighteen *reales* and is now sold for twenty-three ... ". On January 15, 1628, the list of fifty-nine points agreed in the nine Board meetings in the Count-Duke's rooms was drawn up again and in the margin against each point the degree of compliance was written with possible warnings. Most of the annotations on the various points coincided in expressing the same succinct, "so it was done."

The economic deficiencies did not end with this statement of accounts. The royal chamber could not meet the salaries and pensions

[73] The monarch himself recognized as much, when, at the end of 1623, he ordered: "His Majesty issued a decree for the Councils, ordering that, in their proposals, they should make a list of the servants among the aspirants, or of their past service, and if they are, or have been, at Court and for how long; for he does not want their claims to be met simply by request, but on merit." (Almansa y Mendoza, *Cartas*, 164). On this topic, see *La Monarquía de Felipe II*, vols. 1 and 2.

[74] AGP, *Administrativa*, leg. 928.

owing to the Monarchy's servants who had received grace and favour payments for services rendered. Concern had been mounting since the death of Philip III, given that the scarcity of income was compounded by the preoccupation with honesty that the new monarch wished to convey by pursuing and removing favours obtained by underhand means.[75] In one "list of people who have pensions drawn from the three thousand ducats paid out every month as ordinary expenses of His Majesty's chamber, and of its other expenses and outstanding debts owing up until today, February 22, 1628," details were shown as follows: "expenditure on pensions [...] amounted to 587,279 *reales* and every month 3,000 ducats in total are paid out, amounting to 396,000 *reales* a year, so that the outgoings are 191,279 *reales*, which is 17,389 ducats." Moreover, 110,149 *reales*, owed to the pensioners, and 155,040 in debts to private individuals, had to be added to this figure.[76] The problem with the debts contracted by the royal chamber was not so much an economic one, as the lack of credibility offered by the Monarchy compared to earlier reigns. The courtiers and secretary themelves were conscious of this when they wrote: "What suffers, when those who depend on this money pester and insist, is not only the patience, but the credibility of those of us who have to deal with it because, accustomed to the punctuality of the chamber, they blame our time because they are not paid with the same [punctuality] and, so, the distribution is our responsibility and while Your Excellency is the master of the order, it will not be out of place to inform Your Excellency what should be remedied and how it could be done."

The following year, 1629, the governing organ of the Burgundy household, the *Bureo*, reviewed the accounts of the royal household from the previous year, pointing out to the monarch at the same time, that it would be impossible to maintain itself in economic terms with the cuts that had been implemented: "As for the posts that in some offices were ordered to be reformed, they have either not yet fallen vacant so that they can be extinguished, or if they have fallen vacant, not only has

[75] "List of pensions that have been consigned to the ordinary expenses of the larder, distinguishing three groups: those granted by letters patent from Philip III (Nov. 1622), which amount to 1,561,420 *maravedís*; by letters patent from Philip IV which increased ordinary expenditure, amounting to 1,142,500 *maravedís*; and by order of His Majesty that have not increased ordinary expenditure (mostly dated between 1625 and 1626) that amounted to 937,000 *maravedís*. To these are added 2,382,320 *maravedís* for 13 valets of the chamber, and 400 *reales* a month entered by mistake for the apothecary are struck from the account" (AGP, *Administrativa*, leg. 364).

[76] AGP, *Administrativa*, leg. 939/1, exp. 12.

it pleased Your Majesty to fill them, but also to make favours of other supernumerary posts and for people to succeed to them in the future." Together with this document, another was presented to the monarch, entitled "what the comptroller reports about the reduction in ordinary expenditure," showing that the royal household could not possibly be maintained on such a budget.[77]

In general, what was more important and far-reaching in the application of such drastic economic measures was the part they were playing in the breakdown of the political structure of the Monarchy, since the integrative function fulfilled by the royal households and service to the monarch for the elites in the kingdoms was disappearing, as the monarch himself recognized in each of two *cédulas* sent to the *Bureo* in 1630 and 1631. In the first one, he ordered that: "henceforward, the *Bureo* will not propose to me any office that has not been vacated, in accordance with the reform of sixteen hundred and twenty-four, nor supernumerary posts, even if they are without stipends, nor swear anybody into a post of *ayuda* [assistant to a superior] with the stipend of a groom." In the second, he insisted that, "When I resolved to reform those things held to be advisable in my household, it was with the intention that it should be carried out [...] and once again, I order and command that it should be adhered to inviolably."

The new reform in 1631

Reducing the number of officers and freezing *quitaciones* [wages] was not sufficient to raise the amount of revenue required to cover the cost of war. Moreover, the depression that the agricultural economy had experienced in Castile between 1629 and 1632 meant that it would not have been wise to request new taxes to pay for the war that the Monarchy was waging in Europe.[78] In view of the impossibility of raising funds, Philip IV ordered a fresh reform of his household in 1631. This reform did not concentrate on reducing offices or drawing up new ordinances

[77] "Your Lordship commanded me to inform him of my opinion on the reduction that His Majesty has ordered to be made each month in the ordinary expenditure of his Royal Household, and in fulfilment of that, I wish to report the following" (AGP, *Administrativa*, leg. 928). The date is Madrid, February 22, 1629.

[78] For the political and economic situation, see Domínguez Ortiz, *Política y Hacienda de Felipe IV*, 37–39; John H. Elliott, *The Count-Duke of Olivares. The Statesman in an Age of Decline* (New Haven - London, 1986), 407–412; Gonzalo Anes and Jean-Paul Le Flem, "La crisis del siglo XVII: producción agrícola, precios e ingresos en tierras de Segovia," *Moneda y Crédito* 93 (1965), 16–18.

of conduct in the service, but focussed on the food to be given to each officer, beginning with the king, by reducing courses and quantities of food. Control of kitchen expenditure and the amount of food for the household officers and the tables of the "estates" had been a recurring theme since the beginning of the reign; however, it had never been stipulated in such detail what each office post could consume to the extent of producing specific ordinances on the matter:

> His Majesty, having seen a proposal by the *Bureo* of February 21, 1630, on the moderation of expenditure on his household and adjusting it to what was done in the households of the lords Emperor Charles the Fifth and King Philip II, his forefathers who are in glory, and another that the Board, which His Majesty had convened for the reform of the royal households, made on this matter on September 25 of the same year, it has pleased him to resolve both and henceforth, let the following be kept and implemented:
>
> 1 That the courses for His Majesty be henceforth, ten at lunch and eight at dinner, and if it were boiled capon and gigot, the remaining courses should not be duplicated, keeping down costs.
>
> 2 That the requirements for sugar, wine, flour and everything else that is used for His Majesty's meal should be issued through official chits from the comptroller and in no other way, according to the food that is ordered, with no excess whatsoever and the same applies to that of the estates.
>
> 3 That the estate of the chamber be reduced to six courses at lunch and four at dinner on meat days, and on fish days, eight for lunch and four for dinner […], and so on.[79]

Such measures were destroying the political underpinning on which the union of the Monarchy was based and made the monarch appear a bad *paterfamilias* for not rewarding the merit and service provided to him by his subjects. For example, in point 37 of this reform, it was ordered that, "henceforth no compensation should be given to the widows of sweepers unless it is once only, and that it should not be charged to the larder." In article 38: "omit the firewood that used to be given to

[79] AGP, *Administrativa*, leg. 928.

the Councils." What was even more surprising was the ban on giving expense allowances to the widows of muleteers and soldiers. The reform ended by ordering a return to the times of Philip II.

The ordinances of 1635–1636: The reform of the Chamber and the appointment of the Count-Duke of Olivares as chamberlain and sumiller de corps

Overall, the economic problem that the royal household represented was not the number of officers (few could be dispensed with), nor the more or less substantial quantities of food that were served up, but the pensions that the monarch granted to individuals for services rendered. Such graces and favours were granted through the *Cámara*, which was the king's most restricted and intimate section in all the households of the European monarchies. It consisted of all those important people who, making use of their friendship and daily contact with the king, advised him on his political decisions and on the appointments and favours that he granted. In the household of Castile, it was always clearly defined, to the point where, in 1588, in the time of Philip II, it was finally constituted as the *Consejo de Cámara* [Council of the Privy Chamber]. By contrast, the household of Burgundy was a confusing organism, with little regulation and, beyond a list of pensioners drawn up annually to pay them their wages, there was no detailed record of the favours and positions granted.

The progress of the Thirty Years War, especially when France entered the conflict in 1635, intensified the tax burden.[80] It was necessary to fall back on resources of all kinds: half-annates were taken from the salaries of ministers and officers of the Monarchy, as well as from the interest on *juros* [bonds] and loans; a general donation was requested to replenish the royal coffers; an appeal was made to the *Cortes* to vote in favour of more *servicios*, stamped paper was introduced and finally, the *vellón* was devalued.[81] In such circumstances, it was of utmost importance, on the one hand, to control expenditure occasioned by the royal household; on the other, it was essential to reward those vassals who were outstanding

[80] The political development has been studied in detail by Elliott, *The Count-Duke of Olivares*, 456–492. For the economic problems, see Ruiz Martín, *Las finanzas de la Monarquía hispánica*, 109–111; Carlos Álvarez Nogal, *El crédito de la Monarquía hispánica en el reinado de Felipe IV* (Valladolid, 1997), 225–239.

[81] All these measures have been studied by Domínguez Ortiz, *Política y Hacienda de Felipe IV*, 2nd ed., 49–53.

in their service to the king, especially at times when great sacrifices were being demanded and when not all the subjects identified with the political strategy followed by the Monarchy. In this situation, in which it was necessary to bring all the resources of the kingdoms together in one common enterprise, complete control of access to the person of the king and the granting of favours was regarded as absolutely essential.

In accordance with the economic cuts imposed on the household, the chamber had been assigned 36,000 ducats a year, the same sum as in the time of Philip II. However, the major problem was that the budget for the chamber had risen to 50,000 ducats a year because of the need to reward services rendered to the Monarchy, making new sources of income necessary. It was imperative to find out how costs had come to outstrip the budget. Consequently, on March 26, 1635, the monarch wrote to the duke of Medina de las Torres, the *sumiller de corps* since 1626,[82] "that the monthly accounts of everything that has been received, issued and paid out, and the fund used for the Royal Chamber from the time when His Majesty succeeded to these kingdoms, should be reviewed, examined and handed to Your Excellency." The *sumiller* sent the note to those who had been secretaries of the chamber during that period (1621–1635), namely, Bernabé de Vivanco, who carried out the duty for the first nine months of 1621; Antonio de Alosa, who was appointed on August 1, 1621, and Antonio de Mendoza, who was in post from September 1, 1625, until he was replaced by Garcigallo on September 9, 1644, asking them, at the same time, to present accounts of every type of revenue that had passed through their hands and of those who had been granted favours.

The secretaries responded speedily and from their replies it emerged that the household of Burgundy had no regulations whatsoever. The statement by Antonio de Alosa exemplifies what all the secretaries alleged:

> The order, sir, with which this money has been collected and paid out, was the general one that all my predecessors received, based on confidence in the secretaries, in those who went before, and in me, on the orders of His Majesty or his favourites, who were usually the *sumillers de corps*, the principal heads of this office and in charge of appointing and dismissing and of demanding

[82] AGP, *Administrativa*, leg. 939/1, exp. 12. The duke of Medina de las Torres left the post of *sumiller de corps*, which he had occupied since 1626, to go to Italy, Elliott, *The Count-Duke of Olivares*, 478.

> whatever they liked, sometimes in writing and at other times verbally, who gave out expense allowances, alms, income and sometimes asked Their Majesties to be allowed to give secret expense allowances or alms with their own hand or to have it in their private offices, and all this in confidence, since it was obvious that His Majesty was not going to be required to give a receipt. And so, nobody will be able to satisfy this question; the rest will be easy for the person whose responsibility it is. The justifications for the collection of this money and for its distribution in the aforementioned manner are two *cédulas*, copies of which are attached to this paper, in which His Majesty commands that no account should be asked for, nor record made. I, sir, keeping to that style and with this security, when I took up the said office, continued to do what my predecessors had done, with the same officers, with the same books, in the same manner and same justifications, but neither do I know who the officers are, nor did I know when I took up the post, nor do I know what books these are, nor have I seen them, nor do I know what they are for, nor do I have any instruction to guide me.[83]

With these reports, the *sumiller de corps* wrote to the monarch, pointing out the economic plight of the chamber and, to avoid this situation in the future, advised the use of a better accounting and control system so that "whenever money is requested or given, it should be accounted for formally with a legitimate justification and likewise, if it would please His Majesty, to kindly identify those pensions on the pension list which

[83] AGP, *Administrativa*, leg. 939/1, exp. 12, dated Madrid, March 31, 1635, and signed by Antonio Alosa Rodarte. The secretary, Antonio Hurtado de Mendoza followed the same course of action, although he added some details: "His Majesty gave the orders to the secretary verbally and, in this case, not only for assistance and ordinary expense allowances for the servants and soldiers and the guards, officers and woodland gardeners and important people in need and helped by his hand, but also for fixed incomes and individuals; and it is not found in the office book, decree or dispatch, that the secretary ordered them to be settled, His Majesty said send it [...]. At the end of each month, and other times halfway through the year, on official paper, the secretary informed His Majesty of everything that had been spent and if anything was left over, he told him what was to be done with it; and if there was not enough, it was arranged for the president of the exchequer to supply it later and not only did the 36,000 ducats enter the chamber, but greater sums and extraordinary amounts which were shared out in the same secret expenditure and when His Majesty was pleased to do so, he signed in the book in his own hand."

he had ordered to be placed there and which not." It was essential, therefore, to carry out a thorough reform of the Burgundy household.[84]

In 1636, Philip IV sent the duke of Medina de las Torres to Italy and appointed the Count-Duke of Olivares in his place. The king himself justified the appointment in the preamble to the title that he was bestowing on him:

> Having recognized the problems that arise from not using the offices of *gran chambelán* (≈great chamberlain) and *camarero mayor* (≈lord chamberlain) of our households of Castile and Burgundy, as regards the appropriate respect due to our royal person, and also because experience has shown that everything dependent and attached to the exercise of this office has not had the proper method for doing things because there was nobody who could fill the post [...].[85]

The impact on the court must have been enormous, to the extent that, two days later, the count of Arcos, lord steward of the household, wrote a memorandum to the Count-Duke, reminding him of the importance of the post and the great esteem in which the household of Burgundy was held among the kingdoms of Europe, at the same time as he justified the pre-eminence of this household within the Spanish Monarchy, to the detriment of that of Castile:

> The office of Lord Chamberlain derives from the grandeur of the House of Burgundy and its Duke Charles, such a great prince, that he surpassed some princes and was not inferior to those of Spain or France. He possessed both Upper and Lower Burgundy, all the Low Countries and the islands of Holland and Zeeland and the rest. The status of his house was so superior that when his blood entered the Emperor's and that of the kings of Bohemia and Hungary and Castile, the services of those households ceased and they introduced Burgundy's. [86]

[84] "Orden que se ha de guardar en la distribución del dinero de la cámara, que es en conformidad de lo resuelto por Su Majestad en consulta del conde mi señor camarero mayor de 23 de diciembre de 1638" (AGP, *Administrativa*, leg. 939/1, exp. 12).

[85] AGP, Administrativa, leg. 939/1, exp. 14. The letters patent ended as follows: "The enjoyment of everything pertinent to the said office is to be made good to you from the eighth of April of last year 1636, when I granted you the favour."

[86] *Ibidem*, dated April 10, 1636.

Don Gaspar de Guzmán put all his effort into regulating the Chamber with the aim of controlling expenditure and the granting of favours. First of all, he drew up new ordinances for the secretary of the chamber, the person mainly responsible for controlling those favours and the officers that served him. Then, he defined the behaviour and duties of each office of the privy chamber, laying down a new "instruction and order which is to be observed henceforth in His Majesty's apartments," which Philip IV proclaimed in March 1637.[87] Finally he set about rectifying the economic imbalance affecting the royal household. The Monarchy's economic crisis was not going to be solved by cutting down on the number of courses served to the royal household's servants or by eliminating a few offices. For this reason, on April 7, 1638, the monarch was obliged to announce a new decree to try and cut back expenditure on the larder of his household. The decree was discussed in the *Bureo* and at the meetings of the board on April 10 and 13 of that year, when a series of comments were added to ensure its smooth implementation. It consisted of twenty-eight articles in which the extent to which the various departments of the royal household had contracted as a result of the budget cuts of earlier years was noticeable. However, the failure of this cost-cutting policy was recognized in article four:

> Likewise, I have ordered that three thousand ducats be made available for the larder every month so that the bureo may distribute them among the merchant and menial officers of my chamber, household and stable to offset in this way the deficits that have been acknowledged up till now and the complaints that are made, apart from the fact that paying promptly may be useful for the prices of things.

In article 6, it was acknowledged that payments were not being made promptly:

> And because I wish the stipends of my servants and those of the chapel and guards to be paid punctually, I have commanded the marquis of Jódar to meet Antonio Campo Redondo and, between them, to rectify whatever may remain unclear about the consignations given to the treasurer of the chamber for this payment, showing the said treasurer of the chamber the

[87] *Ibidem*, exp. 15, Madrid, March 4, 1637. Studies of these instructions are found in: Yves Bottineau, "Aspects de la cour d'Espagne au XVIIe siècle: l'etiquette de la chambre du roi," *Bulletin Hispanique* 74, no. 1–2 (1972), 138–157; Charles C. Noel, "La etiqueta borgoñona en la Corte de España (1547–1800)," *Manuscrits* 22 (2004), 141–150.

> procedures followed in the period of 30 days that have been assigned to it and the amounts that turn out to be wrong; it should then be paid out of the tax on soap and candles and the balance payable in compliance with everything owing until the end of last year, 1637, should be consigned.

But the political problems afflicting the Monarchy prevented it from turning the economy round; so, in 1639, it was decided to tackle the reform of the offices and expenditure of the queen's household as well.[88]

Towards the elimination of the household of Castile: 1644

The fall from power of the Count-Duke of Olivares, in January 1643, did not remedy the economic situation of the Monarchy, nor did it improve the situation in the royal exchequer, but it did raise the spirits insofar as the nobles who had been removed from the king's immediate circle could now return to court. For this reason, the solutions they proposed to avoid the bankruptcy of the royal households were in no way original. On the one hand, tighter control of expenditure on the chamber and the domestic offices of the king was introduced and on the other, all the legislation to do with offices and expenditure that had been passed during the reign was gathered together in the ordinances of 1647 and published in 1651.

In general terms, the reduction in costs naturally led to the idea of reducing the number of other households that, on the face of it, served no useful purpose because they duplicated offices. The household of

[88] "The King our Lord (glory to him), by a resolution of a proposal by the *Bureo* of April 16, 1639, was pleased to command that in the offices of the Household of the Queen, our lady, the number of servants that head each office in this list should be fixed, and that all the rest who exceed the appointed number, should serve and enjoy their stipends, bouche of court, apartments and other emoluments, and that as they fall vacant, they should be extinguished until they are adjusted to the reform. The publication of this resolution of His Majesty was delayed until June 20, 1642 when it was ordered to be implemented by the *Bureo*, and since then it has never been complied with on the grounds that in some offices certain servants were necessary, who were proposed to His Majesty on the recommendation of the Bureo, this with regard to Heads and Assistants; and also His Majesty during this same time granted various favours because it suited his royal service giving supernumerary posts, which as they have fallen vacant, have been filled again so that the number of the reform has never been complied with" (AGP, *Administrativa*, leg. 928).

Castile was a case in point. The first serious attempt at eliminating, or at least, reforming the household of Castile dates from 1644. With this in mind, a Board was formed to study the economic situation of the household and what it would mean in terms of savings if it were reformed or eliminated. The plan seemed suitable and so the Board presented it to the monarch, who turned it down. Philip IV's response to this reform is a perfect example of the contradiction in which the Monarchy was embroiled: struggling on the one hand, to make economic savings, whilst on the other, striving to retain the structural and political organization which previous monarchs, such as Philip II, had used to build on:

> Reforming expenses that can be spared was never more necessary and now could not be a more appropriate moment; but there are things (despite this) that cannot be changed either by resolutions or orders publicly proclaimed by me, either because they constitute ancient customs of my Royal Households which cannot cease to exist without a loss of authority, or, because they have considerations of gracious favours, they also have a share in justice for services having been rendered that deserve fair and proportionate remuneration, or because they are like a stipend and salary which are necessary precisely to sustain those who serve me according to their posts and quality. And so, although I am grateful that the Board has looked so closely at what could be strengthened in the Household of Castile, I find few things among those that are proposed which, from my point of view, do not oblige me to tolerate them as they are. [...] They are servants who serve loyally and they and the rest that you wish to reform live on what they are given to sustain themselves, and when they are paid promptly it is less than what is necessary in these times, and so I resolve that for now no new thing be done over and above what is declared here.

The monarch's reflections effectively prevented the elimination of the royal household of Castile, but the changes that were implemented from that time on were far-reaching and had serious consequences for its structure. The household of Castile became an irritating appendage of the royal service, whose servants were irrelevant to the government of the Monarchy. From an economic point of view, Philip IV began by suppressing the position of paymaster of the royal household of Castile on February 3, 1645;[89] moreover, he placed the income for maintaining the household in those sources of Crown revenue that were difficult to collect, so that from then on the officers did not receive their wages promptly. This meant that the heads of each household section or profession were obliged to meet annually to share out the meagre income that existed.

Meanwhile, the household of Burgundy – the household that represented the dynasty – was emerging as the sole service of the Spanish Monarchy and all members of the royal family. Philip IV had confirmed this in letters to his sister, Maria Anna, when, in 1629, she set off for Vienna to marry the future emperor, Ferdinand III. In them, he told her that she was "my greatest Ambassador to her father-in-law and her husband" and concluded by:

> asking Your Majesty affectionately to endeavour with particular care and attention to keep her service in the style of the Household of Burgundy, which we esteem so much here and wish our infantas not to forget it anywhere, and with great insistence, both with His Imperial Majesty and the King of Hungary, in my name, urge Your Majesty not to allow this to be abandoned nor that Your Majesty, as Infanta of Castile neglect to observe the style of the Household of Burgundy, something that I shall hold as a special favour, which doubtless for the decency of the person of Your Majesty is a great advantage and no less for that of the Emperor and King of Hungary, and for us, the contrary is of great disadvantage. And it seems that at home, where we are all one, it would not be right for me to neglect to achieve something which I desire and prize so highly, as has happened to us with feeling in France.[90]

[89] "It has been put to me that it would be well if the paymaster of my household of Castile, whoever he may be, should be granted before a fixed notary all powers, cessions and other dispatches to do with the said office and household, and with a budget which for this reason is not to produce any cost to my Royal Exchequer; I have resolved that it should be done thus and that it be in the presence of Gabriel Rodríguez de las Cuevas, my royal notary who has been involved in this exercise for some time now. He will be given a dispatch that may serve as title but without a stipend" (AGP, Administrativa, leg. 340).

[90] The instructions can be found in BNE, MS. 2362, fols. 19–22, transcribed by Quintín Aldea Vaquero, *España y Europa en el siglo XVII: Correspondencia de Saavedra Fajardo. I. 1631–1633* (Madrid, 1986), 321–322.

The court of Madrid and the courts of the viceroys

Manuel Rivero
Instituto Universitario "La Corte en Europa",
Universidad Autónoma de Madrid [1]

The unity of the Monarchy

Between autumn 1598 until well into 1599, funeral rites in honour of Philip II were held in every corner of his dominions. The news of the king's death spread westwards as it was dispatched by couriers and messengers across continents and oceans. As the news was received, individuals demonstrated that they were all part of the same whole; they were all subjects of the same sovereign and united by the same grief. Just like Castile, Naples, Catalonia or Portugal, all Spanish America went into mourning. The viceroys of Peru and New Mexico both issued official proclamations that, everywhere, "the outward manifestations [of mourning] customary in such cases should be made." They were expressing that they belonged to a single body politic, a mystic republic held together by royalty. This organic nature made the whole something more than a composite monarchy made up of independent kingdoms and states, since the public ceremonies in each place commemorated three different levels of identity and belonging: city, kingdom and Monarchy, passing from the microcosm to the macrocosm and viceversa.[2]

[1] This paper forms part of the research project funded by the Spanish Ministry of Education and Science "La decadencia de España y la vida italiana en el siglo XVII (1621–1665)," HUM. 2006-11587, coord. Manuel Rivero. Abbreviations: AGS, Archivo General de Simancas; AHN, Archivo Histórico Nacional, Madrid; ASMi. Archivio di Stato, Milan; BL. British Library, Add. *Additional*; BNE. Biblioteca Nacional de España, Madrid; Cs., *Consejos*; E., *Estado*; Leg. Legajo; RAH. Real Academia de la Historia.

[2] Hilda Raquel Zapico, "El poder monárquico y la imagen de la Monarquía en el Buenos Aires de fines del siglo XVI," in *XIII Coloquio de Historia canario-americana / VIII Congreso internacional de Historia de América 1998* (Las Palmas, 2000), 1107–1122. As a counterpoint, the description of the funeral rites in the Americas can be compared with the one written by Ottavio Caputi, charged, on the express orders of viceroy Olivares, with organizing the funeral rites in Naples, see Ottavio Caputi, intro. *La pompa funerale fatta in Napoli nell'essequie del Catholico Re Filippo II di Austria*

The catafalques and commemorative monuments raised between 1598 and 1599 took as their model those that were erected when Charles V died. In 1559 a catafalque was raised in the transept of the church of San Francisco de los Naturales in Mexico. Designed by the humanist, Cervantes de Salazar (author of *Túmulo imperial de la ciudad de México*, published in Mexico in 1560), it was decorated with mythological scenes which emphasized the sovereign's virtues (prudence, justice and fortitude), with paintings and bas-reliefs alluding to the conquest (Ferdinand the Catholic receiving the papal bulls from the pope himself, scenes showing the exploits of Hernán Cortés and his audience with the emperor), and evocations of the Aztec past, to represent the continuity of the present with the past and the future. Such images normalized the representation of the kingdom of New Spain at the heart of the Monarchy. At the same time, the viceregal courts, during both the funeral rites and the celebrations of the new sovereign's coronation, took on the distinctive character of a true royal court, a mirror or reflected image of the seat of the king's power as his subjects visualized it. The king and his court were reproduced through their *alter ego* and *alter domus*.[3]

Nothing in the commemorative representations or funeral rites set Mexico and Lima apart from other courts; there was no suggestion that they were in any way subordinate to a capital. The courts of the viceroys had existed before the court in Madrid, and the fact that we have no date or record of the moment when the city of Madrid was officially regarded as the capital is an indication that there was no consciousness of the Monarchy having any geopolitical centre. It was not yet possible to conceive of a centre and periphery in territorial terms, precisely because it was the viceroyalty that enabled a diversified centre to exist. The Spanish Monarchy had no capital, nor, until well into the seventeenth century, was there any awareness that the only court that existed was in Madrid.[4] This transformation and its significance is what we shall now concentrate on.

(Naples, 1599), 1–8. In the ceremonial, the motto *Non sufficit orbis* would occupy a central and visible place, p.14.

[3] María Jesús Mejías Álvarez, *Fiesta y muerte regia: Las estampas de túmulos reales del Archivo General de Indias* (Sevilla, 2002), 29–38.

[4] José Luis De Pablo Gafas, "La invención de la Corte: La creación de la sala de alcaldes y el proceso de modernización institucional en el reinado de Felipe II (1561–1598)," in José Martínez Millán (ed.), *Felipe II (1527–1598): Europa y la Monarquía Católica* (Madrid, 1998), vol.1, bk. 2: pp. 579–594; Veronique Gerard, *De castillo a palacio: El alcázar de Madrid en el siglo XVI* (Bilbao, 1984), 141–153.

Viceroy: "officer" or "royal person"?

According to a firmly-held tradition, shortly after Philip II had taken possession of his kingdoms, he decided to break with the prevailing diversified centre by concentrating prerogatives in a single seat for the court, which meant permanently fixing his and its residence in one place. This involved a radical reorganization of power, which had a marked effect on the very concept of a viceroy and his functions. Charles V employed pure viceroys, with long mandates, undefined in nature and not limited in time. The reason was that he never stayed in one place for very long; the viceroy was an exceptional figure who ruled during the king's absence, occupying a position that he automatically abandoned when the sovereign returned. The king was supposed to live among his subjects and it was inconceivable that he should not do so; unless, of course, he was a bad governor (hence the irony expressed by prince don Carlos when he gave a book containing blank pages the title of *Philip II's Travels*, thereby showing his father to be a poor governor). The Prudent King, however, was neither as radical as he might appear, from his regulation making Madrid the centre of the Monarchy – the city seems to have been viewed as the court of Castile rather than as the court of all the territories – nor was he perceived as such by his contemporaries. The changes were gradual and silent, and went almost unnoticed, as is clear from the fact that it is impossible to pinpoint the precise moment, the exact date when Madrid was declared the court of the Monarchy.[5]

The resolutions issued on March 10, 1555 by the emperor in Brussels, which limited the mandate of the viceroys of the Indies to three years, anticipated an idea worked on later by his son and given shape during the regency of Joanna of Austria (1554–1559) when she limited the mandates of those of Italy and the crown of Aragon.[6] Limiting the mandate was regarded as a problem to do with the permanent absence of the king, since it implied that the alter egos were not conceived of as temporary substitutes for the royal person but as his delegates with limited attributes, or, as Juan de Vega feared, governors more akin to *corregidores* [mayors appointed by the king] than to kings.

[5] Alfredo Alvar Ezquerra, *Felipe II, la Corte y Madrid en 1561* (Madrid, 1985), 23–37.
[6] Jordi Burieu Juan, *La Corona de Aragón de Carlos V a Felipe II: Las instrucciones a los virreyes bajo la regencia de la princesa Juana, 1554–1559* (Madrid, 2000), 71–73; Manuel Rivero Rodríguez, *Felipe II y el gobierno de Italia* (Madrid, 1998).

Reorganizing the Councils of the Indies and Aragon and creating the Council of Italy were part of a general intention to concentrate the capacity for intervention on the new court, to make it the only source of favours, a place where all the networks of patronage and clientelism would converge and through which the effective government of the Monarchy would be exercised. Fixing the residence of the court of the king, who did not travel except on rare occasions (and never outside the Iberian peninsula), was bound to give a new reading to the authority of the viceroy by restoring to the monarch attributes that those acting in his place had traditionally enjoyed, since the king would no longer go out to the kingdoms to exercise his prerogatives in person. When, in 1558, Philip II introduced the innovation of appointing viceroys for only three years, the proposal to limit viceregal autonomy was precisely in order to give some content to a superior court.[7] The wording of the regulation does not state this explicitly, but it was clarified later, in 1574, when the viceroys of Italy experienced difficulties in reconciling their own courts with the king's. In a letter to the governor of Milan, the nature of the alter ego was confirmed: they were vicars of the king in the exercise of royal authority, his doubles, or "other self," although this did not prevent Philip II from wanting to be informed about everything they did or to approve the decisions they took, particularly with regard to appointments.[8] As time went by, some treatise writers saw this decision to supervise and keep a close eye on matters as a distinctive mark of "restricted otherness in viceregal authority." Pietro Corseto pointed it out by underlining the fact that the king authorized the person of the viceroy in public affairs by conferring *potestad ordinaria* [ordinary authority] on him, but without transferring *potestad absoluta* [absolute authority] to him, since this was inalienable to the person of the king. A clear difference was established, in this way, between the sovereign and his "double." The king recognized no person superior to him in the temporal world and was also above the law, whereas the viceroy had to account for his actions and faculties, abiding by the legal system in force at the time.[9] As a consequence, the viceroy became an instrument of royal authority, not a parallel one (as had been the case in the time of the emperor).

[7] "El tiempo en que se despacharon los títulos de los tres ministros de Italia," n.d. 1563?, AGS, E., Leg. 1046, 210.

[8] Letter written in his own hand by Philip II to the governor of Milan, Madrid, May 10, 1574, BL, Add, 28398, 15.

[9] Pietro Corseto, *Instruccion para el príncipe Filiberto para el gobierno de Sicilia*, ca.1621, BNE, MS. 9412.

However, the modifications carried out in government were not very far-reaching. It was neither easy, nor did it seem desirable, to go beyond overseeing the way the viceroys governed by submitting them to a regime of vigilance and total subordination. A generic mandate could be established but not exhaustive supervision nor, as Juan de Vega had already remarked, was it possible to transform them into *corregidores*. The debate surrounding the foreign viceroy in Aragon may be illustrative of the limits of the subordination of the viceroy, since in that kingdom the local *fueros* did not allow the king's officers to be foreigners. Every post, from the most exalted to the humblest, from the governor to the palace gate-keeper, was reserved for natives of Aragon. Having a viceroy fulfil the role of head of government was an innovation that had not really been accepted and, to avoid friction with the native population, Charles V had done his best to appoint viceroys from the territory in question. In a kingdom dominated by small groups and factions, the notion that the absence of the king was transient meant that the viceroy was limited by the provisional nature of his mandate, whilst the sovereign's frequent visits to the territory restricted the possibility of his viceroy governing solely for the benefit of members of his family and circle of friends. In 1554, the appointment of don Diego Hurtado de Mendoza to occupy the position, demonstrated the sovereign's concern to introduce changes in the viceregal regime. His intention was not to subject the kingdom to a foreign power. The monarch's idea was that it was more effective to put someone neutral in place, given that his absence was likely to be permanent.[10]

His intention was not to alter the delicate checks and balances which kept the kingdoms in equilibrium; the new viceroy of Aragon had to come from outside the place he was going to govern and be free of ties of any kind binding him to those he administered. This purpose is patently clear in prince Philip's instruction to Hurtado de Mendoza; the factional conflicts are described in the text as being at the heart of the kingdom's problems, and it is tacitly understood that only somebody from outside and impartial will be able to resolve them. In Aragon, however, a figure of this kind had never been called upon before and, since Hurtado de Mendoza was not a person of royal blood, the Aragonese soon interpreted this as meaning that without family connections and with limited

[10] Luis González Antón, "La Monarquía y el reino de Aragón en el siglo XVI: Consideraciones en torno al pleito del virrey extranjero," *Príncipe de Viana, Annex* no. 2 (1986), 251–268.

authority, the viceroys were not royal persons, but only officers acting on the king's orders. For this reason, the viceroy ought to be a native of the kingdom, not a foreigner. There were interpreters of civil law, such as Antonio Labata or the public prosecutor, Pérez de Nueros, who strove to prove that the viceroy was not an officer, because, among other things, he was not subject to any ordinance, but a royal person, as the king could appoint him without reference to what was stated in the *fueros* on the subject of offices in the administration and government.[11]

Hurtado de Mendoza went on to preside over the Council of Italy in 1558 and his successors did not have to face the problem of nationality or origins. Between 1566 and 1575, an Aragonese viceroy of royal blood, Hernando de Aragón, archbishop of Saragossa, combined in his person both the wishes of the king and the regulations enshrined in the *fueros*.[12] Nevertheless, the question remained latent, resurfacing in 1590 when viceroy Artal of Alagón, the count of Sástago, tried to prevent his successor, the marquis of Almenara, from taking office on the grounds that it infringed the *fueros*. Sástago was unable to delay the moment when he had to step down from office and, in May, Almenara took possession. Shortly after, the disturbances known as the Revolt of Aragon began and the issue of his appointment was regarded as one of the prime causes triggering the conflict.[13]

Almenara's powers made him subordinate to the king's court, yet, paradoxically, he also owed his authority to the strengthening of the figure of the viceroy, detached from the local powers, which qualified him to set up a bona fide viceregal court in Saragossa that was not incompatible with the king's court in Madrid. In fact, after annexing Portugal in 1580, Philip II had given the final impetus to a model of territorial government whose two fundamental pillars were to be the councils of the court of Madrid and the viceroys.[14] Subsequently, under Philip III and Philip IV, this model was expressed in apparently contradictory terms in the instructions to viceroys:

[11] *Ibidem*.

[12] Gregorio Colás Latorre, "El virrey de Aragón," in Gregorio Colás, Jesús Criado and Isidoro Miguel (eds.), *Don Hernando de Aragón, Arzobispo de Zaragoza y virrey de Aragón* (Zaragoza, 1998), 11–73, for his authority, see 55–56.

[13] González Antón, "Monarquía y el reino de Aragón", 251–268.

[14] On this matter, the undated, anonymous defence of the viceregal government for Portugal, kept in manuscript form in BNE, MS. 904, pp. 268–270, is of the greatest interest.

> The power to exercise this position and office is very wide-ranging and free because, in public, it is well that, since you have to be there in my place, you should have all the authority that is necessary for it. But notwithstanding that power, I hereby declare to you that my intention is that you keep to and comply with all the abovementioned things completely.[15]

Consolidation and development of the courts of the viceroys

There is no doubt that in the final decades of the sixteenth century the courts of the viceroys grew in splendour and pomp. Their presence grew not only at a symbolic level but also as centres of power, as evidenced by the growth in personnel to serve the viceroys. This impetus was obvious in the 1590s in Naples, where the viceroys created forty-two new offices in their household and court between 1585 and 1595 (exactly twice as many as those created from the beginning of the reign).[16] The Neapolitan court was recapturing its character as a political centre. If we look closely at a nearby case, namely Sicily, we notice a parallel development of viceregal power, apparent in the increasing expenditure of the court in Palermo to meet the obligations of the viceroy's household and court.[17] This trend can be discerned even in the most modest viceroyalties, such as Majorca, where the viceroy, Ferrán Sanoguera, requested funds from the king in 1597 to pay for a personal guard, deemed necessary to preserve his dignity.[18]

The development of the figure of the viceroy as the political hub of a large number of states within the Monarchy is only explicable if we look at the role of the Castilian high nobility in government; this role emerges after their function as representatives in the *Cortes* disappears

[15] Instruction to the duke of Alba, viceroy of Naples, Madrid, September 4, 1622, AHN, E., Leg. 2010. We can follow a model drawn up on the death of Philip II, in which the instructions to the viceroys are worded according to a set pattern, in a document from the Council of Italy's secretariat in Milan that used the same draft to word the instructions to the governor issued on November 21, 1610, those of April 1, 1643, March 30, 1645, February 18, 1662, and January 16, 1686, AHN, E., Leg. 1936.
[16] Roberto Mantelli, *Il pubblico impiego nell'del Regno di Napoli: retribuzioni, reclutamento e ricambio sociale, secc. XVI–XVII* (Naples, 1986).
[17] Anon., "Relación de las cosas de Sicilia," n.d. RAH, MS. 9/514.
[18] Josep Juan Vidal, *Els virreys de Mallorca* (Palma, 2002).

and they merge into a symbiotic relationship with royalty. It was a link that went beyond mutual dependence, since the members of the Spanish high nobility eventually accepted their function as partners with the prince in the tasks of government. Quite obviously, harmonious integration had existed since time immemorial (after all, the nobility had its roots in royalty, as it was the Crown that bestowed the rank).[19] But whereas other members of the nobility, in Catalonia, Aragon, Portugal, and so on occupied the first estate within their respective kingdoms, the Castilian nobility extended its power across national borders. It abandoned its position as the first estate of Castile to rise to an even higher level, occupying the highest seats of power and wielding that power in place of the king. At the end of the sixteenth century and the beginning of the seventeenth, the Castilian nobles occupied, as of right, the captaincies general, embassies and viceroyalties, because only they represented the king, whether as executors of his monopolies or as negotiators in his name with other princes or parliaments, that is, with the kingdoms. This characteristic was reinforced because the very position of viceroy implied a way of belonging to royalty, of entering the sovereign's "family," expressed in the formula "our cousin, viceroy and captain general"; this is one reason why visitors in Italy were never allowed to touch the person of the viceroy or his household.[20] We observe this contiguity between king and viceroy in their households, which were associated both symbolically and physically.[21]

This symbiotic relationship was such that it permitted all the wealth of the Castilian high nobility to be placed at the disposal of the Crown so that their monopoly of the most important posts constituted, in fact, a safeguard; in the absence of a well-organized bureaucracy, they provided the structure for government, supplied through their client

[19] Beatriz Cárceles, "Nobleza, hidalguía y servicios en el siglo XVII castellano," in *Hidalgos & Hidalguía dans l'Espagne des XVIe –XVIIIe. Siècles*, various authors (Paris, 1989), 72–79.

[20] Jorge Ignacio Rubio Mañé, *El Virreinato*, vol. 1 (Mexico, 1983); Manuel Rivero, "Doctrina y práctica política en la Monarquía Hispana: Las instrucciones dadas a virreyes y gobernadores de Italia en los siglos XVI y XVII," *Investigaciones Históricas*, no. 9 (Valladolid, 1989), 209; Jesús Lalinde Abadía, *La institución virreinal en Cataluña* (Barcelona, 1964), 247.

[21] The viceroy of Sicily, Philibert of Savoy, died a victim of the plague in Palermo in 1624. Philip IV maintained and paid the expenses of his household for at least the next two decades: "Copia de la cláusula y legado de gajes que el serenísimo príncipe Filiberto, que sea en gloria, dejó a todos sus criados en el testamento debajo de cuya disposición dejó en Palermo a 4 de agosto de 1624," AHN, E. Leg., 2125.

network, their stock of prestige, their honour and their goods. In other words, their personal credit constituted a reserve for the royal service to draw on. On this specific point, for example, the laws of the Indies included some directives relating to the organization of the viceroy's household which, in themselves, demonstrate the way in which the household of the *alter ego* dovetailed with the sovereign's, fulfilling the functions of an *alter domus*: "The viceroys should endeavour to use and have in their households the sons and grandsons of discoverers, peacemakers and settlers and other distinguished people, that they might learn urbanity and have a good education."[22]

An institutional perspective makes it difficult to see this function. If we analysed the government as if it were a modern state, we might well be led to believe that the nobility were kept from power. Nothing could be further from the truth, as Domínguez Ortiz pointed out many years ago.[23] And this is evident if we examine the reflections upon the nature of viceregal power made by eminent members of this estate. From Juan de Vega's letter, written in 1558,[24] to Olivares' memoranda, the aristocrat-viceroys always responded on the assumption that they belonged to a domestic order, one of familiarity with the king, and were, therefore, immune to having their function controlled externally by the law courts and royal officers. They never admitted to being subject to higher administrative powers. Federico Chabod made this point when he saw that the underlying philosophy of viceregal government made it impossible to invest the figure of the viceroy with a bureaucratic conception of his office; the viceroy was inspired by a chivalric ethic and understood his function as deriving from the personal bond that tied him to the king.[25]

[22] Philip II, in Madrid, April 9, 1591, in *Recopilación de las Leyes de Indias mandadas recopilar por la Magestad del Rey nuestro señor Don Carlos II* (Madrid, 1841), lib. 3, título 3, no. 31.

[23] Antonio Domínguez Ortiz, *Las clases privilegiadas del Antiguo Régimen*, 3rd ed. (Madrid, 1985), 140–43.

[24] His indictment of lawyers and their jurisdictionalist claims is well known: "They are base and ambitious, and they have been ill-bred and do not know what it means to be King, nor where the Greatness nor the Authority of the King resides, nor the provinces of the World and the qualities of the People, nor Chivalry nor Honour, nor the Grandeur and Estates of those of us who deserve to be Viceroys, nor what these should be like, nor the captain general and other ministers of this quality," J. de Vega to Philip II, June 8, 1558, BNE, MS. 10300, fol. 53.

[25] *Lo Stato di Milano nella prima metà del secolo XVI* (Rome, 1955).

This is the reason why, both in *Advertimientos del doctor Fortunato*, written at the end of Alba de Liste's viceroyalty in Sicily, as well as in the report written by Olivares when his mandate on that same island came to an end, the position of the viceroy as the apex of all life in the kingdom was underlined, since this was what made it possible for the king not to be absent.[26]

Lawyers and viceroys

Linked to the problem of redefining the office of viceroy was the issue of the inexorable rise of the lawyers and the development of the machinery of royal councils in Madrid. Philip II's plans for reform came together in the creation of a blueprint that would be reproduced in similar terms throughout his possessions, and whose most refined form was the viceroyalty in the Indies. The viceroys of Peru and New Spain embodied all the sovereign's functions at the highest levels: military ones as captains general, judicial ones as presidents of the assize court, and ecclesiastical ones as vice-patrons of the church in the Indies. The governor-presidents of the assize courts who exercised similar functions in Chile, New Granada, Guatemala, Terra Firma, and so on were in their turn "their viceroys." Lalinde emphasized the fact that from the king and his councils right down to the last viceroy with his assize court, the entire government of the Monarchy was organized along binary lines; he termed this a "viceregal-senatorial regime," and its special feature in each of the kingdoms was to act as a check and keep a careful eye on the viceroys.[27] He cited the case of Catalonia, whose assize judges were appointed directly by the king with the aim of counteracting the power of the viceroy and limiting his autonomy. This interpretation appears to be confirmed by the serious conflicts that arose in 1599 and 1626 between the viceroys and their officers on the one hand and the judges of the assize court on the other. At the same time, this schema was imposed in the rest of the Crown of Aragon's domains, so that it is reasonable to conclude that correcting the law courts was the prerogative of the king: they were directly accountable to him. As has been observed, this model was valid outside Catalonia and

[26] "Relación del Conde de Olivares sobre el gobierno de Sicilia," 1596, RAH, MS. 9/3947, fol. 54.

[27] Jesús Lalinde Abadía, "El régimen virreino-senatorial en Indias," *Anuario de Historia del Derecho español*, no. 37 (Madrid, 1967), 5–245.

Aragon, and was applied universally from what can be deduced from the texts of Italian jurists, such as Carlo Tapia, or experts in institutions in the Indies, like Solórzano.[28]

It is very common to confuse the voice and stance of the assize courts with "central government"; the fact remains, though, that they only ever showed one very limited aspect of royal authority. In the sixteenth century, the concept of tyranny shifted away from the ruler who merely followed his own whim – while holding the common good in contempt – towards the king who ignored the laws and ruled without counsel. The act of providing advice had been transformed into a legal ruling and entailed compliance with the law. The effect of the legal arguments supporting judicial reviews was to underline what was forbidden to the "idiots," those untutored in the law who would fall into despotism if they took decisions without knowledge of the law.[29] Around the year 1600, lawyers acquired a visibility in public previously enjoyed only when carrying out their functions in the courts; this can be deduced from many testimonies, such as the letter written by the Council of Italy to the viceroy of Sicily, the duke of Maqueda, reminding him that, according to the "pragmatic sanction of judges' gowns of 1599," they should "wear their official dress" to all public ceremonies and not only when going to court.[30] Wherever they happened to be, they were always judges, the living embodiment of the Law.

Furthermore, the magistrates, together with the Castilian nobility and the military, constituted an inherently itinerant social group, firstly, because their careers ordinarily took them to all the courts the length and breadth of the kingdom, and, secondly, because the court of Madrid was the pinnacle of their professional lives. There was a constant stream of judges passing through the councils, courts and assizes, on visits both private and general, making enquiries, compiling reports, carrying out investigations and so forth. In 1606, the learned Ochoa de Luyando, with abundant experience of the courts of the Indies, was commissioned to

[28] Jesús Lalinde Abadía, *La institución virreinal en Cataluña, 1471–1716* (Barcelona, 1964), 154–159.

[29] Silvio Zotta, *Giovan Francesco de Ponte: Il giurista politico* (Naples, 1987), 33–34; Eduardo Martiré, *Las Audiencias y la Administración de la Justicia en las Indias* (Madrid, 2005), 46–49; Pier Luigi Rovito, *Respublica dei togati: Giuristi e società nella Napoli del seicento* (Naples, 1981); Gaetana Intorcia, *Magistrature del Regno di Napoli: Analisi prosopografica, secoli XVI–XVII* (Naples, 1987); Vittorio Sciuti Russi, *Astrea in Sicilia: Il ministero togato nella società siciliana dei secoli XVI e XVII* (Naples, 1983), 104–111.

[30] Giovanni di Blasi, *Storia cronologica dei vicerè, luocotenenti e presidenti del Regno di Sicilia* (Palermo, 1867), 263–269.

make a visit of inspection to the courts in Sicily; in 1607, the Castilian, Felipe de Haro, was sent to visit Milan; Beltrán de Guevara was sent to Naples, also in 1607; in 1610, Giacomo Maynoldi, from Milan, was dispatched to Valencia to carry out an inspection (there had been a similar visit to officers who had not submitted accounts in 1599, and another general visit in 1606). The Aragonese lawyer, Clavero, visited Catalonia between 1603 and 1605; the Catalonian, Monserrat Rosselló visited Sardinia in 1601, as did Cristóbal Monterde in 1604, Miquel Major in 1606, and Joan Estalrich went to the kingdom of Majorca in 1614, and so on.[31] Lawyers trained in Bologna, who completed their *cursus honorum* in the Milanese magistracy, ended their days as presidents of the assize court in Charcas, in Peru.[32] The various local judiciaries, apart from being subject to constant vigilance, also enjoyed a high degree of intercommunication, enabling the transfer of procedures and a tendency towards standardization of practices, illustrated by the attempt to create a Sicilian Consiglio Collaterale in 1612, or the reform of the Sardinian assizes in 1606 which separated civil from criminal action.[33]

[31] For Valencia, see Teresa Canet Aparisi, *La magistratura valenciana* (Valencia, 1991), 214–219; for Naples, see Mireille Peytavin, *Visite et gouvernement dans le Royaume de Naples, XVIe.–XVIIe. siècles* (Madrid, 2003); for Milan, see Massimo Giannini, "Politica spagnola e giurisdizione eclesiástica nello Stato di Milano: Il conflicto tra il cardinale Borromeo e il visitador regio Felipe de Haro (1606–1607)," *Studia Borromaica*, no. 6 (1992), 195–227; Marco Ostoni, "Prassi amministrativa e abusi del magistrato straordinario nella visita di don Felipe de Haro (1606–1612)," *Studi e fonti di Storia Lombarda. Quaderni Milanesi*, year 13, no. 33–34 (Milan, 1993), 5–42; Mario Rizzo, "Finanza publica, impero e amministrazione nella Lombardia spagnola: le 'visitas generales,'" in Gianvittorio Signorotto and Paolo Pissavino (eds.), *Lombardia borromaica: Lombardia spagnola*, 2 vols. (Rome, 1995), 1: 303–361; for Sicily, Sciuti Russi, *Astrea in Sicilia*; Pietro Burgarella and Grazia Fallico, *L'Archivio dei Visitatori Generali di Sicilia* (Rome, 1977); for the Franche Comté, Joseph Lefèvre, "Le Tribunal de la visite (1594–1602)," *Archives, Bibliothèques et Musées de Belgique*, 9 (1932), 65–85; for the Indies, Guillermo Céspedes del Castillo, "La Visita como institución indiana," *Anuario de Estudios Americanos*, no. 3 (1946), 984ff.; Pilar Arregui Zamorano, "Visita en Indias," *Anuario de historia del derecho español*, no. 49 (1979), 661–664.

[32] Pascual Tamburri, "La nación de las Indias en la Universidad de Bolonia (siglos XIV–XIX): raíces medievales de la cultura hispanoamericana," *Espacio, Tiempo y Forma*, Historia Moderna, no. 13 (Madrid, 2000), 339–364.

[33] The reform of the assize court of Sardinia was recorded by Francisco Vico, *Historia General de la isla y Reino de Cerdeña*, ed. Francesco Manconi (Cagliari, 2004), 1: 190–191; for the Sicilian *Collaterale*, Sciuti Russi, *Astrea in Sicilia*, 128–136; for the assize court of Valencia and its reforms of 1604 and 1607, Canet Aparisi, *Magistratura valenciana*, 207; for Catalonia, see Pere Molas Ribalta, *Catalunya i la Casa D'Àustria* (Barcelona, 1996), 95–126; for the assize courts in the Indies, see Ernst Schäfer, *El Consejo Real y Supremo de las Indias* (Salamanca, 2003), 2: 65–143.

The result of all this was that the lawyers, together with the Castilian nobles, formed a social group able to visualize the Spanish Monarchy as a political and jurisdictional unit, not as a composite of free-standing states with no connections between them. The practice of judges being co-opted onto the councils of Madrid (which began to be common from 1595 onwards, and general from 1600) demonstrates this fact. The attendance of co-opted judges and councillors at council meetings arose from the practice of calling in members of a council working in another area to ask for their opinion as legal experts. Jurisprudence and legal practice made it possible to discuss matters of law or government which went beyond the scope of the laws of each individual kingdom, with the Italian, Castilian, Portuguese and Aragonese magistrates exchanging knowledge and experience or finding common ground in law.[34]

The unitary vision that the lawyers displayed implied a perception of the king's council that was not tied to a single place; when the judges of the Mexico assizes introduced themselves in public, they stated after their name that they were "from the Council of His Majesty in New Spain," a similar affirmation to the one made by the judges of the *Consiglio Collaterale* in Naples or those of the assize court in Catalonia. They situated themselves in an intermediate position between the king and the kingdom: before the king, they were the voice of the kingdom; before the kingdom, the voice of the king and before everyone, they represented the Law.[35]

Helmut Koenigsberger, one of the best known experts on government practice in the Monarchy, pointed out that the main causes of conflict in the seventeenth century centred on the defence of the Law and the dispensation of justice, matters in which the different legal bodies, competing among themselves, claimed roles which the others either did not recognize or did so only grudgingly.[36] Following this explanation of the situation, we can regard the incidents between viceroys, standing committees of representatives, assize courts, chapter houses, town halls, and bishoprics as conflicts born of emulation or rivalry rather than as a manifestation of a king-kingdom, centre-periphery dialectical relationship.

[34] Pietro Giannone, *Opere postume*, 2 vols. (Italy, 1821), 2: 219–227.

[35] Horst Pietschmann, "Los principios rectores de la organización estatal en las Indias," in Antonio Annino, Luis Castro Leiva and François-Xavier Guerra (eds.), *De los imperios a las naciones: Iberoamérica* (Zaragoza, 1994).

[36] Helmut Koenigsberger, "Dominium regale or dominium politicum et regale: Monarchies and Parliaments in Early Modern Europe," in *Politicians and virtuosi: Essays in Early Modern History*, (London, 1986), 1–26.

Conflicts over jurisdiction were endemic and choral in nature. They appeared and disappeared, the main figures changed, sometimes involving civil and inquisitorial courts, at other times viceroys and assizes, or viceroys and bishops, and so on. It was a question of jurisdictional spaces that ebbed and flowed like a magma of states in unstable equilibrium, continually negotiating their scope and their boundaries. These conflicts cannot be read simply as a tug-of-war with opponents pulling in their own direction. When the Sardinian parliament requested and obtained the limitation of causes that were open to appeal to the assize court in 1603, it did not argue its case on the basis of a king-kingdom opposition, but as a question of jurisdiction.[37] So, when one jurisdictional conflict was resolved, another one was triggered because the resolution of one problem nearly always sparked off another. When the count of Fuentes, the governor of Milan, resolved the jurisdictional conflicts with the archbishopric at the beginning of the seventeenth century, he set in train a difficult, problematic relationship with the Milanese senate.[38]

The immaterial court

In the shrewd analysis of the society of New Spain with which he prefaced his magnificent biography of Sor Juana Inés de la Cruz, Octavio Paz defined the singularity of Mexico at the time of the viceroys in terms of the non-correspondence of its history with European modernity. He made the point that "the Modern Age is distinguished by two features that we do not find in New Spain (…) The first is the growth of the centralized state (…) The second is equality before the law." In his view, what took place there was an inverted modernity, which was neither re-feudalization nor a return to medievalism, but the compartmentalization of power, the fragmenting of public space into isolated segments, producing "an intricate mosaic of influences, powers and jurisdictions."[39] He observed that there was no State, only states, and pointed to this unusual origin as the reason for Mexico's unhappy history.

[37] Bruno Anatra, "*Dall'Unificazione aragonese ai Savoia*," in John Day, Bruno Anatra, Lucetta Scaraffia (eds.), *La Sardegna medioevale e moderna*, vol. 10 of *Storia d'Italia*, ed. Giuseppe Galasso (Turin, 1984), 534; Luis Corteguera, *Per al bé comú: La politica popular a Barcelona, 1580–1640* (Vic, 2004), 185–202; Miquel Pérez Latre, *El poder polític a Catalunya al segle XVI* (Vic, 2003), 223–258; Pietro Lanza, *Considerazioni sulla Storia di Sicilia* (Palermo, 1836), 53.
[38] Giannini, "Politica spagnola e giurisdizione eclesiástica", 211–223.
[39] Octavio Paz, *Sor Juana Inés de la Cruz o las trampas de la fe* (Barcelona, 1982), 23–41.

The Mexican Nobel Laureate attributed this singularity to distance, to the need to establish checks and balances. A distant king needs to fetter the authorities to prevent them from taking control of the territory and what better way of doing this than by playing them off against each other. Nevertheless, Paz himself was inconsistent when he compared the court of the viceroy with Louis XIV's. It seemed as if he was able to reconcile the existence of the court with the power wielded by the chapter houses, town halls, assizes, archbishoprics, and so on, only as a place indifferent to politics, alien to administration and innocent of the real world. In his description, it was a meeting place for high society, detached from the real world, immersed in pomp, luxury and festivities.[40]

Well acquainted with the work of Norbert Elias, Paz was unable to get around the fact that the court was the centre of absolutist power and his arguments tend to be a little confused when he tries to reconcile that central role with the fragmentation of power. Naturally, in the few lines in which the writer attempted to describe the political life of the viceroyalty, the difficulties of fitting historiographic concepts and schemas to the reality of the situation are obvious. He resolved the dilemma by thinking that the concepts and schemas were the fruit of analysing the history of Europe, and convinced himself that it was for this reason that the history of New Spain was so abnormal. Instead of checking whether the method was sufficient to explain reality, he saw reality as an anomaly because it did not match what he considered to be the correct version, the norm of modernity. He was unaware that Spanish America was no different from Europe, for which he cannot be reproached, since knowledge of and interest in the viceroyalties of Europe were scanty in the extreme when he wrote his work. Italian and Spanish historiographies have filled this void in the last twenty years with the result that, today, we are in a position to undertake comparative studies and set out the main features of a model of the Spanish viceroyalty in the sixteenth and seventeenth centuries.

In the second half of the twentieth century, histories of institutions sustained an interpretation that paid privileged attention to the bureaucracy and origins of the modern state. In line with this type of analysis, it was taken for granted that the power of the viceroys waned to the benefit of the court in Madrid. From 1561, central power was strengthened as a result of fixing a permanent seat of government, and the power relations within the vast Catholic Monarchy became an interplay of opposing forces, of the centre versus the periphery, a

[40] *Ibidem*, 43–44.

state of tension between centrifugal and centripetal impulses. This reading of the situation saw administrative renewal at the level of the state cancelling out particularisms, developing anti-noble and anti-constitutional policies (in other words, contrary to the representative assemblies of the Estates and the laws emanating from them), in favour of absolutism. A well-known series of studies on the kingdom of Naples has pointed out that the build-up of power at the centre converted the potestas viceregia into something residual, the resultant stripping away of authority being linked to the expulsion of the Neapolitan aristocracy from high office. The judicial institutions, that is, the Neapolitan high courts, the *Collaterale*, the *Sommaria*, the *Vicaría*,[41] and the provincial assizes wielded power because they were state institutions.[42]

But when the social and political processes are scrutinized more closely, these analytical schemas do not work. Earlier we described how, at the end of the sixteenth century, the concept and practice of government was consolidated as a duality between gubernaculum and jurisdictio, making the paired viceroy-judiciary model universal and that this relationship was more complex than the one expressed as a system of mutual surveillance. In "uni reddatur," maxim 57 of the *Empresas morales y políticas para un príncipe Cristiano* [Moral and Political Maxims for a Christian Prince], Saavedra Fajardo emphasized that "the government of the Monarchy of Spain [is] founded on such sound judgement that the kingdoms and provinces that Nature separated have been brought together by prudence. Everyone has their respective Council in Madrid: one each for Castile, Aragon, Portugal, Italy, the Indies and Flanders."[43] But he also advised, "The king of Spain does not rule in Italy as a foreign prince, but as an Italian prince."[44] The point he was making was that thanks to the viceroys, Italy was governed in Italy and from Italy.

[41] The three most important law courts in the kingdom of Naples were the *Consiglio Collaterale* (the political council presided over by the viceroy), the *Sommaria* (the court of auditors, also called the court of Capuana because it was situated in Castel Capuano), and the *Vicaría* (the Great Court, or supreme court of justice which, because it was originally located in the part of town called the Vicaria Vecchia, was commonly referred to as the *Vicaría*). Finally, the kingdom was divided into twelve provinces, in each of which the corresponding assize court exercised maximum jurisdiction.

[42] Pier Luigi Rovito, *Il viceregno spagnolo di Napoli* (Naples, 2003), 77–130; Aurelio Musi, *L'Italia dei vicerè: Integrazione e resistenza nel sistema imperiale spagnolo* (Cava de'Tirreni, 2000), 167–204.

[43] Diego de Saavedra Fajardo, *Empresas políticas*, ed. Francisco Javier Díez de Revenga (Barcelona, 1988), 392–393.

[44] *Ibidem*, s.v. maxim 95, 637.

Saavedra was not proposing a game of riddles. In the seventeenth century, the power of the viceroys was anything but residual. In protocol, the style of address for a viceroy was equivalent to that for a prince, because a viceroy with plenipotentiary status was the king. In Noticia general de el Estado de Milán, su gobierno y forma año 1645, it says: "only two bodies represent the king in this State, the governor in the natural form and the Senate in the mystic."[45] The quotation in itself is quite enlightening. In Covarrubias's dictionary, natural is defined as "Everything that is according to the nature of each one" where 'nature' is a condition, whereas mystic means "much the same as figurative: that which gives shape to matter." (In the Vocabulario de las dos lenguas, toscana y castellana by Cristóbal de las Casas, místico [mystic] is translated into Italian by figurativo [figurative]). Mystic representation is none other than that manifested by the rege-patria identity, embodying the defence of the Law and its observance;[46] a natural representation which, coming directly from God, subjects the population to the obedience of his person.

Both these representations of the sovereign, the natural and the mystic, neither transmit a distant central power nor are they extensions of it. We find ourselves, in fact, in a Monarchy with a diversified court, where the king is absent, but at the same time, present on account of the duality of his nature. To understand this, the Neapolitan jurist, Pietro Giannone, set out very briefly what the Spanish system was like, in order to make a comparison with the absolutist regimes after the War of Spanish Succession of 1701–1714. The most significant factor was the existence of a virtual court, so that a Neapolitan could live in and experience Madrid as if he were in Naples, because the important thing was the access to the king that his subjects could enjoy at all times. The territorial councils "si riputavano fondati come in proprio territorio" [were established as if they were in their own country], for "tali consigli eretti in Ispagna, alla quale furono incorporati i regni nuovamente acquistati, si reputavano stabili come in proprio territorio e per conseguenza poteano vicendevolmente comunicarsi gl'interventi e mescolarsi insieme" [these councils, set up in Spain, created as new territories were incorporated, were established in the same way as in their own countries and therefore were able to communicate with each other about their work and mix together]. This

[45] ASMi, *Confini p.a.*, cart. 5, eds. Massimo Carlo Giannini and Gianvittorio Signorotto, *Lo Stato di Milano nel XVII secolo: Memoriali e relazioni* (Rome, 2006), 45.
[46] The obligatory reference here is Ernst H. Kantorowicz, *Los dos cuerpos del rey: Un estudio de teología política medieval* (Madrid, 1985), 248–259.

order did not proceed solely from the will of the king; the councils were not passive subjects because, apart from their consultative function, they possessed jurisdiction and they exercised it.[47] This analysis coincided almost word for word with a legal ruling that the Council of Aragon sent to the Count-Duke of Olivares, explaining to him the nature of the territorial councils: "the court is a *patria* common to all, where everybody is considered for the business of the provinces as if they were actually in those provinces, and as if the court were part of each province in any matters which concern the natives of those provinces."[48] In this way, the kingdoms were permanently in the presence of the king and he could attend to them in person, for the magistrates kept the patria alive in the royal retinue. Conversely, the viceroys with their courts kept the presence of the natural lord alive among his subjects. The relationship between the court in Madrid and the courts of the viceroys was based on this dual interplay. This relationship, however, gradually became unbalanced because of the changes wrought during Philip III's reign. The duke of Lerma set in motion changes that delegated greater executive power to the viceroys at the same time as the law courts became more autonomous. It is not beyond the bounds of possibility – it is a working hypothesis that we are exploring in current research – that the revolts of 1640 were not the result of a reaction against centralization, but quite the reverse; they were a reaction to an imbalance in which the courts of the viceroys were gradually cutting their ties with the court of the king. In the strictest sense, they were revolts of loyalty, at least in Italy. The popular cry: "long live the king, death to bad government" called, precisely, for the restoration of the figure of the king as father and protector, one that had become increasingly remote and mediated by local elites.[49]

[47] Pietro Giannone, *Breve relazione dei Consigli e dicasteri della città di Viena*, in *Opere postume*, 2: 219–227.
[48] (n.d. ?1630), AHN, Cs., Lib. 1991, fols. 368r–369v.
[49] Manuel Rivero, "*Viva Rè di Spagna e muora mal governo:* Discursos sobre la legitimidad y el ejercicio tiránico del gobierno durante la rebelión siciliana de 1647," in Guido Capelli and Antonio Gómez Ramos, *Tiranía: Aproximaciones a una figura del poder* (Madrid, 2008), 187–214.

The economic foundations of the royal household of the Spanish Habsburgs, 1556–1621

Carlos Javier de Carlos Morales[1]
Universidad Autónoma de Madrid
Instituto Universitario "La Corte en Europa"

In historiographic terms, the resurgence in recent years of studies on the court of the early modern era has been something of a Europe-wide phenomenon. Research on this topic has also blossomed in Spain, although, in my view, here it has displayed two distinctive features of its own: firstly, it has taken comparatively longer to develop and publish research than in Italy, France, or Great Britain; secondly, both the approach to topics in this area and their treatment have been widely divergent, which may be attributable to a less solidly based historiographic tradition than is found in other countries.[2]

These two characteristics of Spanish research are apparent in the recent "rediscovery" of one of the basic institutions of the court, the royal households, especially with regard to economic issues.[3] After being virtually neglected by historians for decades,[4] the economics of the royal households is now proving to be fertile ground for researchers in Spanish historiography. We have, for example, a brief yet extremely detailed article by Ladero Quesada about the economic foundations of the court and royal households during the reigns of the Catholic

[1] This study has been carried out as part of the research group "Solo Madrid es Corte": CAM-HUM-2007-0045.

[2] For a historiographic synthesis, see José Martínez Millán and Santiago Fernández Conti (eds.), *La monarquía de Felipe II: la Casa del Rey*, 2 vols. (Madrid, 2005), 1: 17–51; and José Martínez Millán, "La corte de la monarquía hispánica," *Studia Historica. Historia Moderna*, no. 28 (2006), 17–61.

[3] Cf Maurice Aymard and Marzio A. Romani (eds.), *La Cour comme institution économique* (Paris, 1998), both their introduction "La cour comme institution économique," 1–13, and the individual studies.

[4] Antonio Domínguez Ortiz, "Los gastos de la corte en la España del siglo XVII," in *Crisis y decadencia en la España de los Austrias* (Barcelona, 1969), 75–96.

Monarchs;[5] a doctoral thesis, later published, by Jurado Sánchez, setting out the trends and characteristics of royal household expenditure during the whole of the early modern period;[6] another earlier doctoral thesis, as yet unpublished, centring on the reigns of Philip III and Philip IV;[7] my own research on the way the royal household was set up and maintained in the sixteenth century, published in two compilations devoted to the court in the reigns of Charles V and Philip II, and also a recent article on the financing of Philip III's household;[8] and last, but not least, a substantial monograph on the Bourbon dynasty.[9]

With this wealth of historiographic material available to us, now seems an appropriate moment to try and synthesize what we know about the royal households: how they were sustained economically, their costs in terms of amounts and trends, how they were organized institutionally, and where their funds came from during the reigns of Philip II and Philip III.[10] The choice of period is not arbitrary, since I believe that

[5] Miguel Angel Ladero Quesada, "L'Hotel du roi et la Cour comme institutions économiques au temps des Rois Catholiques: 1480–1504," in Aymard and Romani, *La Cour comme institution économique,* 43–49. Interesting data can also be found in Rafael Domínguez Casas, *Arte y etiqueta de los Reyes Católicos: Artistas, residencias, jardines y bosques* (Madrid, 1993).

[6] José Jurado Sánchez, *El gasto de la Casa Real, su financiación y sus repercusiones hacendísticas y económicas* (Madrid, 2000), republished with slight corrections as *La economía de la corte: El gasto de la Casa Real en la Edad Moderna,1561–1808* [hereafter, *La economía de la corte*], (Madrid, 2005). This is the version cited from now on.

[7] Richard Giles Trewinnard, *The Household of the Spanish Monarch: Structure, Cost and Personnel, 1606–1665* (PhD diss., Univ. of Wales, Cardiff, 1991).

[8] For the first, see Carlos Javier de Carlos Morales, "La llegada de Carlos V y la división de la Casa de Castilla," "La cuestión de la financiación de la corte y la defensa del modelo de Casa castellana durante las Comunidades," "Las reformas de las casas reales en 1522–1525," and "La problemática definición de los soportes hacendísticos de las casas reales," in José Martínez Millán (ed.), *La corte de Carlos V,* 5 vols. [hereafter *Corte de Carlos V*], (Madrid, 2000), 1: 166–177, 190–97, 221–231, 251–259; also "La evolución de la Casa de Borgoña y su hispanización," "Castilla y el sostenimiento financiero del Imperio de Carlos V," "La continuidad de la Casa de Castilla y su presencia en el séquito imperial," and "Los últimos años de las Casas de Castilla y de Borgoña del emperador," in Ibidem, 2: 67–77, 77–83, 85–93, 259–266; for the second, see also Carlos Javier de Carlos Morales, "El sostenimiento económico de las Casas de Felipe II," in *La monarquía de Felipe II,* Martínez Millán and Fernández Conti, 1: 78–119; and finally, Carlos Javier de Carlos Morales, "Gasto y financiación de las Casas reales de Felipe III," *Studia historica. Historia Moderna,* no. 28 (2006), 179–209.

[9] Carlos Gómez-Centurión and Juan A. Sánchez Belén (eds.), *La herencia de Borgoña: La hacienda de las Reales Casas durante el reinado de Felipe V* (Madrid 1998).

[10] In addition to the studies above, it should be remembered that there are valuable data on the costs of the royal households in the historiography specializing in the study of the

the institutional development of the royal households of the Spanish Habsburgs was marked by three phases. During the first phase, in the time of Charles V, the system gradually took shape; in the second, between 1556 and 1621, which is the period that concerns us here, the organs and ceremonials of the domestic palace service were consolidated in line with the process which had turned the Spanish Monarchy into an institution; the third phase, under Philip IV and Charles II, saw successive reforms carried out in response to the increasing maturity of the institutional organs of the royal households.

An economic assessment of the royal household

The growth of research into the economics of the royal household is hardly surprising given that its institutional position rested directly on two main cornerstones of the Monarchy of the Habsburgs: the court, and the royal treasury or the *hacienda real.* It formed part of the court through its socio-political significance as the focal point of patronage, whilst it was an integral part of the royal finances as a substantial section of ordinary non-financial expenditure (financial expenditure or costs being the interest and fees paid to lenders). Consequently, the way the royal households were maintained economically was an important point of contact between both politico-institutional structures, and simultaneously reflected their circumstances and characteristics.

From this initial scenario, various basic questions arise, which studies on the economics of the royal households are now attempting to resolve: the first is to determine the magnitude of the cost of the royal household, and how it evolved in current and constant values; the second concerns the percentage it represented of the *hacienda*, and lastly, its socio-economic importance as a major area of court expenditure. In order to make these assessments, it is necessary to begin by recalling, first of all, how royal household and court expenditure were defined in accounting and economic terms, since they have occasionally posed difficulties of understanding and application, even though they appear not to be very complex.

royal exchequer of each reign: Modesto Ulloa, *La hacienda real de Castilla en el reinado de Felipe II*, 3rd ed. (Madrid, 1986), 93–96; Ildefonso Pulido Bueno, *La Real Hacienda de Felipe III* (Huelva, 1996), 217–221.

Basic definitions from the perspective of economic accounting: royal household and court expenditure

It should be pointed out first of all that the institutional characteristics of the royal household, particularly its economic accounting aspects, were established in a process which lasted, approximately, from 1515 to 1559. The first date marks the formation of Charles V's household in the style and customs of Burgundy. The first years of his reign are recalled as the time when his royal household, in the broadest sense of the term, came into being and the principles were laid down of the way the Monarchy's court expenditure should function in economic and financial terms.

The emperor decided to preserve the household of Castile almost in its entirety, and some sections of it, such as the chapel, the hunt, and the *monteros de Espinosa* guard, were absorbed directly into his service.[11] However, the *Casa de Borgoña*, with an increasing complement of Spanish nobles and courtiers, continued to form the nucleus of his domestic palace support and its cost was charged from that time to the *hacienda real* of Castile.

In short, Charles V basically used two centres, each with its own administration, financing and accounting methods, to support his domestic palace service: the *Casa de Borgoña*, and a secondary one, the *Casa de Castilla* (the latter divided, in turn, into two sections, one in Tordesillas and another which accompanied the emperor). Although the *Casa de Castilla* remained in the service of Charles V, it was overshadowed in economic, political and social importance by the *Casa de Borgoña*, as can be seen from the fact that the latter household, at that time, cost more than 200,000 ducats and the former, 35,000, a lower figure than in the time of the Catholic Monarchs. They were,

[11] Given its nature and the way it was formed, there were numerous testimonies during the early years of Charles's reign from major figures fearful that the change of dynasty might entail the disappearance of the traditional *Casa de Castilla*. It did not look as if the household that served his mother, Joanna, in Tordesillas was in any danger, but since the education and customs of the young sovereign had been forged in the heart of the *Casa de Borgoña*, it would not have been surprising if there had been doubts as to whether the new king would use the Castile institutions directly in the service of the palace. For the dynamics of this and the data which follow, see Carlos Javier de Carlos Morales, "La llegada de Carlos V y la división de la Casa de Castilla," "La cuestión de la financiación de la corte y la defensa del modelo de Casa castellana durante las Comunidades," "Las reformas de las casas reales en 1522–1525," and "La problemática definición de los soportes hacendísticos de las casas reales," in Martínez Millán, *Corte de Carlos V*, 1: 166–177, 190–197, 221–231 and 251–259.

therefore, two distinct entities in terms of their origins, the way they operated, and their accounting and financing methods. Despite this, throughout his reign there was mutual influence and interaction between the subsections and constituent parts of the two households in the sharing of court space and the practice of patronage. In other words, the royal household of Charles V in its broadest sense was made up of the sum of the departments of the two households, although we should also point out that, properly speaking, 'the household,' to his contemporaries, referred to the *Casa de Borgoña*. At the same time, the royal household of Aragon also continued in existence, albeit in symbolic form, out of respect for the political and legal code of this Crown, although this was not a burden on the *hacienda real* of Castile (as was also the case with the household of Portugal after 1580).

During the reign of Philip II, when the officers of the *hacienda* made their global estimates of the Monarchy's annual financial requirements and noted down the costs under a variety of headings, the terms "casa ordinaria" or "casa de Su Majestad", in the context of personal palace services, were understood as referring to the original *Casa de Borgoña*. In later accounting consultations, the households belonging to the other members of the royal family were added, and, finally, the *Casa de Castilla*. This, therefore, was the network of royal households that made up a substantial part of the court. For this reason, a rigorous assessment of royal household expenditure must specify the particular entity being referred to: whether the *Casa de Borgoña* on its own, this one combined with the *Casa de Castilla*, or a general one including all the households belonging to the royal family.

Accounting for the expenditure of the royal households presents additional difficulties. In the *Casa de Borgoña*, there were some entries classified as expenditure which did not pass through the hands of the treasurer of the chamber (*maestro de la cámara*) so that precise quantification of total costs may be contingent upon the particular documentary source being consulted. At the beginning of Philip II's reign, for instance, the annual expenditure for the *Casa de Borgoña* was estimated at some 250,000 ducats, of which about 217,000 was spending which can be classified as ordinary and foreseeable; the rest arose from funeral rites, journeys and festivities, favours and private chamber expenses.[12] Several authorities in the household, apart from

[12] Carlos Morales, "Sostenimiento económico de las Casas de Felipe II,", 86–87.

the treasurer of the chamber, received funds from the general treasurer (*tesorero general*). A few examples, spread over time, are as follows: in 1559, the *tesorero general* issued 313,502 ducats to the *maestro de la cámara*; 7,231,000 *maravedís* (mrs.) to the *sumiller de corps* (groom of the stool), Ruy Gómez de Silva, for chamber expenses; 432,900 mrs. to the *limosnero mayor* (lord almoner) Lupercio de Quiñones; and various payments to help defray the costs of and pay favours to members of the household who had accompanied the king during his sojourn in the Low Countries.[13] In 1579, in addition to the *tesorero general's* contributions to the *maestro de la cámara* (67,574,728 mrs), a hefty sum was issued to an *ayuda de cámara* (valet of the chamber) Sebastián de Santoyo (94,500,000 mrs.), and a smaller amount to the lord almoner (8,048,327 mrs).[14] Years later, in 1610, the tesorero general, Juan Ibáñez de Segovia, issued 15,375,000 mrs. to an *ayuda de cámara*, Rodrigo Calderón, and 2,400,000 mrs. to the countess of Lemos, the queen's chief lady-in-waiting, in addition to the transfer of 238,742,704 mrs. to the *maestro de la cámara*.[15]

Furthermore, at different periods the *maestro de la cámara* of the *Casa de Borgoña* was also responsible for managing the expenses of other royal households. This was the situation in the final five years of Philip II's reign, and also when Philip III married and the *maestro de la cámara* took charge, first, of the new queen's household and, later, of the palace services of their children. A final demonstration of the occasionally blurred boundaries defining royal household costs is the existence of indeterminate entries which swelled their total amount. It seems beyond doubt that the payments to the lord almoner and to cover chamber expenses referred to earlier were included under household expenditure. Another example, according to Ulloa's calculations, was the periodic transfer of the sum of 20,000 ducats to the empress Maria during her stay at the Imperial court, although the same researcher excludes from his overall total the cost of Philip II's household of Castile.[16]

[13] AGS (Archivo General de Simancas), CMC (*Contaduría mayor de Cuentas*), 1ª época, leg. 1336.
[14] AGS, CMC, 2ª época, leg. 146.
[15] AGS, CMC, 3ª época, leg. 1142.
[16] Ulloa, *La hacienda real*, 94.

On a broader scale, the term *court expenditure* is similarly in need of clarification because of the blurred boundaries of this concept.[17] It is generally understood that, in addition to the various royal households, the court was made up of the councils, the court tribunals, and the palace and retinue of the king. In principle, calculating total court expenditure is simply a matter of determining the amount that corresponds to each of the above entities and adding them all together; in practice, however, and even though quantifying everything this way is dictated by the nature of the documentary evidence, this only takes into account the court from an institutional perspective.

What makes weighing up court expenditure as a whole difficult is putting a value on the dynamic elements, and including or separating out items such as commissions and embassies, expense allowances and favours, royal progresses, maintenance and improvements to royal sites (subject to the jurisdiction of the *Junta de Obras y Bosques*, the Board of building work and woodlands), funeral rites and provisions made in wills.

The quantification and distribution of household expenditure

As we have just stated, the difficulty of indicating and marking boundaries affected the very definition of royal household expenditure. Even so, thanks to existing research, a number of complete series of the nominal costs of the royal households is available covering the reigns of Philip II and Philip III, in both current and constant values,[18] and which I shall not, therefore, repeat here in full. In brief, there was a sharp increase in the first decade of Philip II's reign following the expansion and diversification of the royal family's households: in 1560, total upkeep was already estimated at some 385,000 ducats, of which 250,000 corresponded to the king's *Casa de Borgoña*; by 1565, the amount had reached some 470,000 ducats, with only 220,000 allocated to it. After this expansion, the current values of these outgoings practically stagnated during the following decades; so, for example, in 1591, the estimated amount for the *Casa de Borgoña* was 274,000 ducats and the overall cost of the various households, 418,000. Between 1588

[17] Already noted by Gómez-Centurión and Sánchez Belén, 13–14. For considerations of their historiographic assessment, see Jurado Sánchez, *Economía de la corte*, 91–93.

[18] Jurado Sánchez, *Economía de la corte*, 95–101 is of great help on this point; also, with pertinent comments, in Carlos Morales, "Sostenimiento económico de las Casas de Felipe II" and "Gasto y financiación de las Casas reales de Felipe III,".

and 1598, average spending on the household of Burgundy remained stable at some 240,000 ducats per annum. If we move from current to constant values, we are able to deduce that, after a sharp rise at the beginning of his reign, the cost of maintaining the royal households fell slightly under Philip II; moreover, as a proportion of all the royal exchequer's ordinary expenditure, it decreased in relative terms.

During the reign of Philip III, spending on the royal households averaged out at 600,000 ducats per year. Jurado Sánchez states, with greater precision, that: "the cost of the royal household in current prices quadrupled between the last decade of the sixteenth century and 1618." The major spurt in the royal households' current expenditure took place between 1601 and 1604 (1601: 240,177 ducats; 1604: 606,406 ducats), although the upward trend continued until 1612 (1,174,406 ducats). However, costs then underwent a small but significant reduction until 1618 (1618: 996,789 ducats). Now, it should be mentioned that when these figures are converted into constant values, the general situation looks a little different: indexed spending on the personal palace service of Philip III and the queen fluctuated from 100 in 1599 to 215 in the middle years of his reign (1609–1613), before falling back to 133.5 in the final years.[19]

Jurado Sánchez has also calculated the percentage of the *hacienda real*'s income used to maintain the royal households. According to his data, the figure was around 3% in the reign of Philip II and 10% in Philip III's. I regard it as more appropriate to consider the cost of the royal households against the total annual budget of the hacienda real under the heading of ordinary non-financial expenditure. In general, the officers responsible for making such estimates for the *Consejo de Hacienda*, or Council of the Exchequer, had a solid view of the grouping of payments and for the question that concerns us here, ordinary non-financial expenditure was made up of already consolidated military outgoings, both at sea and on land, at home and abroad; maintenance of the royal households, embassies, councils, and court tribunals; work carried out on fortresses or prisons; and expenses incurred in the grounds or premises of the royal estates.[20]

[19] Jurado Sánchez, *Economía de la corte*, 99.

[20] However we ought to point out that this block of expenditure may vary from year to year depending on the documentary source being consulted, given the constellation of payers and outgoings, in both cash and other types of financial instrument, and the fact that expenditure was not centralized. Ulloa, chap. 3, sec. A, identifies them as "costs of governance": royal households; construction on royal sites; internal governance which

	Budget amount for ordinary non-financial expenditure (in ducats)	Budget amount for royal households (in ducats)	%
1556	1,400,000		
1557	1,348,866	316,667	23.47
1560	1,624,000	385,813	23.75
1561		430,000	
1562	1,581,000		
1565	1,416,670	464,500	32.79
1568		468,000	
1574	3,200,000	400,000	12.50
1575		477,000	
1583		388,500	
1585	2,833,130	422,667	14.90
1587	3,315,833		
1589	4,468,428	370,000	7.11
1591		418,000	
1599		267,000	
1601		487,333	
1603	4,223,333	600,000	14.20
1606	7,400,000	800,000	10.81
1607	7,272,173	934,120	12.84
1610	4,200,000	851,467	20.00
1612	3,060,000	720,000	23.52
1615	3,772,100	1,000,000	26.51
1617	3,730,000	980,000	26.17
1620	3,658,000	914,000	24.98
1621	4,016,200	924,200	23.01

Table 1. Budget for ordinary non-financial expenditure compared to budget for royal households (except *Casa de Castilla*)

On the basis of these figures, the sum budgeted for royal households in the first decade of Philip II's reign increased by 49.8%. As we know, the king's wedding and the setting up of services for his son, Carlos, and his half-brother, don John of Austria accounted for this increase. Meanwhile, ordinary non-financial expenditure barely progressed by

was expressed in the "court payroll" (councils, ministers, officers and their subordinates, the king's local representatives, mayors, and so on); the diplomatic corps and postal service; and the maintenance of a standing army and navy and their installations.

5% as a result of ordinary military commitments stagnating after the peace of Cateau-Cambrésis. From then on, the gradual increase in this item, coinciding with the Monarchy building up its military strength, significantly reduced the contribution of the percentage represented by the royal households. This amount also decreased because there were fewer family members of the king with personal palace services. In the time of Philip III it becomes glaringly obvious that the cost of the royal households was the most significant entry under ordinary non-financial expenditure borne by the *hacienda real* of Castile, since it was effected through "large" or "general" *asientos* [short term credit loans] following the *Medio General* of 1608.

In addition, it is important to match the amounts received by the treasurer of the chamber with the outgoings of the royal treasury.[21] To this effect, I have used and compared three types of contemporary document: firstly, the *cargo* and *data* [charge and discharge] accounts of the treasurer of the chamber and other persons of the household authorized to handle funds, such as the lord almoner; secondly, the proposals of the *Consejo de Hacienda* where the nominal costs of the households for the following year and the total expenditure to be borne by the royal exchequer were estimated; and, thirdly, the accounts of the royal treasurers of Castile, where the annual allocations to the treasurer of the chamber and other members of the royal household were recorded under "discharges."

	Discharges from the royal treasury	Allocation to the royal households	%
1559	1,452,067	313,502	21.50
1566	2,487,207	199,452	8.02
1586	3,487,512	344,000	9.86
1589	2,443,155	236,986	9.70
1605	1,927,705	601,452	31.20
1610	1,850,308	636,647	34.35
1614	1,721,088	649,069	37.71
1618	2,289,428	990,482	43.26

Table 2. Royal treasury discharges and transfers to the royal households (in ducats)

[21] These data are taken from my articles. From 1590, Guillamás Velázquez also took responsibility for the expenses of their Royal Highnesses.

Comparing the data in the two tables enables us to match fluctuations in the royal exchequer and the royal treasury against movements in the assets and liabilities of the royal household. In the first place, there is a difference between the amounts received by the treasurer of the chamber and the estimates made by the Council of the Exchequer, creating a floating deficit carried over from year to year. As the treasurer of the chamber could not disburse more than had been paid to him in each financial year, and this amount was insufficient for him to meet his commitments, a series of cumulative arrears and debt payments arose, whose settlement was deferred to later financial years. In other words, the royal household began each year with defaults and liabilities of unpaid stipends and purchases. This deficit was periodically settled, either by cancelling consignations given to businessmen, or, when some royal progress was planned outside Castile, it was appropriate to make a "general payment" to clear the backlog of stipends.

Finally, I present some data of interest about trends in the distribution of expenses in the *Casa de Borgoña*.[22] At the beginning of Philip II's reign, the bulk of the expenses, at 44%, was accounted for by household salaries of all kinds (except those due to the corps of German and Spanish Royal Bodyguards), followed by *la Despensa* (the larder), at 16.23%, and the stables, at 15.64%. The running costs of the larder, in particular, increased significantly over time. Where monthly consumption was roughly 2,000 ducats at the beginning of Charles V's reign, this figure had risen to 3,000 by 1559 (32,500 ducats per year, equivalent to 66,000 florins). In 1560, this amount rose to 4,000, and again in 1561, to 6,000 ducats per month (72,000 ducats per year). Shortly afterwards, a small additional amount itemized as "extraordinary larder expenditure" was consolidated with "ordinary larder expenditure," so that by 1566, the total annual cost under this heading was some 80,000 ducats. At the end of the sixteenth century, during the transition from Philip II to Philip III, these costs had already risen to 8,000 per month: 6,000 ducats for ordinary larder expenditure and another 2,000 per month for "the extraordinary expenditure of the said larder." In total, then, at 96,000 ducats per year, or 36%, the larder had become the most important section of the *maestro de la cámara*'s spending, ahead of salaries.

[22] It is worth breaking off at this point since Jurado Sánchez, *Economía de la corte*, 107–118 concentrates on the second half of seventeenth century. The data that follow are based on information from my own research, cited in n. 8.

At the turn of the new century, the expenditure soared again, as a result of the celebrations held at court at the beginning of Philip III's reign and the establishment of a household for the new queen, which the king's treasurer of the chamber took charge of, both for accounting and expenses. In 1601, monthly payments of ordinary and extraordinary expenditure on the larder came to 17,000 ducats (204,000 for the year), amounting to 41.86% of total estimated costs. From this date, it becomes difficult to distinguish the volume of expenditure on the larder, since it is run together in the accounts with that of the stables, to form the set of "ordinary" and "extraordinary" expenses of the royal household. Thus, at the end of Philip III's reign, out of a total of 924,000 ducats, 69.9% was ordinary expenditure (646,000), 6.5% extraordinary (60,000), 19.5% household salaries and stipends (180,200), and 3.24% (30,000) was spent on state vehicles. In this respect, the question arises of how much the growth in the nominal cost of the larder was due to price increases and how much to an increase in the volume of goods purchased.

The royal household and distribution of revenue

Quantifying royal household expenses is just one starting point for assessing its economic value. From another perspective, we must situate the royal households in the socio-economic context of the period. In my opinion, and looking at the royal household as a centre where incomes were concentrated, the least important part is the quantification of its payroll, consisting of salaries and bouche of court which, even when they were updated, always lagged behind prices. Since the court had become the focal point of patronage relationships, it is important to stress the role of the royal households as one of the pinnacles of the gift economy that characterized the age. In this respect, we find that when we use documents about the way the royal households functioned, they resonate with the language of the political economy of the time.

On the other hand, as a fundamental part of the court, resources and economic flows were concentrated in and distributed from the royal household, turning it into a centre of consumption that absorbed a significant part of the court's total demand for goods and services. In the mid-sixteenth century, supplies to the royal household were usually channelled through officers responsible for areas of consumption, and who negotiated the quantity, quality and prices of products with particular suppliers and sellers. So, for example, in the fourrier's department, positions existed for baker, water bearer, spice provider, *salsier* (responsible for supplying vinegars and sauces), *busier* (a wood and coal supplier) and so on, whilst the *escuyer de cocina* was responsible for supervision, ensuring that everything that was going to be consumed was of the requisite quality. Meat, wine, dressings, clothing, leather, cloth and textiles, wax, straw, horse accessories, jewels, timepieces, furniture, tapestries and a host of other products constituted the kinds of goods arranged in advance with merchants and suppliers for a particular period of time and at previously agreed prices.

In the reign of Philip II, the supply arrangements for the royal household underwent a few modifications, largely as a consequence of the court being established in Madrid. Hence, the way of obtaining goods and services in the reign of Charles V, which could be characterized as itinerant, now gave way to a market settled in one place. In this way, by the seventeenth century, three means of acquiring merchandise had become established at the same time: purchasing produce direct from specific vendors, undertaken by various royal household officers; secondly, the provision of cereals, coal and wood from within an area of five leagues around the court, which was the responsibility of aldermen in the centres of population concerned, and at prices previously set by the royal officers authorized to seek out the obligation to supply; and thirdly, those purchases which were the object of contracts or of *asientos de abasto* [supply contracts] with private individuals responsible for specific goods or merchandise.[23]

Credit and debt centred on the royal household, giving rise to an intricate framework for managing time schedules, guarantees and revenues. The characteristically erratic payment schedule of the royal treasury conditioned the treasurer of the chamber's actual disbursements: in general, larder expenses were paid with relative punctuality, whilst arrears and debt payments associated with stipends built up. It was, therefore, quite usual for stipends and salaries to be paid with considerable delay. While gentlemen, because of their social background, normally had other means of support so that their difficulties did not prove too arduous, those minor officers and subordinates who relied solely on their remuneration from the royal household to support their families, were constantly forced to ask for credit or the services of the court banks. The accumulation of arrears created obvious difficulties for their families, as was shown, for example, in one petition drawn up in 1607

[23] Jurado Sánchez, *Economía de la corte*, 111.

by various skilled craftsmen who served in the household (chair makers, saddlers, shoemakers, tailors and the like) who received no wages and were only paid per finished article. When they required payment of arrears, they would point out that it was "impossible to serve if they were not being paid for their work, because their debts mounted up and then they became bad payers, and their creditors harassed them."[24]

The administration of the Burgundian household's economic affairs of the *Casa de Borgoña*

An account of the way the royal household of Burgundy managed and administered its economic affairs in the period we are studying necessarily begins with the foundation of Charles V's household, which took Charles the Bold's as its model. The new regulations governing the *Casa de Borgoña* of Charles V, comprising a total of 665 people, were published on October 15, 1515. An extensive hierarchy of positions and palace duties was created which was reflected in the corresponding salaries and payment structures; scant attention, however, was paid to controlling the expenses incurred by the institution. The responsibilities of the *maistre de la chambre aux deniers* [the treasurer of the chamber] were to take receipt of funds and make payments supervised by the first chamberlain or stewards, with the agreement of one of the two *contrerolleurs* [comptrollers] who took it in turns every six months to record transactions.[25]

This scheme gradually took shape during his reign; more detailed functions of the principal officers responsible for administering the household's economy and the sections comprising the household are found in the account written in Philip II's reign by Jean Sigonney, who had been *grefier* [secretary or clerk] since the time of the emperor. It is of great interest, as a complement to Sigonney's description, to use the royal treasury accounts as a document to shed more light on the way the economy of the royal household functioned between 1556 and 1621.

[24] AGS, CJH (*Consejo y Juntas de Hacienda*), leg. 475, fajo 17.

[25] Raymond Fagel, "Un heredero entre tutores y regentes: Casa y corte de Margarita de Austria y Carlos de Luxemburgo (1506–1516)," in Martínez Millán, *Corte de Carlos V*, 1: 135–136. For a translated copy of the ordinance, see ibid., 5: 137–168, in which it is noted: "We are sending more to the above-mentioned treasurer of the chamber for him to pay the items of his office with the monies he has, or will have assigned to him and ordered, having first notified the lord chamberlain, and the lord steward and first steward, and in no other way."

Three levels can be distinguished. Firstly, there were officers responsible for receiving transfers of funds from the royal treasury: the treasurer of the chamber handled funds which were received from this source, and made quarterly distributions for the larder, stipends and wages, pensions and rewards, as well as monthly distributions "on account" for purchases and supplies acquired by the various officers in the fourrier's department. Apart from discharges to the *maestro de la cámara*, the royal treasury also made discharges to the lord almoner, the *sumiller de corps*, and, when he was absent, an *ayuda de cámara*.

The way transactions of this kind worked was associated with a second category of officer that included those with the authority to make decisions about expenditure: the *camarero mayor* (the lord chamberlain), or his immediate substitute the first *sumiller de corps*, the *mayordomo mayor* (lord steward) and other *mayordomos* (stewards) who formed the *Bureo*,[26] the *caballerizo mayor* (master of the horse) and the *limosnero mayor* or lord almoner. These figures were authorized to issue payment orders and direct them to the treasurer of the chamber, always subject to the approval of the comptroller.[27]

[26] The *Bureo* (from the French *bureau*) was composed of the *mayordomo mayor* and the *mayordomos*, but on occasions also the *sumiller de corps*, the *caballerizo mayor* and the captain of the royal guard attended its meetings. The *Bureo* audited the accounts of the royal household and sat as a court upon offences committed within the verge of the palace.

[27] For a contemporary version of the relationship between the *Bureo* and *maestro de la cámara*, see Martínez Millán, *Corte de Carlos V*, 5:188–189: "The said treasurer of the chamber paid all the ordinary and extraordinary larder expenses, stipends, pensions and rewards accounted for by the *bureo* and for these expenses, the treasurer, or His Majesty's general receiver, gave him the necessary monies, and at the beginning of each month, he was given a sum of money to distribute on account amongst the officers who spent according to the orders of the comptroller, with whose payment orders he likewise paid for the things that had been bought for the offices. / Every three months, a book was made up of every amount to do with the larder in that time, which was given to the said treasurer of the chamber, and he was handed the difference between what the items cost and what he had received on account and so he ended up paying everyone what was due to them. / Another book was made up for the stipends, pensions and rewards accounted for by the *bureo* in the same three months and the amount was likewise given to the said treasurer of the chamber to pay everyone what they were owed in the said three months, according to what was set down in the said book; and when the larder and stipends for three months had been paid in this way, the said treasurer of the chamber gave his account to the stewards and officers of the *bureo* who had the power and authority to see, examine and close them, and to consider the paid sum settled. / After this position fell vacant in His Majesty's household, payment of stipends was entrusted to an officer of the royal treasury of Spain who followed His Majesty's court for this purpose, and the payment for the larder to His Majesty's *grefier*."

Finally, there was a third kind of office in the household whose officers were responsible for recording and controlling revenue and expenditure transactions: the board of the *Bureo*, the comptroller and the *grefier*. Control of disbursements was the remit of the *Bureo* committee, made up of the *mayordomos* with the *mayordomo mayor* as its chairman. The duties of the comptroller, and his counterpart, the *grefier*, were set out in some detail in Sigonney's account. The comptroller, whose authority was on a par with a steward's deputy, checked that the expenditure decisions made by the *Bureo* were scrupulously carried out. The indirect result of this was that it was the comptroller who authorized the treasurer of the chamber's payments and reviewed the purchases made by the appropriate officer, as well as their prices. He also checked that the goods consumed at table corresponded with those that had been purchased.[28] The *grefier*, for his part, was responsible for making a daily record of expenses incurred in the larder and of the stipends of servants in active service, and for making up a monthly book of accounts. In short, he was responsible for duly recording any payments made.[29]

[28] For the comptroller, see ibidem: "The said comptroller was responsible for seeing that everything supplied and bought for His Majesty's table, for the estate of the stewards and bouche of court for certain offices was distributed according to the orders given in the *bureo* and nothing was allowed to be spent without the corresponding order. He had authority to oppose everything he understood as not redounding to the service of His Majesty, and whatever could not be remedied personally by himself had to be notified by him to the lord steward, or to the stewards if he was absent, and, if necessary, to His Majesty himself. Each day he had to visit the offices and see the books of the officers in charge of spending and delete from them any unauthorized expenditure, and reprimand the officer who had spent it. He had to know the prices of things that were ordinary expenses to curb the officers' books accordingly. To do this, he often needed to visit the marketplace. And likewise he had to know the dishes planned for His Majesty's table, for the estate of the stewards and find time to meet the kitchen supervisor in the larder to order the said dishes and be present when the food was served. [...] / He also had to see all the chamber and stable accounts, even if they had been signed by the master of the horse and *sumiller de corps*. All the officers obeyed any order he gave concerning His Majesty's service as a deputy steward [...]."

[29] For the *grefier's* functions, see ibidem: 5:188–190: "The said *grefier* was responsible for collecting and setting down in a monthly book all expenses incurred, itemized daily after the comptroller had seen and added them, as the stewards used the book to give a daily account of the larder in the *bureo*, and the same for the stipends, as well as those accounted for in the *acroy's* books, and also for extraordinary expenditure so that the amount of expenses and stipends incurred for that day could be seen every day.

Sources of maintenance and financing of the royal households

As we have pointed out, Charles V's decision to maintain the *Casa de Castilla* in his service and to include Spaniards in his *Casa de Borgoña* coincided, in the early years of his reign, with another decision, no doubt related to the previous one: to assign the economic upkeep of the *Casa de Borgoña* to the hacienda real of Castile from 1516 when transfers of funds from the *tesorero general* to the *maestro de la cámara* and *argentier* (the steward of royal expenditure and court banker) commenced. Within a short period of time, an attempt was made to ensure the annual endowment of the *Casa de Borgoña* by using *asientos* negotiated with merchant bankers; the bankers were to contribute fixed monthly sums and receive, in consignation, remittance orders of payment from the Indies and revenue from the Military Orders. This system, however, failed to produce the desired effect and, from 1525, upkeep of the household was tied definitively to direct transfers from the royal

Extraordinary expenses were also set down in the same book on the last day of the month, and a weekly total of what the larder expenses and stipends had amounted to that month was made; and the said *grefier* could make no entry without the comptroller first seeing it. In the *bureo*, the said *grefier* read out all the entries for expenses and stipends which were accounted for in it, which the stewards, comptroller and the *grefier* himself counted using silver disks, and the said *grefier* set down the sums in his book, and his officer passed the cumulative total to another book that they called the steward's *contrarolo* [control account] that lasted a whole year and which could not be opened or written in without the said stewards being present, as it was sealed with the seal of one of them. And when the *bureo* was over, they read out the sum totals that had been counted, the *grefier* reading them out from his book and the steward for the week looking at them in the control book, and which, when the sums had been read out, was closed again.

The said *grefier* had a note of the gentlemen and officers absent from court, with and without permission, in order to account for each in the *bureo* according to the time they had resided there or had been given leave. And he signed all the proceedings to do with justice, warrants, ordinances, sentences and other matters dealt with in the said *bureo*.

He had to be present when the oath was taken of any servant belonging to His Majesty in order to record it in the said *bureo's* books. He kept all the agreements made in the said *bureo* for the provision of ordinary and extraordinary household expenses.

He also had to keep all the expense accounts accounted for in the *bureo*, as well as those signed by the *sumiller de corps*, lord steward, lord almoner, and those passed by the stewards and the comptroller."

treasury of Castile.[30] From then on, successive treasurers resorted to two procedures to provide the *Casa de Borgoña* with the revenue it needed. The first was to charge expenses directly to the *servicios* of the *Cortes*, which failed, nonetheless, to prevent the frequent delays in supplies and stipends. The second was to negotiate *asientos* with merchant bankers who advanced money in exchange for orders of payment on ordinary and extraordinary *servicios*, the *Casa de Contratación* in Seville, and the sale of *juros* [interest-bearing state bonds]. Until the final years of the reign of Charles V, annual contributions fluctuated between 150,000 and 250,000 ducats. The difference between these two amounts is explained by the accumulated arrears from previous financial years being added, in the second case, to the average annual cost of 200,000 ducats.

At the beginning of Philip II's reign, with annual costs of 250,000 ducats, the financial situation of the household gave cause for concern. It was decided to fix a large part of the expenses, up to 200,000 ducats, on ordinary and extraordinary *servicios*, although the crisis in the royal exchequer ruined any expectations to that effect. So it was that, despite the suggestion of a measure which would guarantee the treasurer of the chamber resources for the household in one annual payment or in quarterly instalments, the royal treasury had no alternative but to make irregular payments which gave rise to arrears and overdrafts. To give an example, in 1559, Domingo de Orbea made out twenty-four orders of payment to the treasurer of the chamber, Francisco de España, on widely differing dates and for varied amounts: with up to five payments some months, and just one in others. The following year, we find thirty-two discharges from the royal treasury recorded as paid to the treasurer of the chamber, also in differing amounts and on irregular dates.[31] In those days there was still no permanent source of sustainable income and the royal treasury had no other choice but to resort to external, even exceptional financing methods, such as the cancellation of consignations to the businessmen, in 1561, after suspension of

[30] See details in the works cited above; also Carlos Javier de Carlos Morales, "Juan de Adurza," in *La Corte de Carlos V*, 3:17–20. It seems that, from 1517, the position of treasurer of the chamber remained vacant and the court banker was given responsibility for meeting household expenses. Between 1525 and 1530, Adurza carried out the functions of both treasurer and court banker so that the financing of the Burgundian household passed once and for all to the exchequer of Castile. After Adurza's death, a treasurer of the chamber was once again appointed.

[31] AGS, CMC, 1ª época, legs. 1336 and 1385; Archivo General de Palacio (AGP), *Administrativa*, leg. 6723.

payments in November 1560, as a way of facing the mounting arrears in paying stipends and even larder expenses. This measure would be repeated in each of the later "bankruptcies" of Philip II and Philip III.

Given the difficulties posed by the absence of a firm financial basis and the resulting dependence on transfers of funds from the royal treasury, plans were repeatedly drawn up in the reigns of Philip II and Philip III to find some fixed consignation to bear the economic brunt of maintaining the royal households. In 1561, plans were made for royal household funding to be based on the *encabezamiento general de alcabalas,* or sales taxes, which rose sharply from that year. However, this attempt was a failure and there was no other way out than to resort once more to bank loans; after negotiations with the treasurer, the *asentistas* (creditors) undertook to make monthly payments, which Orbea transferred to the treasurer of the chamber, Francisco de España. In consignation, the Gentiles, Grimaldis, and other Genoese bankers received orders of payment on the extraordinary income of the *hacienda real* of Castile and even on the recent increase in the *alcabalas.* From 1566, coinciding with Diego de Espinosa's presidency of the *Consejo de Hacienda,* new projects were drawn up to provide stable financing for the royal households. More specifically, there was a proposal to base the endowment for the *Casa de Borgoña* on revenue from the salt deposits, with queen Isabella's household charged to the *almojarifazgo mayor de Indias* (a trade tax levied on goods from the Indies), and those of don Carlos and don John of Austria on sea tithes and the *almojarifazgo mayor.*[32] It seems that, indirectly, the exploitation of the salt deposits eventually met a large part of the expenses of the *Casa de Borgoña,* since it was to serve as consignation for the contracts agreed by the *tesorero general* to provide the treasurer of the chamber with funds; however, the assigning of expenses to fixed income did not become institutional practice on that occasion either. From 1574, coinciding with another crisis in the royal exchequer of Castile, fresh plans were drawn up. It was proposed this time that the financial basis of the royal households should be the ordinary and extraordinary *servicios* of the *Cortes,* a measure which would undoubtedly have been to the liking of the *procuradores* (procurators), but was, once again, deferred.

It was quite apparent, though, that, after they had passed through the crucible of the *asientos* negotiated by the Council of the Exchequer, the *servicios* of the *Cortes,* and even such unreliable sources of income

[32] IVDJ (Instituto de Valencia de Don Juan), Madrid, *Envío 50,* fol. 252.

as *arbitrios* (discretionary taxes levied to raise funds for public expenditure) and the selling of *juros*, all implemented in Seville at the beginning of the 1580s, served as consignation for bankers supplying the stream of funds to the treasury which were then made available to the treasurer of the chamber.[33] The major innovation affecting the way the royal households were financed concerned the new treasury regime instituted in 1584: the three coffers with three keys (ordinary income, extraordinary income, and the Three Graces). It was initially hoped that ordinary expenditure, such as that represented by the royal households, would be met out of the coffer of ordinary income, but it was not long before this was shown to be a pipe dream. As a result, the new treasurer, Portillo de Solier, used the ordinary coffer to give the treasurer of the chamber funds for the larder and stipends, and the extraordinary coffer for arrears and outstanding debt. Shortly afterwards, from 1588 onwards, there is evidence of the existence of new coffers which had been split off from the original extraordinary coffer (made up of *juros*, the treasure fleet and the new mint in Segovia) and that the royal households received their finances from any one of these coffers, no matter which, although the principal amount came from the ordinary coffer.[34] Nonetheless, between 1590 and 1592, the major sources of revenue employed by the royal treasurer to finance the royal households were the treasure fleets and the recently inaugurated Segovia Mill Mint. The same irregularity in the treasury's revenue was reflected in the provision made for the royal households, so that, in 1593, the situation was modified and the treasurer of the chamber, Guillamás Velázquez, received 61.66% of royal treasury transfers from a new source, known as the "emergency coffer". This coffer supplied the royal treasury with the surplus from the *millones*, borrowings and the treasure fleets. The remaining 38.34% came from the extraordinary coffer.[35]

In the reign of Philip II, the result of the irregular and insufficient revenues to the royal household was an increase in debt and arrears, mostly stipends, so that liabilities constituted an ongoing deficit, transferred from one financial year to the next. This dynamic was less the result of expenditure on the royal household increasing, since it virtually stagnated under Philip II, and more the corollary of having no fixed sources of sustainable income to serve as consignation when needed. The treasurer of the chamber's dependence on the treasury of

[33] Carlos Morales, "Sostenimiento económico de las Casas de Felipe II,", 105–108.
[34] Ibidem, 109–115.
[35] AGS, CMC, 2ª época, leg. 117.

Castile gave rise to a deficit between expenditure contracted and funds received.

This situation continued, with barely any modifications, during the reign of Philip III. The *maestro de la cámara* dependence on whether the royal treasury was in liquidity or in penury could only be overcome by resorting to credit to bring funds into the royal households. In the early years of the reign, increased court expenditure was the reason why even the consignations that could be offered to the bankers were as precarious in nature as they had been unusual in earlier times. So, the profits from Portuguese pepper, leasing the royal monopoly of black slaves, surpluses from the dry ports and sea tithes were used in 1600 and 1601 as guarantees for the *asientos* that the royal exchequer was obliged to take out with the businessmen with the object of finding money for the treasurer of the chamber. In the end, in 1601, as an obligation contracted by the king with the *Cortes* when the new *servicio de millones* was granted, the royal exchequer came to terms with the fact that provision for the royal households and other ordinary expenses had to be allocated in a permanent manner from a fund consisting of *Cruzada* income and the ordinary and extraordinary *servicios*. This resolution was soon deferred; the following year, it was a struggle to obtain any kind of financing for the royal households at all and increases in *juros* and an advance on rental income from the *maestrazgos* [lands belonging to the military orders] were proposed.[36]

In short, signing *asientos* was the only way of ensuring that the royal treasury could supply a regular amount to the treasurer of the chamber. The greater the sum contracted in the loan, the further into the future it could be extended, and in fact, at the end of 1602, an *asiento* was signed with Octavio Centurión guaranteeing, in exchange for various consignations on extraordinary revenue, that Castile's external and internal expenditure would be met for three years and that a substantial proportion of it would be assigned to the royal households. As an extra complement to this deposit, the *maestro de la cámara* received hefty payment orders against the *arbitrio del vellón*, which was preferentially assigned during these years for the maintenance of the royal households. Until 1606, these were the main financial instruments used; nonetheless, there was no way of staving off the accumulation of debts and arrears, which had swollen once more with the unfortunate demise of the *Junta de Desempeño*, or Recovery Committee.

[36] Carlos Morales, "Gasto y financiación de las Casas reales de Felipe III,", 185–187.

As long as the cost of providing services for the royal family continued to increase, finding a more solid source of income was a matter of urgency. In fact, there was no doubt about this in the plans of the *Consejo de Hacienda*, and the renewed *servicio de millones* became the new mainstay of the royal household's finances. After recovering the consigned securities when payments were suspended in 1607 (an amount which had been largely earmarked for neglected internal expenses, amongst which, of course, figured royal household arrears), the cost of maintaining the various households of the royal family fell on the new *servicio* of 17.5 *millones*.[37] Although the Castilian *Cortes* favoured the *millones* being regarded as the foundation for ordinary internal expenditure when drawing up budgets, two factors did not take long to thwart this idea: the first was that the *sisa* tax brought in too little income, and the second, that too many consignations and orders of payment were tied to this source of income. So, once again, no fixed income had been found to maintain the royal households, nor had the deficit problem disappeared. The only procedure, albeit temporary, to prevent arrears and debts from accumulating over several financial years, was to sign *asientos* which brought in rapid liquidity and settled outstanding balances in the various departments of the households; but by assigning repayment to future instalments generated by the *millones*, an ongoing deficit was produced; this had to be faced in the medium term by declaring partial moratoria on payments to creditor bankers, the recovery of which served, precisely, to pay off debts and arrears associated with various ordinary expenses.

From 1612, the attempt to assign internal expenditure directly to the *millones* having failed, a new idea was applied to financing the Monarchy's compulsory payments. Having accepted that the best (or, probably, the only) way to obtain liquidity was to resort to the businessmen, it was decided at least to avoid the proliferation of minor *asientos* by concentrating most of the credit financing and the corresponding consignations into a single contract, one large or general *asiento*, that would be binding on the royal exchequer and the moneylenders over one or even two annual payments. In this way, every general *asiento* signed from then on undertook to guarantee a regular stream of payments to cover the various regular internal and external outgoings facing the royal exchequer. In particular, one of the stipulations was that the banker be obliged to pay a fixed amount each month to the treasurer which he,

[37] ACC (*Actas de las Cortes de Castilla*), vol. 24: 752, 754, 757 and 764.

for his part, had to allocate to the royal households. In the end, despite this, the funds received by the treasurer of the chamber turned out, year after year, to fall short of those initially forecast at the beginning of the financial year. When the bankers advanced a loan, the general *asiento* could fix the assignee (Habsburg Netherlands, royal households, and so on), as well as the consignations and interest to be received. Shortfalls were inevitable, however, as long as there was no way of ensuring that the treasurer was obliged in his budget to make identical payments for each purpose. And as soon as something unexpected occurred, or there was some war necessity abroad that had not been anticipated, the fund initially earmarked for the treasurer of the chamber, was reassigned, either partly or entirely, and used to finance the new outlay required in Italy, the Netherlands or Germany.

In short, the general *asientos* drawn on between 1612 and 1621 failed to guarantee the *maestro de la cámara* a regular supply of money or to wipe out the chronic deficit afflicting the royal households. To resolve the problems and deal with the arrears and debts, partial measures at least were adopted: making general payments of stipends whenever there was a royal progress; making sporadic cost reductions; taking out *asientos* for lower amounts; and seeking out various sources of extraordinary income. Yet despite everything, the finances of the royal households did not cease to be insufficient, irregular and constantly in deficit.

Conclusions

Some reflections by way of conclusion are called for now that the general characteristics of the economic foundation of the royal households of the Spanish Habsburgs during the reigns of Philip II and Philip III have been outlined. My own opinion is that, although advances have been made in recent years in economic studies of the court and royal households, we can see that numerous topics still remain to be analysed. Broadly speaking, I think future research will have to address some aspects which are largely unknown at present; to indicate some questions of interest, it would be well worthwhile studying, one by one, the economic administration and expenditure of the major departments of the household; how the wages of their members developed in relation to general price levels; how the presence of the court influenced the supply of goods and services; and what repercussions there were on price trends. In sum, I think we can feel satisfied with what we know of the position of the royal households with respect to the royal exchequer, but there is still a good deal of ground to be covered with respect to relations between the court and the development of the economy during the period.

The household of archduke Albert of Austria from his arrival in Madrid until his election as governor of the Low Countries: 1570–1595[1]

José Eloy Hortal Muñoz
Universidad Rey Juan Carlos /
Instituto Universitario "La Corte en Europa"

Archduke Albert of Austria was one of the most important figures in the Spanish Monarchy of the *Austrias* during the reigns of his uncle, Philip II, and his cousin Philip III. Until recently there was no complete modern biography of him and, apart from his period as co-sovereign of the Habsburg Netherlands with Isabella Clara Eugenia, there are very few studies about particular episodes of his life.[2] This represents

[1] This article has been funded as part of the project: "La contradicción de la Monarquía Católica: la fijación de las ordenanzas y etiquetas cortesanas en el periodo de su declive", (Ref: HAR2009-12614-C04-02/HIST), directed by Professor F. Suárez Bilbao, Universidad Rey Juan Carlos, and financed by the Spanish Ministry of Economy. Abbreviations: AGS: Archivo General de Simancas; CJH: Consejo y Juntas de Hacienda, DGT: Dirección General del Tesoro and E.: Estado; AHN: Archivo Histórico Nacional, Madrid; Consejos: *Consejos Suprimidos* and E.: *Estado*; ASV: Archivio Segreto Vaticano, Spagna: *Segreteria di Stato, Spagna*; BNE: Biblioteca Nacional de España, Madrid; BPRM: Biblioteca del Palacio Real de Madrid; IVDJ: Instituto Valencia de Don Juan, Madrid; RAH: Real Academia de la Historia, Madrid.

[2] See the political biography of Albert by Luc Duerloo, *Dynasty and Piety. Archduke Albert (1598-1621) and Habsburg Political Culture in an Age of Religious Wars* (Farnham, 2012). There are two seventeenth century biographies: Aubert le Meere (Lemire), *De vita Alberti Belgarum principis* (Antwerp, 1622), and Jean-Chrysostome B. de Montpleinchamp, *Histoire de l'Archiduc Albert gouverneur général et puis prince souverain de la Belgique*, 1693, the edition by Aimé Louis Philémon Robaulx de Soumoy (Brussels, 1870) being the one consulted here. On different periods of his life: for his stay in the court in Madrid in his youth, José Martínez Millán, "El archiduque Alberto en la corte de Felipe II (1570–1580)," in Werner Thomas and Luc Duerloo (eds.), *Albert & Isabella, 1598–1621 Essays* (Louvain, 1998), 27–37; the outstanding study on his travels as governor of Portugal is by Francisco Caeiro, *O archiduque Alberto de Austria, vice-rei de Portugal* [hereafter, *O archiduque Alberto de Austria*] (Lisbon, 1961), with comments by Domingos Mauricio in: "O Arquiduque Alberto de Áustria, Vice-Rei de Portugal (1583–1593)," *Brotéria* 24, no. 4 (1962), 422–9. Also, as a collector and patron of art, Annemarie Jordan Gschwend, *Archduke Albert in Lisbon (1581–1593):*

an enormous gap in the bibliography of the reigns of Philip II and Philip III, and a complete study of his life would help clarify many points concerning the histories of Portugal, the Habsburg Netherlands, the Holy Roman Empire and the Spanish Monarchy itself. The aim of this essay is to make a contribution to this endeavour by studying the members of his entourage and the changes in its composition from the time the archduke arrived in Castile with his brother, Wenceslas, until his election as governor of the Low Countries in 1595, as well as examining the political background during his upbringing and his function as an integrator of territorial elites in the different places he served.

The creation of the household for archdukes Albert and Wencelas in Madrid: 1570–1576

Archduke Albert was born in Neustadt on November 13, 1559, the ninth child of emperor Maximilian II and his wife Maria of Spain, and hence nephew of Philip II.[3] He very soon revealed how useful he could be to his uncle's political strategies and, when he was eleven years old, it was decided to have him educated, together with his brother Wenceslas at the court in Madrid, where they took over from their older brothers, Rudolph and Ernest. Philip II's intention was to ensure an orthodox Catholic upbringing for the future emperors, and possible successors to the Spanish throne, whilst, at the same time, instilling in them his own

A question of patronage or emulation? (Ph.D. diss. Brown Univ., 1985). Relating to his brief period as archbishop of Toledo, BNE, MS 13027, Anon., *Vidas de los Arzobispos de Toledo,* (n.d. ca. 1620), 3: 201–8ff. For his stage as governor of the Low Countries from 1595 to 1598, Juan Roco Campofrío, *España en Flandes, trece años de gobierno del archiduque Alberto, 1595–1608,* [hereafter, *España en Flandes*] (Madrid, 1973), 1–219. There are, however, many studies about him as sovereign of the Habsburg Netherlands, particularly on the occasion of the fourth centenary of the Act of Cession in 1998. A good summary of studies about the Archdukes can be found in Werner Thomas, "La corte de los archiduques Alberto de Austria y la infanta Isabel Clara Eugenia en Bruselas (1598–1633): Una revisión historiográfica," in Ana Crespo Solana and Manuel Herrero Sánchez (eds.), *España y las 17 provincias de los Países Bajos: Una revisión historiográfica (XVI–XVIII),* 2 vols. (Cordoba, 2002), 1: 355–386. Lastly, Luc Duerloo, *Dynasty and Piety* (mentioned above), which in its first chapter speaks briefly about Albert´s life before his appointment as sovereign of the Netherlands.

[3] For a short biography of the archduke, José Martínez Millán and Carlos Javier de Carlos Morales (eds.), *Felipe II (1527–1598): La configuración de la Monarquía hispánica* [hereafter, *Configuración de la Monarquía hispánica*], (Valladolid, 1998), 318.

political view of Christianity. The empress Maria, Philip II's sister, was a great help to him in this endeavour by doing everything possible to further his aims.

Archdukes Rudolph and Ernest had been in Madrid since 1564 and their retinue, with Adam von Dietrichstein in charge as lord steward,[4] was composed largely of servants from the Holy Roman Empire.[5] However, what had been suitable for the older brothers was not going to be so for the younger ones and even before the names of the archdukes who would relieve Rudolph and Ernest were known, Philip II had decided that those in their service would be Castilian so that he could better control their immediate circle. This, naturally, did not convince the emperor, who did his utmost to ensure that some Imperial servants remained in Madrid with the archdukes.[6] With this hope in mind, a small party of servants was assembled for the brothers in the Holy Roman Empire, much fewer in number than the group which accompanied their sister, Anne, the future wife of Philip II, and hence the future queen of the Spanish Monarchy.[7]

[4] For this figure, Friedrich Edelmayer, "Honor y dinero: Adam de Dietrichstein al servicio de la Casa de Austria," *Studia Historica. Historia Moderna* 10–11 (1992/ 93), 89–116.

[5] For the stay of the two archdukes in Castile, see Erwin Mayer-Löwenschwerdt, "Der Aufenthalt der Erzherzoge Rudolf und Ernst in Spanien," *Sitzungsberichte der philosophisch-historischen Klasse der Österreichische Akademie der Wissenschaften* 206 (1927), 1ff. As for the political evolution of archduke Ernest and his service during his stay in the Low Countries, José Eloy Hortal Muñoz, "La casa del archiduque Ernesto durante su gobierno en los Países Bajos (1593–1595)," in Antonio Álvarez-Ossorio Alvariño and Bernardo García García (eds.), *La Monarquía de las Naciones: Patria, nación y naturaleza en la Monarquía de España*, (Madrid, 2004), 193–213, and its bibliography.

[6] In a missive to Philip II dated May 29, 1570, the empress Maria expressed her view on this matter: "It seems to me that the emperor has decided to send two sons as you command. I think they will be the middle ones of those over here, although I don't know this for sure (...). The emperor approved everything you said to him about this matter, but later, I saw that he thought it strange that they weren't going to have any Germans. I blame others, and I think that if they were to have some, so that they don't forget the language, for he is right about that, he will be very happy about the great favour you are doing him and them." Cf. Juan Carlos Galende Díaz and Manuel Salamanca López, *Epistolario de la emperatriz María de Austria: Textos inéditos del Archivo de la Casa de Alba* (Madrid, 2004), 181–182.

[7] For Anne´s entourage, José Eloy Hortal Muñoz, "Organización de una Casa. El Libro de Veeduría de la reina Ana de Austria," in José Martínez Millán and María Paula Marçal Lourenço (eds.), *Las Relaciones Discretas entre las Monarquías Hispana y Portuguesa: Las Casas de las Reinas (siglos XV-XIX)* (Madrid, 2008), 1: 275-309.

The two archdukes and the archduchess began their journey at the end of July 1570, finally arriving in Madrid in October.[8] From there, they moved on to Segovia, the venue chosen for the wedding, where arrangements were set in train to establish a household for the archdukes, the whole process no doubt influenced by the political climate then prevailing at the court of the Prudent King.

The Alba faction that had been dominant until a few years earlier had lost power when its principal patron, the duke of Alba, left to put down the revolt in the Low Countries. Cardinal Espinosa exploited the duke's absence to advance in the administration, using the new policy that made the Monarchy confessional to his advantage. Despite the cardinal's promotion being endorsed by members of the Eboli faction, he seconded the duke of Alba's policy in the Low Countries because of the religious and ideological ties that united them. The court faction that had initiated the confessional policy lost power towards 1570 following the failure of the Morisco Rebellion of 1568, and because of the enormous sums of money that Alba required in Flanders. The result was that Espinosa's influence declined, as did the duke's, while Philip II searched for different ways of solving his problems. The new situation favoured the rise of the old members of the Eboli faction and their influence is apparent in the creation of the Holy League against the Turks in 1571, a formation that ran counter to Alba's interests since it diverted funds away from the Habsburg Netherlands.[9]

Given this situation, it is easy to understand why it was decided that the household of the archdukes should be controlled by two figures who were close to the prince of Eboli, with links to Eraso and who also had the blessing of the empress Maria: the secretary Gaztelu and don Juan de Ayala,[10] who was recalled from his quiet life as the governor of

[8] There is an account of the journey in J. Báez de Sepúlveda, *Relación verdadera del recibimiento que hizo la ciudad de Segovia a la majestad de la reyna nuestra señora doña Anna de Austria, en su felicísimo Casamiento que en la dicha ciudad se celebró* (Segovia, 1998). For political implications, see our article "La estancia del Prior de Castilla, Don Hernando de Toledo, en la Corte de Bruselas (1567–1570): Las luchas cortesanas," in Francisco Ruiz Gómez and Jesús Molero García (eds.), *La orden de San Juan entre el Mediterráneo y la Mancha* (Alcázar de San Juan, 2009), 327-50.

[9] For factional struggles during this period, José Martínez Millán, "Grupos de poder en la corte durante el reinado de Felipe II: la facción ebolista, 1554–1573," in José Martínez Millán (ed.), *Instituciones y élites de poder en la Monarquía Hispana durante el siglo XVI* (Madrid, 1992), 183–97.

[10] See his biography in Martínez Millán and Carlos Morales, *Configuración de la Monarquía hispánica,* 329–30.

Aranjuez to be named tutor and lord steward, with an annual stipend of 375,000 *maravedís*.[11] Between the two of them, they drew up a plan for the household and proceeded to choose the courtiers, although in queen Anne's household it was cardinal Espinosa who succeeded in appointing the principal officers.[12]

In total, the household services that were arranged for the archdukes, consisted of some seventy servants plus pages, although some of the servants carried out several offices at the same time. Thanks to the set of documents kept in the Archivo General de Simancas, under *Contaduría Mayor de Cuentas, 1ª época, legajo* 1024, we know the members of the household service in its entirety, from May 1, 1571, when it started up, until the end of 1576. Looking at the way it was made up, it is possible to infer that the service assigned was on a par with that received by royal princes of tender years but inferior to that, for example, of the heir to the throne, prince don Carlos.[13] Some household sections were not provided at all, for instance the palace Guard or the Hunt, or they were very small, as in the case of the Stable; no master of the horse was appointed, and the Chapel comprised only one confessor, Gómez Manrique, and a chamberlain, George of Austria,[14] since the archdukes could use the appropriate section of the queen's household, or even the king's if need arose.[15] What follows is a breakdown of this service, although citing only the names of the figures occupying the principal offices.[16*]

[11] Martínez Millán, "El archiduque Alberto en la corte de Felipe II", 28–9.

[12] José Martínez Millán, "La corte de Felipe II: la casa de la reina Ana," in Luis Antonio Ribot García (ed.), *La Monarquía de Felipe II a debate* (Madrid, 2000), 164–70.

[13] For the members of the said service and its structure, José Martínez Millán (ed.), *La Corte de Carlos V*, 5 vols. (Madrid, 2000), 5: 130–3; José Martínez Millán and Santiago Fernández Conti (eds.), *La Monarquía de Felipe II: la Casa del Rey* [hereafter *Monarquía de Felipe II*], 2 vols. (Madrid, 2005), 2: 663–8.

[14] He was the illegitimate son of Leopold of Austria, former prince-bishop of Liège, and served Albert as chamberlain until 1598.

[15] For the use made by the royal princes or queens of the king's guards, especially the old guard of the Spanish guard, José Eloy Hortal Muñoz, "Las guardas palatino-personales de Felipe II," in *La Monarquía de Felipe II*, 1: 477.

[16] *Translators' note: For the offices 'below stairs' we have used the names of the corresponding positions in the English royal household contemporary with the Burgundy household. On occasions, this has meant using the title of 'serjeant' for the person in charge of each office, for example, 'serjeant of the bread pantry' for *sumiller de la panetería* and 'yeoman' as the equivalent of *ayuda*, for example, 'yeoman of the bread pantry' for *ayuda de la panetería*. With regard to the offices of the chamber, the Spanish names have been translated more literally, e.g. 'gentleman of the table' for *gentilhombre de la boca*, to avoid any confusion with the English system, except where

The only steward assigned to them was Juan Pacheco y de Navas with an annual stipend of 56,100 *maravedís*; he also served as gentleman sewer.[17] He naturally maintained a fluid relationship with the lord steward, don Juan de Ayala, and enjoyed his confidence, as was essential, given that he had to run the household whenever the lord steward was away. He had, in addition, extensive experience of royal domestic service since he had been Philip II's gentleman of the table since 1555, whilst Philip was still a prince.

The Chamber did no have very many servants either. It comprised a physician, with an annual wage of 112,200 *maravedís*; four valets of the chamber with a stipend of 36,000 *maravedís*, one of whom, Bautista Mola, was also yeoman of the great wardrobe and jewels; a barber, with a salary of 36,000 *maravedís*; and four doorkeepers of the chamber who belonged to the king's household but served the archdukes during 1571 and 1572 with an expense allowance of 2,500 *maravedís* over and above their usual stipends.

As for the Fourrier's department, the preceptor was a prominent figure since Philip II paid a good deal of attention to his nephews' education during these formative years. For this purpose he relied on the three men who had introduced the archdukes to legal affairs in the Holy Roman Empire: Nicolas Coret, Mateo de Otthen and Augier Guilain Busbeque (or Augerio Busbecq),[18] to whom were added the castilian, Sebastián Pérez, and between them, they set about preparing Albert and Wenceslas for making the leap into active political life. Although we have evidence of the importance of the other three in the education of the archdukes, only Mateo de Otthen appears as their preceptor in the household accounts, with a stipend of 90,000 *maravedís*; Otthen, moreover, was one of those closest to the

clear equivalents existed. *Sumiller de corps* has been left untranslated, however, following the example of eminent historians, such as John H. Elliott, while indicating for lay readers that his role had some things in common with the groom of the stole's. As for the system of emoluments used by the Spanish monarchs to pay those who served them, we have opted for the following equivalents: 'stipend' has been used for *gajes*, 'wages' for *quitaciones*, 'vantage' for *ventaja*, and 'bouche of court' for *ración*. 'Entertained' (*entretenido*) describes a person who received an 'entertainment' (*entretenimiento*), that is a monthly retainer.

[17] For a biography, Martínez Millán and Fernández Conti, *La Monarquía de Felipe II*, 2: 343.

[18] Montpleinchamp, *Histoire de l'Archiduc Albert*, 20–1.

archduke.[19] The treasurer of the chamber was also an important official position, occupied by Justo Valter with a total stipend of 200,000 *maravedís*. His task was to keep records of monies assigned to the chamber as well as to take responsibility for the payment of the salaries of the members of the household every four months, as in the other royal households.[20] To help him in his duties, there was the comptroller, Diego de Olarte, with a stipend of 150,000 *maravedís*, and the *grefier*, García Álvarez Osorio, with a stipend of 125,000 *maravedís* and a grace and favour payment of another 50,000, who replaced Mattheus de Ocáriz on November 1, 1571, and went on to become the treasurer of the chamber, in 1576, after the death of Justo Valter. The *grefier* also had the help of an officer with a stipend of 25,000 *maravedís*. Other members of the Fourrier's department were the two yeomen of the great wardrobe and jewels, who received stipends of 15,000 *maravedís* annually, supported by two grooms who earned 7,200. In addition, there were two household physicians in charge of the health of the members of the retinue, Suárez de Luxán and Luis de Rivera, with stipends of 60,000 *maravedís*, increasing to 80,000 in 1578, and an apothecary, Rafael Arigón with a stipend of 15,000. As for the harbingers, there was one for the palace, Diego de Arze, who also combined the offices of serjeant of the chandlery and serjeant arras-worker, with a salary of 50,000 *maravedís*, and two for the household and court, with 40,000. To take care of hygiene, we find a groom of the closet who had a salary of 7,200 *maravedís*, a sweeper, who earned 7,300 until 1576, when it was raised to 12,000, and two laundresses, one for the body linen and another for the table linen, earning 45,000. Finally, there is evidence of a head water bearer who earned 75,000 *maravedís*, a food-bearer, paid 18,250, and a shoemaker with no stipend although he was awarded expense allowances during his service.

With reference to positions that formed part of the Fourrier's department, those concerning the arrases and chandlery were combined

[19] Descended from a Danish family, he began to teach the archduke Latin when the latter was nine years old. He accompanied the archdukes on their journey to Madrid and was their private tutor until he became Albert's secretary during his stay in Portugal, remaining with him until Albert departed for the Habsburg Netherlands. Afterwards, in Madrid he was put in charge of his master's affairs. Philip II granted him a pension of 1,500 ducats in the archbishopric of Toledo and appointed him a beneficed clergyman in the diocese of Mechlin; see AHN, *Consejos*, lib. 174, fol. 91r, and Caeiro, *O archiduque Alberto de Austria*, 129–30.

[20] For household expenses and accounts from its creation on May 1, 1571 to 1574, see IVDJ, *Envío 7*, fol. 446.

and the office holders were the same. It was headed by Diego de Arze, and he was aided by five servants: two yeomen with stipends of 35,000 *maravedís*, one of whom, Miguel de Gurrea also served as sewer to the pages, and three grooms, with 27,000; they all had permission to eat any food left by the pages. The Bakehouse, for its part, was included with the Cellar and both were headed by the serjeant of the cellar, Rodrigo de Castro, who enjoyed a stipend of 50,000 *maravedís*. The office of yeoman was nominally split until Bernabé de la Peña combined them in October 1572. Both offices, whether separate or combined, received a stipend of 34,400 *maravedís*. For their part, the grooms always worked for both the Cellar and the Bakehouse, with a wage of 27,200 *maravedís*. The only position that differentiated between the Cellar and Bakehouse was the pantler's, in charge of the bread, and with a stipend of 7,300 *maravedís*. The salsery was headed by Francisco de Portilla, who was also steward of the estate for the table; he received a stipend of 50,400 *maravedís*. He had a yeoman to help him, whose stipend was worth 15,000 *maravedís*, and two grooms who earned 7,300. The number of servants in the larder was fixed at three, with a serjeant of the acatry and larder to prevent pilfering. The serjeant of the acatry and larder, Amaro Márquez, had a wage of 56,400 *maravedís*; there was also a clerk of the larder, paid 40,400 *maravedís*, a post occupied by Santiago Jiménez until January 20, 1573, Pedro de Mendoza from that date until January 16, 1576, and Alonso de Salmerón thereafter; and a yeoman of the larder, who was paid 34,000 *maravedís*. Finally, the Kitchen employed a buyer, Juan de Torres, between May 11 and July 7, 1571, and Hernando de Zabala from then on, with a stipend of 27,373 *maravedís*, plus 7,300 for the stipend of a groom who led the mule with the pack saddles; both buyer and groom also received bouche of court, consisting of two pounds of mutton and one of beef, eight loaves of bread and an *azumbre* [some two litres] of wine per day. There were also two cooks with stipends of 35,000 *maravedís*, a porter who was paid 35,350 *maravedís*, two grooms earning 25,300 *maravedís* and a pastry cook, 35,000.

The Stable, as we noted, was very small and only the Pages' House attained any size. We do not know their exact number but we do know that, in order to attend to them, a teacher was appointed at 40,000 *maravedís*, to teach them catechesis and Latin, a position which was filled by Master León until his death on March 13, 1575; they also had a tutor, Juan (Johann) Fritznaver, until the end of September 1571 and Pedro Romano Corbino from 1573. There was also a sewer, a groom with a stipend of 6,000 *maravedís*, and a servant, from 1574, for another 6,000 *maravedís*. Finally, there were six footmen with 20,250 *maravedís* each in stipends.

The stipends were not particularly high, especially if we compare them with those granted in the household of the king or queen. To take a striking example, in the queen's household, the lord steward earned one million *maravedís* a year and only 375,000 in the archdukes' household. The paltriness of the stipends may be one reason why a number of servants held several offices at the same time. Another explanation is that the archdukes' tender years and their, as yet, scant belongings meant that certain sections of the household, such as the Jewel Office, the Cellar and other similar offices had not yet assumed great relevance.

Many of the servants who comprised the archdukes' first household were serving for the first time in a royal household, although we are in a position to confirm that a considerable number did have experience and came from three different areas of service: Imperial servants who formed part of the retinue that the archdukes themselves brought with them from the Holy Roman Empire, former servants of the deceased prince Carlos, and servants from the household of queen Isabella of Valois.

The presence of servants drawn from the retinue that had accompanied the archdukes on their long journey from the court of Vienna to Madrid, had been, as we saw, a stipulation of emperor Maximilian, anxious not to lose control over his sons' immediate circle. The empress Maria had warned her brother that the emperor would not tolerate a household that had no German speakers in it, and his mind was only set at rest when he had checked that that there were, in fact, several being appointed.[21] There is no doubt at all that the empress Maria's opinion carried weight in the choice of servants; meanwhile, the rest returned to their home countries, together with those of her daughter Anne's retinue who did not join any royal household. The Pages' House was one of the areas with the greatest number of prominent figures from the Imperial court, as Juan (Johann) Fritznaver was the preceptor and tutor to the pages until the end of September 1571 and Roberto Olacher was the pages' groom until March 28, 1573, when he was replaced

[21] As can be seen in the letter from the empress to her brother, dated July 31, 1571: "And the Emperor is happy that there remain some who can speak their language," cf Galende Díaz and Salamanca López, *Epistolario de la emperatriz María de Austria*, 220–1.

by another Imperial servant, Jorge Alemán until December 31, 1573. By the same token, we find various footmen, such as Jacques Lanze or Adrianis de Merica, or valets of the chamber, such as Paulo Quenobel or Pedro Poinsot. Other examples were the groom of the kitchen, Tomás Rolet; the laundress of the body linen, Juliana Rubin; the barber to the person, Tomás Remelli; and, of course, the preceptor and secretary, Mateo de Otthen and the chamberlain, George of Austria. There were various cases of Imperial servants who were assigned permanently to Madrid but who, in the end, preferred to return to the Holy Roman Empire with archdukes Rudolph and Ernest in the summer of 1571. This was the case of the previously mentioned Juan (Johann) Fritznaver, and the laundress, Isabel de Buce.

As for those figures who had originally served prince don Carlos, who had died in 1568, it should be stressed that it was not only when the household was first set up that they were given appointments, but in stages until 1577. When the heir to the throne died, his servants were given annual monetary compensation in the form of a lifelong *juro* [a perpetual bond], rather lower than what they had received in their former positions, or until they were granted another position in some royal household; and this was also the case in queen Isabella of Valois' household.[22] So, in general, we may consider that those figures who went on to form part of the archdukes' household improved their positions in comparison with the offices they had held in the household of the heir to the throne, although their stipends did not improve in proportion, since those offered in don Carlos's household were substantially higher than those in that of Albert and Wenceslas; and some even earned less in the archdukes' service than from the *juro* they had been granted. We actually know the names of twelve servants who moved from don Carlos household to serve the archdukes, beginning, in May 1571, with the sweeper, Enrique Joyman, who formerly swept for prince don Carlos; the comptroller, Diego de Olarte, former keeper of the jewels to the heir; the clerk of the larder, Santiago Jiménez, formerly groom of the

[22] A record of *juros* granted on the dissolution of the two households can be found in AHN, *Consejos*, lib. 251 with the title "Libro primero de la cámara desde el 19 de septiembre de 1568 hasta el 24 de septiembre de 1570. Libro de despachos de la cámara en el qual están particularmente todas las mercedes que su Majestad hizo a los criados del príncipe don Carlos y reina Doña Isabel nuestros señores que sean en gloria y a otros." First book of the chamber from September 19, 1568 until September 24, 1570. Book of despatches from the Chamber in which can be found in particular all favours made by His Majesty to the servants of Prince Don Carlos and Queen Isabella, our lord and lady, may they be in glory, and to others, trans.

larder; and the yeomen arras-workers and yeomen of the chandlery and sewer to the pages, Miguel de Gurrea and Pedro Rodríguez, who were previously grooms to the arras-workers. Later, and in chronological sequence, the following entered into service: the buyer, Hernando de Zabala, the prince's groom in the fourrier's department; the yeoman of the salsery and the estates, Domingo de Valdés, formerly a groom of the bakehouse; the *grefier*, García Álvarez Osorio, valet of the chamber to the prince and who would acquire importance later as treasurer of the chamber; the clerk of the larder, Alonso de Salmerón, formerly water bearer and serjeant of the woodyard to don Carlos; the yeoman of the larder, Juan de Arroyo, previously groom to the yeoman of the cellar; and the *grefier*, Pedro Álvarez de Casasola, who had been the heir's valet of the chamber. Finally, and now in 1577, Alonso Velázquez de la Canal, a person with a long tradition in the service of royal households, since he served in several of them for thirty-six years, turned up in the archdukes' household as comptroller.[23]

The servants from the former household of queen Isabella de Valois joining the archdukes' household, just six, were fewer in number than those from prince Carlos's since most of those joining another royal household went to queen Anne's. They found themselves in the same situation as the servants of prince Carlos: their position improved but not their stipends. In May 1571, Rodrigo de Castro, who had been the former deputy of the master of the mules, was taken on as serjeant of the cellar and bakehouse. There was also Francisco Luçero, the yeoman of the salsery and estates, a former yeoman sewer to the ladies-in-waiting of the deceased queen; and Juan de Santiago, the yeoman of the jewel office, a former groom of the great wardrobe. Later, on July 1, Juan Francés was taken on as pantler, a post he had also held in Isabella of Valois' household; Luis de Laguna, formerly fourrier of the pack animals, entered as yeoman of the cellar and pantry, and Adán de Cornechin, a former groom of the larder, entered as a yeoman in the same office.

[23] More specifically, he was serjeant of the bakehouse in the Burgundy household between 1558 and 1559 at least, and in the household of prince Carlos in 1557 and 1564. In 1564, he became *grefier* of the second household, serving there until the death of the heir to the throne. Later, in 1577, he became comptroller of archduke Albert's household and remained in this position until his death on July 23, 1592. He was also *contino* in Castile from February 29, 1556 until his death, see AGS, CJH, leg. 250, carpeta 17, and DGT, *Inventario 24*, leg. 903; AHN, *Consejos*, leg. 4408, no. 98, year 1578, lib. 251, fol. 50r, and lib. 252, fols. 115v–116r; RAH, MS A-61, fol. 47v.

The reform of 1577: Albert's service is separated from Wenceslas's

After their household service had been set up, both archdukes, Albert and Wenceslas, were groomed in readiness for the moment when Philip II should determine their future roles in political life. This decision was about to be made for Albert in 1576 when the allies of the duke of Alba proposed him as a candidate for governor of the Low Countries in place of the deceased Requesens. However, the members of the papist faction, who were still firmly in control, imposed the choice of don John of Austria. In exchange, Antonio Pérez, at the request of Philip II, pulled strings in Rome so that Albert would be named Cardinal-Deacon, which came about on March 11, 1577, and the following year he was appointed Cardinal-Priest. Similarly, he was considered for appointment as archbishop of Toledo after the death of Carranza on May 2, 1576, but Antonio Pérez preferred someone with more experience and closer to his own way of thinking, like Gaspar de Quiroga, who was appointed on August 17, 1577.

Whilst Albert was being steered towards offices of this importance, his brother Wenceslas received certain privileges from the Order of St John and he was thought of as its future prior, this move being part of Philip II's strategy of controlling the Order by using members of his family. However, the archduke's death in 1578 put paid to that idea.[24]

Even before the death of Wenceslas, some thought had been given to the need for separating the services of the two brothers, particularly in view of the growing importance of archduke Albert within the court. His appointment as Cardinal-Deacon set that process in motion and it was decided to make the necessary changes to provide him with his own household and include in it certain positions hitherto not considered necessary.[25] The whole process, of course, was carried out under the watchful eye of the papist faction.

[24] Ignacio Ezquerra Revilla, "Tentativas de la corona por controlar la orden de San Juan en tiempo de Felipe II: la "expectativa" del archiduque Wenceslao de Austria en el gran priorato de Castilla y León (1577–78)," in Ruiz Gómez and Molero García, *La orden de San Juan entre el Mediterráneo y la Mancha*, 401-30.

[25] We know the key members of the household in 1577, thanks to the account given by ambassador Hans Khevenhüller in *Diario de Hans Khevenhüller, embajador imperial en la corte de Felipe II* [hereafter, *Diario*], intro, Sara Veronelli, trans. and ed. Félix Labrador (Madrid, 2001), 125, which Martínez Millán mentions in "El archiduque Alberto en la corte de Felipe II", 35.

To be specific, the positions of gentleman of the table and of the chamber were introduced for the first time into Albert's retinue and, because of his own association with the church, gentlemen of the cloth or chamberlains, who lived outside the palace. The number of stewards also increased.

The five gentlemen of the table appointed were: Diego de Guzmán, Jerónimo de Mendoza, Juan de Ludeña, Francisco de Vargas (a teacher of theology), and a professor from Salamanca, Bazán Pérez. As for the appointments of gentlemen of the chamber, these were: Cosme de Meneses, Gabriel Niño and Luis Enríquez.[26] As has already been mentioned, three more men in religious orders were appointed as gentlemen of the cloth or chamberlains who would not reside within the palace because of Albert's status as a cardinal, and who joined George of Austria. The new incumbents were: Martín de Alarcón, named chaplain of the king's Castile household on June 25, 1580, Miguel de Ayala, a member of the lord steward's family and dean of the chapel in Granada from 1582, and Andrés Pacheco, who eventually became bishop of Segovia and Cuenca. The final three ended their service before the archduke's progress to Portugal to assume the position of viceroy, and received in return pensions in a number of bishoprics: Miguel de Ayala 300 ducats from Granada, Martín de Alarcón, another 300 from Santiago and Andrés Pacheco, 500 from Cuenca.[27] Finally, Luis de Ayala, who was related to the lord steward, and Juan Gaitán joined the steward, Juan Pacheco y de Navas.

We do not know who exactly formed the rest of the new entourage since the documents kept in *legajo* 1024 from the first period of the *Contaduría Mayor de Cuentas* stop at the end of 1576, just before the archdukes' household was split. However, we may infer that, compared to the earlier one, the number of office holders would not have varied greatly, since the death of Wenceslas prompted Albert to provide posts for those servants who had been assigned to his brother. From July 26, 1577, the new household was endowed with 20,000 ducats per annum in income from Toledo for its maintenance, an amount considered spartan by the lord steward, don Juan de Ayala, whose request for more was turned down.[28]

[26] A short biography can be found in Martínez Millán and Fernández Conti, *La Monarquía de Felipe II*, 2: 145.

[27] AHN, *Consejos*, lib. 174, fols. 89r and 91v.

[28] Martínez Millán, "El archiduque Alberto en la corte de Felipe II", 34.

Appointments to the new household were controlled by the papist faction, as has been mentioned, and, in fact, several members of don Juan de Ayala's family entered the service. However, this group found itself isolated from power after the downfall of Antonio Pérez in 1579 and although many figures took advantage of the cover afforded by their service to Albert to survive at court, the new situation made itself felt. The appointment as page, in 1579, of Juan de Toledo y del Águila, son of the Castilianist judge of the household and court (and so a member of the fifth court of the Council of Castile), Alvar García de Toledo,[29] is just one small symptom that the trend that had favoured the papists was beginning to turn down.

Archduke Albert's sojourn in Portugal and his return to Madrid: 1583–1593

During the time Philip II spent in Badajoz and Portugal from 1580 to 1583, the Castilianist group of courtiers, which had helped to impose a confessional ideology in line with Castilian interests, gradually shaped the organization of the government, and attempted to weed out the remnants of the papist faction from important positions. Mateo Vázquez began to stand out from the other principal courtiers, although the relentless rise of other figures, who would eventually eclipse the secretary, began to be apparent on their return to Madrid in 1583. Juan de Zúñiga was one of the most ambitious, although his decease in 1586 brought his career to an abrupt end. His death, together with cardinal Granvelle's in the same year, catapulted Juan de Idiáquez into the post, converting him into a principal courtier with no need for assistance from Mateo Vázquez. Along with the secretary, he grew very influential, taking over from his father, the third count of Chinchón. Finally, the figure of Cristóbal de Moura deserves special mention. He was situated on the side of those whose ideology was opposed to the Castilianists, but, in the end, was party to many of the ideas that they advocated.[30]

[29] For a biography, see Martínez Millán and Fernández Conti, *La Monarquía de Felipe II*, 2: 720–2.

[30] For the court struggles during this period, Santiago Fernández Conti, *Los consejos de Estado y Guerra en el reinado de Felipe II, 1548–1598* (Valladolid, 1998), 172–84; Martínez Millán and Carlos Morales, *Configuración de la Monarquía hispánica,* 138–47.

Despite the control exerted by both the Ebolists and the papists in the first decade of his service, Albert never favoured the political and religious convictions of either group, and set about developing ideas that tended to be more in harmony with the new dominant faction. This affinity made it possible for archduke Albert to be appointed to the difficult post of viceroy of Portugal. It had been speculated that empress Maria, recently arrived in the Iberian Peninsula, would take charge of the government but the eventual decision favoured her son. Although Antonio Danvila y Burguero puts forward other reasons,[31] we believe that the choice fell upon Albert because the main task that Philip II wanted the viceroy to perform was to establish Confessionalism in Portugal, and the kind of spirituality that the empress practised was not the most suitable for accomplishing this task. Her son's, on the other hand, did approach what the king wanted, and an example of this is that his confessors were always of the Dominican Order, instances being Juan Velázquez de las Cuevas, Fray Juan Vicente and Fray Íñigo de Brizuela. With a view to carrying out the task entrusted to him by the monarch, Albert gradually accumulated the titles of viceroy, Inquisitor General, and the pope's *legatus a latere* during his ten-year stay in Portugal.

Unfortunately, our knowledge of the structure and members of archduke Albert's household during his Portuguese sojourn is very incomplete with no source to give us an overall view. Thanks to memoranda written at later dates and held in the *personal* section of the *Archivo General de Palacio*, manuscript A-61 of the *Real Academia de la Historia* or other sources, we have been able to pinpoint some of the servants, albeit only in part. However, some interesting general conclusions can be drawn.

During the creation of the viceroy's household, the archduke expressed his preference for keeping a Castilian majority amongst his servants, as had been the case up until that time.[32] As a way of attracting the sympathies of the elites of the neighbouring kingdom towards their recent annexation, Philip II was conscious of the need to organize the service in accordance with the customs of Portugal, that is, in the image and likeness of the way he had set up his own Portuguese

[31] Antonio Danvila y Burguero, *D. Cristóbal de Moura, primer Marqués de Castelrodrigo, 1530–1613* (Madrid, 1900), 539–40, says in his book that Albert was preferred because the empress was a spendthrift, because Maria's character and intelligence might cause problems and because Philip II wanted someone trustworthy close to him to take care of the infantas.

[32] Khevenhüller, *Diario,* 270.

household.[33] So, although the office holders of the most important positions of the archduke remained the same, Portuguese gentlemen of the chamber were appointed and new positions introduced peculiar to Portugal, such as *crucífero* or Abbreviator.[34]

Another measure adopted was to endow the household with those areas it did not possess on the grounds that they had previously been considered unnecessary, such as, the Hunt and the Guard, or to complete others, such as the Chapel and the Stables. Consequently, a master of the horse was appointed, a position that fell to the archduke's gentleman of the chamber, Luis Enríquez, and huntsmen such as Manuel Pimienta and Juan Issino. The area we know best is the Guard, thanks to the ordinances issued on October 20, 1586, for the new corps of halberdiers;[35] the monarch having already made provision, in the instructions he left for the archduke in 1583, for part of Albert's stipend to be used to pay the said guard.[36] These ordinances laid down that the Guard would be composed of a captain, with more limited powers than in the royal guards, being unable to take on or dismiss any halberdier without the consent of the archduke; there would also be a lieutenant and six officers, namely, four squadron corporals, a notary, and a harbinger with a wage of ten gold florins and the cost of the uniform, as well as fifty-eight halberdiers and a drummer, who would receive eight gold florins and with a supplement in their wages to help offset the cost of the uniform. The wage was spread over three payments, as in the royal guards, and the captain or lieutenant had to draw up a roll of these payments. After ten general articles, the instructions also introduced forty articles explaining internal administrative functions. Finally, the last part prescribed the way justice was to be administered, which, according to the text, was the same as that used in the royal guard.

33 For Philip II's Portuguese royal household, Labrador Arroyo's study in *La Monarquía de Felipe II*, Martínez Millán and Fernández Conti, 1: 820–945, see also *Ibidem*, 2: 593–663 for its members.

34 This position, equivalent to a secretary of religious affairs, was held by Roco de Campofrío from 1592.

35 "Institución y ordenanzas de la Guarda Alemana que mandó fundar el señor Archiduque Cardenal Alberto legado a la de S.M. en el reino de Portugal, Lisboa, 20 de octubre de 1586," AHN, E. lib. 728. It is already published in Félix Labrador Arroyo, *La Casa Real en Portugal, 1580-1621* (Madrid, 2009), 214-21.

36 Caeiro, *O archiduque Alberto de Austria*, 514. In chapter 31 of these instructions, it says: "Hey por bem que depois de entenderdes no Governo em diante enquanto o tiverdes se dê de minha fazenda para a despeza de Vossa meza, e pagamento de Vossa Guarda."

The archduke dispensed with this guard when he left the kingdom of Portugal to go, first to Madrid, and then to the Low Countries, although some of its members, such as Jacques Ruypacher, continued to serve him.[37]

Albert's governorship in Portugal was generally satisfactory; from 1588, however, there was speculation about his departure, as the Monarchy needed him.[38] After the failure of the Armada against England, Philip II became quite pessimistic and looked weary; he began to think that he was incapable of carrying the workload that he had until then. Following the advice of Moura and Idiáquez, who saw the archduke as someone who would defend their ideas, the king deemed it necessary for his nephew to return to help him in Madrid, placing him close to prince Philip to instruct him in business matters. In fact, Philip II confirmed this point with his ambassador, Olivares, and entrusted him with the mission of asking Rome whether the archduke's offices of nuncio and inquisitor would be maintained if Albert left Portugal.[39] This first attempt to bring Albert back to Madrid did not prosper due to the threat of English expeditions against Lisbon and other coastal areas of Portugal. Nevertheless, rumours about his return to Madrid or to the Low Countries as governor were constant for the rest of his time as viceroy in Portugal.[40]

After the first attempt, Philip II was more careful about the preparations for Albert's return and consulted with important figures in Portugal, such as the count of Portalegre, to sound out opinions on the advisability of his nephew giving up the post of viceroy.[41] Furthermore,

[37] He was a halberdier with a place reserved for him in the archduke's German guard when he was in Portugal until 1593; in 1595 we find him in Flanders as a clock-mender in the household, RAH, MS A-61, fols. 65r, 72v, 79r, 99v and 108r.

[38] Buongiovanni to Montalto, November 5, 1588, ASV, Spagna, leg. 36, fol. 456r: "Qui s'e levata voce, ch'in breve S. A. sia per andare in fiandra, però non se n'ha que anche certezza." Here there have been rumours that H.H. is soon to go to Flanders, but not if it is also certain, trans.

[39] Philip II to Olivares, December 1, 1588, AGS, E. leg. 951, fol. 166.

[40] Among other testimonies, Biglia to Montalto, January 20, 1590, ASV, Spagna, leg. 36, fol. 197r. "Dicono che S. A. partirà in breve per fiandra, e che in suo luoco verra a questo governo il Marchese figliuolo dell'Arciducca Ferdinando, il che da gran noia a tutto questo regno." They say that HH will soon leave for Flanders and that the Marquis son of the Archduke Ferdinand will come to this government in his place, which is tedious for the whole of this kingdom, trans.

[41] Portalegre to Philip II, March 1591, RAH, MS K-9, fols. 74v –75v. Displaying his proverbial pessimism, the count expressed the view that it was not a good moment and that he thought it necessary for Albert to stay there for at least two more years.

he used his ambassador in Rome to secure income for him from a church in Castile so that the archduke's servants could receive some financial benefits when he left Portugal,[42] although this situation was sufficiently well covered by the lucrative Priory of Crato, which enabled Albert to award favours charged against that income even during his time in the Low Countries.[43] Notwithstanding this, Philip's ambassadors in Rome managed to obtain for him the possibility of providing for his followers from the income of Sigüenza cathedral.[44] It should be remembered that the income from the Monarchy's richest archdiocese, Toledo, was subsequently added to the income from Crato and Sigüenza, so that the archduke had a generous supply of resources available to reward those who served him. This was a great incentive to anyone seeking to enter his household.

Everything pointed to the fact that Albert would return to Madrid sooner or later and this was confirmed on March 5, 1593, when Philip II communicated to the archduke that both he and his household should return to Castile. From Madrid, precise arrangements were made for the progress; several carts for the luggage, a judge of the household and court and a royal harbinger were sent to Portugal and the frontier posts were notified.[45] At the same time, Philip II prepared lodgings in the Madrid court to accommodate the more than 400 retainers who were expected to travel with his nephew. This caused considerable upheaval as it meant taking over the accommodation of a number of royal servants, mostly those in menial posts and harbingers.[46] Once these vicissitudes were overcome, the entourage left Lisbon on August 16

[42] Philip II to Sessa, July 10, 1591, AGS, E. leg. 958 (no pagination).

[43] Caeiro, "O Archiduque Alberto no Priorado do Crato," chapter 7 of *O archiduque Alberto de Austria*, 321–44.

[44] Olivares to Philip II, September 22, 1591, AGS, E. leg. 957 (no pagination).

[45] IVDJ, Envío 92, fol. 84r, in a note to Juan Vázquez, July 21, 1593, "His Majesty commands that a warrant be despatched so that the ports of Castile give free passage to the clothes of the Lord Prince Cardinal Albert and his servants without paying duty of any kind, and because it would be difficult to send a private list of the said clothing as there is much of it, with small things and belonging to different people, His Majesty says that it should be stated in the said warrant that everything should be allowed through freely on the authorization of don Joan de Ayala, his lord steward, with no other surety required."

[46] This can be seen in various notes to the harbingers in ibid, fols. 89r–91r, also in the impressions of some contemporaries, such as Diego Ochoa de Avellaneda to the count of Gondomar on July 28, in BPRM, MS II/2149, doc. 12, or the nuncio to Aldobrandino, in ASV, Envío 92, leg. 44, fols. 263–4.

and, a little over a month later, the archduke arrived at the monastery of San Lorenzo de El Escorial to pay his respects to Philip II and his mother, the empress Maria.[47]

Archduke Albert's second sojourn in Madrid: 1593–1595

Upon his arrival in Madrid, Albert was informed that he was going to be included in the Council of State and the *Junta de Gobierno* [Board of Government], giving him a leading role at court together with the heir to the throne, and he was even entrusted with the mission of receiving nuncios and ambassadors.[48] However, it was not simply the dispatching of business that had prompted his recall; there were at least two other missions that he had to fulfil.

The first was to contribute to the dynasticism that Philip II had begun to discern as necessary to the preservation of his immense empire. The development of a closer relationship between the two branches of the Habsburgs since 1587 enabled the Spanish monarch to further the idea of consolidating a network of territories with similar interests and joined by dynastic ties which, in the long term, would be the only way to achieve a stable and lasting peace. The figure of the archdukes Ernest and Albert was fundamental to this and that is where the germ of the idea of the Act of Cession of 1598 lay.[49]

The other mission that Philip II had in mind for his nephew was to appoint him archbishop of Toledo. This idea, as we have seen, had been broached before but on this occasion it came to fruition. The incumbent at the time was still Gaspar de Quiroga who was steeped in the ideas of the papist faction, which had never been to the liking of his Castilianist opponents. Furthermore, Philip II wanted his nephew to be named coadjutor of the archbishopric so that he could control with a firm hand the unrest that appeared to have gripped Toledo in those

[47] A description of his arrival can be found in a letter from the nuncio to Aldobrandino, on September 25, in *Ibidem*, fols. 291–3.

[48] Cabrera de Córdoba mentions this in Luis Cabrera de Córdoba, *Historia de Felipe II, Rey de España* [hereafter, *Historia de Felipe II*], 3 vols. ed. José Martínez Millán and Carlos Javier de Carlos Morales (Valladolid, 1998), 3: 1483–4. On the reforms taking place in the Council of State and the Board of Government, see Fernández Conti, *Los consejos de Estado y Guerra*, 222–3.

[49] Martínez Millán and Carlos Morales, *Configuración de la Monarquía hispánica*, 257–61.

years.[50] The monarch had tried to have the archduke named as successor to the archbishopric on several occasions after the first attempt failed in 1576 and, on January 12, 1581, he succeeded in persuading Gregory XIII to agree to it, even though twenty-seven was the minimum age stipulated for acceding to the post. So, in 1594, Philip II gave Sessa the task of ensuring that he was appointed coadjutor with an income of 20,000 ducats a year, which Clement VIII granted on November 7 of that year; the papal bull, however, was not delivered until the taxes and *media annata* [half annates] had been paid.[51] While the archduke was waiting for the bull of his appointment as coadjutor, Quiroga died. Philip II hastened to name his nephew archbishop, even though the requirement of appointing him a priest had not been fulfilled. However, the death of his brother Ernest in Flanders cut short the entire process.[52]

Ever since his arrival in Madrid, the different factions at court had tried to win the archduke over to their side, but the Castilianists had a distinct advantage as Philip II had told Moura to stay close to his nephew and advise him.[53] The empress Maria, for her part, attempted to take advantage of family ties and during her son's first week in Madrid, she held meetings with him on two occasions and even had him lodge near the Descalzas with her lord steward, the noted papist, Juan de Borja, count of Mayalde. The empress likewise managed to get the Imperial ambassador, Hans Khevenhüller, count of Frankenburg,[54] to be appointed the archduke's lord steward and *sumiller de corps* during his period in Madrid, after Juan de Ayala had resigned from office on the grounds of age, shortly before his death in 1594. The empress was confident that the proximity of the ambassador, who closeted himself with the archduke every day for an hour to show Albert how the Castilians discussed business, would serve to control the circles that her son moved in and to instil in him his view of the Spanish Monarchy,

[50] The state of unrest in Toledo can be seen in the anonymous manuscript kept in BNE, MS 12974, no. 23, "Representación al Archiduque Alberto de Austria, Arzobispo de Toledo, en el año 1595, sobre varios abusos que se notaban en el Arzobispado y su remedio" Representation to Archduke Albert of Austria, archbishop of Toledo, in the year 1595, concerning various abuses that were noted in the archbishopric and their remedy, trans.

[51] Philip II to Sessa, November 28, 1594, AGS, E. leg. 964 (no pagination).

[52] Caeiro, *O archiduque Alberto de Austria*, 360–70.

[53] Martínez Millán and Carlos Morales, *Configuración de la Monarquía hispánica*, 274.

[54] A biography of this renowned diplomat is found in the introduction to his diary.

which was similar to the empress's.[55] In the event, it did not work and Albert stuck to his own political and religious ideas.

Throughout 1593–4, Albert grew in importance and he seemed destined for greater things than he actually attained. However, both Idiáquez and, especially, Moura tried to keep a close eye on the archduke's activities to prevent him from acting independently and so gradually taking over the management of affairs. The proximity of the Portuguese nobleman began to irritate the king's nephew and their mutual distrust became obvious. The allies of Philip II's favourite also began to have disagreements with Albert and lent their weight to Moura's complaints about the archduke's attitude. These complaints could not be too acrimonious since Philip trusted his nephew implicitly and the latter had never acted illegally or done anything untoward. So, the situation began to be reminiscent of the Madrid court in 1576 when don John of Austria became a thorn in the side of Antonio Pérez and the rest of the papist faction. In this case the players were different but the situation remained the same. Albert had become an irritant for important people of his own persuasion and for those of the opposing one; he even upset prince Philip himself, with whom he clashed on a number of occasions. These disagreements led people to wonder whether his return to Madrid had been such a good idea after all; consequently, when news of his brother Ernest's death arrived, Philip II's favourites did not hesitate to support his dispatch to the Habsburg Netherlands.[56] After a series of negotiations and the appearance of several possible candidates, the pressure brought to bear by Moura and Idiáquez on Philip II and the negotiations held with the empress Maria enabled the decision to be taken that the new governor of Flanders was to be archduke Albert.[57]

The decision was actually taken on April 22, 1595, although it was not made public until April 26. In this way, Moura and Idiáquez achieved two very important personal objectives: the removal of a

[55] *Ibidem*, 24–5, emphasizing his friendship with Antonio Pérez, and their ideological closeness.

[56] The Patriarch of Alexandria to Aldobrandino, April 26, 1595, ASV, Envío 92, leg. 46, fol. 269r–v: "Questa grave infirmita e stata causa che hoggi si sia publicata la deputatione del Cardinale Arciduca al governo delle stati di Fiandra in luogo del Arciduca Ernesto (...) Li spagnoli pretendenti in Corte non mostrano dispiacere alcune della partita di S. A." This serious illness has been the reason why the Cardinal Archduke's deputation has been published today to the government of the states of Flanders in the place of Archduke Ernest (...) The Spanish pretenders at Court show no displeasure whatsoever at H.H's departure, trans.

[57] Cabrera de Córdoba, *Historia de Felipe II*, 3: 1544–5.

member of the royal family who could prevent them from gaining access to the monarch, and the placing of someone with a similar ideology to their own in the government of one of the Monarchy's most important territories. Albert´s personal household was going to ocuppy such a relevant place in his new tasks, as it did in the former ones.[58]

[58] The continuation of this study in "The Household of Archduke Albert of Austria from His Election as Governor of Flanders until His Investiture as Sovereign Prince of the Low Countries: 1595-1598", *Revue belge de philologie et d'histoire / Belgisch Tijdschrift voor Filologie en Geschiedenis,* 91-4 (2013)

Flemish elites under Philip III's patronage (1598-1621): household, court and territory in the Spanish Habsburg Monarchy*

Alicia Esteban Estríngana
University of Alcalá

The constitutional diversity of the Spanish Habsburg Monarchy, the way in which it was managed, and how this was perceived by each of its constituent territories, generated political conflicts throughout the sixteenth and seventeenth centuries. As time went by, these conflicts led the Crown to continually reconsider how best to approach such diversity in order to bring greater cohesion to the whole. This process of re-examination was necessary, if we bear in mind that some territorial components of the Monarchy, the "loyal provinces" of the Netherlands in particular, underwent significant jurisdictional changes between the last year of Philip II's life (1598) and the first year of the reign of his grandson, Philip IV (1621).

The Monarchy of Philip IV (1621-1665) was even more diverse than that of his predecessor Philip III (1598–1621), because Philip IV, unlike his father, was also sovereign of the Southern Netherlands, a sovereignty recovered by him following the death of archduke Albert of Austria on July 13, 1621. Even though the expansion of the Crown's patrimony by adding new territories was no novelty in 1621, the process represented a considerable political challenge for the monarch, because the incorporation of the Archducal Netherlands with the Spanish Monarchy involved incorporating its population into the "community of subjects" at the service of a common sovereign and

* This essay was produced within the framework of a Ramón y Cajal research contract at the University of Alcalá and two research projects funded by the Spanish Ministry of Science and Innovation (HAR2009-12963-C03-02) and the Spanish Ministry of Economy and Competitiveness (HAR2012-39016-C04-02: *Building loyalty, preserving loyalty. Sovereignty and elites in the Spanish Habsburg Monarchy, 16th and 17th centuries*), and carried out in the same university. Monetary equivalences: 1 ducat (around 55 *pattards*, currency of Brabant); 1 *escudo* (between 50 and 55 *pattards*); 1 florin (20 *pattards*).

dependent in common on his patronage.[1] Smooth incorporation with the whole territory of the Monarchy required integration, understood in terms of volition and feeling, the consciousness of being a part of that community, and the Crown had to adopt an active role to encourage it. The subjects of the archdukes Albert and Isabella had received this encouragement from Philip III before Albert died, which paved the way for the Archdukes' patrimony to be reincorporated in 1621.

Encouragement meant effective inclusion of the territorial elites in those areas where their service was being carried out, and always subject to the monarch's patronage. The offices and honours that constituted that service formed part of the royal patrimony and royal patronage, and found expression in spheres of activity and political relations – administration and justice, religion and church, armies and navies, and the royal household – which, to a large extent, occupied the same space and were superimposed on each other within the specific framework of the court, since this was where the monarch sought to effectively centralize the overall management of each and every sphere of activity.

Within this framework, the Crown had taken pains to reflect the heterogeneous nature of the Monarchy. It had created a common representational space, shared and recognized by each one of the territories, given the Crown's status as the head of the individual political communities that inhabited those territories.[2] This space was the basis for numerous institutions and offices designed for the political, ecclesiastic and military government of the Monarchy, as well as the domestic government of the personal and family departments of the sovereign. For that very reason, it was a service space, constructed to employ, and therefore, welcome and reward the subjects that populated the Monarchy.[3] In other words, its purpose was to generate (or increase) personal obligations, and win over (or confirm) equally personal wills, which could be used later by the Crown to secure its own particular interests (within an individual territory) or the general one of promoting the cohesion of the Monarchy as a whole.

[1] Alicia Esteban Estríngana, "El servicio: paradigma de relación política en los siglos XVI y XVII," in *Servir al rey en la Monarquía de los Austrias. Medios, fines y logros del servicio al soberano en los siglos XVI y XVII*, ed. Alicia Esteban Estríngana (Madrid, 2012), 11-45.

[2] Antonio Álvarez-Ossorio, "Introducción", in Antonio Álvarez-Ossorio and Bernardo J. García García (eds.), *La Monarquía de las naciones: Patria, nación y naturaleza en la Monarquía de España* (Madrid, 2004), 29–36.

[3] Manuel Rivero Rodríguez, *La España de Don Quijote: Un viaje al Siglo de Oro* (Madrid, 2005), 241.

The efforts of Spanish historiography are currently directed towards demonstrating the role that the royal household played in the Crown's policy of integrating the Monarchy's territorial elites.[4] Entering the royal domestic service enabled the members of these elites to distance themselves from their own, political communities of origin, by moving to the common court of the sovereign, where reserving palace offices for the natives of the various territories remained in force. It was the influential political thinker Baltasar Álamos de Barrientos who, at the beginning of Philip III's reign, recommended to him the measure of having in his household "people of all the tongues of his monarchy, and that favour and admission be extended to native speakers of them." By applying it, the young monarch would be able to "calm the humours" of some of his dynastic states, whose elites were discontented at the time, because they felt at a disadvantage by being excluded from the prince's domestic service.[5] This feeling was justified because of a change in policy during the Philip II's reign towards the household of Burgundy. Whereas under Charles V this essential component of the king's household, originally consisting of Flemish and Burgundian personnel, had become increasingly "international" as a result of incorporating servants from other territories under his sovereignty, once the court had finally settled in Madrid in 1561, in Philip II's reign, it had become progressively more "Castilian". The Castilian elites ended up monopolizing the palace offices, and hence displacing the elites from other territories, who were obliged to keep away from the court. At the end of the sixteenth century, this situation revealed the crisis in the policy of integration of territorial elites practised in the past.[6] After the Aragonese rebellion of 1591, the decision taken by Philip II to increase the number of natives of the kingdom of Aragon in his domestic service demonstrates that the Crown's confidence in the old policy had been restored. It continued to keep faith with the same policy in 1609, when it assessed the possibility of reinstating not only the nobility of the

[4] Especially, José Martínez Millán, "Las naciones en el servicio doméstico de los Austrias españoles (siglo XVI)," in *La Monarquía de las naciones*, 131–161; José Martínez Millán (ed.), *La Corte de Carlos V*, 5 vols. (Madrid, 2000); José Martínez Millán and Santiago Fernández Conti (eds.), *La Monarquía de Felipe II: la Casa del Rey*, 2 vols. (Madrid, 2005); José Martínez Millán and María Antonietta Visceglia (eds.), *La Monarquía de Felipe III: la Casa del Rey*, 2 vols. (Madrid, 2008); and José Martínez Millán and José Eloy Hortal Muñoz (eds.), *La Monarquía de Felipe IV: La Casa del Rey*, forthcoming.

[5] Baltasar Álamos de Barrientos, *Discurso político al rey Felipe III al comienzo de su reinado* (Madrid, 1990), 95 and 97.

[6] Martínez Millán, "Las naciones en el servicio doméstico", 135-156.

kingdom in that service but also the municipal oligarchies of Saragossa and Teruel, in order, finally, to bring peace to the Aragonese territory and provide its elites with a tangible and continuing presence in the household and court of Philip III.[7]

The reconsideration of this policy of integration should be linked to the recommendation made by Álamos de Barrientos, and also to another of his suggestions, namely to "bring, under any colours whatsoever, all the grandees and lords from them[8] to your Court." This obviously utilitarian intention contained several objectives. The first was "to become acquainted with their talent, their understanding, their inclinations, in order to use or employ them in different ministries"; the second was to prevent those who were dissatisfied from placing themselves at the head of groups of potential malcontents and leading any movement of opposition to the sovereign's authority that might arise in their territories of origin, arguing that "removing the grandees and lords from their sight, without them, the common people will wish rather than do"; and the third objective was to ensure that the beneficiaries of this favourable treatment – which included the possibility of establishing family links (understood as the set of family members and servants) with the sovereign, of starting or consolidating personal relationships in the most influential court circles and, even, of influencing the decisions and distribution of royal favours by being at court – were transformed into a valuable publicity weapon aimed at promoting the image of the Crown in their regions of origin, since they would send them "the pleasure of their prince,"[9] in other words, the satisfaction afforded them by their proximity to him and relationship with him.

[7] Rivero, *La España de Don Quijote*, 95.

[8] He is referring here to the states of Italy, but the suggestion must also apply to all the "far-flung states," that is, the states of the Habsburg Netherlands, Italy and the Indies, as opposed to the "united states," which are "those within the confines of Spain" (Castile, the kingdoms of the Crown of Aragon, Navarre and Portugal), see Álamos de Barrientos, *Discurso político*, 9 and 96.

[9] All quotations in the paragraph are from Álamos de Barrientos, *Discurso político*, 96.

Household, court and royal patronage in a context of territorial incorporation

Being invited to enter the royal domestic service was the perfect excuse for more or less outstanding members of the nobility from various states of the Monarchy to move to the court. Philip III, throughout his reign, also endeavoured to include subjects of the archdukes Albert and Isabella in his royal household, especially those belonging to the middling and high titled nobility of the Archducal Netherlands. The idea behind this measure was to establish bonds of personal obligation with a foreign sovereign's subjects who could well become his own subjects in the not too distant future. Hence, the monarch tried to establish these ties with subjects of rank of the highest quality possible: social rank was an *a priori* determinant of the extent and importance of the *parentela* (the complete set of blood relations, dependants and kin forming an interrelated network of interests, friendship and kinship within a territory), and establishing bonds of obligation with the key members of the *parentelas* scattered across the hinterland of these states would multiply its effects.

Once it was assumed that sovereignty over the Archdukes' territories would subsequently be returned to the Spanish monarch because they had no issue, some were quick to provide Philip III with precise instructions on how he should go about securing it. Particular importance was attached to the recommendations made in 1610 by Philippe de Croÿ, count of Solre (master of the horse to the Archdukes and gentleman of the chamber to Albert), and Felipe de Cardona, marquis of Guadaleste (the monarch's ambassador in Brussels), who journeyed to Spain at the beginning of the year for personal reasons.

Each of them took advantage of the journey to hand the king a set of written observations aimed at successfully addressing the restitution issue, and they coincided in recommending the entry of the titled nobility of the Archducal Netherlands into the royal household. In Solre's opinion, the monarch ought to facilitate this entry at once by assigning them posts of gentlemen of the chamber and gentlemen of the *boca*, that is, including them as soon as possible in the most select circle of his domestic service, "because in this way, they will see the love and good will that Your Majesty has towards them and the trust you place in them and [...] seeing that Your Majesty has a mind to honour them, it would console and inspire them and Your Majesty would have servants to employ when it were necessary."[10]

Guadaleste's proposal was very similar: to offer the Flemish nobles, and not only titled ones "positions in the royal household in accordance with the quality of their persons, and not only to those who live at court, but also to those who live outside it." The object was for the monarch to establish ties with the territorial nobility least attached to the court of the Archdukes, instead of confining himself to establishing them only with the court nobility integrated into the household of both sovereigns or tied to the central government institutions based in Brussels. However, among the measures proposed by the ambassador to win the hearts and minds of the Flemish elites in the lead-up to the restitution of sovereignty, he included awarding habits of the Spanish Military Orders (Santiago, Calatrava and Alcántara) to some of its members.[11]

Possession of the military habit carried with it the option of a lifetime income provided by the king in the form of an *encomienda*, or 'commandery,' the number of which was limited.[12] It also connoted traditional, old-established nobility. It was, therefore, an indisputable guarantee that anyone who possessed one was of noble blood. From Guadaleste's proposal, it can be deduced that the members of the Flemish elites would gladly accept the habits because possessing one could bring distinction and social recognition in their community of origin: a mark of honour, in addition to the customary ones, that could be esteemed for its rarity value within the Archducal Netherlands, quite apart from a second reason, namely, the fame that the favour obtained from Philip III would acquire there once the process of admission to any of these Orders was initiated. The fame went with the nature of the proceedings, explicitly involving many members of that same community.

[10] To Philip III, Valladolid, April 11, 1610, summing up the content of various short tracts presented by the count of Solre after his arrival at court, Archivo General de Simancas [hereafter, AGS], *Estado* [hereafter, E.], leg. 2868.

[11] Guadaleste to Philip III, March? 1610, two copies in AGS, E. leg. 2026.

[12] The majority of the commanderies used to have endowments of between 1,000 and 3,000 ducats a year; at the beginning of the seventeenth century, there were only one hundred and eighty-three commanderies: ninety-four of the Order of Santiago; fifty-one of the Order of Calatrava; thirty-eight of the Order of Alcántara, Lorraine Wright, "Las Órdenes Militares en la sociedad española de los siglos XVI y XVII: La encarnación institucional de una tradición histórica," in John H. Elliott (ed.), *Poder y sociedad en la España de los Austrias*, (Barcelona, 1982), 28 and 30.

The prerequisite was for the habit to be authorized. Selection of the fortunate foreign recipients was made in the Council of State or in decision-making circles close to the monarch. It was the task of the secretaries of state, of the king's chamber and, even of the favourite himself or his private secretaries, to inform the secretaries of the Council of Military Orders, via official note or decree, of the identities of those to be awarded habits. The secretaries issued the letters patent which made the awards official, and instructed the Council to set the procedure in motion; and this was done at the behest of the interested parties, who had to pay the corresponding secretarial dues. The procedure began when the letters patent, accompanied by the candidate's genealogy, reached one of the two Clerk's Offices of the Council Chamber (the Order of Santiago's, or that of the Orders of Calatrava and Alcántara). After the presentation of both documents and the payment of further dues,[13] the admission formalities proper began.

These formalities centred on judicial verification to check that the candidate complied with all the qualities and requirements for acceptance. In order to gather "the information about the qualities and purity" of the aspirant, two "informants," commissioned by the Council of Military Orders by means of a royal provision, interrogated witnesses in his place of birth and that of his parents and grandparents. The testimonies of those who were summoned to testify – more than eighty witnesses in total in many cases – had to prove the following: the noble credentials of the aspirant, with the first degree of nobility through both the paternal and maternal lines for several generations, at the very least; his legitimacy, that he belonged to a specific family group, with a clearly defined lineage or ancestral line; the "purity of his blood," free from the contamination of Moorish or Jewish forebears, or ancestors condemned by the Inquisition; and "purity of occupation," meaning remoteness from professional activities or practices that were degrading, and apt to bring loss of honour or nobility in their wake. This "information," subject to the approval or disapproval of the Council of Military Orders, acquired the status of legal proof, allaying any doubts that might be cast on the nobility and purity of anyone who had passed the "qualification tests" and the rigorous screening of the Council.

[13] For the set of procedures involved in the process of admission, see María Jesús Álvarez-Coca González, "La concesión de hábitos de caballero de las Órdenes Militares: procedimiento y reflejo documental (siglos XVI–XIX)," *Cuadernos de Historia Moderna* 14 (1993), 277–297.

The habit was synonymous with nobility, accredited before others and dignified by a third party, the Council of Military Orders, and could be a source of undeniable social prestige in any community. For this reason, there was no doubt about the esteem in which it was held in the heart of a community, like the Flemish one, which was relatively alien to its tradition.[14] The commandery that could eventually accompany the habit would always be desirable, and this combination – of both habit and the expectation of revenue – would also bring the Flemish elites symbolic recognition in territories other than those of their origin, in this case, Spain and the whole of Philip III's Monarchy. This necessarily expanded the horizons of political reference for elites who had seen their own shrink to the very local level when the Southern Netherlands ceased to form part of Philip II's Monarchy in 1598.[15] Thanks to such measures, the opening up of horizons could be more and more attractive as the time approached for their likely reincorporation into the Monarchy of Philip III.

Philip III's domestic service and the Spanish Military Orders

The offer of military habits in the Archducal Netherlands in the years prior to the return of sovereignty to the Spanish Monarchy in 1621 would confirm the monarch's intention to deliberately boost the appeal of reincorporation among the Flemish elites, but so too would the offer of posts in the royal household. And he formally implemented both in the spring of 1613, while Albert was still convalescing after the serious deterioration in his health at the end of the previous year.

In a letter addressed to Ambrogio Spínola, *maestre de campo general* of the Army of Flanders and superintendent of the military treasury on March 31, 1613, Philip III gave orders for habits and posts as pages, *meninos* and gentlemen of the *boca* to be offered in his name,

[14] Relatively alien, but not completely so. During the reigns of Charles V and Philip II, some Flemish had already been admitted to the Orders of Santiago and Calatrava, see Francisco Fernández Izquierdo, "Los flamencos en las Órdenes Militares españolas: Algunas notas sobre la integración en el sistema nobiliario de la Monarquía Hispánica," in Ana Crespo Solana and Manuel Herrero Sánchez (eds.), *España y las 17 provincias de los Países Bajos: Una revisión historiográfica*, 2 vols. (Cordoba, 2002), 1: 101–136.

[15] For the cession of the Low Countries to Albert and Isabella in 1598, see Alicia Esteban Estríngana, "Los estados de Flandes. Reversión territorial de las provincias leales (1598–1623)," in José Martínez Millán and María Antonietta Visceglia (eds.), *La Monarquía de Felipe III: los Reinos*, (Madrid, 2008), 593-682.

announcing his willingness to grant them to all those who aspired to them "in accordance with their quality" and also his wish to receive "some daughters of the principal gentlemen of the country" as ladies-in-waiting for his daughter-in-law, princess Isabella of Bourbon, the young betrothed of the prince, the future Philip IV. In the opening of the letter, the monarch admitted he was proceeding "in imitation" of his father, Philip II, former sovereign of the Low Countries, and emphasized his determination to "continue to do so henceforth, demonstrating this to a greater extent"[16] by progressively including more Flemish in his domestic service.

Awarding habits of the Spanish Military Orders to the Flemish and inviting them to enter the royal household prior to 1613 might suggest that offers had been made at an earlier date, and also that members of the high and middling nobility of the Southern Netherlands had already shown an explicit interest in obtaining honours of this kind and had actually sought them with the approval and recommendation of the Archdukes. The count of Solre and the marquis of Guadaleste would have echoed this same interest before travelling to Spain in 1610. Whatever the case, the letter sent to Spínola at the end of March 1613 represents a decision taken after a process of due deliberation, and by reconstructing that process, it is possible to discover the true objective behind the royal offer.

In the spring of 1612, don Rodrigo Calderón, count of Oliva, had travelled to Brussels. One of the missions of his embassy was to draw up the necessary reports for implementing a new general reform (*reformación*) of the army of Flanders, as ambitious as the one undertaken in 1609–1610, after the signing of the Twelve Years' Truce. The primary reason for the reform was to reduce military expenditure, which included discharging soldiers, dissolving units, and eliminating pensions, entertainments [monthly retainers] and salaries paid by the army's paymaster-general which were funded by transfers from Philip III in the form of bills of exchange and known as "Spanish provisions". Upon his return to Madrid in January 1613, Calderón brought with him numerous reports and proposals for cutbacks, as well as a large number of letters of recommendation in which archduke Albert interceded on behalf of private individuals petitioning Philip III. On the orders of the king, this pile of papers was organized and subjected to a preliminary evaluation by Calderón and the Knight Commander of Leon (of the

[16] Philip III to Spínola, Madrid, March 23, 1613, AGS, E. leg. 2228, 8.

Order of Santiago), don Juan de Idiáquez, who was president of the Council of Military Orders, and one of the longest-serving and most influential councillors of State. The papers were then examined further, this time by the Council of State, although not in every particular. The "things of private individuals" were discarded and, in February 1613, based entirely on the opinions of Calderón and Idiáquez, Philip III made his decisions.

Among the many claims from private individuals that don Rodrigo had to lend his support to in Madrid, were those of Hendrik van den Bergh, an outstanding cavalry officer in those days. The count aspired to a military habit because he was interested in exchanging the revenue of eight hundred ducats a year, assigned by the monarch in the kingdom of Sicily in 1602, that he was already receiving, for a commandery that would yield more. Calderón made it clear that it was advisable to favour van den Bergh in order to "win him over and secure him" in the service of the Archdukes and Philip III, but also so that the Dutch "would not trust [...] this man to be of use to them." He acknowledged, besides, that van den Bergh was not asking for this favour (habit and commandery) on his own initiative, but had been influenced by someone in Brussels.[17]

From don Rodrigo's words, it would seem that by joining a Spanish Military Order, Hendrik van den Bergh (Maurice of Nassau's first cousin) would be confirming his willingness to remain loyal to the service of the Catholic cause. It would confirm it, because acceptance of the military habit created a subjective moral obligation, committing the holder to the foundational objectives of the Order, which included the active defence of Catholic Christianity against the threat represented by the expansion of other religious creeds. It was a commitment voluntarily assumed and measured in terms of allegiance and personal obedience to the Grand Master of the corresponding Military Order, who was Philip III,[18] which would not go unnoticed in the United Provinces. With the publicity that his membership would acquire there, the States-General would lose all hope of seeing count van den Bergh at their service.

Another commandery was claimed by Robert de Ligne-Arenberg, baron of Barbançon (younger brother of the prince-count of Arenberg, gentleman of the chamber to archduke Albert, captain of

[17] "El comendador mayor de León y el conde de la Oliva," Madrid, January 16, 1613, AGS, E. leg. 2027.

[18] Elena Postigo Castellanos, "Caballeros del Rey Católico: Diseño de una nobleza confesional," *Hispania* 55, no. 189 (1995), 169–204.

the Bodyguard of *Archeros* of the Archdukes and former colonel in the Walloon and German infantry),[19] and Antoine Schetz de Grobbendonk (baron Grobbendonk; governor of Bois-le-Duc; son of the late Gaspard Schetz, treasurer general of the Council of Finance of Brussels between 1561 and 1580; brother of the deceased Jean-Charles Schetz, member of the, by then, extinct Supreme Council of Flanders and former chancellor of the Order of the Golden Fleece between 1588 and 1595). They made their claims on their own initiative, with no outside influence whatsoever, because they had both already obtained the habit: Barbançon in 1601 and Grobbendonk in 1612.[20] Another habit was aspired to by Conrad Schetz de Grobbendonk (baron Hoboken; elder brother of baron Grobbendonk, member of the Council of Finance of Brussels and the Archdukes' ambassador in London until 1609), and Guillaume Richardot (Lord Lembeek, son of the late president of the Privy Council, Jean Richardot and brother-in-law of Hoboken, who was married to Richardot's eldest daughter).

According to Calderón, they all ought to receive a favourable response to their claims "for being people of standing in the country and sons of such well-known ministers." The reply to baron Grobbendonk should be "that if he wishes, he will be able to send his son to be brought up in Spain, where Your Majesty will receive him as a page."[21] Don Rodrigo must have known whether the baron had expressed his wish to place one of his sons in the domestic service of Philip III, but did not clarify the point, confining himself to pointing out that the moment had arrived to encourage that same desire in other members of the Flemish nobility in order to secure the interests of the monarch within their territory.

Calderón warned that the reform was going to deprive many Flemish of quality of their pensions, salaries and posts enjoyed to date. For that reason, it was advisable to compensate them for the loss in some way: first of all by whetting their appetite for symbolic recognition in order to satisfy it later, by offering and awarding posts in the royal household, military habits, and collars of the Golden Fleece, one of the honours held in greatest esteem by the titled nobility in the

19 Albert to Philip III, Brussels, October 15, 1600 and Isabella to Philip III, Brussels, October 6, 1600, with a memorandum from Barbançon, AGS, E. leg. 617, fols. 69–72; Calderón had already interceded on his behalf from Brussels: Calderón to Philip III, Brussels, August 8, 1612, AGS, E. leg. 2294.

20 See below.

21 "El comendador mayor de León y el conde de la Oliva," Madrid, January 16, 1613, AGS, E. leg. 2027.

Southern Netherlands. To put it another way, it was advisable to offer the Flemish elites opportunities for advancement and improvement in rank because this would feed their expectations of promotion in the future, once sovereignty had been returned to the Spanish Monarchy when Albert disappeared from the political scene. As to what the return of sovereignty might hold in store for them, the aforementioned elites would safeguard their future on the information available to them before it took place. And those who benefited from royal patronage, making the most of the opportunities afforded in the present (those who saw their current expectations being fulfilled), would raise their expectations of the future, actively working, by mobilizing their kith and kin, so that the restitution of sovereignty was completed successfully. The resources of royal patronage enabled this strategy to be used without it costing Philip III's royal exchequer anything. Increasing the symbolic capital of the Flemish elites required very little outlay and that was crucial for the Crown after the financial crises of 1610–1612, which were on the point of causing the second general suspension of consignations in the kingdom.[22]

With respect to admission to the Order of the Golden Fleece, there were three aspirants backed by archduke Albert in 1613, and all three obtained the prized collar of the Order: Frederick count van den Bergh, governor of the province of Guelders and captain of the Archdukes' halberdiers; the Burgundian marquis of Marnay, Charles-Emmanuel de Gorrevod, gentleman of the chamber to Albert and *maestre de campo* [commander of a *tercio*] of the Walloon infantry in the army of Flanders; and the count of Hoogstraten, Antoine de Lalaing, head of the House of Lalaing. Calderón and Idiáquez recommended the award of the collars for weighty reasons.

The collar was the ideal means to reward Frederick count van den Bergh for his record of service, especially as his first cousin, Maurice of Nassau, aimed to win him over to the cause of the Republic by reminding him of the humiliations suffered in the service of Albert and Philip III, who had denied him the right to the two senior posts in the army high command (those of *maestre de campo general* and cavalry general) some years before, despite his unquestionable merit and proven capabilities.[23]

[22] Bernardo J. García García, *La Pax Hispanica: Política exterior del Duque de Lerma* (Leuven, 1996), 223.

[23] Alicia Esteban Estríngana, *Madrid y Bruselas: Relaciones de gobierno en la etapa postarchiducal, 1621–1634* (Leuven, 2005), 144–145.

With regard to Marnay and Hoogstraten, admission to the Order of the Golden Fleece would serve to encourage subsequent services, ensuring that, with the collar, they would be "won over and obliged," because, as Calderón and Idiáquez warned the monarch, "Your Majesty might have need of them one day," an obvious reference to the imminent restitution of sovereignty over the Archdukes' territories.[24] This warning demonstrates that, by distributing certain resources of royal patronage, Philip III was trying to extend his relations among the Flemish elites and that he too was placing his hopes on this strategy. It was a question of relations that generated expectations for both parties, for the monarch and also the elites; and the moment to make use of these expectations in negotiations had arrived.

A first set of letters designed to set the negotiations in motion and satisfy the aspirations of some individuals was sent off on March 31, 1613, although preceded by a dispatch to Albert, alerting him to a list of favourable resolutions from Philip III and authorizing him to announce the favours granted to the interested parties.[25] This set included a letter to Spínola on March 31, 1613, requiring him to "let it be known that His Majesty will receive into his Household some noble people from the country" and offer military habits and specific posts in the domestic service of the princess of Asturias, Isabella of Bourbon.[26] It also included the letter informing Albert that the aspirations to commanderies of the barons Barbançon and Grobbendonk would be borne in mind at a later date (when the moment arrived to provide some vacant commandery), and inviting Grobbendonk to "send his son to be brought up over here" so as to include him as a page in the royal household,[27] and the letter announcing the award of the habit and future award of a commandery to Hendrik count van den Bergh. This future award was granted to him on condition that he would renounce the income that he already enjoyed in Sicily, but Philip III authorized Spínola to increase the value of this revenue as an inducement to him to accept the habit before obtaining the commandery.[28]

[24] "El comendador mayor de León y el conde de la Oliva," Madrid, January 16, 1613, AGS, E. leg. 2027.

[25] Philip III to Albert, n.p., February 20, 1613, AGS, E. leg. 2228, fol. 2.

[26] AGS, E. leg. 2228, fol. 8.

[27] Philip III to Albert, Madrid, March 31, 1613, AGS, E. leg. 2228, fol. 9.

[28] Philip III to Spínola, Madrid, March 31, 1613, AGS, E. leg. 2228, fol. 1.

The success of the negotiations mentioned earlier depended on van den Bergh's acceptance, and on all the others benefiting from royal patronage during this period doing likewise. Success depended on their acceptance, because these favours were granted with the explicit purpose of winning them over and creating obligations, that is, winning their hearts and minds and pleasing and gratifying the beneficiaries. Moreover, the recipients were well aware of this purpose, since they had addressed specific petitions to Philip III, expressing in this way their willingness to develop a relationship of obligation born of mutual appreciation and confidence, that is *confianza* (understood as keeping faith with the other) that a favourable response from the beneficiaries (favourable to the interests of the monarch authorizing the favours to be accepted) would undoubtedly become stronger over time.

Flemish elites and Philip III's patronage

Albert and Spínola undertook to pass on the responses of the beneficiaries to Philip III in letters that reached Madrid in the course of the summer of 1613. The first to show their satisfaction with the favour received from the monarch were the barons Hoboken and Grobbendonk. The former, because of his advanced age, expressed the wish to assign his habit to his heir. Philip III acceded to this as it seemed "perfectly reasonable that this be done, since the aim of it is to win over the country's nobles," and it was obvious that passing on the royal favour implied passing on the obligation to his descendants. Grobbendonk declared his intention to send one of his sons to Madrid as soon as he was old enough to serve as a page. Count van den Bergh was unable to voice his opinion at that time; Spínola and Albert had sound reasons for deciding to defer informing him of the terms in which the king had agreed to satisfy his aspirations to a habit and commandery. Van den Bergh had never been able to collect the revenue assigned to him in Sicily and he would be sceptical of being able to collect any other sum that was added to it. He would think that, once he had accepted it, the subject of the commandery would never be raised again, and that Philip III's real objective was for him to be satisfied with the habit. So, it was better to wait until a commandery of the necessary standing became available before approaching the count; otherwise, they would have no bargaining counter. The reasoning was sound; nonetheless, Philip III issued the order to offer him the habit for its immediate acceptance "with which it becomes impossible for the rebels to look to him [for support]," and assuring him that the commandery associated with it would be awarded shortly.[29]

These three selected examples show that the resources of patronage employed to negotiate with the Flemish elites in the final years of the Archdukes' regime were welcomed by the middling nobility, made up of lords (holders of seigneuries, that is, jurisdictions, and many of whom were members of urban elites) who, in certain cases, had obtained the rank of baron and transformed their seigneuries into baronies with the object of stepping onto the lowest rung of the ladder of the titled nobility. This was the case of the barons Hoboken and Grobbendonk,[30] who accepted admission to a Spanish Military Order and responded favourably to the offer to send their sons to Madrid to enter the domestic service of Philip III.

These resources of patronage were not sufficient to negotiate with the high nobility, consisting of titled nobles at the top of the social hierarchy of the territory. For nobles like count van den Bergh, opportunities for advancement and improvement in rank did not always exist. Admission to the Order of the Golden Fleece was a legitimate resource when the noble to be favoured was not already a member of the Order; however, there was only a limited number of collars which meant that they were not always available. To award one, therefore, it was advisable to apply relatively strict criteria of eligibility, which not all candidates were in a position to meet. In general, only the first-born son of the most distinguished lineages normally obtained the collar, and this criterion, for the moment, closed the door to the Order on count van den Bergh (the youngest of seven brothers, although few were still alive in 1613), whose eldest brother, Frederick count van den Bergh, had just received one. Something similar also occurred at the time, and for the same reason, to Christoph von Emden (from East Frisia), who had served in Flanders at the head of a High-German infantry regiment. When he was told that he was to be favoured with the habit and future commandery awarded by Philip III in that same context, he showed

[29] For the whole paragraph, Spínola to Philip III, Mariemont, June 30, 1613, AGS, E. leg. 2298 and "El comendador mayor de León y el conde de la Oliba, sobre particulares de Flandes," Madrid, July 26, 1613, AGS, E. leg. 2027.

[30] They had obtained the title of baron in 1600 and 1602 respectively, Paul Janssens and Luc Duerloo, *Armorial de la Noblesse Belge: Du XVe au XXe siècle*, 4 vols. (Brussels, 1992-94), 3: 449.

his dissatisfaction and protested because he had not been able to collect the revenue that had already been assigned to him in the duchy of Milan. The possibility of awarding him the Golden Fleece was considered, since he had the quality to be admitted to the Order, but the view was that the habit, the future commandery and payment of the income were sufficient "because he was the third son in his household."[31]

To negotiate with the titled nobles of the Archducal Netherlands, Philip III also had to use resources from the royal exchequer, as Albert and Spínola confirmed in a number of letters to Madrid early in 1614. In these, they both admitted not having urged counts van den Bergh and Emden to accept the habits, because they knew only too well "that they do not want them without being given the commanderies at the same time." This attitude was understandable because if the habit was not accompanied by a commandery, the cost of being admitted to a Military Order – defrayed entirely by the interested party in silver coins – could not be recovered.[32] So, van den Bergh could only be given an increase in the value of the revenue that he possessed (another 600 ducats per year), while the count of Emden's request was held in abeyance.[33]

In those letters, Albert and Spínola also communicated the identities of other members of the middling nobility prepared to send their sons to Madrid to serve as pages in the household of Philip III: Lord Pierre-Ernest de Raville, a former captain of the Walloon infantry who governed the province of Luxembourg in the name of the titular governor (count Florent de Berlaymont), and baron Hoboken himself. They were both given permission to organize the journey of their sons, of twelve and thirteen years of age, to Spain. It was a journey that aroused great expectations in Madrid, as Idiáquez and Calderón made

[31] "Sobre particulares de Flandes," Madrid, July 26, 1613, AGS, E. leg. 2027; Spínola to Philip III, Mariemont, June 30, 1613, AGS, E. leg. 2298.

[32] For comment on the cost of habits, see Elena Postigo Castellanos, *Honor y privilegio en la Corona de Castilla: El Consejo de las Órdenes y los caballeros de hábito en el siglo XVII* (Almazán, 1988), 172–176. The monetary deposits stipulated by the Council of Military Orders for the Flemish analysed in this study fluctuated between 200 and 400 ducats. These deposits were used by the Council to finance the two "informants" who questioned witnesses in the places where the aspirants to a habit, and both sets of maternal and paternal parents and grandparents were from. See below.

[33] "Sobre particulares de algunas personas de Flandes," Madrid, April 16, 1614, AGS, E. leg. 2028; Albert to Philip III, Brussels, January 31, 1614 and Spínola to Philip III, Brussels, February 11, 1614, AGS, E. leg. 2296.

clear to the king after deliberating on the content of the letters from Brussels:

> That Your Majesty receives as servants the sons of principal vassals of Flanders [...] is held to be beneficial and necessary so that they and their parents and relatives feel affection for, and are more inclined and obliged to Your Majesty's service.[34]

This statement is very revealing. The physical transfer of young Flemish to Spain to be brought up at the court of Philip III was considered crucial to strengthening the relationship that they, their parents and all the members of their extended family network would maintain with the monarch in the future, because it would win their hearts and minds, encourage their interest in service to Philip III, in short, predispose them to place everything they had – their lives, wealth, offices, personal relations and social rank – at the monarch's disposal whenever necessary. This was precisely what serving the king meant, and service became a sign of worth that deserved recompense. The recompense was effected within the framework of a bilateral political relationship which would benefit Philip III and those Flemish who decided to place themselves at his disposal. It was a relationship that even some who were not vassals of the Archdukes showed interest in strengthening at that point, paving the way for their sons to be sent to Madrid. The case of count Jean de (Johann von) Ritberg (brother of the count of Emden, from East Frisia in the Lower Rhine-Westphalia area, who had served in Flanders as a cavalry captain) is paradigmatic in this respect: in the spring of 1614, he requested, and obtained a post as *menino* to the prince (the future Philip IV) for one of his sons.[35]

This post attached to the service of the chamber rather than the stable – like that of the pages – and reserved for aspirants of greater social distinction, also aroused the interest of some members of the Flemish high nobility, such as count Florent de Berlaymont (Knight of the Golden Fleece, member of the Council of State in Brussels and governor of the province of Luxembourg-Chiny from 1604). He sought and obtained a post of *menino* to the prince and another of lady-in-waiting to the princess for two of his children in the summer of 1615,

[34] "Sobre particulares de algunas personas de Flandes," Madrid, April 16, 1614, AGS, E. leg. 2028.
[35] "Sobre recibir por menino del príncipe nuestro señor a un hijo del conde de Ritberg," Madrid, May 17, 1614, AGS, E. leg. 2028.

and authorization to send them to Spain in the company of Isabella of Bourbon herself.[36] However, the impression is that Berlaymont was an exception.

The high titled nobility

The exceptional nature of Berlaymont can be explained by one significant fact, not commonly found among Flemish nobles of his rank: the count was not a member of the Archdukes' household. This was rather unusual, because he did form part of the select minority of titled nobles who, from the beginning of the Archdukes' sovereignty, received a pension paid out of the revenue from the embassy that Philip III maintained in Brussels.

These pensions started to be assigned in the time of ambassador don Baltasar de Zúñiga (1599–1603) to preserve ties with some members of the Flemish high nobility so that they would help secure the government regime of the Archdukes, which it was imperative to consolidate in order to negotiate the longed-for peace with the Republic, and which benefited Philip III as much as the Archdukes themselves.[37] The pensions fluctuated between 600 and 3,000 ducats a year, but their payment was stopped during the costly Frisian campaign (1605). Although Philip III ordered the payments to be restored and the accumulated arrears owing to the pensioners (five in 1610,[38] and visibly distressed by the lack of

[36] Council of State, Valladolid, September 3, 1615, "Por los condes de Barlamont," AGS, E. leg. 2777; Philip IV to Albert, Burgos, November 21, 1615, Archives Générales du Royaume de Belgique (hereafter, AGRB), *Secrétairerie d'État et de Guerre* (hereafter, SEG), registre (hereafter, reg.) 178, fol. 301.

[37] Esteban Estríngana, "Los estados de Flandes,".

[38] According to a report by the marquis of Guadaleste, Philip III's ambassador in Brussels at the time, two were of the House of Croÿ: Charles de Croÿ, duke of Arschot (Knight of the Golden Fleece, member of the Council of State in Brussels and governor of Hainaut), and Charles-Philippe de Croÿ, marquis of Havré (Knight of the Golden Fleece, member of the Council of State and the first head of the Council of Finance in Brussels), nephew and uncle respectively, and both gentlemen of the chamber to Albert. Another was of the House of Berlaymont: count Florent de Berlaymont, and there was also Frederick count van den Bergh (governor of Artois until 1610 and subsequently of Guelders), and Philippe de Rubempré, Lord Vertaing (gentleman of the chamber to Albert and master of the hunt of Brabant), "Del marqués de Guadaleste: Los que tienen renta sobre la embaxada de Flandes," 1610, AGS, E. leg. 2026.

payments)[39] to be reimbursed by the paymaster-general of the army in 1611,[40] the arrears were still unpaid when don Rodrigo Calderón arrived in Brussels in 1612.

On his return to Madrid in 1613, Calderón passed on to the monarch the request of Charles-Philippe de Croÿ, marquis of Havré – one of only, by then, four pensioners, to be paid his arrears (assessed at 15,000 ducats, at the rate of 2,000 a year),[41] and also the wish of Charles de Ligne, prince-count of Arenberg (gentleman of the chamber to Albert and member of the Council of State in Brussels), to benefit from a pension of 3,000 ducats per year, the same one that had remained in abeyance after the death of his brother-in-law, Charles de Croÿ, duke of Arschot in June 1612. He was granted a pension on account of "his great quality and services and the other considerations that there are for it," although duly reduced to 2,000 ducats a year (the same amount as the marquis of Havré was receiving) and a personal title, suggesting that the number of pensioners was not fixed, but depended entirely on the will of Philip III, who assigned pensions according to the merits and qualities of each person.[42] This implied admitting that the assignment of a pension was not subject to any condition and that the monarch used the allocation of one sum or another to establish a hierarchy of rank between all the pensioners.

These pensions were not affected by the reform carried out in the summer of 1613, in the sense that they did not disappear nor was their value reduced to save costs. There were, in fact, cases where their value increased, such as the prince-count of Arenberg's, whose wife, Anne de Croÿ, inherited part of her brother Charles de Croÿ's estate and the title of duke of Arschot as the result of a judicial ruling issued in July 1614. After assuming the title of duke of Arschot, Arenberg asked for

39 Don Rodrigo Niño de Lasso, count of Añover, to Philip III, Brussels, June 2, 1610, AGS, E. leg. 2292.

40 Guadaleste to Philip III, Brussels, October 2, 1611, AGS, E. leg. 2293; CE, Madrid, February 11, 1612, and Lerma to Antonio de Aróztegui, from the palace, February 16, 1612, AGS, E. leg. 2026.

41 In 1603, the initial value of his pension had been raised to 2,000 ducats a year, according to the testimony of two memoranda addressed by the marquis of Havré to Philip III in 1608 and 1610, and a letter from Albert to Philip III, Brussels, August 7, 1608, in AGS, E. legs. 1750 and 1751. For the 15,000 ducats in arrears, see Albert to Philip III and to the duke of Lerma, Mariemont, November 30, 1612, AGRB, SEG, reg. 177, fols. 124–125.

42 "El comendador mayor de León y el conde de la Oliva," Madrid, January 16, 1613, AGS, E. leg. 2027; Philip III to Albert, Madrid, March 31, 1613, and Philip III to Albert, n.p., February 20, 1613, AGS, E. leg. 2228, fol. 28 and 2, respectively.

his pension to be raised to the level of the late duke which exceeded his own by 1,000 ducats a year. His request was granted in 1615.[43]

The reform, however, did affect the entertainments enjoyed by some members of the high nobility who were part of the domestic service of the Archdukes, headed provincial governments, or did both things at the same time. Many of these entertainments, paid by the paymaster-general of the army, had been assigned within the framework of the earlier reform, after the titled nobles had lost their military commands when their units disappeared and it was considered opportune, in 1613, to eliminate them, since their beneficiaries were already receiving a provincial governor's salary, a wage as a servant to the Archdukes, or both incomes at the same time. But from the beginning, the will existed to reintroduce the provincial governors' entertainments after a decent interval, and they were reintroduced, unofficially, in June 1614. From this date they were paid out of secret expenses so as not to publicly contravene or compromise the policy of austerity and restraint in military expenditure imposed from Madrid. They were also restored because it was a good idea to have the governors in a position of being "very grateful for what was offered and, in particular, for the question of the succession of those states."[44] Succession was understood in terms of the future restitution to the Spanish Monarchy of sovereignty over the territories of the Archdukes as well as recognition in advance of Philip III's right to succeed to that patrimony. The idea was for this recognition to be confirmed by swearing a reciprocal oath of allegiance with the various assemblies of the States-Provincial. The ceremonies, in fact, took place in the middle months of 1616, with the consent and backing of Albert, who swore the oath and took it in the monarch's name.[45]

After the oath-swearing, two of the principal titled nobles of the Southern Netherlands, the duke of Arschot-prince/count of Arenberg and the marquis of Havré, both gentlemen of the chamber to the archduke, were honoured with the collar of the Golden Fleece for their

[43] Council of State, Madrid, October 7, 1614, and February 11, 1615, with a memorandum from Arenberg to Philip III, AGS, E. leg. 2029.

[44] "Sobre particulares de Flandes," Madrid, July 26, 1613, AGS, E. leg. 2027; "El comendador mayor de León y el conde de la Oliba [...] sobre aclarar los sueldos a los gobernadores de provinçias en Flandes," Madrid, April 27, 1614, AGS, E. 2028; Alicia Esteban Estríngana, *Guerra y finanzas en los Países Bajos católicos: De Farnesio a Spínola, 1592–1630* (Madrid, 2002), 161.

[45] For this oath and its preparations, begun in 1614, see Esteban Estríngana, "Los estados de Flandes,", 656-674.

memorable contribution to the success of the oath ceremony.[46] The duke of Arschot's contribution was especially valuable, as Spínola testified to Philip III when he praised the roles of two provincial governors: the governor of Artois, prince Lamoral de Ligne, and the governor of Tournai-Tournaisis, Charles de Lalaing, who had succeeded his nephew, Antoine de Lalaing, at the head of the county of Hoogstraten at the end of 1613.[47]

Arschot proposed the oath in the province of Hainaut, which his uncle Charles de Croÿ had governed, since the then titular governor, Charles de Longueval, count of Bucquoy, was away on an embassy to Madrid (to congratulate the monarch on the occasion of the prince's recent marriage to Isabella of Bourbon); he also played a crucial role in Brabant province, as one of the members of the States-Provincial. The actual admission of Arschot and Havré into the Order of the Golden Fleece was delayed till 1618, but Philip III was in a position to use this resource of patronage with them at that juncture, because they had both just succeeded their fathers as heads of their estates (Charles-Alexandre de Croÿ, marquis of Havré, at the end of 1613 and Philippe-Charles d'Arenberg, duke of Arschot, at the beginning of 1616) and neither of them was a member of the Order. Not surprisingly, most provincial governors were already members, and although there were some who had not been awarded a collar,[48] their pre-eminent rank justified the award of those honoured in 1616, and which would stay in the memory of other titled nobles, predisposing them to work to obtain the collar when sovereignty over of Flanders was restored to the Spanish Monarchy after Albert's death.

[46] "Memoria de frai Yñigo de Briçuela sobre la orden que trae del señor archiduque Alberto a propósito de los Tussones que ha supplicado Su Alteça a Su Majestad," end of 1616, AGS, E. leg. 2030; Alicia Esteban Estríngana, "El collar del Toisón y la grandeza de España. Su gestión en Flandes durante el gobierno de los Archiduques (1598-1621)," in Krista De Jonge, Bernardo J. García García and Alicia Esteban Estríngana (eds.), *El legado de Borgoña. Fiesta y ceremonia cortesana en la Europa de los Austrias* (Madrid, 2010), 507-561.

[47] Spínola to Philip III, Brussels, May 14, 1616, AGS, E. leg. 2299.

[48] One who did not have the collar was the governor of Limburg-OutreMeuse and lord steward to the Archdukes, count Maximilien of Sainte-Aldegonde, but simply baron Noircarmes until 1605, Janssens and Duerloo, *Armorial*, 3, 419; nor did the governor of Tournai-Tournaisis and gentleman of the chamber to Albert, Charles de Lalaing, count of Hoogstraten, but simply baron Achicourt until the end of 1613, when he succeeded his nephew Antoine de Lalaing, who left no legitimate issue, Albert to Philip III, Brussels, March 8, 1616, AGRB, SEG, reg. 179, fol. 107, and AGS, E. leg. 2299.

The case of Charles de Lalaing, count of Hoogstraten, gentleman of the chamber to the archduke, is paradigmatic in this respect. A few months before the oath ceremony was held, he had been refused admission to the Order of the Golden Fleece, requested on his behalf by Albert in March 1616; nevertheless, just after the oath was sworn, Philip III granted him an entertainment of eighty *escudos* a month, charged to the "Spanish provisions."[49] The award was justified on the grounds that Charles de Lalaing had been governor since January 1615[50] and probably was not in receipt of any entertainment. Philip IV granted him the collar of the Golden Fleece in April 1621, a few months before Albert's death, albeit in the context of the extravagance that marked the opening of the reign of the king who held the right of succession to the Archdukes.

The way Philip III managed the resources of patronage at his disposal with the high titled nobility – resources from his royal exchequer and offers of the rank of Knight of the Golden Fleece, which implied an increase of rank within the internal hierarchy of the nobility itself – produced the desired effects, since that same nobility showed its enthusiasm for serving the monarch, that is, a readiness to defend his interests when these were at stake. This occurred in the year 1616, the start, to some extent, of the process of reincorporating the Archducal Netherlands into the Spanish Monarchy.

Middling nobility

The middling nobility were also represented in the States-Provincial and their determination to support the monarch's interests in the same context, the reincorporation of the Archducal Netherlands into the Spanish Monarchy, seems beyond question. Following the offer made by Philip III in 1613, their desire to obtain military habits and posts in the monarch's domestic service confirms the success of the negotiations entered into with them and explains their resolve in defending those interests. Even so, it is worth considering whether the expectations negotiated at the time with the middling nobility were created by the

[49] Albert to Philip III, Brussels, March 8, 1616, "Que se omita la respuesta," AGS, E. leg. 2299; and Philip III to Albert, San Lorenzo, September 10, 1616, AGS, E. leg. 1853.

[50] Edmond Poullet, "Les gouverneurs de province dans les anciens Pays-Bas catholiques," *Bulletin de l'Académie Royale de Belgique*, vol. 35 (1873), 918.

monarch, or merely encouraged by him. The admission of Flemish into the Spanish Military Orders and royal household prior to 1613 might suggest that the expectations already existed and that Philip III confined himself to encouraging them whenever it would clearly benefit him to do so, that is, the monarch retained certain ties and bonds with the former Flemish subjects of his father after 1598 but decided to increase and strengthen those bonds from 1613 onwards. Bearing in mind that admission to Philip III's service meant voluntarily and publicly embracing the ideological values that inspired and defined it, sharing them with all those who formed part of the community of subjects placed at his service throughout the Monarchy, it is worth finding out whether he had sparked off interest among the Flemish elites before 1613.

In the summer of 1601, don Rodrigo Niño de Lasso (future count of Añover and, at the time, lord steward to the Archdukes, gentleman of the chamber to Albert and commander of the two companies of light cavalry of the personal guard that attended him in his capacity as captain general of the army of Flanders) travelled to Valladolid to explain the financial problems being experienced by the army, which was partially deployed around Ostend. The official purpose of the journey was to request an increase in the monetary remittances that Philip III sent to the provinces, but, just as with don Rodrigo Calderón in 1613, Niño de Lasso arrived at the monarch's court with the task of supporting a host of claims by private individuals in Albert's name. Among them, were those of baron Barbançon (habit and commandery); lord Grobbendonk (habit); Philippe de Croÿ, count of Solre (habit and commandery for one of his sons); Philippe de Rubempré, Lord Everberghe – gentleman of the chamber to Albert, master of the hunt of Brabant and first-born of baron Vertaing, Antoine de Rubempré – (habit); and the marquis of Havré (post of honorary gentleman of the chamber to the king).[51]

It is evident, then, that the interest of the Flemish in military habits had arisen before 1613. After 1598, it looks as if some of the Archdukes' vassals still remembered the prince who, had the right of succession been followed, would have been their legitimate sovereign on the death of Philip II, and that Philip III had not forgotten them. The marquis of Havré, who did not have a key to Albert's chamber, obtained the

[51] Council of State, Valladolid, September 20, 1601, "Por las personas encomendadas del señor archiduque Alberto,"; "Los encomendados del señor Archiduque," n.d; also "Relación de las personas que ha encomendado don Rodrigo Niño de Lasso en nombre de Su Alteça para ávitos y encomiendas," all in AGS, E. leg. 2764.

rank of gentleman of the chamber to Philip III.[52] To the list of aspirants to a habit must be added Charles de Lalaing, baron Achicourt (future count of Hoogstraten, but uncle of the titular head of the county at the time, Antoine de Lalaing), who requested and was granted a habit of Santiago in 1601.[53] As we will see below, the list was made up of members of the untitled middling nobility, and second and third sons of titled nobles. The overall number of those recommended for habits and commanderies in 1601 was very high, and there was a risk that favours of honour of this kind would become devalued if they were handed out without applying rigorous criteria. Philip III opted, therefore, to favour the sons of titled nobles first.[54] The barons of Barbançon and Achicourt and one of the count of Solre's sons – there were three of them in 1601 and it is very unlikely that the habit was requested for the first-born, Jean de Croÿ – obtained habits, although their claim to a commandery was deferred.

—Baron Barbançon processed his admission to the Order of Calatrava between September 1606 and May 1607, after depositing 300 ducats with the Council of Military Orders. He processed it without having obtained the commandery, which Albert requested again on his behalf, but without success, in 1606 and 1609.[55]

—Baron Achicourt (gentleman of the chamber to Albert and first, colonel, then *maestre de campo* of the Walloon infantry) was admitted to the Order of Santiago in 1612, seven years after depositing 400 ducats to initiate the admission process.[56]

—The count of Solre's son, Charles-Philippe de Croÿ, honoured with a habit of the Order of Calatrava, was a third son (the second of his second marriage); his identity was revealed to the Council of Military Orders in June 1605, although the admission procedure was delayed until June 1607. At that point, the young Croÿ informed the Council

[52] Philip III to don Baltasar de Zúñiga, Valladolid, June 10, 1601, AGS, E. leg. 2224/2, 174.

[53] *Ibídem*.

[54] Philip III to Albert, n.p., March 16, 1602, "Relación de las personas que ha encomendado don Rodrigo Niño de Lasso," AGS, E. leg. 2764.

[55] Archivo Histórico Nacional de España (hereafter, AHNE), *Órdenes Militares*, expedientillo 9572. His file has not been preserved. Albert to Philip III, Brussels, December 10, 1606 and September 28, 1609, AGRB, SEG, reg. 176, fols. 91, 207; Janssens and Duerloo, *Armorial*, 2, 601.

[56] AHNE, *Órdenes Militares*, Santiago, exp. 4283, expedientillo 97, and lib.125, fols. 15r, 38v.

that Philip III had authorized him to change his Calatrava habit for one of the Order of Santiago. A new award certificate was dispatched in August 1607, shortly before his deposit was fixed at 300 ducats. The qualification evidence for admission to the Order of Santiago was assembled in the second semester of 1608, when he was about fifteen years old; he inherited the title of marquis of Renty on the death of his mother, Anne de Croÿ, when he was in Madrid serving as a page to queen Margaret of Austria. The evidence was approved in February 1609, when his title to a habit of a Knight of Santiago was dispatched.[57]

With respect to the other aspirants in 1601:

—Baron Grobbendonk requested the habit of one of the three Military Orders yet again in 1610. Despite the favourable opinion of the Council of State, Philip III was reluctant to grant it at that time. The letters patent that made the award of a habit of Santiago official are dated November 1612. In February 1613, Grobbendonk's deposit was fixed at 200 ducats to pay for the qualification evidence. His title was dispatched in July 1615.[58]

—Lord Everberghe obtained the habit in September 1603, thanks to the persistence of the archduke, who had requested it again on his behalf, once he had become baron Vertaing in August of the same year. He obtained it at the same time as the annual pension of 600 ducats, payable through the royal embassy in Brussels, for being "one of the principal and most qualified" gentlemen without title in the Archducal Netherlands, head of the House of Rubempré (holder of the hereditary title of master of the hunt of Brabant) and "a man of great power and influence" throughout the States of Brabant.[59] The letters patent authorizing a habit of Santiago are dated November 1604. The Council of Military Orders received, along with his genealogy, a memorandum from Philippe de Rubempré requesting Philip III "to obtain the information on his qualities with the least cost and deposit

[57] Andrés de Prada to Francisco González de Heredia, Valladolid, June 15, 1605, and Pedro de Gamboa to the same, from his home, June 25, 1605, with the genealogy of Charles Philippe de Croÿ, AHNE, *Órdenes Militares*, leg. 1396/1, Santiago, exp. 2225, expedientillo 175 and lib.125, fols. 15r, 37v, and lib.126, fol. 54v; Georges Martin, *Histoire et généalogie de la Maison de Croÿ* (Lyon, 2001), 102.

[58] Council of State, Madrid, November 24, 1610, AGS, E. leg. 2782; AHNE, *Órdenes Militares*, expedientillo 316 and lib.125, fols. 181v, 205v, 211v and 261v. His file has not been preserved.

[59] Council of State, Valladolid, September 20, 1603, AGS, E. leg. 2765.

possible" since he was serving "close to the person of the [...] Most Serene Archduke and on the occasions of war occurring in the Low States spending his wealth there, and as he has lost it, so he is suffering need." The deposit amounted to 300 ducats. His qualification evidence was processed between January and May 1609, but the Council of Military Orders ordered it to be repeated in 1610 because each and every one of "the places of origin of his parents and grandparents given by the aspirant" had not been visited. The second investigation, to fill in the gaps of the first one, was carried out in April 1614 and his title dispatched in October of the same year. By then, Philippe of Rubempré had obtained the title of count Vertaing (in February 1614).[60]

But there were more Flemish who joined one or other of the three Spanish Military Orders before Philip III had offered military habits to subjects of the Archdukes at the end of March 1613:

—Richard de Mérode, Lord of Ognies and younger brother of Philippe de Mérode, baron Frentzen (governor of Bruges and grand master of the hunt in the county of Flanders from 1615, count of Middelbourg from 1617 and later, lord steward to the Archdukes). Richard de Mérode had served as an infantry and cavalry captain, as governor of a stronghold and as lieutenant colonel of a regiment of fifteen companies of Walloon infantry. He obtained the habit in 1602 and was admitted to the Order of Calatrava in 1604, after making a deposit of 300 ducats. At that date, he was a gentleman of the *boca* and lieutenant in the Bodyguard of *Archeros* of Philip III, a post he held between 1598 and 1612, when he returned to Flanders to serve as governor of Bapaume.[61]

—Jean Pyramus, page to archduke Albert and a native of Antwerp. He had German ancestors on his father's side. His father, Conrad Pyramus, captain of the German infantry and a native of Brussels, was the son of don John of Austria's mother, Barbara Blomberg, originally

[60] AHNE, *Órdenes Militares*, Santiago, exp. 7262, expedientillo 118 and lib.125, fols. 118v, 176v, 232v; Janssens and Duerloo, *Armorial*, 3, 398. For Philippe and Antoine de Rubempré, see Alphonse Wauters, *Histoire des environs de Bruxelles ou description historique des localités qui formaient autre fois l'ammanie de cette ville*, 3 vols. (Brussels, 1855–57), 3: 213–214.

[61] AHNE, *Órdenes Militares*, expedientillo 9518. His file has not been preserved; Council of State, Valladolid, October 11, 1603, AGS, E. leg. 2765; a memorandum from Mérode to Francisco de Idiáquez, n.p., January 11, 1600, AGS, E. leg. 1743; another memorandum from Mérode, seen in February 1612, AGS, E. leg. 1757; Janssens and Duerloo, *Armorial*, 2, 752.

from the Imperial city of Regensberg, and Hieronymous Pyramus Kegel, a native of Villach, in the archduchy of Carinthia. On his mother's side, his roots were in the provinces of Hainaut and Tournai, since he was a nephew of Charles de Cottrel, baron Saint-Martin and Lord of Bois-de-Lessines, and grandson of Nicolas de Cottrel and Louise Rubempré, sister of Antoine de Rubempré, baron Vertaing. He obtained the habit of Santiago in October 1607. To join the Order, he paid a deposit of 200 ducats and his qualification evidence was gathered between January and April 1609, when he was about eighteen years old. His title was dispatched in June 1609. In the spring of 1608, Philip III had assigned him an entertainment of fifty ducats a month, to be received in Antwerp Castle and, in the autumn of 1612, the monarch sent a letter of recommendation to Albert in support of Pyramus's aspiration to obtain a post as gentleman of the *boca* in his household "as he was of an age to stop being a page."[62]

—Charles-Albert de Longueval, son of the artillery general of the army of Flanders, Charles-Bonaventure de Longueval, count of Bucquoy, and gentleman of the chamber to Albert. He obtained the habit of Calatrava in 1612 and processed his admission to the Order between July 1612 and 1614, after depositing 200 ducats.[63]

—Antoine de Beaufort and Goignies, son of the late Louis de Beaufort, Lord of Boisleux and Walincourt, governor of Quesnoy, captain of the lancers and "lieutenant general of the mounted gendarmes of the country of Artois." He obtained the habit of Santiago in March 1613 and began the process of admission to the Order that same month, paying a deposit of 200 ducats.[64] In December 1612, he had replaced Richard de Mérode as lieutenant of the Bodyguard of *Archeros* and obtained a post as gentleman of the *boca* to the king. At that time, he was about twenty and had been in Madrid for several years, having entered the royal household as a page in December 1611. He was one

[62] AHNE, *Órdenes Militares*, Santiago, exp. 6516, expedientillo 178 and lib.125, fol. 102r; Philip III to Albert, Madrid, May 17, 1608, AGRB, SEG, reg. 176, fol. 174; memorandum from "Don Juan de Piramus, sobrino del Serenísimo don Juan de Austria," May 24, 1613, AGS, E. leg. 1770.

[63] Antonio de Aróztegui to the duke of Lerma, with a reply from the duke in the margin, n.p., March 2, 1612, AGS, E. leg. 2294; AHNE, *Órdenes Militares*, expedientillo 9618. His file has not been preserved.

[64] AHNE, *Órdenes Militares*, Santiago, exp. 925, expedientillo 328, and lib.125, fols.19r, 184v and 192r, and lib.126, fols. 19r, 38r, 79v and 141r; Archivo General del Palacio Real (hereafter, AGPR), reg. 5730 (no pagination).

of the few Flemish who did so before Philip III offered specific posts in his domestic service for subjects of the Archdukes, also at the end of March 1613.[65]

Antoine de Beaufort's habit ought to be considered the first to be awarded to a Flemish after the offer was formalized; the royal provision designating the informants, whose responsibility was to gather the qualification evidence, is dated April 1613. The evidence was assembled between July and August of the same year and his title was dispatched the following December. The speed with which it was processed leads us to think that Philip III may have used it as an incentive for possible aspirants to a knight's habit in a Military Order, especially for well-placed aspirants like young Beaufort. The testimonies included in his evidence identify him as a relative of the count of Solre's first wife, daughter of baron Philippe de Beaufort, an ordinary general deputy of the corps of nobility in the States of Artois, and head of the House of Beaufort, the first family of Arras and one of the most important in the county of Artois. According to several witnesses questioned in the city of Arras, this was a House of knights-bannerets, "which means that they have privileges to raise levies in the service of their prince and there are other knights and gentlemen who follow them."[66] In fact, Antoine's father, Louis de Beaufort, had been the lieutenant of one of the fifteen companies of mounted gendarmes assembled in 1602 to prevent the relief of Ostend, the company captained by the count of Solre.[67]

The number of aspirants to a habit who were natives of the Archducal Netherlands identified between mid-1613 and Albert's death, in July 1621, indicates that Philip III's incentive was not in vain. Two of those aspirants were sons of baron Hoboken, and there were also twelve others.

—Jean Charles de Grobbendonk, Hoboken's eldest son. Born in 1590, he obtained the habit in 1613, passed on by his father. He began the admission process to the Order of Santiago in December 1616, with a deposit of 300 ducats. His title was dispatched in October 1618. In 1621, he served in Flanders as a cavalry captain.[68]

[65] Martínez Millán and Visceglia, *La Monarquía de Felipe III*, 2: 735.

[66] AHNE, *Órdenes Militares*, Santiago, exp. 925.

[67] Henri Louis Gustave Guillaume, "Lettre sur les bandes d'ordonnances adressée à l'Académie," *Bulletin de l'Académie des Sciences, des Lettres et des Beaux-Arts de Belgique*, vol. 8, no. 1 (1851), 101 and 112.

[68] AHNE, *Órdenes Militares*, Santiago, exp. 3625, expedientillo 461 and lib. 80, fol. 27v; lib.125, fol. 271v; lib. 126, fols. 64r and 257r.

—Charles d'Oignies, son of Eustache d'Oignies, Lord Gruzon, *maestre de campo* of the Walloon infantry, acting governor of Ostend between 1605 and 1617, and governor of Hesdin after 1617. Charles processed his admission to the Order of Calatrava between May 1614 and December 1616, after paying a deposit of 300 ducats. According to the testimonies included in his qualification evidence, he was twenty-one years old and a soldier in the Spanish infantry *tercio* under the command of the *maestre de campo*, Simón Antúnez.[69]

—Jean Moulert, gentleman of the *boca* to the Archdukes and lieutenant in the Bodyguard of *Archeros*. He obtained the habit in July 1614. The letters patent that made the award of the Order of Calatrava official were issued in October of that year and his genealogy was presented in May 1615. The deposit was fixed at 300 ducats and his qualification evidence, gathered in the course of 1616, was approved in April 1617. His title was dispatched in August 1617.[70] He died at the end of 1625 as the count of Hautrepe.

—Ferdinand van Boisschot, auditor general of the army of Flanders, member of the Privy Council of Brussels and baron Hoboken's replacement at the head of the Archdukes' embassy in London, a position he held until 1615. He requested the habit of one of the three Military Orders that same year and processed his admission to the Order of Santiago between May and October 1616,[71] at the same time as he was starting his period as ordinary ambassador of the Archdukes in Paris (1616–1621), with an entertainment of forty *escudos* a month assigned by Philip III.[72] In 1622, he obtained a judge's position on the Council of State in Brussels and, in 1626, the post of Chancellor of Brabant.

[69] AHNE, *Órdenes Militares*, Calatrava, exp. 782, expedientillo 9646 and lib. 356, fols. 502r–504r. For the inclusion of Flemish soldiers in the Spanish infantry, see Alicia Esteban Estríngana, "Las provincias de Flandes y la Monarquía de España: Instrumentos y fines de la política regia en el contexto de la restitución de soberanía de 1621," in *La Monarquía de las naciones*, 237.

[70] AHNE, *Órdenes Militares*, Calatrava, exp. 1745, expedientillo 9647 and lib. 204, fols. 136v, 298v and 301r; and lib. 357, fols. 87r, 374v–375r and 449r.

[71] Council of State, Madrid, August 20, 1615, AGS, E. leg. 2777; AHNE, *Órdenes Militares*, Santiago, exp. 1123, expedientillo 15396 and lib. 125, fols. 241v and 263r; and lib.126, fol. 7r.

[72] Philip III to Albert, San Lorenzo, September 10, 1616, AGS, E. leg. 1853; Jules Delecourt, "Ferdinand de Boisschot," *Biographie Nationale de Belgique*, 44 vols. (Brussels, 1868), 2: 621–624; Joseph Lefèvre, "Ferdinand van Boisschot," *Nationaal Biografisch Woordenboek*, 17 vols. (Brussels, 1964), 1: 216–219.

—Philippe de Laloo, gentleman of the household to Albert and son of Alonso de Laloo, secretary of the former Supreme Council of Flanders and *grefier* of the Order of the Golden Fleece between 1580 and 1598. The letters patent awarding the habit are dated September 1616 and the admission procedure to the Order of Santiago, once the deposit of 300 ducats had been paid, continued until April 1618, when his title was dispatched.[73]

—Maximilien de Houchin, Lord Gulzin or Goeulzin, *sargento mayor* of a Walloon infantry *tercio* (from 1611) and the count of Bucquoy's cousin. He had laid claim to a habit at the beginning of 1613 and obtained it at the end of 1616, having become by then *maestre de campo* of his own *tercio* (he was promoted in July 1614).[74] A note addressed to the secretary of the Council of Military Orders in November 1618 showed that it was a Calatrava habit. The letters patent awarding the habit are dated in March 1619.[75] He distinguished himself in the Palatine expedition in 1620 and Spínola entrusted him with the government of the town of Oppenheim on the Rhine.[76]

—Pierre de Gomiécourt, Lord Lagnicourt and gentleman of the *boca* to the Archdukes. He obtained a habit early in 1617 and his qualification evidence to gain admission to the Order of Santiago was gathered in the course of 1618 when he was thirty years old. It was approved in December of that year and his title to a knight's habit was

[73] AHNE, *Órdenes Militares*, Santiago, exp. 4284, expedientillo 15398 and lib. 125, fol. 261r; lib. 126, fols. 38v, 39v, 123r and 167r.

[74] "El comendador mayor de León y el conde de la Oliva," Madrid, January 16, 1613; "Mos de Gulsin, sobrino del conde de Bucoy, que pretende otro ábito. Al conde [de la Oliva] le pareçe que lo podría acordar adelante. Al comendador mayor de León [Juan de Idiáquez] le pareçe lo mismo," AGS, E. leg. 2027; Spínola to Philip III, Brussels, January 29, 1613; AHNE, *Diversos* [Miscellaneous], Autógrafos [Autograph] collection, 10, n. 820; Albert to Philip III, Brussels, January 27, 1617, AGS, E. leg. 2301. He was a cousin and not a nephew of the then (second) count of Bucquoy, Charles-Bonaventure de Longueval, because he was the son of Éléonore de Longueval, the younger sister of the first count of Bucquoy, Maximilien de Longueval, the father of Charles-Bonaventure, see Louis de Haynin, seigneur du Cornet, *Histoire générale des guerres de Savoie, de Bohême, du Palatinat et des Pays-Bas, 1616–1627*, ed. Aimé Louis Philémon de Robaulx de Soumoy, 2 vols. (Brussels, 1868), 2: 90.

[75] AHNE, *Órdenes Militares*, lib. 205, fol. 67v. His file has not been preserved. There is however, a note from the duke of Uceda to the secretary, Alonso Núñez de Valdivia, from el Pardo, 8-11-1618, in the same section, Calatrava, exp., n. c. 95 (this catalogue number is provisional).

[76] Philip IV to Albert, Madrid, August 11, 1621, AGS, E. leg. 1781.

dispatched in March 1619.[77] His father, Adrien de Gomiécourt, had been governor of Maastricht and Hesdin, a gentleman of the *boca* to Philip II and also a knight of the Order of Santiago (from 1582).[78]

—Jean Alegambe, son of Jean d'Alegambe, Lord Vertbois, and grandson of the councillor of the Great Council of Mechlin (or Malines), Jean du Bois. He obtained the habit of the Order of Calatrava in May 1617. The letters patent making the award official were dated August of that year and the admission procedure to the Order, once the deposit of 300 ducats had been paid, lasted till August 1618, when the title was dispatched.[79]

—François de Mérode, eldest son of Richard de Mérode (a knight of Calatrava since 1604) and *menino* to the infanta Isabella. He obtained the habit in July 1619 at the age of ten. The letters patent granting the Calatrava habit are dated October 1620. He paid a deposit of 300 ducats and the title was dispatched in September 1621.[80]

—Pierre de Grobbendonk, baron Hoboken's son. Born in 1601, he obtained the Order of Calatrava habit in September 1620. The royal letters patent granting it are dated the same month. He paid a deposit of 200 ducats, his qualification evidence was approved in April 1621, and his title dispatched in the following May. By then, he had spent several years in Madrid serving as a page in the royal household, but he had been careful to prepare for his return to Flanders; late in 1619, he was granted a vantage of twelve *escudos* a month to be paid there once he had decided to serve as an infantryman in his national army.[81]

[77] Albert to Philip III, Brussels, March 29, 1617, AGS, E. leg. 2301; AHNE, *Órdenes Militares*, Santiago, exp. 3493 and lib. 125, fol. 311v; lib. 126, fols. 82v, 106r–v. His *expedientillo* has not been preserved. In 1633, when he was governor of Béthune (Artois), he obtained from Philip IV the title of count of Gomiécourt. For this Artois seigneury, see Janssens and Duerloo, *Armorial*, 2, 203. In 1635, he was appointed governor of the province of Artois.

[78] AHNE, *Órdenes Militares*, Santiago, exp. 3494.

[79] AHNE, *Órdenes Militares*, expedientillo 9671 and lib. 204, fol. 301r; lib. 205, fols. 30v, 31r, 82v, 102r, 105r and 193r; lib. 357, fol. 368r; lib. 358, fols. 39v, 127r–128r and 380v. His file (Calatrava, 78bis) has not been preserved; Jean Charles Joseph de Vegiano and Jacques S. de Herckenrode, *Nobiliaire des Pays-Bas et du comte de Bourgogne* 4 vols. (Ghent, 1865-1868), 1: 23-24.

[80] AHNE, *Órdenes Militares*, Santiago, exp. 1638, expedientillo 9707 and lib. 205, fols. 143r, 196r–v; lib. 358, fol. 406v. Eugène Duchesne, "Ongnies (Anne-François, comte de Merode de D')," *Biographie Nationale de Belgique* (Brussels, 1901), 16: 183–189.

[81] AHNE, *Órdenes Militares*, Calatrava, exp. 1117, expedientillo 9706 and lib. 205, fols. 141r, 183v; lib. 206, fols. 20v, 99r; lib. 358, fols. 350r–352r, 359r–v. For the

—Florent de Noyelles, baron Rossignol, gentleman of the chamber to Albert, captain of the Walloon infantry, captain of the lancers, and son of Adrien de Noyelles, Lord Marles, lord steward to the Archdukes, *chef* of the Council of Finance in Brussels and governor of Arras. Early in 1620, he applied for a pension using two supporting letters of recommendation from archdukes Albert and Isabella. In the spring, Philip III finally agreed to grant him a pension of 600 *escudos* in the kingdom of Naples, which he asked to collect from the paymaster-general of the army of Flanders, "in the same form and manner as is done with the other knights of his nation who enjoy similar pensions there." His aspirations were satisfied in December of that same year and communicated to Albert in February 1621. By then, he had already obtained the habit of Santiago with no expectation of receiving a commandery. He obtained it in the summer of 1620, a year before inheriting the title of the count of Marles, which Adrien de Noyelles obtained in January 1621. In his case, the Council of State emphasized the advisability of mixing favours of honour with those of revenue, that "he might feel very confident,"[82] but no documentation has come to light to vouchsafe his admission to the Order.

—Charles de Bourgogne, baron Wacken, captain of the Walloon infantry, captain of the lancers and *haut-bailli* in the city of Ghent. He was the son of the Vice-Admiral of the Sea, Antoine de Bourgogne, Lord Wacken, and grandson of Jean de Bonnières, Lord Vichte, hereditary marshal of the county of Flanders and governor of Termonde. In 1620, he applied for the post that his father had held and a pension while he obtained promotion. He was granted a habit of Santiago in April 1621 and, in December of the same year, a standard letter of recommendation in his favour was sent to Isabella. After depositing 200 ducats, he processed his admission to the Order between August 1621 and January 1623, the date when his title was dispatched.[83]

favour of the habit, see *Órdenes Militares*, leg. 99/1, 28; letters patent of Philip III, Madrid, December 31, 1619, "Doze escudos de ventaja a don Pedro de Grobendoncq," AGS, E. leg. 1782.

[82] Council of State, Madrid, February 20, 1620, April 9, 1620 and December 24, 1620, AGS, E. leg. 2782; Philip III to Albert, Madrid, February 5, 1621, AGS, E. leg. 1781; Juan de Ciriza to Alonso Núñez de Valdivia, San Lorenzo, August 24, 1620; AHNE, *Órdenes Militares*, leg. 99/1, 50; Janssens and Duerloo, *Armorial*, 3, 77.

[83] Philip III to Albert, n.p., January 1, 1621, and Aranjuez, May 18, 1622, AGS, E. legs. 1781 and 1782; Philip IV to Isabella, Madrid, December 16, 1621, idem, leg.

—Charles-Philippe de Liedekerke, Lord of Ackeren and Nieuwerkerken, viscount of Bailleul and gentleman of the *boca* to the Archdukes. He was the son of Antoine de Liedekerke, baron Heule, Lord of Moorsele, Axel and Gracht and lieutenant of one of the fifteen companies of mounted gendarmes assembled to prevent the relief of Ostend in 1602, the one captained by the marquis of Havré. He obtained the habit in June 1621 and began to process his admission to the Order of Santiago in April 1622, having paid a deposit of 300 ducats. His qualification evidence, gathered between June 1622 and June 1623, was approved by the Council of Military Orders in September 1623 and his title dispatched in the following October.[84]

—Charles de Courteville, Lord Sasbroek (perhaps Assebroek), gentleman of the household to the Archdukes. Albert requested a military habit for him early in May 1621, appealing to the services inherited from his forebears, his own and to provide an incentive to future services.[85] There is no record of the habit being granted nor any record of his being admitted to any Military Order.

All those aspirants before and after 1613[86] were members of the middling nobility or second sons of titled houses with links to the administrative bureaucracy, the army or the domestic service of the Archdukes, with one exception: Charles-Bonaventure de Longueval's son and heir, who would inherit the title of count of Bucquoy on the death of his father in 1621. His admission to the Order of Calatrava can be explained by

1781; Juan de Ciriza to Alonso Núñez de Valdivia, Madrid, April 29, 1621, AHNE, *Órdenes Militares*, leg. 99/1, 65; lib. 80, fols. 351v–354r; lib. 84, fol. 20v; lib.126, fol. 238v; lib. 127, fols. 45v, 46v, 193r; Santiago, exp. 1162 and expedientillo 628; Janssens and Duerloo, *Armorial*, 1 [see n. 30], 361; Du Cornet, *Histoire générale des guerres de Savoie*, 2: 100.

[84] Guillaume, "Lettre sur les bandes d'ordonnances"; AHNE, *Órdenes Militares*, Santiago, exp. 4404, expedientillo 612 and lib. 83, fol. 170r; lib. 126, fol. 229v; lib. 127, fols. 114r, 115v; Jean-Chrisostome Bruslé de Montpleinchamp, *Histoire de l'archiduc Albert, gouverneur général et puis prince souverain de la Belgique*, ed. Aimé Louis Philémon Robaulx de Soumoy (Brussels, 1870), 543.

[85] Albert to Philip IV, Brussels, May 8, 1621, AGRB, SEG, reg. 185, fol. 215.

[86] Six of them (Robert de Ligne, Richard de Mérode, Charles-Albert de Longueval, Maximilien de Houchin, Florent de Noyelles and Charles de Courteville) do not appear on the list published by Fernández Izquierdo, "Los flamencos en las Órdenes Militares españolas". Nor do all of these appear in Fortuné Koller, *Les Belges admis dans les Ordres Militaires espagnols* (Brussels, 1952), and idem, *Gens de chez nous dans les divers Ordres de Chevalerie sous l'Ancien Régime* (Dison, 1974).

the fact that his father had been a member the same Order, and with a commandery, since 1586. In the spring of 1611, he accompanied Spínola to Madrid to pursue his claim at the court of Philip III; during that journey, he obtained a collar of the Golden Fleece for himself and authorization to cede the commandery to his son,[87] since membership of two orders of chivalry was not permitted.

Admission of the middling nobility from the Southern Netherlands to the Orders of Santiago (which brought together the military nobility and nobility associated with local power and urban patricians) and Calatrava (which drew together the administrative nobility with political and courtly careers) but not to Alcántara (reserved for traditional nobles of the blood),[88] is quite revealing. The examples subsequent to 1613 confirm that the greatest interest of the middling nobility in military habits was at this time, meaning that Philip III's incentive policy had been a notable success. He had been able to convert the favour of a habit into an honour both sought after and highly-esteemed by the elites of a territory soon to be added to his Monarchy. It was a policy that could be regarded as profitable if one considers the apparent approval and acquiescence[89] with which the same elites accepted the return of sovereignty to the Spanish Monarchy in 1621.

Posts in the royal household

Certain posts in the royal household (pages, *meninos*, ladies-in-waiting and gentlemen of the *boca*) were offered by Philip III in 1613 to attract young Flemish to come and live temporarily at the court in Madrid. It is worth recording who eventually did occupy them, or simply felt tempted to do so, in order to evaluate whether the attempt to convert admission to the royal household into a desirable and highly-prized honour for the Flemish elites was equally profitable for the king.

The post of gentleman of the *boca* was associated with the post of captain of the Bodyguard of *Archeros*; for this reason, it is not necessary to comment on the cases of Richard de Mérode (from 1598) and Antoine de Beaufort (from the end of 1612), or on the entry of anybody

87 Antonio de Aróztegui to the duke of Lerma, n.p., March 2, 1612, with response from Lerma in the margin, from the palace, March 1612, "La merced que S. M. ha hecho al conde de Bucoy del Tusón," AGS, E. leg. 2294.

88 Postigo, *Honor y privilegio en la Corona de Castilla*, 189–196.

89 Esteban Estríngana, *Madrid y Bruselas*, 22.

into the royal household prior to 1613. There is one significant case, however: Charles-Philippe de Croÿ, marquis of Renty, the third son of the count of Solre, which goes a long way to clarifying the reasons that led the monarch to offer those posts.

When the evidence qualifying him for admission to the Order of Santiago was being collected, in the second half of 1608, the young Croÿ was living in Madrid. The date of his arrival at the court of Philip III is uncertain. He might have arrived with his father in the autumn of 1604,[90] because, in May 1605, he entered as a page in the queen's household.[91] Two years later he was still at court in the care of his uncle, Jacques de Croÿ, marquis of Falces, captain of the Bodyguard of *Archeros*.

In a memorandum addressed to the duke of Lerma in March 1607, Falces sought the payment of a pension of 12,000 *escudos* a year that the count of Solre had been assigned in Sicily since 1599, and confessed his concern at his nephew Charles's ill health. He did not want to see him "die in his care, and so, because he did not have the wherewithal to make him appear in the palace and court like the son of whom he is, he would wish to send him to his parents this spring." The marquis communicated to the favourite his decision to return the boy to Flanders and asked Lerma to intercede with Philip III on his behalf to obtain permission, and also "some favour from his royal hand that might oblige the count, his father, always to take great pains in his royal service."[92] The memorandum was passed on to a Board that understood that it was impossible for Falces to support his nephew in accordance with his quality but stated it was not advisable to authorize the return of the young Croÿ. The reason was that his father had:

> great influence and credit [...] in Flanders, and having sent his son here to be brought up in the Palace, and it being convenient to the service of Your Majesty that it be done thus, it seems that in no manner is it meet to occasion his departure, but that since Your Majesty has done him the favour of a habit, it may please you to give him a commandery with which to maintain himself, because with this the marquis of Falces will be relieved

[90] For this journey by Solre, see Bernardo J. García García, "Ganar los corazones y obligar a los vecinos: Estrategias de pacificación en los Países Bajos (1604–1610)," in *España y las 17 provincias*, 1: 150–156.
[91] Martínez Millán and Visceglia, *La Monarquía de Felipe III*, 2: 815.
[92] "A Su excelencia el duque de Lerma. El marqués de Falces por su hermano el conde de Solre y su sobrino el marquesillo de Renty," March 1607, AGS, E. leg. 1939, 17.

> of the need to send him away, [and] he will be brought up in the devotion and service of Your Majesty and his father will be obliged.[93]

He was not awarded the commandery, but Philip III ordered the Council of State to look into the payment of Solre's pension to ensure that the young Croÿ had suitable means of support to keep him in Madrid. Keeping him in Madrid had a twofold objective: to provide him with an upbringing that would promote affection and obedience towards Philip III, and strengthen the obligation that his father already had towards the monarch.

The count of Solre's decision to have one of his sons brought up at Philip III's court is understandable because he himself had been attached to Philip II's domestic service as the titular captain of the Bodyguard of *Archeros* between 1588 and 1596[94] and formed part of a family branch of the House of Croÿ that had openly supported maintaining links with Philip III after 1598. But for other nobles of his rank to do the same during the Archdukes' lifetime, as the monarch was trying to persuade them to do when he issued his offer in 1613, was not so easy, because a post in the royal household in Brussels could satisfy any expectations the high and middling nobility might have of obtaining a post in royal domestic service. And the impression is that neither body of nobles showed much interest in taking up posts in Philip III's royal household between 1613 and 1621.

As far as the titled nobility is concerned, only the count of Berlaymont's petition has been located. This was for a post of *menino* and another of lady-in-waiting to the prince and princess of Asturias for a son and daughter, in 1615. His request may be explained by the fact that he himself had not managed to obtain a post in the royal household in Brussels, although the count did not in the end send his children to Madrid: the two males died young and the surname Berlaymont does not appear among Isabella of Bourbon's ladies-in-

[93] Board of Two, Madrid, March 18, 1607, AGS, E. leg. 1938, 16.

[94] For the designation of Philippe de Croÿ to occupy this post and his management at the head of the guard, see Alicia Esteban Estríngana, "¿El ejército en Palacio? La jurisdicción de la guardia flamenco-borgoñona de corps entre los siglos XVI y XVII," in Antonio Jiménez Estrella and Francisco Andujar Castillo (eds.), *'Los nervios de la guerra': estudios sociales sobre el ejército de la Monarquía Hispánica, siglos XVI-XVIII* (Granada, 2007), 195–228.

waiting.[95] Neither lord Raville's son – the young Hartard of Raville, according to a letter of recommendation in his support addressed by Albert to Philip III in October 1615[96] – nor baron Grobbendonk's are listed among the pages of the royal household. This leads us to suppose that the middling nobility did not respond to Philip III's appeal either, in spite of the fact that some of them sought posts for their offspring in his domestic service after 1613. Two more examples support this view:

—Maximilien de Mérode, son of baron Philippe de Mérode, Lord Petersheim. In 1615, the baron requested and obtained a position of page for his son, who was fourteen years old,[97] although there is no record of his having entered the royal household.

—Alexandre de Beaufort, younger brother of Antoine de Beaufort. He obtained a post as page to Philip III before 1618. When he was old enough to serve, he opted to stay in Flanders and join the Spanish infantry as a soldier. In 1620, he had been in the army for a year and a half and asked for an entertainment or vantage to pursue his military service in the Palatinate campaign. He was granted a vantage of twelve *escudos* a month to serve in his national infantry (the Walloon).[98]

There is, in fact, only one recorded entry of a page of Flemish origin in the royal household of Philip III after 1613: baron Hoboken's son, Pierre de Grobbendonk, who served in 1618, and was sworn in as a *coustillier* [who accompanied the king to chapel or church or on journeys] in May 1622.[99] He left Spain in the course of that same year, for in March 1623, he was serving in the army of Flanders, and in January 1624, he was placed on reserve with the rank of captain of the Walloon infantry in the *tercio* of the *maestre de campo*, Paul-Bernard de Fontaine.[100]

As for the post of gentleman of the *boca*, one entry is recorded in 1614: Charles de Bonnières, baron Auchy, first son of the former baron Auchy, Jean de Bonnières, governor of Lens and Hénin. The Twelve Years' Truce obliged him to abandon the Southern Netherlands and

[95] Vegiano and Herckenrode, *Nobiliaire des Pays-Bas*, 1: 163; Martínez Millán and Visceglia, *La Monarquía de Felipe III*, 1: 1109–1110.

[96] Albert to Philip III, Brussels, October, no day, 1615, "Por Hartardo de Raville, su paje," AGRB, SEG, reg. 518, fol. 80r.

[97] Albert to Philip III, Brussels, September 17, 1615, AGRB, SEG, reg. 178, fol. 251.

[98] Council of State, Madrid, August 2, 1620, AGS, E. leg. 2782.

[99] Martínez Millán and Visceglia, *La Monarquía de Felipe III*, 2: 736.

[100] AHNE, *Órdenes Militares*, lib. 359, fol. 389v; "Reformaçión de la gente del pays deste exército (1624)," AGRB, *Audience*, 2812.

move to the duchy of Milan, where he began his military service by recruiting an infantry company with a captain's commission issued, in 1609, by don Pedro Enríquez de Acevedo, count of Fuentes, governor and captain general of the duchy of Milan between 1600 and 1610. He travelled from Milan to Spain in the spring of 1611 with a letter of recommendation from Fuentes's successor, the constable of Castile, don Juan Fernández de Velasco, duke of Frías, to further his claims. At that time, he expressed his wish to continue to serve in the army of Flanders with an entertainment, but he aspired to the post of lieutenant in the Bodyguard of *Archeros*, left vacant by Richard de Mérode when he returned to the Southern Netherlands in 1612. When he did not obtain this post, he sought a position as gentleman of the *boca* to the king, which Philip III granted in February 1614, with the approval of the Archdukes. When his father died that same year, he was attached to the royal household in Madrid and he informed the monarch of his decision to return to Flanders to serve in the Spanish infantry. He returned in late 1614 with letters of recommendation from Philip III and high hopes of occupying the governorships that his father had just left vacant. Archduke Albert did not comply with his wishes, however, and so his ambitions turned towards securing a command in a cavalry company. He obtained one in 1616, the same year he married Ursula de Mancisidor, daughter of the archduke's secretary of State and War, Juan de Mancisidor. He took part in the Palatinate campaign at the head of a company of cuirassiers, and in the Flanders campaigns of 1621 and 1622, distinguishing himself in the failed siege of Bergen-op-Zoom.[101]

[101] Memorandum from baron Auchy, Carlos de Bonyeres [Charles de Bonnières] (to Juan de Ciriza), September 28, 1612, with a list of his own services and those of his forebears and a dispatch from Philip III to Albert, no day, no month, end of 1612, AGS, E. leg. 1770; Albert to Philip III, Brussels, May 2, 1611 and May 15, 1613; Isabella to Philip III, n.d. [1611]; Albert to Lerma, Brussels, May 18, 1613; memorandum from Carlos de Bonyeres (to Juan de Ciriza), August 9, 1614; "Relaçión de los serviçios de don Carlos de Boyeres, barón de Auchy" [1614]; Memorandum from baron Auchy (to Antonio de Aróztegui), April 10, 1615, all in AGS, E. leg. 1772; "El comendador mayor de León y el conde de la Oliva: Por don Carlos de Bonieres, barón Dauchi," AGS, E. leg. 2028; Philip III to Albert, Madrid, June 20, 1615 and Albert to Philip III, Brussels, August 5, 1615, AGRB, SEG, reg. 178, fols. 144, 191–192; Albert to Philip IV and don Baltasar de Zúñiga, Brussels, May 17, 1621; idem., reg. 185, fol. 241; Isabella to Philip IV, Brussels, March 11, 1622; idem., reg. 187, fol. 114; Joseph Lefèvre, "Charles de Bonnières, baron d'Auchy," *Biographie Nationale de Belgique* (Brussels, 1956–1957), 29: 317–319.

As for the position of *menino*, Nicolas de Montmorency is a case in point. He was the eldest son of the count of Estaires, Jean de Montmorency, lord steward to the Archdukes and governor of the town of Aire, who improved his status considerably between 1617 and 1619 when he came into the estate of his elder brother, the Jesuit, François de Montmorency, and that of his uncle, Nicolas Montmorency, count of Estaires, *chef* of the Council of Finance (1603–1617) and member of the Council of State in Brussels (1609–1617).[102] Young Nicolas, who was born in 1603 and died during the 1629 campaign,[103] must have been attached to prince Philip's service of the chamber, first as a *menino*, and later, as an honorary gentleman, a rank with which, in the course of the 1620s, he must have returned to Flanders, in possession of the symbolic key to the chamber.[104]

The future reconstruction of the household of the heir to the throne, established in 1615 after the celebration of his marriage to Isabella of Bourbon, might hold a few surprises and confirm the inclusion of more members of the Flemish elites in the domestic service of the family of Philip III; it is quite possible that the sons of Raville, Grobbendonk and Petersheim entered it. After all, the establishment of his household and the princess's generated a demand for domestic servants which Philip III doubtless intended to satisfy through the offer of posts that he made in Flanders in 1613, that is, with a view to the subsequent establishment of the two households. But the presence of Flemish in two of the three royal households that coexisted in Madrid between 1615 and 1621[105] was negligible, if the members of the monarch's Bodyguard of *Archeros* are discounted, since their posts were reserved specifically for natives of the Southern Netherlands and of the Franche-Comté. This enables us

[102] Vegiano and Herckenrode, *Nobiliaire des Pays-Bas*, 3: 1390; J. N. Paquot, *Mémoires pour servir à l'histoire littéraire des dix-sept provinces des Pays-Bas, la principauté de Liege et de quelques contrées voisines*, 3 vols. (Louvain, 1764), 3: 165–166.

[103] Detlev Schwennicke, *Europäische Stammtafeln: Stammtafeln zur Geschichte der Europäischen Staaten, Neue Folge* (Marburg, 1991), 14: table 129.

[104] Two memoranda addressed to Philip IV by the count of Estaires, Jean de Montmorency, in 1630: "Lo que el conde de Esteres [...] representa con toda humildad" and "El segundo memorial del conde de Esterres [...]." Also a letter from Isabella to Philip IV, n.p., n.d. [1630], AGS, E. leg. 2044, fols. 84, 86 and 87; Martínez Millán and Visceglia, *La Monarquía de Felipe III*, 1: 551–552.

[105] Until 2013, the research group led by prof. José Martínez Millán has reconstructed two of these three households: that of the king Philip III and that of the princess Isabella of Bourbon, but not that of the prince Philip, also formed under a logic of the reign of Philip III, Martínez Millán and Visceglia, *La Monarquía de Felipe III*.

to state that, unlike the situation with the habits of the Spanish Military Orders, the success of the policy of patronage practised by Philip III in the sphere of his domestic service was moderate. And the reason was the fierce competition offered by the household of the Archdukes during that period: the Flemish elites increased their presence there after 1615, and not so much because of the additional number of posts in the service – which certainly increased slightly in all departments – as because of the proportional increase of Flemish among the total number of domestic servants.[106]

Conclusions

After analysing two key moments in the reign of Philip III – which coincide with the beginning of the sovereignty of the Archdukes (1601) and the early part of the final phase (1613), after the halfway point of this period – and reconstructing the main lines of patronage policy implemented by the monarch to maintain and boost his relations with the Flemish elites, it is possible to draw certain conclusions.

Between Philip III and the Flemish elites, personal ties survived which the Archdukes consciously and deliberately helped to preserve from 1599 to 1621. From the outset of the Archdukes' sovereignty, Albert and Isabella adopted the role of inevitable intermediaries on behalf of the Flemish elites, who constantly used their own sovereigns to seek favours from Philip III, basing their requests on their own service and merits, with the endorsement of the Archdukes expressed in the customary letters of recommendation addressed to the monarch. By the same token, Albert and Isabella always undertook to make their subjects aware of the graces and favours conferred by Philip III, since only with their approval or leave could they receive rewards or gifts from a foreign sovereign.

The patronage resources that Philip III employed with the Archdukes' subjects were of two types, honour and wealth, because the offices that provided legal and institutional means of action within the territory were at Albert's entire disposal and also because, in his position as captain general of the army of Flanders, Albert also controlled the

[106] Werner Thomas, "La fiesta como estrategia de pacificación de los Países Bajos meridionales (1598–1621)," in *El legado de Borgoña*, 267-303.

advancement and military promotion of his vassals.[107] Ennobling his subjects and promoting members of the Flemish nobility in rank were likewise exclusive prerogatives of Albert as sovereign prince, although Philip III was prepared to grant certain honours which would enhance the prestige of the Flemish elites. Such honours could be used to advance positions in the rank hierarchy in the Southern Netherlands: the accolade of Knight of the Order of the Golden Fleece among the high titled nobility; the honour of Knight of any of the three Spanish Military Orders (Santiago, Calatrava or Alcántara) among the middling and lower nobility; and the privileged status of domestic servant to the monarch, through the admission of these three types of nobility into the royal household (or royal households, as there were three between 1615 and 1621) in Madrid.

As for the Order of the Golden Fleece, Albert was always commissioned by Philip III to present the collars to his vassals, because, with respect to this Order, the monarch had delegated to Albert the power to carry out and fulfil the favours he had granted in 1599.[108] Delegation occurred when those Knights of the Golden Fleece who were vassals of Albert requested of Philip III exemption from the oath of allegiance that they owed him as sovereign of the Order, since now they owed allegiance to their own territorial sovereign, archduke Albert. The resolution, taken by Philip III in 1599, astutely resolved the conflicting or competing loyalties that had arisen in the context of the cession of sovereignty of the territory: the loyalties were given a hierarchical structure. The allegiance due to Philip III was the direct consequence of a prior, more fundamental one: that due to archduke Albert.

In the case of the Spanish Military Orders, delegation was not necessary, since the Grand Master of the Order did not take part directly in the induction ceremony of the new knights of the military habit. But the bond of personal allegiance also operated in these Orders since their members owed allegiance and obedience to the monarch as the administrator in perpetuity of the offices of Grand Master and swore an oath to this effect during the induction ceremony. In addition,

[107] In the aforementioned army, Philip II and Philip III only reserved for themselves the appointment of the two most senior posts in the military organization chart (the *maestre de campo general* and the cavalry general), the appointment of the governors and castellans of Antwerp, Ghent, Cambrai, Ostend and two or three other (indeterminate) towns, and the superintendent of military justice, Esteban Estríngana, *Madrid y Bruselas*, 38–39.

[108] Esteban Estríngana, *Madrid y Bruselas*, 58, n. 121.

knights of the habit who were not natives of the kingdoms of Spain did not only have to swear the oath; the certificate granting the habit and the title itself of knight of the habit included an ordinary clause which established a prerequisite for admission. This was the signing, before a notary, of a deed of obligation stating that the new knights were committed to "remaining subject and obedient" to the "establishments and definitions of the Order" (their statutes and chapter laws) and to their perpetual administrator. It can be said that they contractually obliged their persons and all their possessions, goods and revenues, both present and future, to the maintenance of obedience due to the Grand Master, in other words, to maintaining an attitude of permanent willingness to defend with deeds the causes of the service of Philip III. These causes could be defended in several ways; the military way was one, but it was not the only one that interested the monarch, as is demonstrated by the award of the favour of a habit to Flemish with no experience, either personal or among their ancestors, of military service.

For the Flemish, this obligation did not take precedence over any other, since Philip III was not their natural sovereign. Therefore, it did not serve to strengthen any other obligation with a prior claim on them but to establish a new one. Using the offer and award of habits, Philip III invited the Flemish elites to enter into this obligation in 1613. The Flemish who joined the Spanish Military Orders established it voluntarily and consciously, although some did so before this offer was officially formalized in 1613. This shows that they were confident of profiting in some way from the rank of knight of the habit much earlier, even, than when it began to look likely that Philip III would be the Archdukes' successor because they had no issue. The offer boosted this confidence when it became clear that Philip III was the indisputable successor.

The Flemish who became members of the Spanish Military Orders after 1613 were from the middling nobility. Seemingly, the offer of favours enabled these nobles to negotiate their expectations directly with the monarch, with the Archdukes acting as intermediaries, but dispensing with other mediators traditionally used in the territory, such as the high titled nobility, who acted as heads of the principal kinship groups, in other words, as patrons of client networks that coexisted throughout all the provinces. These were patrons who acted as intermediaries between their network of dependants and the territorial sovereign and who, to a certain extent, Philip III was concerned to identify and classify hierarchically by assigning pensions payable out of the Spanish provisions during the period of the Archdukes' sovereignty.

The favours of honour offered in 1613 were not only military habits, but also posts in the royal households in Madrid. Occupying these posts served to establish and strengthen bonds of allegiance and personal obedience with the monarch–entry into the household also demanded an oath of loyalty–and responsibility for making the offer in the name of Philip III, was given to Spínola. This shows that the policy of moving closer to the Flemish elites, set in train by Philip III with a view to the future recovery of sovereignty over the Southern Netherlands, required the traditional mediation by the Archdukes to be reduced and the obligation to Philip III to become a priority rather than a subsidiary reference for those elites. For those Flemish who responded to the offer, the journey to Madrid and service in the royal households would allow them to establish a direct relationship with Philip III, without mediation on the part of the Archdukes. From this point of view, the "assault" by Flemish elites on the household of the Archdukes after 1615 cannot only be interpreted as Albert yielding to pressure from his subjects because he was committed to rewarding all those who had contributed to the success of the 1616 oath.[109] It can also be interpreted as a conscious gesture of resistance to a policy of patronage that appeared to harm his interests as a sovereign prince. Albert did not object to his subjects entering Philip III's domestic service and interceded on behalf of all those who showed interest in it, but he tried to ensure that as few as possible were seduced by the idea.

Some of the Flemish who had joined the Spanish Military Orders before 1621 had obtained posts in the royal households in Madrid. Therefore, an attempt was made to deliberately reinforce the bonds of allegiance and personal obedience in certain cases and the example of the pages is the most revealing. Flemish pages in the kingdom of Philip III received habits (Charles-Philippe de Croÿ, Antoine de Beaufort and Pierre de Grobbendonk). It would appear that an upbringing suited to the interests and aims of the service of Philip III was rounded off by taking up the ideological values of the Military Orders. These values revolved round the enhancement and defence of a religious cause and specific policy, identified with the Catholic monarch, that the young sons of prominent members of the Flemish elites would have to put into practice when they returned to the Southern Netherlands and

[109] Thomas, "La fiesta como estrategia de pacificación".

occupied political and military posts. There, they would make public display of their status as "crusading knights," wearing the emblem of their Order – the red cross of Santiago, the vermilion of Calatrava or green of Alcántara – on their chests, which distinguished both them and their lineage as noble and *limpios* (here, untainted by dealings with heretics and rebels). Membership of the Order was an element of social distinction, and also of ideological and political identification: the crusading knight shared and represented the interests, ways of life and ideals of the Catholic Nobility.[110] They formed an outstanding and exemplary elite of a "community of combatants" committed to actively fighting for the same causes. They were, in other words, "a community of servants" at the disposal of the Catholic monarch and voluntarily defending, with deeds, the causes of his service.

[110] Postigo Castellanos, "Caballeros del Rey Católico", 196–204.

The 'Spanish Faction' at the court of the archdukes Albert and Isabella

Werner Thomas
Katholieke Universiteit Leuven

At the end of his life, Philip II made great diplomatic efforts to bring to an end the military conflicts in which Spain was involved. He negotiated a peace treaty with France and sought rapprochement with his Protestant enemies. However, the most expensive conflict of all was the civil war in the Netherlands, a war that for the Northern provinces had become a struggle for independence. In the past, several solutions had been considered, among them the idea of creating a separate principality or of ceding the rebellious provinces to a friendly prince.[1] In order to free his son of the war in the North, Philip ultimately put into effect a plan that had been discussed before at the Spanish court: the Netherlands would be given to his daughter Isabella, as her dowry. Philip hoped that this would bring the Northern provinces to recognize the new sovereigns. This would logically lead to the unification of the country under the authority of the infanta and her future husband, archduke Albert.

However, it was never intended that the cession would lead to the creation of an independent state. On the contrary, all earlier projects foresaw that the Netherlands would remain firmly rooted in the Spanish-Habsburg constellation, and the solution on which Philip finally settled also included arrangements that prevented the new princes from turning their backs on the king of Spain. Moreover, several conditions guaranteed that even future generations of Flemish princes would

[1] Rafael Valladares, "'Decid adiós a Flandes': La Monarquía Hispánica y el problema de los Países Bajos," in Werner Thomas and Luc Duerloo (eds.), *Albert and Isabella, 1598-1621: Essays* (Turnhout, 1998), 47-54. See also Paul Bonenfant, "Les projets d'érection des Pays-Bas en royaume du XVe au XVIIIe siècle," *Revue de l'Université de Bruxelles* 41, no. 2 (1935-1936), 151-169.

remain loyal to the Spanish-Habsburg cause.[2] Still, although the treaty made a change in religious ideology impossible, archducal sovereignty would almost inevitably lead to the emergence of a different perspective on how the Spanish Monarchy should deal with its problems. Moreover, Madrid would be obliged to take full account of this perspective, as it was no longer the opinion of subordinate governors general that could be recalled when their personal viewpoint was at odds with the king's, but of sovereign princes.

One method to avoid discrepancy between Madrid and Brussels was to surround the Archdukes with advisers that shared the king's vision and could, if need be, restrain them from developing a policy contrary to Spanish interests. At the same time, these advisers should keep Madrid informed about any development at court and in the provinces. As local institutions, due to their privileges, were usually controlled by the Flemish and Burgundian elite, the court was an important structure from which royal agents operated. Therefore, close attention was paid to its composition. This 'technique' of counterbalancing the power of the head of the Brussels government by the presence of royal confidants, especially when the head of government was not a Spaniard, had already been applied before, in the case of archduke Ernest of Austria, although with varying success.[3] Later in the seventeenth century, it would be repeated at least one more time, when archduke Leopold-Wilhelm was appointed governor-general of the Netherlands in 1647.[4]

In the case of Albert and Isabella, the Spanish agents at their court gained even greater importance. Although Isabella's half-brother, Philip, had approved the cession of the northern territories, he soon regretted his father's decision. Events in the Netherlands, and in particular Albert's defeat at Nieuwpoort, convinced him that the archduke needed an assistant by his side in case he should die or be

[2] Werner Thomas, "La corte de Bruselas y la restauración de la casa de Habsburgo en Flandes, 1598-1633," in Alejandro Vergara (ed.), *El Arte en la Corte de los Archiduques Alberto de Austria e Isabel Clara Eugenia, 1598-1633: Un Reino Imaginado* (Madrid, 1999), 46-63; Alicia Esteban Estríngana, "Los estados de Flandes. Reversión territorial de las provincias leales (1598–1623)," in José Martínez Millán and María Antonietta Visceglia (eds.), *La Monarquía de Felipe III: los Reinos* (Madrid, 2008), 593-682.

[3] José Eloy Hortal, "La casa del archiduque Ernesto durante su gobierno en los Países Bajos (1593-1595)," in Antonio Álvarez-Ossorio Alvariño and Bernardo J. García García (eds.), *La Monarquía de las naciones: Patria, nación y naturaleza en la Monarquía de España* (Madrid, 2004), 193-213.

[4] Renate Schreiber, *Ein Galeria nach meinem Humor: Erzherzog Leopold Wilhelm* (Vienna, 2004), 73-79.

unable to govern in person. At the same time, it soon became clear that the Archdukes would not have children, which thwarted the solution Philip II had given to the Flemish problem. The Netherlands would eventually return to the Spanish crown, and the new king was of the opinion that the reincorporation should not occur at the passing of one of the Archdukes, but, on the contrary, as soon as possible. From 1601 onwards, the Spanish Council of State discussed different scenarios, but Albert resisted any arrangement that would affect his *reputación* or that of his wife. Philip first advocated the election of Albert as king of the Romans, thus providing for an elegant exit to the Holy Roman Empire.[5] Next, he proposed supporting Isabella's rights to the English throne, so that once the Archdukes became sovereigns of England, they could be convinced to give up the Netherlands in order to avoid the Flemish provinces becoming part of the English heritage at their deaths, and thus falling under the sway of a non-Habsburg monarch.[6] When he realized that Albert and Isabella would not easily agree to abandoning either their inheritance or their sovereign status, he took a series of measures that would prevent the Netherlands from being separated from Spain in the event of one of the Archdukes dying without issue. At the same time, he tried to increase his hold on the archducal government. The Spanish courtiers in Brussels played an important role in this process, and it is precisely the composition of this 'Spanish faction' that will be discussed here.

[5] Henri Lonchay, Joseph Cuvelier and Joseph Lefèvre (eds.), *Correspondance de la Cour d'Espagne sur les affaires des Pays-Bas au XVIIe siècle,* 6 vols. (Brussels, 1923-1937), 1: 50-51, 55, 57 (hereafter cited as *CCE*).

[6] *Consulta* of the Council of State, Valladolid, 17 November 1601, in Mariano Alcocer y Martínez (ed.), *Consultas del Consejo de Estado,* (Valladolid, 1930-1932), 1: 164 (hereafter cited as *Consultas*): "El medio de la subçesion [of England] es muy suabe para boluer a incorporar aquellos Estados [the Netherlands] con la Corona de Vuestra Magestad." See also Instructions from Philip III to Baltasar de Zúñiga concerning the English succession, Madrid, 28 February 1601, in *CCE*, 1: 63-64, 71, 86-87 (as in note 5). The Spanish Council of State even had a book written on the rights of the infanta to the English throne, which was to be printed and distributed in England among "personas de buena intençion" (*Consultas*, 1: 110). Another project of these initial years, debated in 1602, planned a marriage between the Spanish infanta Ana Mauricia and the French heir to the throne, with the Netherlands as dowry, this in case the Archdukes should remain childless. See Valladares, "'Decid adiós a Flandes'," 48 (as in note 1); Alicia Esteban Estríngana, "Los estados de Flandes. Reversión territorial de las provincias leales (1598-1621)» (as in note 2).

Spanish presence at the archducal court

Before analyzing the positions the Spaniards occupied at the archducal court in Brussels, it would be interesting to know the proportions of local office-holders – that is, those of Flemish and Burgundian origin – to courtiers of Spanish origin. In order to calculate this ratio, several lists of the archducal court personnel can be used. Three of them reproduce the composition of the court of Albert as governor-general and date from 1595[7] and 1598.[8] Two other lists were drawn up in 1605: one was sent to the town council of Ghent in preparation for the Archduke's planned visit,[9] another was probably compiled to provide the city government of Brussels with a list of members of the court entitled to exemptions from civic taxes.[10] A sixth list dates from 1611 and contains the names of the servants given mourning clothes on the occasion of the obsequies held in Brussels in honor of queen Margaret of Austria.[11] For the period from 1612 to 1618, the pay lists of the Brussels court, the so-called *libros de razón,* give per *tercio* the complete wage-sheets of the court

[7] Archives Générales du Royaume (henceforth AGR), *Audience,* no. 23/10, fos. 61r-65r. The second list from 1595 is AGR, *Audience,* no. 33/4, fos. 61r-72v. As the names on this list correspond almost entirely to the description of the court provided by Juan Roco de Campofrío at the moment Albert left Madrid for the Netherlands, one may conclude that it must have been drawn up at the beginning of Albert's 1595 journey to the Netherlands. Although Roco de Campofrío mentions two courtiers that do not appear on the list, this omission can be easily explained: neither the count of Solre nor Maximilian von Dietrichstein traveled with the archduke; Solre went from Flanders to Metz in order to join the court there, Dietrichstein probably awaited the arrival of the archduke in Brussels. See Eloy Hortal, "La casa del archiduque Ernesto," 201 (as in note 3); Juan Roco de Campofrío, *España en Flandes: Trece años de gobierno del archiduque Alberto, 1595-1608,* ed. Pedro Rubio Merino (Madrid, 1973), 70.

[8] Archivio Segreto Vaticano (henceforth ASV), *Fondo Borghese,* ser. 1, no. 913, fos. 352r-356r (old numbering: fos. 340r-344r). This list reflects the composition of Albert's court during his journey to Spain in 1598, as the writer records among the "personajes que vienen con el Archiduque" the presence of "dos señoras viudas y seis damas las quales an de ir siruiendo a España a la Regina y Reyna [*sic*]." In other words, the list dates from after the death of Philip II. It is conceivable that this list was compiled during Albert's sojourn in Ferrara in November 1598, where Pope Clement VIII officiated at his marriage by proxy. This would explain its presence in the Vatican Archives.

[9] AGR, *Audience,* no. 33/3. The list was sent to the city of Ghent on 25 February 1605.

[10] AGR, *Audience,* no. 33/4. This list was drawn up by Pedro and Antonio de Mendoza, respectively *greffier* and *veedor y contador de la caballeriza,* on 6 and 9 March 1605.

[11] AGR, *Conseil d'État,* no. 157/2. Queen Margaret died on 3 October of that year.

personnel.[12] A similar document survives for the months January to April 1622, concerning the personnel serving the archduchess after the death of her husband.[13] In combination with the 1624 list of Albert's *criados reformados* – dismissed servants granted a life pension – and the engravings of the funeral procession of the archduke by Jacques Francquart, this document offers a splendid overview of the Brussels household at the end of the archducal reign.[14]

However, when comparing numbers, it is important to bear in mind that the summaries of the court personnel drawn up in 1598 and 1605 reflect the court on a journey. They only list the people actually traveling with the Archduke(s).[15] They therefore include neither the servants that stayed at the palace in Brussels, nor the office-holders who were absent for one reason or another. Obviously, the 1595 and 1598 lists also omit the servants of Isabella. The 1611 overview and the engravings of the 1622 cortege, in their turn, only include the people that actually took part in the funeral ceremonies, or that had been expected to do so.[16] The numbers these documents mention thus refer to the minimum size of the court. The *libros de razón* and the second list of 1605, in contrast, give a more complete survey of the court, although the wage-sheets do not contain the honorary offices, such as the *capellanes de honor*, nor the offices that where financed by other means, such as, for example,

[12] AGR, *Chambre des Comptes*, nos. 1837 and 1838. The denominations *libros de razón* and *livres de raisons* derive from the Italian business term *libri della ragione* (account books). See Peter Burke, *The Italian Renaissance: Culture and Society in Italy* (Cambridge, 1987), 198-199. A financial year at court was divided into three *tercios* (thirds) of four months each (January-April, May-August and September-December).

[13] AGR, *Audience*, no. 20, fos. 16r-27v.

[14] AGR, *Conseil d'État*, no. 157/3; Jacques Francquart, Erycius Puteanus and Cornelius Galle, *Pompa funebris optimi potentissimique principis Alberti Pii, archiducis Austriae* (Brussels, 1623). The work contains 65 engravings.

[15] The higher offices were, however, almost always mentioned. For example, the 1598 list includes don Francisco de Mendoza, *mayordomo mayor* of the archduke, who did not travel to Spain, but stayed in the Netherlands to command of the Army of Flanders. Gilles du Faing in his account of the journey, also lists Mendoza among the "dames, seigneurs et cavalliers qui firent le voyage aux mariages de leurs Majestez et leurs Altèzes Sérénissimes," but at least added that "lequel ne fit le voyage, ains demeura aux Pays-Bas pour service." See Louis-Prosper Gachard and Charles Piot (eds.), *Collection de voyages des souverains des Pays-Bas* (Brussels, 1882), 4: 459.

[16] Indeed, the engravings of Francquart mention several servants who, given their particular position at court, should have participated, but were prevented by reasons of practicality or health. Pedro de Mendoza and Manuel de Arinzano, for example, "ne cheminèrent pas à cause de leurs indispositions." See Francquart, *Pompa funebris*, plate xxv (as in note 14).

the Spanish guards, the gardeners of the archducal palaces, or much of the staff of the stables, whose wages were paid out by its own *furriera*.[17]

Table 1 reflects the composition of the archducal court at six different moments with an interval of more or less six years, using the list of the 1598 journey, the 1605 exemption list, the clothing list of 1611, the wage-sheet of the first *tercio* of 1617,[18] and a combination of the 1622 wage-sheet with the 1624 list of *criados reformados*. The different departments of the court are examined separately. The archducal guards are not included: the guards of *archeros* and *alabarderos* did not include any Spaniards, while very little is known about the Spanish guard. As for the calculation of the Spanish courtiers, the numbers are, of course, minima. Only the office-holders clearly of Spanish origin have been counted. Finally, one should take into account that, apart from the unidentified Spaniards, the remaining group not only includes Flemish and Burgundian courtiers, but also German, French and Italian servants.

It is not my intention to repeat Diederik Lanoye's analysis of the presence of Spanish courtiers at all levels of the archducal household.[19] I would only like to point out that certain departments had a relatively high percentage of Spanish servants during the entire archducal reign, namely the *Casa* and the *Cámara*. The powerbase of the Spaniards thus lay here. Other sections were more oriented towards local people: the stables, and above all the *Capilla*. This is hardly a surprise, given the musical tradition of the Netherlands in the fifteenth and sixteenth centuries that influenced court chapels all over Europe, and the abundance of outstanding composers and vocalists in Flemish choirs, who were recruited by many European courts. In Madrid, the most important royal chapel was the *Capilla Flamenca*, and employed Flemish choristers only.[20]

[17] The 1605 exemption roll is the only document that contains a separate list of the personnel paid by the *furriera* of the stables. It records the names of more than half of the servants of this department – 78 out of 148 – showing that, as regards the stables, the other lists are very incomplete.

[18] AGR, *Chambre des Comptes*, no. 1838, fos. 244v-245v and 254v-264v.

[19] Diederik Lanoye, "The Structure and Composition of the Household of the Archdukes," in Thomas and Duerloo, *Albert and Isabella*, 107-119 (as in note 1). However, Lanoye bases his study on fewer sources and presents just one general overview that does not reflect the numerical evolution of the Spanish presence at specified intervals.

[20] See Edmond Vander Straeten, *Les musiciens néerlandais en Espagne du douzième au dix-huitième siècle*, 2 vols. (Brussels, 1885-1888); Paul Becquart, *Musiciens néerlandais à la cour de Madrid: Philippe Rogier et son école, 1560-1647* (Brussels, 1967); Juan José Carreras and Bernardo José García García (eds.), *La Capilla Real de los Austrias: Música y ritual de corte en la Europa moderna* (Madrid, 2001).

	1598[21]			1605[22]			1611[23]			1617[24]			1622-1624[25]		
	T	*S*	*%*	*T*	*S*	*%*	*T*	*S*	*%*	*T*	*S*	*%*	*T*	*S*	*%*
Capilla	17	13	76,4	53	12	22,6	56	7	12,5	70	11	15,7	23	7	30,4
Casa	119	78	65,5	151	76	50,3	149	68	45,6	170	73	42,9	151	60	39,7
Cámara A	37	26	70,2	53	31	58,4	65	28	43,0	99	36	36,3	76	29	38,1
Cámara I	-	-	-	32	18	56,2	44	17	38,6	38	16	42,1	45	19	42,2
Caballeriza	45	31	68,8	148	32	21,6	28	8	28,5	45	17	37,7	82	25	30,4
Total	***218***	***148***	***67,8***	***437***	***169***	***38,6***	***342***	***128***	***37,4***	***422***	***153***	***36,2***	***377***	***140***	***37,1***

Table 1. Spaniards at the archducal court
T = total number of courtiers; S = number of Spanish courtiers; % = percentage of Spaniards

[21] The Vatican list contains 220 offices and 216 names, with don Fernando de Saavedra mentioned twice: once as *gentilhombre de la casa* and once as *caballerizo*. Thus, the archducal retinue consisted of 215 individuals. Four people are listed only once, but held two offices: Juan de Frías, *capellán* (*Capilla*) and *secretario de la cámara* (*Cámara*); Diego Ruiz, *capellán* (*Capilla*) and *maestro de los pajes* (*Caballeriza*); Hernando de Zavala, *furrier* and *aposentador de palacio* (both *Casa*); and Miguel de Pianza, *salsero* and *mayordomo del estado de la boca* (both *Casa*). Because the table also reflects the divisions between the court departments, the office-holders that belonged to two different sections are counted twice. In that way, the table contains 218 (and not 215) individuals. In addition, the list also includes 15 people that accompanied the court (fo. 356r), namely 3 nobles, 2 captains of the archducal guard, the *caballerizo mayor* (who also appears among the staff of the *Caballeriza*) and the above mentioned anonymous ladies. These people are not included in the table. In reality, the archducal court was even bigger, as the document, when naming the *gentilhombres de la boca*, states the presence of "otros caualleros que se an reciuido de nueuo que no uan aquí scriptos" (fo. 353r).

[22] The 1605 exemption roll lists 606 offices, including 155 archducal guards and 5 *pensionarios*, while the office of another 9 servants is unmentioned.

[23] The 1611 overview enumerates, besides 83 notables (members of central and provincial councils, etc.) and their 31 servants, a total of 723 members of the court: 415 courtiers, 172 servants of courtiers, and 136 guards. Of the 415 court offices, 342 office-holders are named, the other 73 appearing anonymously.

[24] The 1617 combined wage-sheets of the *capilla* and the *criados* list 419 servants holding 422 offices: don Rodrigo Niño Lasso de la Vega was simultaneously *mayordomo mayor*, *sumiller de corps* and *caballerizo mayor*, while don Diego Mexía, *gentilhombre de la cámara*, was also *primer caballerizo*.

[25] The wage-sheet of the first *tercio* of 1622 includes 251 names, of which 2 belonged to the guards, 87 to the *Casa*, 52 to Albert's *Cámara* and 45 to Isabella's, 23 to the *Capilla*, and 42 to the *Caballeriza*. The 1624 list contains 137 names, 128 being those of courtiers (64 of them from the *Casa*, 24 from Albert's *Cámara* and 40 from the stables) and 7 widows of former cooks of the Archdukes.

It is also clear that, in general terms, the total number of Spaniards at court decreased over the years. Whether this evolution is due to the efforts of Albert to limit the influence of Spanish courtiers and to stress a certain degree of sovereignty and independence is, however, doubtful. One should always bear in mind that from 1602/1603 onwards the Archdukes were well aware of the fact that the Netherlands were bound to return to the Spanish crown. The major part of their reign is characterized by their efforts to create favorable military and political circumstances for this reincorporation, although Brussels and Madrid many times disagreed on the terms of this policy. If they did not concur with Madrid's viewpoint that this reintegration should occur as soon as possible, it was mainly because they feared a complete and definite loss of *reputación*. The incorporation of a higher number of Flemish and Burgundian courtiers from 1613 – at the beginning of that year Albert became seriously ill and almost died[26] – and especially from 1616 – the year the Provincial States swore allegiance to Philip III[27] – should therefore be interpreted from this perspective. By attaching the local nobility and members of the city councils to the court, the Archdukes were trying to prevent them from opposing the reversion of the Netherlands. In short, they were not so much binding the Flemish notables to their own person, as to the king's.

The powerbase of the Spaniards at court

When analyzing the composition of the archducal court and the division of offices between Spaniards and locals, Lanoye argues that, although the court had a very strong Spanish configuration at the beginning of their reign, the Archdukes gradually replaced Spanish office-holders with Flemings or Walloons. At the same time, important offices otherwise occupied by Spaniards were left vacant. In this way, the Flemish nobility strengthened its powerbase at court, while at a lower level the different departments slowly acquired a more local character.[28] Lists of courtiers confirm this general evolution towards a more Flemish court. Nevertheless, there were key positions that the Spaniards never gave up. They can be divided into four different sets.

[26] *CCE*, 1: 417-418 (as in note 5).

[27] Henri Lonchay, "Le serment de fidélité prêté par les Belges à Philippe III en 1616," in *Mélanges Paul Frédéricq* (Brussels, 1904), 311-317.

[28] Lanoye, "Structure and Composition," 116-118 (as in note 19).

Leading office-holders

The first nucleus of Spanish offices comprised the management of the court. Only a very limited group of people bore full responsibility for the proper functioning of the archducal household, the structure of which followed the Burgundian etiquette introduced in Spain by Charles V. Four court departments – the *Casa* (Palace), the *Cámara* (Chamber), the *Capilla* (Chapel) and the *Caballeriza* (Stables) – were directed by their respective administrators, namely the *mayordomo mayor* (High Steward), the *sumiller de corps* (First Gentleman of the Bedchamber), the *capellán mayor* (High Chaplain) and the *caballerizo mayor* (High Marshal). Besides these four sections, the three companies of archducal guards, usually but incorrectly considered part of the stables, constituted a fifth court department, although it had not one, but three commanders. These leading positions at court obviously put the holders in a potentially powerful position. Their duties allowed them to have direct and almost unlimited access to one or both sovereigns. This daily contact was an important element of their power, as the Archdukes were the source of almost all favors that were accorded at court. It allowed them to solicit *mercedes* for members of their patronage network. Moreover, they enjoyed large autonomy when candidates for offices of a lower rank were selected. They could even engage and discharge such servants as they did not have to take an oath, the so called *criados no jurados*. All this gave them the opportunity to exercise a kind of patronage and to build a network of clients. When they combined their position with other functions at court or in the administration of the Army of Flanders, they were even, to some degree, able to influence the archducal decision-making process.

In theory, there was no hierarchical relation between the heads of the three domestic departments (*mayordomo mayor, sumiller de corps* and *caballerizo mayor*). In his analysis of the Brussels court, the papal nuncio Guido Bentivoglio even stated that all three of them claimed precedence.[29] In other words, they were theoretically autonomous. Conflicts of competence were to be resolved in consultation.[30] In practice, however, the *mayordomo mayor* was held in higher esteem and

[29] Guido Bentivoglio, *Relaciones del cardenal Bentivollo*, translated by Francisco de Mendoza y Céspedes (Madrid, 1638), fo. 54v. The analysis of the court forms part of his *Relación de Flandes; que toca a las Provincias suietas a la obediencia de los serenissimos archiduques*, which fills fos. 47r-80v of his book.

[30] AGR, *Manuscrits divers*, no. 821, fo. 61r.

therefore occupied the first rank. This was not so much the consequence of the pre-eminence of his office, as of the fact that he was responsible for the internal organization of the court, for the court regulations, and for discipline among the court personnel. Moreover, he administered justice to the members of the court and punished the crimes that were committed within the walls of the palace. In fact, these were his main duties at court, while he usually left the daily administration of the *Casa* in the hands of the *mayordomo semanero* (steward in waiting). At the same time, he operated as a contact person between the Archdukes and the outside world, which also contributed to his prestige. Indeed, all embassies and representatives had to address themselves to him first.[31] Finally, he controlled access to the private apartments of the archduke when there were no public audiences or official ceremonies, such as the *lever* and the *coucher*, or public repasts.[32]

During the archducal reign from 1598 to 1621, three out of five court departments were almost continuously headed by Spanish courtiers. For instance, Spanish influence was very strong in the *Casa*, although the position of *mayordomo mayor* remained vacant for a large period. When the archduke was appointed governor-general of the Netherlands, Philip II chose don Francisco de Mendoza, Admiral of Aragon, as the successor of don Juan de Ayala, who had been Albert's *ayo* and *mayordomo mayor* since he arrived in Spain in 1570, but who had died shortly before.[33] At the same time, Mendoza became *de facto* the second in command in the Army of Flanders, being appointed general of the cavalry in 1597.[34] During the interim governorship of cardinal Andreas of Austria from September 1598 to September 1599, Mendoza was even charged with the military government of the country. Difficulties with Andreas, the envy of more eminent army officers, the defeat at Nieuwpoort imputed to the poor performance of the archducal cavalry, his imprisonment after the battle, his efforts to negotiate a peace with the Republic without the approval of the king of Spain, and the loss of

[31] AGR, *Manuscrits divers*, no. 821, fos. 27r-29v.

[32] AGR, *Manuscrits divers*, no. 821, fo. 54v.

[33] José Martínez Millán, "El archiduque Alberto en la corte de Felipe II (1570-1580)," in Thomas and Duerloo, *Albert and Isabella*, 27-37, esp. 30 (as in note 1); Roco de Campofrío, *España en Flandes*, 6 (as in note 7).

[34] Alicia Esteban Estríngana, *Guerra y finanzas en los Países Bajos católicos: De Farnesio a Spínola, 1592-1630* (Madrid, 2002), 91. In theory, the *maestre de campo general* Pierre-Ernest of Mansfeld ranked above him, but he had retired to the duchy of Luxemburg, of which he was the governor, and did not play an active role in the Army of Flanders anymore.

Grave in September 1602, led to his fall from favor. In October he was recalled to Madrid and subsequently banished from court.[35] Although in the summer of 1604 there were apparently plans to send him back to the Netherlands, he never resumed his function at the Brussels court.[36] Nevertheless, his name continues to appear on the archducal payroll until the first *tercio* of 1612, albeit as "ausente".[37]

This peculiar situation was probably a result of the attempts made by Philip III to increase his influence at the Brussels court. From the summer of 1600 onwards, the king and the Council of State in Madrid conceived the plan to send a Spanish confidant to Albert in order to assist him in his task as supreme commander of the Army of Flanders and to replace him during the periods of his physical incapacity. This arrangement was motivated by the outcome of the Battle of Nieuwpoort, during which the archduke narrowly escaped being taken prisoner, and was wounded in the head.[38] Pressure increased with Albert being seriously ill, and unable to perform the tasks of government, in February 1601 and throughout the summer of 1602.[39] The siege of Ostend even came to a complete standstill as a consequence of his indisposition. Madrid argued that if the archduke should be unable to govern, it was important to have somebody in Brussels that could take over. As Mendoza was at that time still Albert's *mayordomo mayor*, this assistant would be appointed *mayordomo mayor* of Isabella.[40] However, it was important that the *reputación* of the Archdukes as sovereign princes of the Netherlands remained intact. Although the archduke resisted the

[35] *Consultas*, 1: 30 (as in note 6); "Cartas del archiduque Alberto a don Francisco Gómez de Sandoval y Rojas, marqués de Denia y duque de Lerma, desde 1598 hasta 1611," in *Colección de Documentos Inéditos para la Historia de España*, vols. 42-43 (Madrid, 1863), 42: 276-574, 43: 5-232; especially 42: 431 (hereafter cited as *Codoin* 42 or 43). See also Antonio Rodríguez Villa, *Don Francisco de Mendoza, Almirante de Aragón* (Madrid, 1899).

[36] Luis Cabrera de Córdoba, *Relaciones de las cosas sucedidas en la corte de España desde 1599 hasta 1614* (Salamanca, 1997), 223.

[37] AGR, *Chambre des Comptes*, no. 1837, fo. 39r.

[38] Roco de Campofrío, *España en Flandes*, 270 (as in note 7); Isabella to the duke of Lerma, Ghent, 12 July 1600, in Antonio Rodríguez Villa, ed., *Correspondencia de la infanta archiduquesa Doña Isabel Clara Eugenia de Austria con el Duque de Lerma y otros personajes* (Madrid, 1906), 18-20.

[39] *Consultas*, 1: 257 (as in note 6).

[40] *Consultas*, 1: 37, 53, 60, 62 (as in note 6); *CCE,* 1: 49-50 (*consulta* of the Council of State, 13 August 1600); 80-84 (*consulta* of the Council of State, 26 September 1601) (as in note 5). See also Esteban Estríngana, *Guerra y finanzas,* chapter 2 (as in note 34).

plan mainly because of his reputation, in February 1602 he partially yielded and accepted an assistant at the head of the army. Nevertheless, it was not until October 1603 that Ambrogio Spínola arrived in Brussels as supreme operational commander of the troops besieging Ostend. By that time, Mendoza was already in disgrace, but Spínola neither replaced him as Albert's *mayordomo mayor* nor was named *mayordomo mayor* of Isabella. There were practical reasons for this decision. Spínola's main task was to command the troops at Ostend. In order not to interfere with his authority, Albert ceased to observe the progress of the siege on the spot and took to following it from his residences in Brussels, Bruges or Ghent.[41] This meant that the positions of supreme commander and *mayordomo mayor* became incompatible, as the latter had to be present at court. But Madrid also wanted to avoid giving any occasion for the Archdukes to be seen as a puppet government directed by Philip III through the Genoese general.[42]

Between 1603 and 1613, the position of *mayordomo mayor* was therefore left vacant.[43] Burgundian etiquette provided no solution for the absence of this office. The day-to-day management of the *Casa* was probably undertaken by the *mayordomos*, who relieved each other in a rotation system that was also applied in the *Cámara* and the stables.[44] The role of the *mayordomo mayor*, however, was not only to administer the *Casa*, but also to supervise the other court departments, a task that was too important to put into the hands of lower court officers. Alternative arrangements therefore had to be made. After the departure of don Francisco de Mendoza, don Gerónimo Walter Zapata, son of a German nobleman and *veedor general* (inspector-general) of the Army of Flanders, at Albert's request took his place *ad interim*. Zapata was a former page of Rudolf II and had been a member of the Council of War in the Netherlands since 1593, loyally serving archduke Ernest. In 1595 he became *pagador general* (paymaster-general) of the army, and during Albert's absence in 1598-99 he formed part of the council that assisted cardinal Andreas of Austria. As *veedor general* since 1600, Zapata superintended the finances of the army. Being directly responsible to the king, he was completely independent of its supreme

[41] Werner Thomas, "Het beleg van Oostende," in Werner Thomas (ed.), *De val van het Nieuwe Troje: Het beleg van Oostende, 1601-1604* (Leuven, 2004), 81-99, esp. 97-98.

[42] Esteban Estríngana, *Guerra y finanzas,* 93-94, 107-128 (as in note 34).

[43] The lists of 1605 and 1611 do not mention the name of the *mayordomo mayor*.

[44] AGR, *Manuscrits divers*, no. 821, fos. 29v-32r, 61v-62r.

commander, the archduke himself.[45] Hence, he was one of the most powerful men at court and a potential supervisor of archducal policy.

However, Zapata soon became Albert's confidant in the army and a reliable executor of his directives.[46] The decision to integrate him into the archducal court might even have been an attempt by Albert to strengthen his personal position at a moment when Philip III was questioning his capacity to govern. Moreover, by doing so he prevented the king of Spain from imposing a candidate of his own. Nevertheless, Madrid soon undermined Zapata's position. It first opposed the combination of the offices of *mayordomo mayor* and *veedor general*, as impacting negatively on Zapata's work in the army.[47] Moreover, in 1603 he was accused of fraud and fell into disgrace. In April of that year Philip III recalled him to Spain without even consulting the archduke. Albert complained bitterly, but without getting any answer from Madrid on this matter.[48]

After Zapata's departure, Philip III apparently seemed determined to send his own candidate to Brussels. In fact, rumors circulated at the Spanish court that don Sancho de la Cerda, marquis of La Laguna de los Cameros, who was about to leave for the Netherlands in order to condole with Albert on the passing of his mother, would stay there and succeed Mendoza and Zapata as *mayordomo mayor* of the archduke.[49] Events prevented this plan from being put into practice. In May 1603 the Council of State in Madrid decided that don Baltasar de Zúñiga, the Spanish ambassador to the archduke, who at that moment was reporting to the king in person on the situation in the Netherlands, should not return to Brussels. Instead, he was to head the Spanish embassy in Paris. La Laguna succeeded him at the court of the archduke and was therefore out of the running as *mayordomo mayor*.[50] It seems that from that moment on, Brussels blocked any attempt to appoint a new

[45] Geoffrey Parker, *The Army of Flanders and the Spanish Road, 1576-1659* (Cambridge, 1978), 282-283.

[46] Cabrera de Córdoba, *Relaciones*, 174 (as in note 36).

[47] "Consulta sobre la asistençia del veedor general y el contador de Flandes al exerçiçio de sus offiçios," Valladolid, 1 September 1601, in *Consultas*, 1: 159-160 (as in note 6).

[48] *Codoin*, 42: 450, 455-456 (as in note 35); Cabrera de Córdoba, *Relaciones*, 202 (as in note 36). Albert's later attempts to obtain a *merced* (favor) for his former *mayordomo mayor* all failed. See *Codoin*, 42: 569; *Codoin*, 43: 7, 23, 74.

[49] Cabrera de Córdoba, *Relaciones*, 183 (as in note 36).

[50] Joseph Lefèvre, "Les ambassadeurs d'Espagne à Bruxelles sous le règne de l'archiduc Albert (1598-1621)," *Revue belge de philologie et d'histoire* 2 (1923), 61-80, esp. 68-69; Roco de Campofrío, *España en Flandes*, 285 (as in note 7).

mayordomo mayor of the archduke and that the most senior *mayordomo* became acting *mayordomo mayor*.[51] When, for example, the Venetian ambassador Giorgio Justiniani traveled to Brussels in December 1604, he was received by Maximilian count of Saint-Aldegonde, baron of Noircarmes, "maggior domo maggior" of the Archdukes.[52] Noircarmes was still at the head of the *Casa* when the English ambassador Sir Thomas Edmondes visited the court in May 1605 as a consequence of the Treaty of London. Indeed, on that occasion he organized the production of a new livery for 260 servants, musicians and soldiers from several court departments.[53] On the other hand, both 1605 lists place him among the *mayordomos* and give no name for the function of *mayordomo mayor*.[54]

Given the increasing concentration of power, over the years, in the hands of don Rodrigo Niño Lasso de la Vega, it is not impossible that Albert's *sumiller de corps* already started to act as a semi-official *mayordomo mayor* after his return from Spain in 1605.[55] On the other hand, his frequent journeys to Spain – in 1608, 1609 and 1611 – weigh against this. In any event, at the beginning of 1613 Lasso received his formal appointment as *mayordomo mayor*, a position he would hold for the next seven years.[56] At his death, at the beginning of October 1620,[57] the Archdukes replaced him with their confidant, Ambrogio

[51] See also Dries Raeymaekers, *One Foot in the Palace. The Habsburg Court of Brussels and the Politics of Access in the Reign of Albert and Isabella, 1598-1621* (Leuven, 2013). This book was published seven years after this paper was presented at the Constellation of Courts Conference, and several years after the final version of this paper was submitted to the editors.

[52] Gustave Hagemans, *Relations inédites d'ambassadeurs Vénitiens dans les Pays-Bas sous Philippe II et Albert et Isabelle* (Brussels, 1865), 68.

[53] AGR, *Conseil d'État*, no. 157/1, fo. 1v: Noircarmes is called "maitre de leur hostel." This livery is depicted in Jan Brueghel the Elder's *Wedding Banquet presided over by the Archdukes*, painted around 1612-1613 (Madrid, Museo del Prado, inv. 1442).

[54] AGR, *Audience*, no. 33/3, fo. 5v; AGR, *Audience*, no. 33/4, fo. 67r.

[55] In 1604 Niño Lasso de la Vega traveled to Spain several times in order to inform the king about the situation in the Netherlands. See *Codoin*, 42: 472 (as in note 35); *Consultas*, 2: 22 (as in note 6); Armand Louant (ed.), *Correspondance d'Ottavio Mirto Frangipani, premier nonce de Flandre, 1596-1606* (Rome, 1942), 3: 457, 472; Cabrera de Córdoba, *Relaciones*, 216 (as in note 36); Hagemans, *Relations inédites*, 67 (as in note 52).

[56] AGR, *Chambre des Comptes*, no. 1837, fo. 104v: wage-sheet of the first *tercio* of 1613, Brussels 24 April 1613; Bentivoglio, *Relaciones*, fo. 54v (as in note 29).

[57] Niño Lasso de la Vega died in Brussels on 5 October of that year. See the letter of the marquis of Bedmar to king Philip III (Brussels 11 October 1611) in *CCE*, 1: 569 (as in note 5).

Spínola. However, before accepting the offer, the Genoese general asked for the approval of Philip III, who accepted the nomination on the one condition that he would always attend first to his duties as commander in chief of the Army of Flanders.[58]

The second department, the *Cámara*, was divided into two sections: the service of Albert and that of Isabella. The *sumiller de corps* directed the first section. This post was assigned in 1595 to Maximilian von Dietrichstein, son of Adam von Dietrichstein, who was an imperial diplomat in the service of Ferdinand I, Maximilian II and Rudolf II, and since 1560 *caballerizo mayor* to empress Maria of Austria, Albert's mother.[59] Several of Maximilian's sisters served in different royal households in Spain,[60] and Maximilian himself became *caballerizo mayor* of archduke Ernest of Austria in the Netherlands.[61] His career lasted only a few years. During Albert's absence in 1598-99, the anti-Spanish faction in Brussels headed by cardinal Andreas of Austria, temporary governor-general until the return of the Archdukes, started to defend a more on Castile orientated policy which soon affected the interests of the Spanish Monarchy, defended by the commander in chief of the Army of Flanders, Admiral Francisco de Mendoza. This foretaste of the possible consequences of looser ties between Madrid and Brussels shocked Philip III, who tackled the archduke on the question. After the arrival of the Archdukes in the Netherlands, this so-called 'Austrian faction' was eliminated, and Maximilian von Dietrichstein probably returned to the Empire.

Dietrichstein was replaced by don Rodrigo Niño Lasso de la Vega, who would direct the *Cámara* for more than twenty years, until his death in 1620. It is not clear whether there was opportunity to appoint his successor Charles-Emmanuel de Gorrevod before the passing of

[58] See the *consulta* of the Spanish Council of State, 16 January 1621, in *CCE*, 1: 574 (as in note 5); Antonio Rodríguez Villa, *Ambrosio Spínola, primer marqués de los Balbases: Ensayo biográfico* (Madrid, 1904), 379.

[59] José Martínez Millán and Santiago Fernández Conti (eds.), *La monarquía de Felipe II: La casa del Rey* (Madrid, 1998), 2: 699.

[60] Hypolitha von Dietrichstein was *dueña de honor* of Isabella and Catalina Micaela until 1585; Beatrix was *dama* of Isabella until her death in 1597; and Maria was *dueña de honor* of queen Anna. See Martínez Millán and Fernández Conti, *La monarquía de Felipe II*, 2: 675, 680, 692 (as in note 59).

[61] AGR, *Audience*, no. 33/4, fo. 59v; Joseph Lefèvre (ed.), *Correspondance de Philippe II sur les affaires des Pays-Bas*, 2nd part (Brussels, 1960), 4: 233, 235, 241, 242, 247-249, 252, 259, 272, 279-281, 284; Hortal Muñoz, "La casa del archiduque Ernesto," 196 (as in note 3).

archduke Albert in July 1621. The description of his funeral procession of 1622 does not mention a *sumiller de corps*, and nor does the list of Albert's courtiers that were granted a pension, a document that was drawn up in 1624.[62] Nevertheless, this list is not conclusive evidence, as it is highly likely that only lower-level functionaries received financial support from the court.

Isabella's chamber was headed by doña Juana de Jasincourt (Jeanne de Chassincourt). She was a former *dama* of the infanta's mother, Isabel de Valois, and had accompanied her to Spain after her marriage to Philip II in 1559. She stayed on in Spain after the death of her mistress in 1568, and in 1570 was appointed to the household of queen Anna of Austria. When the latter died in 1580, Jasincourt was incorporated into the joint household of the princesses Isabella and Catalina Micaela. After the marriage of the youngest of the sisters to the duke of Savoy in 1585, Jasincourt was transferred to the joint household of prince Philip and the infanta Isabella, whom she finally accompanied to the Netherlands in 1598, receiving her promotion to *camarera mayor* during the final months of Philip II's reign.[63] She served Isabella in this capacity until her own death in the spring of 1614,[64] although from 1610, if not before, she was being assisted by her niece, doña Catalina Livia.[65] Jasincourt was followed in office by Antonia-Wilhelmina of Arenberg and the countess of Saint Vitrés, who continued to serve Isabella after archduke Albert's death.[66]

The court chapel was briefly headed by a non-Spaniard between 1603 and 1605, when the duties of *capellán mayor* were performed by Karel Maes, dean of Antwerp Cathedral and brother of the rising star Engelbert Maes, future president of the Privy Council,[67] during

[62] Francquart, Puteanus and Galle, *Pompa funebris* (as in note 14); AGR, *Conseil d'État*, no. 157/3.

[63] Martínez Millán and Fernández Conti, *La monarquía de Felipe II*, 2: 679, 680, 686, 692 (as in note 59).

[64] The last payment to Jasincourt was made on 31 January 1614 and included her salary for the last *tercio* (September-December) of 1613. She died on 25 January 1614. On 24 May of that year, 13,000 guilders were paid to the executors of her will (AGR, *Chambre des Comptes*, no. 1837, fos. 219r and 257r; no. 1838, fo. 32v).

[65] Bentivoglio, *Relaciones*, fo. 55r (as in note 29).

[66] AGR, *Audience*, no. 20, fo. 17r.

[67] For Engelbert Maes, see Louis Tierenteyn, "Engelbert Maes," *Biographie nationale* (Brussels, 1894-1895), 13: 131; Hugo de Schepper, "De Kollaterale raden in de Katholieke Nederlanden van 1579 tot 1609: Studie van leden, instellingen en algemene politiek" (doctoral thesis, Leuven, 1972), 292-294. Another brother of Charles was Philippe, from 1610 archducal representative in Rome.

the absence of the holder of the position, don Pedro de Toledo, as the diplomatic representative of the Archdukes in Rome.[68] Maes, however, never bore the title, although he was formally appointed *limosnero mayor* on 2 May 1603, a few days after the departure of don Pedro for the Holy See.[69] Toledo, *sumiller de la cortina* and therefore one of the first-rate chaplains of Albert since 1595,[70] became head of the chapel in October 1596,[71] when he replaced Pedro de Alarcón, who had directed the chapel since Albert came to Brussels in 1595 and who had died in Antwerp on 28 August 1596.[72] Toledo would lead the chapel until the end of the Archdukes' reign. In the autumn of 1619 he was sent to Madrid to remind the king of the necessity of keeping up payment for

[68] Don Pedro de Toledo was appointed at the end of March or the beginning of April 1603 and was recalled on 29 January 1605. The death of Pope Clement VIII delayed his return to the Southern Netherlands. Finally, Toledo left Rome on 22 May 1605. See L. V. Goemans, "Het Belgische Gezantschap te Rome onder de regeering der aartshertogen Albrecht en Isabella (1600-1633)," *Bijdragen tot de Geschiedenis* 7 (1908), 350-358; Léon Van der Essen, "Les origines de la légation belge auprès du Vatican," *Revue latine*, IIIe année, 5, no. 23 (1922), 41-46; Victor Brants, "Pedro de Tolède," *Biographie nationale* (Brussels, 1901), 16: 801-803.

[69] Neither list from 1605 mentions a *capellán mayor*; and indeed "el licenciado Carlos Maes" is referred to only as *limosnero mayor* (AGR, *Audience*, no. 33/3, fo. 1r; AGR, *Audience*, no. 33/4, fo. 66r). On Christmas Day, 1605, Maes was appointed bishop of Ypres, and in 1610 he became bishop of Ghent. See Michel Cloet (ed.), *Het bisdom Gent, 1559-1991: Vier eeuwen geschiedenis* (Ghent, 1992), 58-59.

[70] Jules Chifflet, *Aula Sacra Principvm Belgii, sive Commentarivs Historicvs de Capellae Regiae in Belgio Principijs, Ministris, Ritibus atque Vniuerso Apparatu* (Antwerp: Officina Plantiniana, 1650), 41. In a letter to Aldobrandino, papal Secretary of State, written in April 1597, the papal nuncio in Brussels, Ottavio Mirto Frangipani, refers to him as "uno de primi camerieri ecclesiastici di questa Alt[za]." See Louant, *Correspondance*, 2: 88-89 (as in note 55).

[71] And not in 1605, as stated by Lanoye, "Structure and Composition," 108 (as in note 9). See Chifflet, *Aula Sacra*, 41 (as in note 70). Chifflet's version is confirmed by other documents. Indeed, don Pedro de Toledo appears in a letter from Albert to the duke of Lerma, written on 19 July 1602, as "mi limosnero y capellán mayor" (*Codoin*, 42: 424, as in note 35). The apostolic brief of Clement VIII, dated 13 August 1602, permitting don Pedro to translate some relics from the Netherlands to Spain, also refers to him as "eleemosinario maiori Principum Flandriae." See Goemans, "Het Belgische Gezantschap," 350 (as in note 68).

[72] Chifflet, *Aula Sacra*, 41 (as in note 70); Roco de Campofrío, *España en Flandes*, 7: "Y las [plazas] de clérigo de su cámara [of Albert's] en [...] Don Pedro de Alarcón, hijo del señor de Valverde, al qual se dio tambien el offiçio de cappellán [*sic*] y limosnero mayor" (as in note 7). A letter of recommendation written by Albert on 10 November 1606 to the duke of Lerma, confirms this: "y son los [años] que me ha servido once" (*Codoin*, 43: 20, as in note 35).

the provisions of the Army of Flanders.[73] He died at San Lorenzo de El Escorial on 7 September 1620.[74] Only then did the Archdukes appoint a non-Spaniard as *capellán mayor*, namely François de Rye, member of an eminent but impoverished Burgundian family,[75] nephew of Archbishop Ferdinand de Rye of Besançon and future Bishop of Caesarea.[76] De Rye had arrived in Brussels in 1606, representing the *Chambre des Nobles* of the States General of Franche-Comté. Very soon he became *sumiller de la cortina* of the archducal chapel.[77] He would remain *capellán mayor* and *limosnero mayor* until the death of his uncle in 1636, having been his coadjutor with the right of succession since the end of 1621. He finally died in Brussels on 17 April 1637 while preparing his journey to Besançon.[78]

In fact, the stables were the only department of the archducal court that was for most of the time directed by a local nobleman. This had not been the initial intention of Philip II. His plan in 1595 was to send Albert's *caballerizo mayor* don Luis Enríquez de Almansa to Flanders, but this younger son of the marquis of Alcañices requested the king not to have to accompany the archduke, in light of his old age.[79] Instead, he was promoted *mayordomo* at the Spanish court and was created count of Villaflor.[80] As his substitute, Philip appointed the count of Solre, Philippe de Croy, who was captain of the royal *archeros de corps* in Madrid and had since 1590 been governor of the duchy of Artois.

[73] *CCE*, 1: 544 (as in note 5).

[74] Jules Finot, *Inventaire sommaire des Archives départementales antérieures à 1790*, vol. 5-6: *Nord. Archives civiles, série B. Chambre des Comptes de Lille* (Lille, 1885-1888), 6: 97-98.

[75] For this reason the infanta repeatedly asked the pope to exempt Rye from the registration rights of his coadjutorship. See Bernard de Meester (ed.), *Correspondance du nonce Giovanni-Francesco Guidi di Bagno, 1621-1627* (Rome, 1938), 2: 135, 332.

[76] He was appointed bishop on 9 January 1623 and consecrated in the Brussels court chapel on 17 May 1626. See P. Gauchat, *Hierarchia Catholica Medii et Recentoris Aevi*, vol. 4: *1592-1667* (Munster, 1935), 126; De Meester, *Correspondance*, 2: 742 (as in note 75).

[77] Chifflet, *Aula Sacra*, 67 (as in note 70). Rye was appointed *sumiller de la cortina* at some point in 1611. His name does not appear on the list of the court members that received mourning clothes at the occasion of the obsequies of queen Margaret of Austria in that year, but he does figure in the wage-sheet of the first *tercio* of 1612 (AGR, *Manuscrits* divers, no. 1837, fo. 37v).

[78] Chifflet, *Aula Sacra*, 41, 62, 119 (as in note 70).

[79] Roco de Campofrío, *España en Flandes*, 7 (as in note 7).

[80] *Ibidem*; Martínez Millán and Fernández Conti, *La monarquía de Felipe II*, 2: 145 (as in note 59).

This was no great risk. Solre had fought under Farnese and had proven himself a loyal servant of the king.[81] Indeed, the royal historiographer Luis Cabrera de Córdoba described him as a "hechura del Rey," a creature of the king.[82] By 1610 Solre had become one of the firmest advocates of the reincorporation of the Netherlands into the Spanish Monarchy.[83]

Once the Archdukes became sovereign princes of the Netherlands, the presence of a Flemish nobleman at the head of the stables turned out to be a potentially important factor in the image-building of the court. Indeed, Burgundian etiquette assigned a prominent role to the *caballerizo mayor.* Once the court left the palace, he ranked above the *mayordomo mayor* and the *sumiller de corps*, at least for the duration of the journey.[84] Moreover, in times of war, that is, during the first half of the archducal reign, the staff of the stables formed the personal retinue of the archduke, and the *caballerizo mayor* became his first assistant. As such, he carried the archducal standard, which he had to show and defend at all times,[85] and was assigned the room nearest to Albert's. During the siege of Ostend, for example, Solre's lodgings were pitched at the entrance of Fort Albertus, where Albert resided when personally directing operations, and where the general staff assembled twice a day.[86] Moreover, tradition required that he ride just before the Archdukes during the Joyous Entries, and that he direct the entrance

[81] Victor Brants, "Solre (Philippe de Croy, premier comte de)," *Biographie nationale* (Brussels, 1921-1924) 23: 126-129. In 1599, Solre was created a knight of the Golden Fleece by king Philip III.

[82] "El Conde de Sorle [*sic*] era hechura del Rey, pues de caballero particular le hizo señor y puso en alto punto." See Luis Cabrera de Córdoba, *Historia de Felipe II, Rey de España*, ed. José Martínez Millán and Carlos Javier de Carlos Morales (Salamanca, 1998), 3: 1554.

[83] Esteban Estríngana, "Felipe III y los estados de Flandes" (as in note 2); Bernardo José García García, *La Pax Hispanica: Política exterior del Duque de Lerma* (Leuven, 1995), 71-72; *Idem*, "Ganar los corazones y obligar los vecinos: Estrategias de pacificación de los Países Bajos, 1604-1610," in Ana Crespo Solana and Manuel Herrero Sánchez (eds.), *España y las 17 provincias de los Países Bajos: Una revisión historiográfica (XVI-XVIII)* (Cordoba, 2002), 1: 157-165.

[84] Christina Hofman, *Das Spanische Hofzeremoniell von 1500-1700* (Frankfurt am Main, 1985), 87.

[85] In the Battle of Nieuwpoort on 2 July 1600, the only battle in which the archduke participated directly, the Dutch captured the archducal standard, but the count of Meghen was able to recover it from the enemy, saving Albert a considerable loss of *reputación*. See Jules de Saint Genois (ed.), *Dagboek van Jan de Pottre, 1549-1602,* Maetschappy der Vlaemsche Bibliophilen, 3rd ser., 5 (Ghent, 1861), 200.

[86] Stadsarchief Antwerp, *Verzameling Iconografie*, no. Ic.15/24.

of the court into the different cities, informing local authorities of the procedure to follow.[87] In the duchy of Brabant, he also held the ducal sword (*l'estoc d'armes*) in his hands and displayed it to the public.[88] In this way, at least outside the palace, it appeared that the court was directed by a local nobleman and not by a foreigner, thus creating an important bond between court and subjects, and mitigating the image of the Archdukes as vassals of the Spaniards. The fact that Solre also enjoyed the confidence of the Flemish States General strengthened this image.[89] Later, in 1604, when the Flemish population's discontent with the archducal government had reached its peak,[90] the Archdukes would stress even more the role of Solre as their and the country's confidant by sending him to Spain in order to defend the interests of the Netherlands.[91]

Solre would remain *caballerizo mayor* until his death in February 1612, while staying in Prague after attending the wedding of archduke Matthias of Austria, king of Hungary and Bohemia. Between 1612 and 1615 no *caballerizo mayor* was appointed. Finally, at the beginning of 1615 don Rodrigo Niño Lasso de la Vega added the title to his already impressive curriculum, thus crowning and consolidating his rise at

[87] Alfred De Ridder, "Une relation inédite de l'inauguration des Archiducs Albert et Isabelle aux Pays-Bas," in *Messager des Sciences historiques*, 1892, 274-287, 408-430, esp. 279-280.

[88] AGR, *Manuscrits divers*, no. 821, fo. 68r-v.; Edmond Geudens, "'Blijde Inkomst' der aartshertogen Albertus en Isabella te Antwerpen in 1599," *Bijdragen tot de geschiedenis, bijzonderlijk van het aloude hertogdom Brabant* 10 (1911), 120-140, esp. 130: "ende ten lesten de Grave van Solre, als grand escuier oft grooten stalmeester, dragende het sweert bloothoofts, als te Loven ende te Brussel." At the funeral of archduke Albert, the *caballerizo mayor*, duke Ottavio Visconti, held the archducal crown. See Francquart et al., *Pompa funebris,* plate 52 (as in note 14).

[89] In 1598 the States General sent him to Spain, together with representatives of the cities and the clergy, in order to congratulate the infanta upon the Cession of the Netherlands. See Brants, "Solre," 126 (as in note 81). During the States General of 1600, Albert appointed Solre as one of the negotiators to fix the *tanteo* (war budget) in concert with the Flemish deputies. See Louis-Prosper Gachard (ed.), *Actes des États Généraux de 1600* (Brussels, 1849), 204, 468. At that time, Solre even pleaded for the creation of a 'national,' and thus, a non-Spanish army, formed by Flemish and Walloon soldiers and paid for by the Provincial States. See Alicia Esteban Estríngana, *Madrid y Bruselas: Relaciones de gobierno en la etapa postarchiducal, 1621-1634* (Leuven, 2005), 90-92; *Codoin*, 42: 242-276, esp. 263-272 (as in note 35).

[90] Louant, *Correspondance,* 2: 272, 276, 290, 346, 350 (as in note 55).

[91] Victor Brants, "Une mission à Madrid de Philippe de Croy, comte de Solre, envoyé des archiducs en 1604," *Bulletin de la Commission royale d'histoire* 77 (1908), 185-203; García García, "Ganar los corazones," 1: 137-165 (as in note 83).

court.[92] Indeed, from that moment onwards, Lasso combined the functions of *mayordomo mayor*, *sumiller de corps* and *caballerizo mayor*. At his death in 1620, Ottavio Visconti, count of Gamalerio, replaced him at the head of the stables.[93]

Apart from the five court departments, the three companies of archducal guards constituted relatively independent units within the court structure. Their captains only obeyed the *bureo*, having a high degree of autonomy concerning the internal organization, the recruitment of new members, the preservation of discipline, the administration of justice, and the leaves of absence.[94] The *archeros de corps* consisted of fifty archers, a lieutenant and a captain, supported by their personnel.[95] The *alabarderos* numbered five detachments of eighteen halberdiers each, commanded by five corporals, a sergeant, a lieutenant and a captain. After 1610, the number of archers was reduced to forty, and that of halberdiers to eighty-four, corporals included. Following the Burgundian tradition, all archers were subjects of the Archdukes born in the loyal territories of the Southern Netherlands and Burgundy. Candidates from the Northern Netherlands and the prince-bishopric of Liège were excluded. The halberdiers were recruited in the Holy Roman Empire. Their commanding officers were all local noblemen. The *archeros* stood under the command, successively, of Guillaume II de Bauffremont, baron of Sombernon (died 1599), Robert de Ligne, baron of Barbançon (died 1614), and margrave Christian of Emden. Count Frederick van den Bergh and, after his death in 1618, his son Albert, stood at the head of the *alabarderos*.[96] Both corps were important to the

[92] His name appears on the wage-sheet of the first *tercio* of 1615. AGR, *Chambre des Comptes,* no. 1837, fo. 397v.

[93] Lille, Archives départementales du Nord, *Chambre des Comptes de Lille,* series B, no. 2913, fo. 221r: "comte Octavio Visconti, grand écuyer de l'hostel de Son Altèze"; AGR, Audience, no. 20, fo. 23v.

[94] AGR, *Audience*, no. 20, fos. 31r-34v: "Lo que parece se ha de ordenar para la compañía de archeros"; Eloy Hortal Muñoz, "Las guardas palatino-personales de Felipe II," in Martínez Millán and Fernández Conti, *La monarquía de Felipe II*, 2: 453-495 (as in note 59).

[95] The *archeros de corps* of the Spanish king numbered sixty members, plus personnel. See Hortal Muñoz, "Las guardas palatino-personales," 459 (as in note 94)

[96] ASV, *Fondo Borghese,* Serie I, no. 913, fo. 356r; AGR, *Audience*, no. 33/4, fo. 67r; AGR, *Chambre des Comptes,* no. 1837, fo. 268v; no. 1838, fo. 256v; AGR, *Audience*, no. 20, fo. 18v. Between the death of Barbançon and the entrance into office of Emden on 5 March 1614, Frederick van den Bergh was acting captain of the *archeros* (AGR, *Chambre des Comptes,* no. 1837, fo. 268v). Until 1610 Emden was commander of a German regiment and fought, for example, in the Battle of Nieuwpoort. See B. Cox,

public profile of the archducal court, as they accompanied the court every time it left the palace.

In addition to the *archeros* and *alabarderos*, Albert also disposed over a third guard that is hardly mentioned in the literature. As commander in chief of the Army of Flanders, he was protected by two troops of cavalry, one of lancers and another of harquebusiers, all of whom were Spaniards, as was their commanding officer since 1595, don Rodrigo Niño Lasso de la Vega.[97] While *archeros* and *alabarderos* fulfilled a more ceremonial role, the *lanceros* and *arcabuceros* were the real bodyguards of the archduke. For example, they fought at his side during the Battle of Nieuwpoort, and prevented the archduke from being captured by the enemy. On that occasion, Lasso was seriously injured and was almost left for dead on the battlefield.[98] As captain of these two units, he also formed part of Albert's council of war. Thus he was an important confidant of Albert long before he reached the highest position at court.

Control of court finances

The second cluster of powerful positions at court controlled by Spanish courtiers included the offices involving financial administration. Indeed, the management of the court was not an exclusive competence of the *mayordomo mayor* and his colleagues at the head of the court departments. An important part of the court administration was reserved for the so-called *bureo* (Office). Every day this institution authorized the expenses of the different paymasters, and every month it verified their accounts. The wage-sheets of the court personnel were inspected at the end of every *tercio*.[99] The *bureo* also supervised the daily provision of wine, food, candles, firewood and medicines to the departments and members of the court, as these were expensive items that could easily

Vanden Tocht in Vlaenderen: De logistiek van Nieuwpoort, 1600 (Zutphen, 1986), 126-127.

[97] Cabrera de Córdoba, *Historia de Felipe II*, 3: 1545 (as in note 82); Bentivoglio, *Relaciones*, fo. 54v (as in note 29); Alonso Vázquez, *Los sucesos de Flandes y Francia del tiempo de Alejandro Farnese*, Colección de Documentos Inéditos para la Historia de España 74 (Madrid, 1880), 380.

[98] Sara Veronelli and Félix Labrador Arroyo (eds.), *Diario de Hans Khevenhüller, embajador imperial en la corte de Felipe II* (Madrid, 2001), 528; Roco de Campofrío, *España en Flandes*, 271: "Don Rodrigo Niño Lasso, capitán de la guardia de su Alteza, que le hallaron entre los muertos tan mal herido, que se juzga estava sin vida, y al no dar señales de vivo, le libró de que no le acavassen de matar" (as in note 7).

[99] See note 12 above.

be used for private purposes. When the court set out on a journey, it hired the mules that were necessary for the transportation of the furniture and the other requisites of the *Casa*. Apart from this financial responsibility, the *bureo* was also in charge of the implementation of the internal decrees and directives on the functioning of the court that were issued by the Archdukes. Finally, it had legal jurisdiction over the members of the court. When functioning as a law-court, it was presided over by the *mayordomo mayor*.[100]

The *bureo* was composed of the *mayordomos*, the *tesorero de la cámara*, the *contralor* and the *greffier*. The ordinary meetings were conducted by the most senior *mayordomo*, who also had the authority to summon extraordinary sessions. Decisions were mainly taken by him and the other *mayordomos*. In fact, neither the *contralor* nor the *greffier* had the right to vote, but the *contralor* could raise objections. This difference in influence was also expressed in a physical way. During the meetings, the *mayordomos* gathered around the main table, while the *tesorero*, the *contralor* and the *greffier* were installed around a second table.[101] Their function was more administrative. The *contralor* verified daily the so called *livres de dépenses* in which the *mayordomo semanero* noted the sums that had been entrusted to the *comprador* (the person responsible for the purchase of provisions) and the *oficiales de boca* (the various heads of the service of the palace), and checked whether they had spent the money correctly. Afterwards, he entered the expenses in the day-book and the register by name.[102] The *tesorero* calculated, although in collaboration with the *mayordomo semanero*, the expenses and drew up the necessary lists. Finally, the *greffier* wrote the receipts and certificates, organized the wage-sheets and the list of town houses that were rented for the court members.[103]

When one examines the origin of the office-holders that formed part of the *bureo*, it becomes clear that it had a strong non-Flemish or even Spanish configuration. Among the lower personnel, only *contralor* Charles de Hertoghe was Flemish. He is first mentioned in both lists of 1605 and was probably engaged in 1598, Pedro de Mendoza having been *contralor* during the period that Albert was governor-general.[104]

100 AGR, *Manuscrits divers*, no. 821, fos. 29v-30r, 32r-35v, 44v, 46r, 56r-v, 58r.

101 AGR, *Manuscrits divers*, no. 821, fos. 32r-35v.

102 Hofman, *Das Spanische Hofzeremoniell*, 84-85 (as in note 84).

103 AGR, *Manuscrits divers*, no. 821, fos. 29v-30r, 32r-35v; Hofman, *Das Spanische Hofzeremoniell*, 85 (as in note 84).

104 ASV, *Fondo Borghese*, Serie I, no. 913, fo. 353r; AGR, *Audience*, no. 33/3, fo. 12r;

Mendoza was later appointed *greffier*, which he stayed until at least 1622.[105] Hertoghe would also survive the archduke and ended his career as a councilor of Finance.[106] The position of *tesorero* or *maestro de la cámara*, on the contrary, was never occupied by a local. When Albert left Spain in 1595 it was assigned to Joseph Hartelieb, who died in 1605.[107] He was succeeded by Juan Jacomo Fleccamer (Fleckhamer), who occupied the post only during a very brief period.[108] As early as 1607 he had been replaced by Antonio Rovelasca, previously the Archdukes' *sumiller de la cava*. Rovelasca was a member of an Italian merchant family that had operated from Milan, Seville, Antwerp and Madrid since the first half of the sixteenth century. Antonio resided at the Spanish court from at least 1581, a year in which he and his brother Giovanni Batista, together with the Flemish merchant Giraldo Paris, negotiated the Lisbon pepper contract with Philip II, a monopoly that was prolonged in 1585.[109] He was introduced into Spanish court circles through Paris, but also through Jehan Lhermite and Pedro van

AGR, *Audience,* no. 33/4, fo. 67v. In 1598, he held the office of *contralor* together with Manuel de Arinzano.

105 AGR, *Audience,* no. 20, fo. 20v. His name does not appear in the 1624 list of *criados reformados* of archduke Albert.

106 Francquart et al., *Pompa funebris,* plate 25 (as in note 14), describes him as "controleur de la Maison Conseillier et Comis des Finances."

107 The accounts of the *Chambre des Comptes* of Lille register his name in 1596, 1597, 1598, 1599, 1600, 1602 and 1603 (Finot, *Inventaire,* 5: 350, 358, 363, 370, 377; 6: 10, 13; as in note 74), while the 1605 lists also mention a Josephe Hertevliet (AGR, *Audience,* no. 33/3, fo. 12r; AGR, *Audience,* no. 33/4, fo. 67v). The 1606 list of textiles delivered at the Brussels court in order to make a new livery for the court servants on the occasion of the arrival of the English ambassador refers to him as "feu nostre tresorier et maitre de la chambre Josepho Hartelieb." It also mentions "Jean Jacomo Fleccamer a present nostre tresorier et maitre de nostre chambre" (AGR, *Conseil d'État,* no. 157/2, fos. 31v-32r).

108 This would explain why the 1605 account of the *Chambre des Comptes* only mentions the function of *tesorero* without naming the holder of the office (Finot, *Inventaire,* 6: 24; as in note 74). Unfortunately, the account of 1606 has been lost, which makes it impossible to confirm whether at that time Fleccamer was still *tesorero*, or whether he had already been replaced by Rovelasca. This was probably the case, as in October 1606 Fleccamer became *secrétaire d'État aux affaires d'Allemagne.* See Edgar De Marneffe, "La Secrétairerie d'État allemande aux Pays-Bas," in *Mélanges d'histoire offerts à Charles Moeller* (Louvain and Paris, 1914), 2: 141-148, esp. 146. Fleccamer was a former *ayuda de cámara* of Albert's. ASV, *Fondo Borghese,* Serie I, no. 913, fo. 352v; AGR, *Audience,* no. 33/3, fo. 10r (among the *ayudas de cámara*: Juan Diego Flegamer); AGR, *Audience,* no. 33/4, fo. 67v (Joan Diego Flecamer).

109 Werner Thomas, *Een spel van kat en muis: Zuidnederlanders voor de Inquisitie in Spanje, 1530-1750* (Brussels, 1991), 62-63.

Ranst, since 1591 both *ayudas de cámara* of Philip II and subsequently of Philip III,[110] and ended up in the household of the Archdukes.[111] Rovelasca held the office of *tesorero* until 1623.[112]

As for the *mayordomos*, it is not quite clear how many there really were. Most of the sources mention four. Lozano's manual describing the etiquette of the Brussels court provided the *mayordomo mayor* with four assistants, and the lists of courtiers from 1598 and 1605 also each contain four names.[113] During the Twelve Years' Truce this number seems to have increased to eight or more. Indeed, the wage-sheets in the *libros de razón* listed eight *mayordomos* for the years 1612 to 1616. From the summer of 1616 to that of 1617 there were nine of them, and from the second *tercio* of 1617 to the first of 1618 the names of no fewer than ten *mayordomos* appear.[114] Nevertheless, Guido Bentivoglio, who wrote chapter III of his *Relaciones* in 1613, still recorded four *mayordomos*.[115] The sources appear to contradict one another, but a closer look at the wage-sheets shows that not all office-holders served simultaneously. In 1612, for example, four of the eight *mayordomos* listed in the wage-sheets were absent, namely the count of Isenghien, don Pedro Ponce de León, the marquis of Montenegro, and don Diego de Ibarra.[116]

110 Martínez Millán and Fernández Conti, *La monarquía de Felipe II*, 2: 547 (as in note 59). Between 1570 and 1571, Van Ranst had already been *ayuda del barbero de corps* (*ibidem*, 548).

111 On the Rovelasca family, see Friedrich Dobel, "Über einen Pfefferhandel der Fugger und Welser, 1586-91," *Zeitschrift des Historischen Vereins für Schwaben und Neuburg* 13 (1886), 125-138; Reinhard Hildebrandt, *Die "Georg Fuggerischen Erben": Kaufmännische Tätigkeit und sozialer Status, 1555-1600* (Berlin, 1966), 146-190; Hermann Kellenbenz, *Fremde Kaufleute auf der iberischen Halbinsel* (Cologne, 1970), 279. When Jehan Lhermite arrived in Madrid in 1587, he stayed at Rovelasca's house, where he was well received: "lesquels [Antonio and Giovanni Batista] m'y receurent fort amiablement, me traictans comme filz de la mayson, jouissant une bonne espace de temps de leur bonne et agréable compaignie, principalement de celle dudict Anthoine." See Jehan Lhermite, *Le Passetemps*, ed. Charles Ruelens, 2 vols. (Antwerp, 1890-1896), 1: 84.

112 Finot, *Inventaire*, 6: 33 (1607), 38 (1608), 59 (1612) (as in note 74); AGR, *Audience*, no. 20, fo. 16r.

113 AGR, *Manuscrits divers*, no. 821, fo. 29v; Gachard and Piot, *Collection de voyages*, 4: 460 (as in note 15); AGR, *Audience*, no. 33/3, fos. 5v-6r; AGR, *Audience*, no. 33/4, fo. 67r. The Vatican list only mentions three majordomos, namely Ibarra, Isenghien and Formensant (ASV, *Fondo Borghese*, Serie I, no. 913, fo. 340r).

114 AGR, *Chambre des Comptes*, no. 1837, fos. 39r (1612), 104v, 160v and 220r (1613), 268v, 305v and 367v-368r (1614); no. 1838, fos. 41v and 97v-98r (1615), 128v, 180r-v and 218r-v (1616), 256r-v, 292v-293r and 337r (1617), 372r (1618).

115 Bentivoglio, *Relaciones*, fo. 54v (as in note 29).

116 AGR, *Chambre des Comptes*, no. 1837, fo. 39r.

The next year, there were again four absentees: Isenghien, Ponce de León, Montenegro and the count of Boussu.[117] The same phenomenon occurred in the years 1614 to 1618. Thus, it seems that at the Brussels court there were always more than four noblemen holding the title of *mayordomo*, but not all of them served the archduke at any one time. The others were granted leave of absence.

This arrangement must have been implemented much earlier than 1609, and it is even possible that there were eight *mayordomos* from the beginning of the archducal reign. Don Diego de Ibarra, for example, was appointed *mayordomo* in 1595, and was still holding the office in 1622.[118] His name furthermore appears in the list of 1598 and in the *libros de razón* between 1613 and 1618.[119] On the other hand, the wage-sheet of 1612, the lists of 1605 and 1611 and the description of Albert's funeral do not include him. It is nevertheless completely unimaginable that somewhere between 1598 and 1612, and again between 1619 and 1622, Ibarra would have lost his title, regaining it in 1613 and again in 1622. On the contrary, it is much more plausible that he held the office continuously from 1595 to 1622, and that his absence in the lists of 1605, 1611 and 1612 was due to the journeys he frequently made to Spain. This means that in 1605 there were at least five *mayordomos*: the four that are mentioned in the 1605 lists, plus Ibarra.

The case of the count of Isenghien, Jacques Philippe Vilain de Gand, is identical. He is referred to as *mayordomo* for the first time in 1598 and held the title until 1622.[120] The 1605 lists and the *libros de razón* mention him, although in the wage-sheets from 1612 to 1618 he is marked "ausente."[121] However, his name does not appear in the 1611 list. In fact, this document, in which the count of Saint-Aldegonde, Philippe de Mérode, Ferdinand d'Andelot and the count of Marles are given as *mayordomos*, should be completed with the names of the absentees, namely Ibarra, Ponce de León, Isenghien and Croÿ. The 1611 document clearly confirms once more that only the *libros de razón* give

[117] AGR, *Chambre des Comptes*, no. 1837, fos. 104v, 160v.

[118] Roco de Campofrío, *España en Flandes*, 70 (as in note 7); AGR, *Audience*, no. 20, fo. 18r.

[119] ASV, *Fondo Borghese*, Serie I, no. 913, fo. 352r; AGR, *Chambre des Comptes*, no. 1837, fos. 39r, 104v, 160v, 219v, 263v-264r, 268r, 305v, 367v, 397v; no. 1838, fos. 41v, 97v, 128v, 180r, 218r, 256r, 292v, 337r, 372r.

[120] ASV, *Fondo Borghese*, Serie I, no. 913, fo. 352r. He died in 1628.

[121] AGR, *Audience*, no. 33/3, fo. 5v; AGR, *Audience*, no. 33/4, fo. 67r; AGR, *Chambre des Comptes*, no. 1837, fos. 39r, 104v, 160v, 220r; no. 1838, fos. 41v, 97v, 128v, 180r, 218r, 256r, 292r, 337r, 372r.

a complete overview of all the office-holders, and that the lists of 1605 and 1611 only mention the *mayordomos* actually on duty.

Bearing all this in mind, it becomes clear that, at least for the years from 1595 to 1611 and from 1619 to 1621, one can only analyze the composition of the quartet of *mayordomos* on duty. Until probably 1609, half of them were Spaniards or members of families originating in the Aragonese kingdom of Naples: don Luis de Ávalos, the most senior, and don Diego de Ibarra in 1598, don Pedro Ponce de León and Gerónimo Carafa, the Neapolitan marquis of Montenegro in 1605.[122] In 1611, on the contrary, all four were local noblemen, headed by the count of Saint-Aldegonde. This was probably no more than a coincidence. Between 1613 and 1617 the *libros de razón* again mention one Spaniard, don Diego de Ibarra. In 1617 a second Spanish *mayordomo* appeared, don García de Pareja, the ambassador extraordinary of Philip III who was sent to Brussels at the beginning of that year in order to thank the archduke for having organized the oath of allegiance of the Flemish provinces to the king in 1616. He would stay in Brussels until the end of 1617.[123]

While local office-holders had a certain – and from 1609 a great – influence on the decisions of the *bureo*, they were almost completely kept out of the financial transactions at court. Payments at court followed a strict procedure. Above all, the *mayordomo mayor* had to approve the transaction. Then, the *secretario de la cámara* would write out a payment order, which would be verified by the *greffier*. Finally, the *tesorero* would pay the creditor. The names of the holders of three out of four offices have already been mentioned: the *mayordomos mayor* Mendoza, Zapata and finally Lasso; the *greffier* Pedro de Mendoza, and the *tesoreros* Joseph Hartelieb and Antonio Rovelasca. The *secretario de la cámara* was also a Spaniard. In 1595 this office was assigned to Juan de Frías.[124] He was recalled by Philip III after he had exposed the abuses of a servant of the army's *pagador general* Gabriel de Santisteban, and returned to Madrid in 1604.[125] His replacement was Diego Ruiz, who

[122] Gachard and Piot, *Collection de voyages*, 4: 460 (as in note 15).

[123] See note 114; *CCE*, 1: 495, 497, 499, 509 (as in note 5).

[124] Roco de Campofrío, *España en Flandes*, 7 (as in note 7); Cabrera de Córdoba, *Historia de Felipe II*, 3: 1545 (as in note 82); Louant, *Correspondance*, 2: 263 (as in note 55).

[125] *Consultas*, 1: 370 (as in note 6); *Codoin* 42: 477, 483 (as in note 5). At his arrival in Madrid, Frías served as *oidor* of the *Real Chancillería de Valladolid* and later, in 1613, was promoted councilor of the *Consejo Real*. See Cabrera de Córdoba, *Relaciones*, 528 (as in note 36).

did not last long. By 1611 Antonio Suárez de Argüello was holding the office, and he continued to do so until at least 1622.[126]

The Spaniards not only dominated the central administration of the finances of the archducal court. At a lower level they also held most of the offices that handled the money coming from the *bureo* in order to provide the departments with the supplies they needed. The *despensero mayor*, for instance, the man responsible for the distribution of the *raciones* among the different sections of the *Casa* (the so called *oficios de boca*) and the administrative head of the kitchen, was at all times a Spaniard: Bernardo Gómez in 1598, Juan del Poyo in 1605, Cristóbal de Lonzón from 1612 to 1622.[127] The same was true of the *comprador*, the official charged with the acquisition of the provisions for the kitchen. In 1598 this position was occupied by Miguel de Guevara, who was succeeded before 1605 by his former assistant, Pascual Navarro.[128] At the end of May 1615, Navarro's aide Lucas Hernández would, in his turn, replace his master.[129] The section of the *Casa* that handled not money, but precious objects, was the *salsería*, the service in charge of the silver and pewter plates and dishes. The *salsero mayor* was even held personally responsible for the loss of any of them.[130] No local servant ever occupied this position. From 1598 to at least 1618 Miguel de Pianza – possibly of Italian origin – held the office, being succeeded by his assistant Tomás de la Riva at the end of the archducal reign.[131] In fact, the only section in Flemish hands involving precious objects was the *tapicería*, whose head, the *tapicero mayor* Herman Vermeren, outlived the archduke.

[126] AGR, *Conseil d'État*, no. 157/3, fo. 9v; AGR, *Audience*, no. 20, fo. 19v. In 1606, Ruiz was still secretary (*Codoin* 43: 21, as in note 35). From 1612, Suárez de Argüello also held the position of *Secrétaire d'État aux affaires d'Allemagne*, thus administering the relations of the Archdukes with the Empire. He died in 1635. See De Marneffe, "La Secrétairerie d'État allemande aux Pays-Bas," 146 (as in note 108).

[127] ASV, *Fondo Borghese*, Serie I, no. 913, fo. 354v; AGR, *Audience*, no. 33/3, fo. 20v; AGR, *Audience*, no. 33/4, fo. 68v; AGR, *Chambre des Comptes*, no. 1837, fo. 110v; AGR, *Audience*, no. 20, fo. 23r.

[128] ASV, *Fondo Borghese*, Serie I, no. 913, fo. 354v; AGR, *Audience*, no. 33/3, fo. 20v; AGR, *Audience*, no. 33/4, fo. 68v.

[129] Navarro died on 21 May 1615. AGR, *Chambre des Comptes*, no. 1838, fo. 187v; AGR, *Audience*, no. 20, fo. 23r.

[130] AGR, *Manuscrits divers*, no. 821, fos. 47v-48r.

[131] ASV, *Fondo Borghese*, Serie I, no. 913, fo. 354r; AGR, *Chambre des Comptes*, no. 1838, fo. 378r; AGR, *Audience*, no. 20, fo. 22r. On the wage-sheet of the first *tercio* of 1618 Miguel de Pianza still appears as *salsero mayor*.

In the *Cámara*, apart from the administrative offices discussed above, both *guardajoyas y ropa* of the Archdukes handled a fortune in jewels and precious stones. They supervised and negotiated the manufacture and acquisition of jewelry, golden and silver art objects and religious silverware with local goldsmiths, jewelers and merchants. Albert's *guardajoyas* Joachim Denzenhear was also responsible for the gold and silver objects and ornaments of the court chapel.[132] He served the archduke from 1595 until after 1618 and was succeeded, not by one of his assistants, but by the former *ayuda de cámara* Juan Laynez.[133] At the passing of his master, Laynez was dismissed in 1624.[134] Isabella's *guardajoyas* was the Spaniard Juan Elordi de Silva, who was first mentioned in 1604 and was still serving the archduchess in 1623.[135] In the stables, most of the resources were administrated by the *veedor y contador*. Of course, any financial transaction was to take place with the knowledge of the *caballerizo mayor*, but the *veedor y contador* kept the accounts and submitted them to the *bureo*.[136] He also paid the wages of some of the servants of the stables. Once again, this office was held by a Spanish servant, in 1598 Cristóbal de Paredes, and from at least 1605 to 1622, Antonio de Mendoza. Finally, one should not forget the *limosnero mayor*, who administered up to 20,000 Flemish pounds in alms every year. He drew up the lists of people that would receive archducal charity, for example, when the court sojourned outside Brussels. Old people, poor prisoners, sick women, orphans, poor girls who were about to marry, "gens bruslez du feu" ('covered in burns'), and merchants "distruict par la fortune" were given priority. The Archdukes approved and signed the list, and might sometimes distribute the alms in person. Be that as it may, a high proportion of their charitable donations passed through the almoner's hands.[137] As the office of *limosnero mayor* was usually combined with that of *capellán mayor*, the first local clergyman in this position was to be François de Rye in 1620, aside from the short interim of Karel Maes in 1603-1605, referred to above.

132 AGR, *Manuscrits divers*, no. 821, fos. 36r-37r.

133 AGR, Audience, no. 33/4, fo. 61v ("Joachim de Encenar"); AGR, *Chambre des Comptes*, no. 1838, fo. 374.

134 Laynez already figures as an *ayuda de cámara* on the 1598 list, ASV, *Fondo Borghese*, Serie I, no. 913, fo. 352v.

135 Finot, *Inventaire*, 6: 20-21, 110 (as in note 74).

136 AGR, *Manuscrits divers*, no. 821, fo. 71v.

137 AGR, *Manuscrits divers*, no. 821, fo. 7r-v.

Direct contact with the Archdukes

The offices that allowed daily contact with the Archdukes or that were involved with the preparation and serving of the archducal repasts constituted a third cluster of Spanish control. Of course there were many courtiers that approached either Albert or Isabella, or even both, on a daily basis. For instance, most of the members of the *Cámara* did. The *barberos* shaved the archduke, the servants of the *guardarropa* helped him to get dressed and the *zapatero* put his shoes on. None of them had the right to address the archduke, and while they were serving there was always the *gentilhombre de guarda* or his substitute present. This type of contact was rather of a 'passive' kind. I am therefore not referring to this group of lower offices, although many of them were in Spanish hands, but to the higher personnel – except the leading offices – that assisted the Archdukes more 'actively,' accompanied them from morning to evening, had the right to speak freely, shared intimate moments or was frequently left alone with them, that is, without anybody else being present.

Indeed, many servants entered the private quarters of the Archdukes, the so-called *retrete*, on a daily basis: the *tapicero mayor*, the cleaners, the water-carrier, the *furrier*, etc. But all of them had to wait until their masters went to mass before they were permitted to carry out their tasks, and they were at all times accompanied by the *ayuda de cámara* on duty. Very few persons were allowed into the *retrete* while the sovereigns were actually present, not even the *Grandes,* the knights of the Golden Fleece, or the generals of the army. Access to the *retrete* was limited to the *sumiller de corps*, the *gentilhombre de la cámara* on duty, and the *ayuda de cámara* on duty. At night, the *ayuda de furriera* on duty locked the doors of the archducal quarters, only to open them again in the morning. The doors of the *retrete* and the *aposento de la alcoba*, on the contrary, were locked by the *mozo del retrete* in the presence of the *ayuda de cámara* on duty.[138] In the private rooms of the archduchess, a similar procedure was in place, but carried out by the women of her retinue, especially by the *camarera mayor*, the *dueñas de retrete,* the *mozas de cámara* and the *mozas de retrete*.

A limited number of servants had the right to reside in the palace building after the closing of the gates, and even to spend the night near the private rooms of the Archdukes. In his quality of *limosnero mayor*, the *capellán mayor,* for example, disposed over a room close to

[138] AGR, *Manuscrits divers,* no. 821, fos. 39v and 43r.

the archduke's.[139] The *sumiller de corps* also had his lodgings next to Albert's, and he even slept on a bed in the room next to the archducal bedchamber. His family and servants, however, lived in a house outside the palace. When he was absent, and only then, his place was taken by the *gentilhombre de la cámara* on duty.[140] The *ayuda de cámara* on duty slept in a bed near the door of the archducal private quarters.[141] Both beds were daily built and removed by the *mozos del retrete*, of which the one on duty also passed the night in the palace. The *gentilhombre de la cámara* on duty furthermore did not budge from the archduke's side during his 24-hour service.[142]

Of all these offices, only that of *gentilhombre de la cámara* was not completely dominated by Spaniards. Indeed, while in 1598 half of the *gentilhombres de la cámara* – five out of a total of ten – were local noblemen, this ratio increased to eight out of thirteen in 1605, ten out of fifteen in 1611, seventeen out of twenty-three in 1617 and finally seven out of eight in 1621. Before 1611, the *ayudas de cámara* and the *mozos del retrete*, on the contrary, were almost never Flemish or Burgundian servants.[143] During the years of the Truce, roughly half of the offices of *ayuda* and *mozo* were occupied by local people. As to the service of Isabella, with the exception of the *camarera mayor* almost all of the positions were in Spanish hands throughout the whole archducal reign.[144]

Spaniards also directed most of the sections of the *Casa*, the so called *oficios de boca*. By doing so, they held control over the preparation, manipulation and presentation of the dishes, beverages and fruit that were reserved for the archducal table and for the other courtiers. Beside the *salsería*, with its Spanish *salsero mayor*, the *cava* (wine cellar), the *frutería* (fruit and marmalades) and the *panetería* (the section

139 AGR, *Manuscrits divers,* no. 821, fo. 7r-v. The *capellán mayor* as such had no right to stay in the palace after closing time.

140 AGR, *Manuscrits divers,* no. 821, fos. 60v-61v.

141 AGR, *Manuscrits divers,* no. 821, fo. 63r.

142 AGR, *Manuscrits divers,* no. 821, fo. 38r.

143 In 1605 only a certain Pedro de Bodens figures among the *ayudas de cámara* (AGR, *Audience,* no. 33/3, fo. 10r-v).

144 1605: all 5 *dueñas de retrete,* 4 of the 5 *mozas de cámara* and 1 of the 2 *mozas de retrete* (AGR, *Audience,* no. 33/3, fos. 3v-4v); 1611: all 4 *dueñas de retrete,* 5 of the 6 *mozas de cámara* and at least 2 of the 4 *mozas de retrete* (AGR, *Conseil d'État,* no. 157/2, fo. 18r-v); 1617: all 4 *dueñas de retrete,* 7 of the 8 *mozas de cámara* and 3 of the 4 *mozas de retrete* (AGR, *Chambre des Comptes,* no. 1838, fos. 215v-216r); 1622: 4 of the 5 *dueñas de retrete,* 6 of the 7 *mozas de cámara* and at least 1 of the 4 *mozas de retrete* (AGR, *Audience,* no. 20, fos. 17v-18r).

responsible for the table linen and the bread) were all directed by non-local officials, mainly Spaniards and Italians.[145] As has already been indicated, the administrative head of the kitchen, the *despensero mayor* – referred to in some documents as the *veedor de vianda* – was at all times a Spaniard, as were the *comprador,* the *guardamanger*, and all of his four assistants.[146] The *guardamanger* administered the delivery of provisions to the kitchen and supervised their quality and use. Indeed, no food was to be sold to any court members; all the meat, fish and poultry purchased by the *comprador* was consigned to the archducal table and the *estados*.[147] And although the *cocinero mayor* was probably of Flemish origin,[148] the Archdukes' repasts might well have been prepared by Spanish cooks only. Indeed, the kitchen consisted of two sections, one for the table of the Archdukes (the *cocina de la boca*) and one for the *estados* (the *cocina de los estados*).[149] Unfortunately, the sources do not specify to which section each cook belonged.[150] Finally, the provisions of the kitchen were guarded by the *ujieres de vianda*, two door-keepers of Spanish origin.[151]

[145] *Cava*: Antonio Rovelasca (mentioned 1598 and 1605), Francisco Rodríguez Agraz (1611 to 1621) and Valeriano Rama (1622); *frutería*: Juan de Cerezo (1598) and Pedro de Aguilera (1605; the lists after 1605 do not mention the position of *frutero mayor*, which probably became a part of the kitchen); *panetería*: Juan del Pueyo (1598), Marcos Obrero (1605), Pedro Aguilera (1611-1618; Aguilera died 30 April 1618, see AGR, *Chambre des Comptes*, no. 1838, fo. 377v) and Gerónimo Gómez (1618-1622).

[146] In 1598 the *guardamanger* was Marcos Obrero (ASV, *Fondo Borghese,* Serie I, no. 913, fo. 354v), in 1605 Cristóbal de Lonzón (AGR, *Audience,* no. 33/3, fo. 20r), in 1611 Miguel de Olivares (AGR, *Conseil d'État,* no. 157/2, fo. 15r), and, finally, between the end of 1612 and 1622, Martín Ruiz de Ezquerecocha (AGR, *Chambre des Comptes*, no. 1837, fo. 110v). Only in 1622 was his aide Christian Vandereycken (AGR, *Audience*, no. 20, fo. 22v).

[147] AGR, *Manuscrits divers,* no. 821, fos. 49v-50r. In fact, the *portadores de la cocina*, the servants that handled the food before the cooks prepared it, were all Spaniards from 1598 to 1622.

[148] Juan Fiel or Fel between 1598 and 1611, and Jean de Termonde from 1612 to at least 1618 (AGR, *Chambre des Comptes,* no. 1838, fo. 379v). The lists of 1622 and 1624 make no further mention of a *cocinero mayor*, but simply enumerate the kitchen staff.

[149] AGR, *Manuscrits divers,* no. 821, fo. 49r-v.

[150] Only the 1595 list, which includes 5 cooks, mentions a "cocinero del estado de los pages y ayudas de camara" among the personnel of the kitchen (AGR, *Audience,* no. 33/4, fo. 64r).

[151] 1598: Martín Pérez (ASV, *Fondo Borghese,* Serie I, no. 913, fo. 355v); 1605: Lorenzo Carrillo and Cristóbal de Arce (AGR, *Audience,* no. 33/3, fo. 15r); 1611: Cristóbal de Arce and Juan Cortés (AGR, *Conseil d'État,* no. 157/2, fo. 13r); 1617: Juan Cortés and Valeriano Rama (AGR, *Chambre des Comptes,* no. 1838, f 261r); 1622: Juan Cortés and Gaspar de Vega (AGR, *Audience,* no. 20, fo. 21v).

However, the courtiers with direct access to the sovereigns, who most enjoyed the Archdukes' confidence, were probably the archducal confessors. They not only molded their penitents' consciences and, as spiritual directors, had a great influence on their personal religiosity, in each case they also intervened in public matters or even in affairs of state, as can be illustrated in the case of Albert's confessor, the Dominican Iñigo de Brizuela. Brizuela served the archduke from 1595, when he was personally selected by Philip II, to 1621.[152] Until 1608 his role at court seems to have been rather discreet. This changed in December of that year, when he was sent to Spain to secure royal approbation of the Twelve Years' Truce. In 1609 he again traveled to Madrid and submitted the final proposal to royal ratification. His political weight in Madrid and Brussels increased considerably as a result of the success of both missions, and he was even appointed councilor of State. From then on, he played an important role in several key issues of the archducal reign. With good reason Bentivoglio wrote in 1613 that:

> aunque por esta suerte de su cargo no tiene negocios particulares y determinados fuera de los que pertenecen a gouernar la conciencia del Archiduque, con todo esso casi se puede dezir, que es el suyo vn tribunal supremo, donde concurren materias de todos generos. Y el Archiduque, que va imitando, como dixe, quanto puede, en todo las acciones de Felipe Segundo, y que se conforma generalmente al estilo de la Corte de España, ha dexado facilmente ganar autoridad a este sujeto.[153]

In 1614, in view of the state of the archduke's health, Philip III requested that the representatives of the Flemish provinces swear allegiance to him; Spínola entrusted Brizuela with the delicate task of convincing Albert of the necessity of this procedure. Later on, he took part in negotiations for the prolongation of the Truce. Brizuela had become indispensable, at least in religious matters. The French geographer Pierre Bergeron, who traveled through the Netherlands and visited the palace in Brussels in 1619, wrote of Brizuela that he "gouverne fort en la court."[154] Brizuela's appointment in 1622 as a member of the Supreme Council for the Netherlands and Burgundy in Madrid reflects the political know-how

[152] Cabrera de Córdoba, *Historia de Felipe II*, 3: 1545 (as in note 82).
[153] Bentivoglio, *Relaciones*, 58v (as in note 29).
[154] Henri Michelant (ed.), *Voyage de Pierre Bergeron ès Ardennes, Liège et Pays-Bas en 1619* (Liège, 1875), 346.

he had built up during his years at the Brussels court.[155] Isabella, on the contrary, chose a Franciscan as her spiritual assistant, namely Fray Andrés de Soto, whose political role was rather modest.[156]

Access to the sovereigns granted to those other than courtiers, knights of the Golden Fleece, *Grandes* of Spain, high-ranked officers of the Army of Flanders and presidents of the archducal councils – who all had structural moments of contact with the archduke – was supervised, as has already been mentioned, by the *mayordomo mayor*, who acted as a filter between the Archdukes and the outside world. He received foreign embassies or representatives, organized the public audiences and controlled access to the private rooms of the archduke. Burgundian etiquette also prescribed that nobody could enter the private rooms of the archduchess without his permission.[157]

Accessibility of the palace

Except for the days on which certain parts of the archducal residence on the Coudenberg were opened to the public, the palace was a restricted area where even the servants of the different court sections were not allowed to circulate freely. Only a limited number of courtiers held a master key (the *llave real*) that opened the doors of every room in the building. The most important of them was the *aposentador mayor*, who carried the key of the archduke and accompanied him everywhere in the palace, together with an aide opening and closing the doors on his way. For obvious reasons, the *gentilhombre de la cámara* on duty also disposed over a master key. Furthermore, the *mayordomo mayor*, the *sumiller de corps* and the *caballerizo mayor* each held a copy, as did the *ayuda de cámara* and the *ayuda de furriera* on duty. The other sections only disposed over a *llave sencilla*, a key that gave access to their own department. The *aposentador mayor* kept strict control over the number of *llaves reales* that circulated and over the use their owners made of them, and reported any abuses to the *bureo*.[158] From the beginning of

[155] See Joseph Lefèvre, "Le Ministère Espagnol de l'Archiduc Albert, 1598-1621," *Bulletin de l'Académie royale d'archéologie de Belgique* 1 (1924), 202-224, esp. 205-209.
[156] Benjamin De Troeyer, "Bio-bibliografie van de Minderbroeders in de Nederlanden, 17de eeuw. Voorstudies. 6. Andreas de Soto," *Franciscana* 37 (1982), 69-96; Cordula van Wyhe, "Court and Convent: The Infanta Isabella and Her Franciscan Confessor Andrés de Soto," *Sixteenth Century Journal* 35, 2 (2004), 411-445.
[157] AGR, *Manuscrits divers,* no. 821, fos. 28r, 55v-56r; Juan de Contreras, *Norma y ceremonia de las reinas de la Casa de Austria* (Madrid, 1958), 90.
[158] AGR, *Manuscrits divers,* no. 821, fos. 38r and 39v.

the archducal reign until its end, the position of *aposentador mayor* was assigned to Spanish courtiers, first Hernando de Zavala and later Manuel de Arinzano.[159]

Circulation of courtiers and visitors in the palace building, as it was established by court etiquette, was supervised by a series of officers that were always Spaniards. Isabella's chamber in particular was heavily guarded to prevent men from entering the private space of the archduchess' retinue, which consisted mainly of unmarried women. In fact, her *guardajoyas* and his assistants, together with her tailor, her embroiderer and her secretary, were the only male members of her *Cámara*. Access to this part of the court was supervised by the *guardadamas*, who was the only person allowed to enter the archduchess's *Cámara* without needing authorization from the *mayordomo mayor* to do so.[160] This position was occupied from at least 1605 – possibly even from 1598[161] – by Juan Fernández de Eyzaguirre, who would continue in office until his death in 1622. He was then succeeded by another Spaniard, Juan Ortiz de Zárate.[162] The *guardadamas* was at the same time *aposentador de palacio*, and probably served as Isabella's equivalent of Albert's *aposentador mayor*. The doors of Isabella's floor were guarded by the *porteros de las damas*, two doorkeepers, again of Spanish origin.[163] The archduke's private chambers were watched over by the *porteros de la saleta*, a palace guard, usually of six men, all of them Spaniards.[164] All of these servants were instructed as to who was to be stopped at the

[159] Zavala's name figures in the 1595 and 1598 list, while Arinzano is mentioned as *aposentador mayor* from 1605 onwards. Before 1598, he was *contralor*. Arinzano would survive the archduke (AGR, *Audience,* no. 33/4, fos. 62r-v, 68v; ASV, *Fondo Borghese,* Serie I, no. 913, fo. 353r-v; AGR, *Audience*, no. 33/3, fo. 18v).

[160] Contreras, *Norma y ceremonia*, 90 (as in note 157).

[161] Fernández de Eyzaguirre was *comprador* at the court of Philip II until 1598. See Martínez Millán and Fernández Conti, *La monarquía de Felipe II*, 2: 682 (as in note 59). His son served the Admiral of Aragon. See *Codoin* 42: 535 (as in note 35).

[162] AGR, *Audience,* no. 33/3, fo. 12r; AGR, *Audience,* no. 33/4, fo. 68r; AGR, *Audience,* no. 20, fo. 20v.

[163] Miguel Veloso and Pedro de Castañeda served as such from at least 1605 to 1622. Their aides, however, were Flemish.

[164] 1598: Domingo de Aguilar, Martín Juárez, Bernardo Añico and Juan Solarno (ASV, *Fondo Borghese,* Serie I, no. 913, fo. 354v); 1605: Diego Martínez, Martín Juárez, Bernardo Añico, Nicolás Correa, Martín de Mendú, Francisco Araujo and Pedro de Hinojosa (AGR, *Audience,* no. 33/3, fo. 19r); 1611: Bernardo Añico, Martín Juárez, Nicolás Correa, Francisco Araujo, Sebastián Ruiz and Alonso Palomino (AGR, *Conseil d'État,* no. 157/2, fo. 14v); 1622: Martín Juárez, Nicolás Correa, Bernardo Añico and Francisco de Ocampo (AGR, *Audience,* no. 20, fo. 22v). See also Hofman, *Das Spanische Hofzeremoniell*, 87 (as in note 84).

entrance of the space they guarded, and who was to be allowed to enter, and they had to report any incident to the *mayordomo mayor*.

A third restricted area at court was constituted by the different *estados*. Contrary to what one might assume, most of the courtiers were obliged to have their meals at home or in the city taverns. Only a limited group of courtiers enjoyed the prerogative of having dinner and supper within the palace. For this purpose, besides the archducal table five or six more tables were served. The *Estado de boca* received the *mayordomos,* the *gentilhombres de la boca,* and the *sumiller de la cortina.* The *Estado de cámara* was reserved for the *gentilhombres de la cámara.* Both *estados* offered meals for up to about twenty-four people a day. The *Estado de ayudas de cámara* was open to eight servants: the *ayuda de cámara* on duty, the *secretario de la cámara*, the *guardarropa* and his aides, and the *ayuda de barbero de corps*. The members of these *estados* had the privilege of bringing a page with them, and the pages were allowed to eat their masters' leftovers. The *Estado de los pajes* received the archducal pages to a maximum of twelve. From 1599 onwards, the *Sala de las damas de la infanta* served meals to between ten and fifteen members of Isabella's *Cámara*. Finally, at the court in Brussels, in contrast to most other Habsburg courts, a sixth *estado* functioned until the Twelve Years' Truce: the *Estado de los capitanes entretenidos*, the high-ranking officers of the Army of Flanders. This *estado* disappears in the documents of 1611 and later. When one takes into account that the *mayordomo mayor,* the *sumiller de corps,* the *caballerizo mayor* and probably also the *camarera mayor* of the infanta did not have their meals in one of the *estados*, but received the same dishes as the Archdukes and were allowed to take them in their private quarters, while the *ayuda de cámara* on duty had his meals in the *retrete* after the archduke had finished eating, the total number of courtiers that were allowed to eat meals from the archducal kitchen fluctuated around a hundred, not counting the pages.[165]

It was at all times important to supervise access to these *estados*, not only from a financial point of view – the more people took their meals in the *estados*, the more provisions the kitchen had to buy – but also with regard to the internal security of the palace. Therefore, only the *mayordomo semanero* was allowed to invite occasional guests to the *Estado de boca*. The other *estados* were exclusively reserved to court personnel, and their members were strictly forbidden to bring anybody

[165] AGR, *Manuscrits divers,* no. 821, fos. 50v-52v.

with them. The *mayordomos de los estados,* the heads of these sections charged with the daily organization, made sure that court regulations were observed and that no unauthorized people entered the *estados* and thus the palace. All of them, with the exception of a few Flemish *mozos* that never advanced to a higher rank, were Spaniards or Italians.[166]

Living encapsulated

The overview of offices held by Spaniards is not exhaustive. Many other courtiers and servants that in one way or another had daily access to the archducal rooms, or that handled personal items of either sovereign, were also of Spanish origin: the sweepers that cleaned the *retrete* (*barrenderos de la casa*), the section responsible for the lighting of the palace building (*cerería*), the *reposteros de camas* that took care of Albert's bed, the personal laundresses: the majority of them were Spaniards, as was at least one of the personal physicians that attended on the archdukes. The point I would like to make is that the Archdukes lived in a kind of Spanish cocoon, in which most of the people they encountered on a daily basis, from the lower personnel to the most important courtiers, were Spaniards. In other words, there was a barrier around the Archdukes, made up of Spanish servants and courtiers, that separated them from the outside, local world. The gates to this inner circle were heavily guarded, and access was watchfully controlled.

This entourage was in large part maintained from the beginning of the archducal reign to its end. Indeed, except for the three groups of *gentilhombres* and their equivalents in the archducal chapel and the stables, the key offices of the system remained in Spanish hands throughout. While other vacancies at court were usually filled with locals, this was not the case with these positions. Here, Spaniards followed Spaniards. Most of the time, the newly promoted servants were already working at court, but on several occasions they were brought from Spain. This demonstrates that the powerbase of the Spaniards at the archducal court was not just carried over from Albert and Isabella's

[166] *Estado de boca*: Miguel de Pianza (1595-1617), Tomás de Riva (1622); *Estado de cámara*: Carlos de Pianza (1595-1624); *Estado de ayudas de cámara*: Francisco de Peña (1595-1605), Diego Martínez de Aguilar (1605), Domingo López de Sosoaga (1612-1617), Ernest du Clarr (1624); *Estado de pajes*: Lorenzo Carrillo (1598), Domingo López de Sosoaga (1605), Diego Martínez de Aguilar (1611-1622); *Sala de damas*: Francisco de Peña (1605-1616), Teodoro Marcelo (1617-1622); *Estado de capitanes entretenidos*: Juan de Aranda (1598), Oracio de León (1605).

former retinues as governor-general and princess, to be undone with the years, but was deliberately maintained in order to conserve a Spanish grip on the Brussels court.

The Spanish faction

The question now is: was this Spanish powerbase at court only an instrument of patronage and clientelism, or did it also facilitate the functioning of a Spanish political faction? Was it just a place to park servants of the king of Spain or of the Archdukes as a reward for services rendered by themselves or their relatives, or did it also try to influence archducal policy? In this context, it is important first to discuss two circumstances that made the situation of the Archdukes very different from that to be found at any other Habsburg court: the peculiar relation between the king and his sister and uncle, and the presence of the Army of Flanders in the Southern Netherlands. Both these factors determined the dynamics of court factions and influenced archducal decision-making.

The particular situation of the archducal court

As has been indicated already, Philip III never really accepted the cession of the Netherlands to his sister. He rather saw the Archdukes as princes that in a certain sense held the country in usufruct from its rightful master, and thought that his own grand strategy should override local interests. From 1601 onwards, Madrid designed a policy that foresaw the immediate reincorporation of the Northern provinces into the Spanish Monarchy. Apart from the consequences this strategy had for the standing of the Archdukes, it also put the king in a very ambiguous position. On the one hand he had to take great care not to undermine the *reputación* of Albert and Isabella. Otherwise, he would only confirm the Protestant view that the archducal regime was no more than a puppet government of the king of Spain. Especially during the first years of the cession, when peace negotiations with the United Provinces might still lead to a definitive resolution of the war in the Netherlands, it was important to avoid any reference to the subordinate – at least in the king's opinion – position of Brussels to Madrid. Indeed, observers reported that the States General were waiting for the birth of an archducal heir, and thus for the consolidation of Flemish autonomy from Spain, before opening discussions on the reunification of the Seventeen Provinces under archducal authority.[167] Any suggestion that Philip had power over the government in Brussels would abort this willingness. It was therefore important, at least outwardly, to stress archducal sovereignty rather than to be seen to attack it.

On the other hand, Philip wanted 'his' northern subjects, and in particular the Flemish and Burgundian nobility, to know that the situation of the Southern Netherlands was exceptional and, in any case, temporary. Although the Archdukes ruled the country, he wanted to make very clear that in the end the Netherlands would return to Spain. Perhaps Philip was not yet technically and rightfully the sovereign of the country, he would be in the near future. Local elites should be made aware of this and should be stimulated to remain loyal to the royal cause. Madrid tried to get this message across as clearly as possible. Already in November 1599, for instance, the Spanish ambassador to the Archdukes, don Baltasar de Zúñiga, organized a banquet in Brussels for the knights of the Golden Fleece on the occasion of Saint Andrew's day, the patron saint of the Order. The Council of State supported the initiative, because it was a signal "en memoria de la soberanidad que reconoçen a Vuestra Majestad."[168] Now the king was of course Grand Master of the Order, and the Order itself had Burgundian roots, but it nevertheless gave evidence of little diplomatic tact to organize a celebration at a sovereign court without consulting the local rulers first. The next year, in the summer of 1600, when Albert was negotiating the subsidies that the Southern States General would grant to the archducal regime, the ambassador extraordinary don Enrique de Guzmán, sent by the king to Brussels in order to congratulate Albert on his performance at Nieuwpoort, suddenly appeared at the Brussels town hall and expressed his thanks to the representatives for the support they had given to Philip III.[169] Similar interventions served the purpose of reminding people of the final destiny of the country.

Spain and the Netherlands were clearly not two completely separate worlds. Madrid defended its interests in Brussels through a variety of channels. On the other hand, the Archdukes tried to bring the Spanish government round to their own political views. In any case, events in the Netherlands – especially the course of the war against the Dutch

[167] Louant, *Correspondance,* 3: 244 (as in note 55).

[168] *Consultas,* 1: 71-72 (as in note 6).

[169] Cabrera de Córdoba, *Relaciones,* 79 (as in note 36); *CCE,* 1: 49 (as in note 5); Gachard, *Actes,* 257-259 (as in note 89).

rebels – affected politics at the Spanish court. Defeat or success in the North respectively weakened or strengthened the government in Spain. Peace negotiations with the rebels were used in a similar way. The results of Spanish policy in the Netherlands had the potential to influence the outcome of the struggle for power at the Spanish court, especially after 1611, when the faction of the duke of Lerma, Philip III's *privado*, was showing its first signs of weakness.[170] The Netherlands offered Lerma's opponents an indirect way to attack his position and to undermine the king's confidence in his favorite. It is therefore no surprise that the struggle between court factions in Madrid – first between *lermistas* and their opponents, and after the removal of Lerma from power, mainly between the former members of the anti-Lerma faction – also had offshoots at the archducal court and thus influenced the formation of factions at the archducal court. The presence of the Army of Flanders would only strengthen this factional division.

A militarized court

If no way was found to guarantee the integrity of the Flemish territory, then the cession of the Netherlands to the Archdukes would eventually lead to the end of a Habsburg presence in Northern Europe. The economic situation of the country did not allow the formation and maintenance of a large army to protect it from the attacks of the United Provinces and, potentially, France. Therefore, the States General in Brussels accepted the secret arrangements that the three most important citadels of the country – Antwerp, Ghent and Cambrai – would remain under Spanish command.[171] At the same time the representatives suggested that the Army of Flanders should not be withdrawn from the Netherlands, but should stay to defend the new government.[172]

It is important not to forget the presence of this organization, completely parallel to the local court and government, ultimately obeying the king of Spain alone. In theory, the Army of Flanders was a

[170] For an analysis of the factions at the court of Philip III and the struggle for power, see Antonio Feros, *Kingship and Favoritism in the Spain of Philip III, 1598-1621* (Cambridge, 2000).

[171] Victor Brants (ed.), *Recueil des ordonnances des Pays-Bas: Règne d'Albert et Isabelle, 1597-1621* (Brussels, 1909), 1: 12-13.

[172] Leo Van der Essen, "Politieke geschiedenis van het Zuiden, 1585-1609," in Jan A. Van Houtte and others (eds.), *Algemene Geschiedenis der Nederlanden*, 12 vols. (Utrecht-Antwerp, 1949-1958), 5: 245-282, esp. 271.

potentially important instrument in the hands of Madrid that could be used to intervene in archducal policy. In practice, the archduke could not be deprived of the high command without affecting his reputation as a sovereign prince. Nevertheless, he would command the army not in his own name, but as the captain-general of the king.[173]

In the past, the captains-general had been given a fairly free hand with regard to disbursements from the military treasury. On several occasions their arbitrary policy, often contrary to the interests of the Spanish Council of State and Council of Finances, had provoked a certain uneasiness in Madrid.[174] Nevertheless, Albert could not be deprived of this competence without causing his displeasure and, even more importantly, without adversely affecting his authority. It was therefore important to surround the archduke with officers loyal to Madrid's policy, and to limit the influence of local opinions about how the war in the Netherlands should be conducted. To attain both objects, a certain degree of integration between the army and the archducal court was pursued.

This meant that the court of the Archdukes became the Habsburg court where the presence of military personnel was probably most strongly marked. Indeed, many of the senior officers in the army also held positions at court. A breakdown of the situation in the period from 1598 to 1605 yields astonishing results. The court and the army were directed by the same individual, don Francisco de Mendoza, *mayordomo mayor*, general of the cavalry, and second in command of the army. His successor at the head of the court, don Gerónimo Walter Zapata, was simultaneously *veedor general* from 1600 to 1603.[175] The *gentilhombre de la cámara* and *sumiller de corps* don Rodrigo Niño Lasso de la Vega was commander of the Spanish *lanceros* and *arcabuceros* that served as Albert's personal guard. Two *mayordomos* were also military men: don Diego de Ibarra was *veedor general* between 1593 and 1599,[176]

173 Esteban Estríngana, *Guerra y finanzas*, 83-85 (as in note 34).

174 Esteban Estríngana, *Guerra y finanzas*, 80-81 (as in note 34).

175 Parker, *The Army of Flanders*, 282 (as in note 45). Most of the highest ranking officers of the Army of Flanders are listed in the appendices on pages 281-286.

176 Don Diego de Ibarra originated from a family with a long military tradition. His father was Francisco de Ibarra, councillor of War to Philip II, who served in the Netherlands under the duke of Alva. His uncle Esteban was even Alva's secretary and later worked for the count of Fuentes and archduke Ernest. He would end his career as *secretario de Guerra*. Another uncle, Pedro, was *contador* of the army in Milan. See José Martínez Millán and Carlos Javier de Carlos Morales (eds.), *Felipe II, 1527-1598: La configuración de la monarquía hispana* (Salamanca, 1998), 406-407.

while the count of Montenegro, captain of the Neapolitan cavalry, took Amiens and later defended it against the troops of Henry IV.[177] Among the *gentilhombres de la cámara* we find don Diego de Acuña, commander of a company of cavalry,[178] don Alonso de Cárdenas, probably occupying a lower rank,[179] don Diego Mexía, captain of the light cavalry and probably a relative of don Agustín Mexía, *maestre de campo* and commander of the citadel of Antwerp,[180] and Gastón Spinola, count of Bruay, *maestre de campo* and since 1597 governor of Limburg.[181] Federico Spínola, admiral of the galleys at Sluis,[182] and don Luis de Velasco, general of the artillery in 1600 and of the cavalry from 1603, were simultaneously *gentilhombres de la boca.*[183] Don Juan de Marquelayn, one of the *capellanes de oratorio* of the archducal court chapel, served as head chaplain of the cavalry.[184] The *licenciado* Juan de Frías, ordinary chaplain and *secretario de la cámara*, combined his court offices from 1600 onwards with that of *superintendente de la justicia militar.*[185] Doctor Juan Roco de Campofrío, also a court chaplain, was at the same time *Vicario General* (head of the military almoners) and administrator of the Royal Military Hospital in Mechelen.[186]

Other senior officers that did not hold court offices were integrated by means of their status as *capitanes entretenidos cerca de la persona*. Geoffrey Parker estimates that there were 52 of them in 1596, and even 138 in 1608.[187] The most important had access to the court through the above mentioned *Estado de capitanes entretenidos*. Among them,

177 Cabrera de Córdoba, *Historia de Felipe II,* 3: 1563, 1597-1601 (as in note 82); Roco de Campofrío, *España en Flandes,* 177-179 (as in note 7).
178 *Codoin*, 42: 355-356 (as in note 35).
179 On 5 April 1600 Albert recommends him to the duke of Lerma because "nunca se le hizo merced en cosas del ejército." See *Codoin*, 42: 340 (as in note 35).
180 During the Battle of Nieuwpoort, don Diego Mexía, at the time a *menino* of Isabella and only twenty years old, prevented the archduke from being captured by the Dutch. See Roco de Campofrío, *España en Flandes,* 270 (as in note 7). During the first months of the siege of Ostend, don Agustín Mexía commanded the troops on the western side of the city. See Thomas, "De val van het Nieuwe Troje," in Thomas, *De val van het Nieuwe Troje,* 82-85 (as in note 41).
181 Roco de Campofrío, *España en Flandes,* 165 (as in note 7); Parker, *The Army of Flanders,* 161 (as in note 45).
182 Cox, *Vanden Tocht in Vlaenderen*, 62-63 (as in note 96).
183 Esteban Estríngana, *Guerra y finanzas,* 88, 95 (as in note 34).
184 *Codoin* 43: 67 (as in note 35).
185 *CCE,* 1: 51, 56 (as in note 5).
186 Roco de Campofrío, *España en Flandes,* 8 (as in note 7); Parker, *The Army of Flanders,* 167-169 (as in note 45).
187 Parker, *The Army of Flanders*, 108 (as in note 45).

the *maestres de campo,* the *veedor general* (when he was not already a member of the court), the *pagador general,* the *contador general* and the commanders of the citadels of Antwerp, Ghent and Cambrai were certainly influential.[188] On the other hand, the court was to some extent integrated in the army structures, as important courtiers also formed part of the rather informal Council of War in the Netherlands, together with senior officers and some local commanders, such as the count of Solre, *caballerizo mayor* of the archduke.[189]

On the other hand, the most important commanders of the Walloon and German regiments of the Army of Flanders also combined their military service with a position at court. Between 1596 and 1606 the baron of Barbançon, captain of the archducal archers, commanded the infantry regiment of colonel Tassis.[190] Count Frederick van den Bergh, captain of the guard of halberdiers, also had his own regiment of German infantry until it was disbanded in 1610. During the first months of the siege of Ostend, he would take charge of the troops attacking the city from the east.[191] Charles de Longueval, count of Bucquoy and *gentilhombre de la cámara*, commanded a regiment of Walloon infantry and was appointed general of the artillery in 1603.[192] René de Châlon, *gentilhombre de boca*, became *maestre de campo* of the baron de Molain's regiment of Walloon infantry after the death of Nicolas Catriz in 1604.[193] From 1597 onwards, the count of Solre was also captain-general of the *bandes d'Ordonnance* (troops of heavy cavalry financed by the States General) until 1602.[194] He was replaced by Charles-Alexander de Croy, count of Fontenoy and future marquis de Havré, *gentilhombre de la cámara* of Albert.[195] Barbançon's eldest brother, Charles, count of Arenberg, also *gentilhombre de la cámara*, was from 1599 Admiral of the Sea.[196]

188 AGR, *Audience*, no. 33/3, fo. 34r-v.

189 Parker, *The Army of Flanders*, 108 (as in note 45).

190 Georges Martin, *Histoire et généalogie des maisons de Ligne et d'Arenberg*, part 1: *Maison de Ligne*, 2 vols. (Lyon, 2003), 2: 187.

191 Thomas, "Het beleg van Oostende," 82-85 (as in note 41).

192 Charles Rahlenbeck, "Longueval (Charles-Bonaventure de)," in *Biographie nationale* (Brussels, 1868), 2: 359-368; Esteban Estríngana, *Guerra y finanzas,* 95 (as in note 34).

193 AGR, *Audience,* no. 33/4, fo. 67v; Jean Bruslé de Montpleinchamps, *Histoire de l'Archiduc Albert, gouverneur général puis prince souverain de la Belgique,* ed. Aimé L. P. de Robaulx de Soumoy (Brussels and The Hague, 1870), 347-348, 579.

194 Roco de Campofrío, *España en Flandes*, 161 (as in note 7).

195 AGR, *Audience,* no. 33/4, fo. 67r; G. Guillaume, "Croy (Charles-Alexandre de)," *Biographie nationale* (Brussels, 1873), 4: 555-558.

196 Louis-Prosper Gachard, "Arenberg (Charles, comte d')," *Biographie nationale* (Brussels, 1866), 1: 380-388, esp. 387.

One consequence of this integration of court and army was that the king of Spain disposed over an instrument to influence the composition of the household and to eliminate individuals that held opinions contrary to those of Madrid. Indeed, while he could not dismiss anybody from the Archdukes' service, he could recall them as officers of the army and then replace them. This happened with don Francisco de Mendoza, and again with don Gerónimo Walter Zapata, who were both called to account for errors they made as army officers, but at the same time left the archduke without a *mayordomo mayor*. The king thus created the possibility to send a candidate of his own to Brussels. At a lower level, Madrid sometimes ordered members of the army to report to the king personally, and obstructed their return, giving them other positions in the royal administration. This happened to, among others, Juan de Frías. All Albert could do in response was to protest, arguing that similar decisions taken without his consent adversely touched his *reputación*, but this did not stop Philip.

However, in the long term the integration of court and army had serious disadvantages. From the end of 1602, the Spanish Council of State reversed its policy completely. In the future, a strict separation of both institutions was pursued. In the first place, differing strategic priorities and the poor performance of Albert as captain-general convinced Philip and his councilors that it had been a mistake to entrust the supreme command of the army to a foreigner, that is, a non-Spanish commander. Poor tactical decisions had led to the defeat at Nieuwpoort. Next, instead of attacking the United Provinces from the east, as most of his Spanish generals had urged, the archduke laid siege to Ostend, a city that even Farnese had not been able to conquer. Once Ostend was invested, Albert proved unable to take the town, and his military adventure became an enormously costly enterprise. Moreover, his ill health several times prevented him from commanding the troops in person. The lack of progress in 1602 was clearly a consequence of this. The second problem derived from the first. When the archduke was not at Ostend, the army was deprived of its senior officers, whose household offices obliged them to reside at court rather than in the camp at Ostend. One of the complaints against *veedor general* Walter Zapata was, as has already been mentioned, his absence from the army.

As the disadvantages of the integration of court and army became ever clearer, a decision was taken in September 1603 to separate the supreme command of the Army of Flanders from the government of the Netherlands. If the senior commanders continued at court, Albert would hold a channel through which to maintain his influence in the army. Therefore, the newly appointed commander in chief did not become *mayordomo mayor* of the Archdukes, and the other army officers and *capitanes entretenidos* were presented with a choice between retaining their military command or their court office.[197] At the same time, the financial administration of the army was separated from the entourage of the archduke. A *Junta de Hacienda* in Brussels would henceforth decide upon military expenses. None of its three members – the *veedor general*, the *contador general* and the *pagador general* – were courtiers. Moreover, funds arriving from Spain were to be kept in a trunk with three locks and, the purpose being to keep the money away from "personas dependientes del Sr. Archiduque," the keys were not to be given to any confidant of Albert.[198] In order to avoid Albert's influence on the *Junta*, all three office-holders were replaced.[199]

The presence of the Army of Flanders and the integration of senior officers into the archducal household during the first years of the reign of Albert an Isabella inevitably influenced the formation of factions at court. One of the major problems of the army was the rivalry between the different 'nations' (*naciones*), specifically between the Spanish *tercios*

[197] The Council of State advised on 18 February 1603 "[...] que los que tienen cargos en el exerçito que requieran asistençia personal en ellos y acudir a las ocassiones, escojan el hazerlo o quedar siruiendo a sus Altezas, y los que agora tienen entretenimientos çerca de la persona del Sr. Archiduque, asistan con su Alteza, pues es aquella su obligaçion y los que no fueren desta calidad vayan a seruir en la infanteria, y en lo venidero se çierre la puerta a que ningun criado de su Alteza tenga offiçio ni sueldo en el exerçito," but the king was of the opinion "[que] no conuiene alargar el remedio, y assi se ordene preçissamente que los que tienen ofiçios y entretenimientos asistan de ordinario en el exerçito y que si tubieren otras ocupaçiones a que acudir, elijan dentro de quinçe dias lo vno o lo otro." See *Consultas,* 1: 315, 322 (as in note 6). However, it took a while before the separation was complete, and apparently several officers and *entretenidos* managed to maintain their position up to and even after the Truce. For example, don Alonso Dávalos, *maestre de campo* of an Italian *tercio*, and don Juan de Meneses, both *entretenidos* in 1605, were appointed *gentilhombre de la boca* after the Truce. Don Diego Mexía continued to combine his position in the army with that of *gentilhombre de la cámara* (AGR, *Chambre des Comptes,* no. 1837, fos. 39v, 105r, 306r).

[198] *Consultas,* 1: 336-338 (as in note 6). The Council of State had Juan de Mancisidor in mind.

[199] "Han proveido por veedor general del ejército de Flandes a don Francisco Vaca y Benavides [...], y por pagador al contador [Martín de] Unzueta, y a otro vizcaino [Asención de Eguigerem] por contador, *mudando los que allá hacian estos oficios, porque seguian las órdenes del Archiduque*, que era en mucho daño de la hacienda que se proveía de acá para las cosas de la guerra [my italics]." Cabrera de Córdoba, *Relaciones,* 174 (as in note 36). See also Esteban Estríngana, *Guerra y finanzas,* 86-106 (as in note 34).

viejos and the Italian, German, Walloon and Irish regiments. This rivalry affected the entire army structure, from the ordinary soldiers to the senior officers. On several occasions, Spanish officers refused to obey orders from their non-Spanish superiors.[200] Moreover, they frequently disagreed with the archduke's strategy. In fact, they had serious, and understandable, reservations about accepting his authority. They and their elite troops had seen many years of active service, and now they were expected to obey the orders of a newcomer with comparatively little experience of warfare in the Netherlands. As a consequence, many Spanish senior officers maintained a direct correspondence with the king of Spain, frequently complaining about the strategic and political decisions being made in Brussels. On the other hand, as commander in chief Albert had to pay special attention to the Spanish *tercios*, the army's elite forces. This provoked discontent among the local regiments and the Flemish nobility, and stimulated the rivalry between the *naciones*, for instance, during the siege of Ostend.[201] It would be surprising if these differences had been contained in the army and had not influenced the formation of factions at court.

Factional struggle at the archducal court

When discussing factions at the archducal court, one should take into account that the struggle between a more nationally orientated party and its Spanish counterparts was not about the 'independence' of the newly created state, as most of the Belgian historians of the nineteenth and the first half of the twentieth century assumed. Of course the Archdukes defended their sovereignty, not least because it was vital to their *reputación*, a word repeated endlessly in the sources. But they never dreamt of detaching their country from the Spanish Monarchy, and very soon the lack of an heir removed any doubt about the future of the country anyway. Albert's main objective was the same as Philip's: to end the war with the rebels as soon as possible and thus free his nephew and the Netherlands from a conflict that was costing the Habsburg Monarchy dearly in human and financial resources.

Of course, both rulers differed on how best to end the war. Philip wanted no less than the full recovery of the rebellious Provinces, and

[200] Parker, *The Army of Flanders,* 116 (as in note 45); Esteban Estríngana, *Guerra y finanzas,* 90-91 (as in note 34); Louant, *Correspondance*, 3: 464 (as in note 55); *Consultas*, 2: 113-116 (as in note 6).
[201] Louant, *Correspondance,* 3: 257 (as in note 55).

therefore insisted on major military campaigns in the Rhineland. His view was endorsed by the senior officers of the army, such as don Luis de Velasco, who thoroughly disapproved of the decision to invest Ostend and, once this had been done, wanted to end the siege as soon as possible, even if this meant simply abandoning it. Albert, aware of the instability of his authority in the South, first wanted to address the grievance of the States General and the States of Flanders by eliminating the only Protestant enclave in southern territory, thus pacifying the country and consolidating his position. He also dreamt of reconquering the North, but soon realized that only a negotiated settlement would put an end to the hostilities. Once a compromise with the United Provinces was reached, soldiers would receive their back pay, and the mutinies that were so damaging to small towns and the countryside would come to an end. Moreover, the Army of Flanders would be downsized and/or employed elsewhere.

In order to reach a settlement with the North, Albert from 1600 onwards sought a peace treaty with the Dutch States General, rather than a truce. Only a treaty would bring a long term solution. The king, on the contrary, wanted to avoid such an arrangement at any price. Instead, he opted for a ceasefire and a truce. This would avoid negotiations on the position of Roman Catholics in the Republic and on religious tolerance in the South. But most of all, Philip suspected that Albert wanted a peace treaty in order to get the Spanish troops out of the country and acquire control of the three citadels that were in Spanish hands.[202] Solre's plans for the creation of a national army only confirmed his conviction.[203] In this way, the influence of Madrid on the archducal regime would inevitably diminish, as power would fall into the hands of the *naturales*. The experiment with cardinal Andreas, interim governor-general during Albert's voyage to Spain, had demonstrated the danger of such policy: his attempts to govern without the Spaniards, in the first place don Francisco de Mendoza, were welcomed by the Flemish population and had occasioned the expression of anti-Spanish sentiment all over the country.[204]

The search for a settlement with the North stimulated the formation of a Spanish faction in Brussels. During the spring and the summer of 1601, to prevent the conclusion of a disadvantageous peace, its members unfolded a major diplomatic offensive, directed by the Spanish Council

202 *CCE*, 1: 75-78 (as in note 5).

203 See note 89.

204 Louant, *Correspondance*, 3: 54-58 (as in note 55).

of State, aimed at changing Albert's mind. At the centre of this group was the Spanish ambassador, don Baltasar de Zúñiga, who confronted the archduke with the views of king Philip and reminded him several times that he was not to pursue a foreign policy at odds with Madrid's.[205] Zúñiga was assisted by Fernando Carrillo, the *superintendente de justicia militar*, who received orders from Madrid to supervise the negotiations of a truce, not a peace treaty, with the rebels. They were to abort the informal talks – including the proposal of religious tolerance and the departure of the 'foreigners,' meaning Spaniards – that the archduke and Jean Richardot, president of the Privy Council, had started with a representative of Maurice of Nassau in the summer of 1601.[206] Attempts to convince the archduke of the virtues of a truce were made by other channels, namely by the courtiers don Diego de Ibarra and don Rodrigo Niño Lasso de la Vega.[207] Niño Lasso de la Vega in particular seems to have been a key figure for those trying to control the archduke.[208]

By the end of October of 1601, Albert finally abandoned the idea of a peace treaty and accepted the solution of a ceasefire.[209] Around this time, the papal nuncio Ottavio Mirto Frangipani observed in one of his letters that although the archduke was the lord of the Netherlands, the

205 *Consultas*, 1: 134 (as in note 6); *CCE*, 1: 59, 68, 73 (as in note 5).

206 *CCE*, 1: 66 (as in note 5).

207 Ibarra was an outspoken opponent of any agreement with the Dutch rebels. In light of his political conviction it is no surprise that in 1607 Philip relied on him to keep him informed about the whole peace process and to ensure that royal interests were not prejudiced, thus trying to regain Madrid's control over the negotiations. He was, above all, to try to prevent Albert and Spínola from recognizing the Northern provinces as independent. Ibarra initially succeeded in steeling Albert not to accept this condition without compensation on matters of commerce and religion. He nevertheless did not participate actively in the negotiations, because the States General of the United Provinces would not recognize him as a representative of Philip III, and he was ultimately unable to stop the peace process. The final reports he sent to Madrid, however, were extremely negative about Albert and Spínola, chiming with the opinion of don Pedro Franqueza. Ibarra stated that Albert was making peace with the Dutch only to revenge himself on the king for having lost the high command of the Army of Flanders and the control over its financial resources, while Spínola was above all promoting his own career at court. See *CCE*, 1: 253-258 (as in note 5); García García, *La Pax Hispanica*, 66 (as in note 83); Van der Essen, "Politieke geschiedenis van het Zuiden," 281 (as in note 172); Feros, *Kingship and Favoritism,* 192 (as in note 170); Paul Allen, *Felipe III y la Pax Hispanica, 1598-1621* (Madrid, 2001), 249-252, 259-261.

208 *CCE*, 1: 81-84 (as in note 5).

209 *CCE*, 1: 88, 93-94 (as in note 5).

Spaniards were as powerful as before the cession.[210] The complete failure of the general assault on Ostend in January 1602, with more than 2500 casualties,[211] discouraged the archduke and was the start of a series of semi-official contacts with agents from the North in order to conclude a *suspensión de armas*, just as the king had urged.[212] Later attempts by the States General to convince Albert of the advantages of a formal peace – not in the least the departure of foreign troops – produced no effect.[213] The Spanish faction seemed to have gained full control over the archduke.

The next step in the recovery of Spanish power in the Netherlands was the separation of the government and the supreme command of the army, to which reference has already been made. By 1602 Albert was willing to accept an assistant bearing the title of general of the cavalry, the rank held by don Francisco de Mendoza before he was captured by the rebels. Philip had in mind don Luis de Velasco, general of the artillery since 1600, but the archduke preferred the Italian *maestre de campo* Giorgio Basta, who at the time was serving the emperor. Finally, in the spring of 1603, Velasco was promoted general of the cavalry without Albert's consent.[214] The arrival of Ambrogio Spínola would temporarily solve the problem, as he offered to direct the troops around Ostend. However, technically Albert was still the commander in chief of the Army of Flanders. Thereupon, Madrid took the next step and decided to replace him at the head of the army. Only somebody close to the archduke would be able to convince him of this, but the same person would also have to enjoy the full confidence of the king. Finally, this difficult task was entrusted to don Rodrigo Niño Lasso de la Vega. At the same time, Niño Lasso had to convince the archduke not to allow the convocation of the States General, which the deputies of Flanders had requested in consequence of the Dutch invasion of the county.[215]

[210] Louant, *Correspondance*, 3: 272 (as in note 55).

[211] The general assault was the archduke's answer to governor Francis Vere's stratagem of agreeing to a ceasefire and pretending a willingness to enter into negotiations for the surrender of the city, solely as a delaying tactic while awaiting reinforcements. Albert considered this ploy to be against the laws of war. See Thomas, "Het beleg van Oostende," 91-92 (as in note 41).

[212] *Consultas*, 1: 183-184 (as in note 6).

[213] *Consultas*, 1: 191-192 (as in note 6).

[214] *Codoin* 42: 446-447 (as in note 35).

[215] *Consultas*, 2: 72 (as in note 6).

Although at first Albert was not willing to accept Madrid's settlement on the *capitanía general* of the army, the loss of Sluis in August 1604, one month before the fall of Ostend, finally made him comply. Albert in practice abandoned the command of the army to Spínola. Later on, Philip appointed don Agustín Mexía to the position of *maestre de campo general*, and once again it was Niño Lasso de la Vega who had to communicate the news to Albert. From 1605, Mexía would direct the Army of Flanders.[216] Nevertheless, a few weeks later Albert rejected the control of the Spanish party over his government. Although Mexía had already been appointed, the archduke wrote the king that another candidate was more eligible: his full support went to Spínola, victor of Ostend. In view of the financial resources over which the Genoese general disposed, and of the willingness of Albert to delegate his authority over the army to Spínola in particular, Madrid appointed him as the new *maestre de campo general* of the Army of Flanders. Thus, a compromise between the king and the archduke had been reached. Although Albert abandoned the supreme command of the army, he was replaced by somebody whom he had chosen.[217]

The arrival of Ambrogio Spínola seems to have consolidated the formation of factions at the Brussels court. Although a confidant of Albert, with his appointment Spínola entered the service of Philip III, as Alicia Esteban Estríngana quite rightly emphasizes.[218] From the beginning, he would be more than just a military commander. Indeed, the king entrusted him with the execution of several royal plans that arranged the transfer of power in the Netherlands in case one of the Archdukes should die, the first of which dates from as early as 1606.[219] From then on, he enjoyed Philip's – and Lerma's – complete confidence, and together with the Secretary of State and War, don Juan de Mancisidor, he put into practice a policy that combined the defense of the interests of the Spanish Monarchy with the archducal desire for peace and the preservation of archducal *reputación*.[220] This had, by then, become less complicated than in 1600. The fall into disgrace in 1607 of Secretary of State don Pedro Franqueza – who firmly opposed any

[216] Esteban Estríngana, *Guerra y finanzas,* 89-106 (as in note 34).

[217] Esteban Estríngana, *Guerra y finanzas*, 107-122 (as in note 34).

[218] Esteban Estríngana, "Felipe III y los estados de Flandes" (as in note 2).

[219] *CCE,* 1: 225-227 (as in note 5).

[220] On Mancisidor, see Joseph Lefèvre, "Don Juan de Mancicidor, secrétaire d'État et de Guerre de l'archiduc Albert, 1596-1618," *Revue belge de philologie et d'histoire* 4 (1925), 697-714.

agreement with the rebels – and the changed climate at the court in Madrid as a result of it, clearly prepared the way for new negotiations with the Dutch.[221]

At the archducal court, Spínola and Mancisidor counted on the good services of Albert's confessor, don Iñigo de Brizuela, referred to above. Brizuela belonged to an order that enjoyed Lerma's patronage and continued to defend him even after his removal from power.[222] Together, Spínola, Mancisidor and Brizuela acted as the extension of Lerma's clique in the Netherlands. For example, they organized the oath of allegiance that Philip III requested of the different Provincial States, thus significantly facilitating the future reincorporation of the Netherlands into the Spanish Monarchy.[223]

In due time Spínola's rise at court gave occasion to the formation of a second Spanish faction in Brussels that was clearly anti-Spínola. Indeed, the promotion to the high command of the army of a non-Spanish general who was not even a subject (*vasallo*) of the king, was received well neither by the Spanish Council of State nor by the senior officers in the Netherlands, and especially not by don Agustín Mexía and don Luis de Velasco.[224] During the campaign of 1604, Velasco and Spínola each tried to blame the other for the loss of Sluis. Albert was also inclined to blame Velasco, but did nothing because he suspected that the Spanish general had the king's full backing.[225] The next year, Velasco accompanied Spínola's army to the North and contributed to the taking of Lingen, Oldenzaal and Wachtendonk, to the entire satisfaction of the commander in chief and of the king.[226] This did not stop him from becoming, over the years, Spínola's fiercest opponent and the centre of a Spanish anti-Spínola faction. He received the support of his brother-in-law, don Iñigo de Borja, *maestre de campo* at Ostend and from 1606

[221] Feros, *Kingship and Favoritism,* 192-197 (as in note 170).

[222] Feros, *Kingship and Favoritism,* 261 (as in note 170).

[223] Esteban Estríngana, "Felipe III y los estados de Flandes" (as in note 2); Henri Lonchay, "Le serment de fidélité prêté par les Belges à Philippe III en 1616," in *Mélanges Paul Frédéricq* (Brussels, 1904), 311-317.

[224] A majority of the members of the Council would have preferred to see the marquis of Montenegro at the head of the army. *Consultas*, 2: 113-116 (as in note 6). Six years later, in 1610, Velasco was still reminding the king of the fact that Spínola had been promoted over his head and that he deserved considerable compensation. See *CCE*, 1: 358 (as in note 5).

[225] *Codoin* 42: 497-498 (as in note 35).

[226] *CCE*, 1: 221-222 (as in note 5).

governor of the citadel of Antwerp,[227] and of don Juan de Ribas, governor of Sluis until 1604, later commander of the citadel of Cambrai. At court, they could count on don Diego de Ibarra and, apparently, on don Rodrigo Niño Lasso de la Vega. Niño Lasso in particular became very powerful after 1609, when he not only combined the leading court offices of *sumiller de corps*, *mayordomo mayor* (1613) and *caballerizo mayor* (1615), but was also created count of Añover and appointed a member of the Spanish Council of War (both in 1609). He probably took advantage of the new political circumstances created by the Twelve Year's Truce. In fact, many senior officers left the Netherlands and when the Jülich-Cleves succession crisis broke out, part of the army was sent to the Holy Roman Empire, thus keeping even Spínola away from the court. In 1619 Pierre Bergeron observed that "celuy qui est le favory de l'archiduc et qui gouverne et traicte toutes sortes d'affaires sous luy, c'est un comte d'Ognavel ou Agnovel, espagnol de grande maison."[228] His capacity of maintaining an intermediate position between the archduke and the king, and of serving as the confidant of both perhaps explains his rapid rise at court.

Factional struggle at the court of Philip III seems to have shaped and consolidated this anti-Spínola party. From 1611 the power of the duke of Lerma was being challenged by his son, the duke of Uceda, and by Fray Luis de Aliaga, Philip III's confessor. They increasingly questioned Lerma's international policy, and above all his decision to conclude an agreement with the king's rebels, which had put *raison d'état* above the duty of the Spanish Monarchy to defend Catholicism at all times and had thus provoked its loss of prestige and power.[229] The example of the opposition to Lerma in Spain stimulated the enemies of Lerma and Spínola in the Netherlands in their struggle for power. Indeed, the Truce had caused much discontent among Albert's military commanders and advisers, as it cost them political and military influence, while Spínola became almost almighty. At the time, not only Velasco and Borja, but also Niño Lasso de la Vega, opposed the ceasefire

[227] They were both married to daughters of Maximilian de Hénin-Liétard, count of Boussu. See Detlev Schwennicke (ed.), *Europäische Stammtafeln: Stammtafeln zur Geschichte der europäischen Staaten*, 24 vols. (Marburg, 1960-2007), 6: 108. It took some years before they met in opposition to Spínola. In 1607-8 they had quarreled so violently over Borja's future spouse that they were imprisoned by the archduke. See *CCE*, 1: 270, 272 (as in note 5).

[228] Michelant, *Voyage de Pierre Bergeron*, 345 (as in note 154).

[229] Feros, *Kingship and Favoritism*, 206, 224-225, 234 (as in note 170).

of 1607 and the subsequent negotiations with the United Provinces.[230] Soon, several members of the faction, among them Velasco and, much more marginally, Niño Lasso de la Vega, were involved in an obscure plan to attack Sluis with the knowledge of the Dutch in order to scuttle the 1609 settlement, employing the services of royal spy Diego López Sueyro. Albert discovered the plot only by chance and had Sueyro arrested, without informing Niño Lasso de la Vega.[231] A few years later, their names turned up in the campaign against the Truce waged by the Carmelite friar Jerónimo Gracián de la Madre de Dios, household preacher to the Spanish ambassador, don Felipe Folch de Cardona y Borch, marquis of Guadaleste, and chaplain to the garrison of the citadel of Antwerp – commanded by don Iñigo de Borja – and probably introduced at court by Niño Lasso de la Vega, whose family supported the Carmelite movement. From his Brussels convent, Gracián provided Philip III and the Council of State in Madrid with reports on the deplorable situation of Catholicism and the growth of Protestantism in the Southern Netherlands, thus bringing the archduke's religious policy and Lerma's *pax hispanica* into discredit.[232] When by 1615, as a result of the Savoy crisis, Lerma's opponents in Madrid openly called for the Spanish Monarchy to take a more active role in European conflicts, and the faction of Uceda and Aliaga strengthened its position at court, in Brussels don Luis de Velasco and don Iñigo de Borja were forming a Spanish 'party' opposed to Spínola.[233] They received the support of Guadaleste, who was a clear supporter of the political viewpoints of Uceda and Aliaga.[234] As a consequence, Spínola countered any moves by Guadaleste to regain pre-eminence at the Brussels court, probably in an attempt to control the attacks on Lerma from the Netherlands. In this, he was supported by Philip III and Lerma himself.[235]

[230] *CCE*, 1: 257-258 (as in note 5).

[231] *CCE*, 1: 360-361 (as in note 5); Miguel Ángel Echevarría Bacigalupe, *La diplomacia secreta en Flandes, 1598-1643* (Leioa, 1984), 148-154.

[232] *CCE*, 1: 432 (as in note 5).

[233] E. K. Purnell and A. B. Hinds, eds., *Report on the Manuscripts of the Most Honourable The Marquess of Downshire formerly preserved at Easthampstead Park, Berkshire*, vols. 2-7: *Papers of William Trumbull the Elder* (London, 1936-1995), 5: 351.

[234] Guadaleste repeatedly criticized the archduke's pacific policy. Calderón's mission to negotiate the transformation of the Truce into a more enduring peace was even held back from him. See Joseph Lefèvre, "Les ambassadeurs d'Espagne à Bruxelles sous le règne de l'archiduc Albert (1598-1621)," *Revue belge de philologie et d'histoire* 2 (1923), 61-80, esp. 72, 74.

[235] Esteban Estríngana, "Felipe III y los estados de Flandes" (as in note 2); Feros, *Kingship and Favoritism*, 210 (as in note 170).

In Madrid, the anti-Spínola faction was supported by several members of the Council of State, among them don Agustín Mexía, who had been appointed councilor to ease the pain of his missed promotion to *maestre de campo general*, and from 1617 onwards don Baltasar de Zúñiga, an ally of the Uceda-Aliaga faction.[236] It was, for example, don Agustín Mexía who proposed in February 1613 that Spínola should be obliged to report on the army and its finances to the Spanish ambassador, as had been the situation before his appointment as commander in chief. Mexía insisted on the necessity of subordinating the Genoese general to Guadaleste, instead of the other way round. Only then could the king's authority in the Netherlands be preserved.[237] In 1620, Zúñiga for his part leaked information to the king on the secret pourparlers between the archduke and Maurice of Nassau concerning the prolongation of the Truce, thus compromising the whole enterprise.[238]

The fall of Lerma in 1618 and the steady rise to power, not of Uceda and Aliaga, but of their former ally don Baltasar de Zúñiga, reinforced the anti-Spínola faction in Brussels and affected the position of Spínola in the Netherlands as an advocate of peace with the Dutch. In 1618, when the Council of War (abolished in 1609) was reinstalled after the death of don Juan de Mancisidor, both Velasco and Añover were appointed, together with Spínola, the count of Bucquoy, and don Fernando Girón, the Spanish ambassador in Paris.[239] With the appointment of the marquis of Bedmar in 1618, the king seemed determined to gain control over Albert and Spínola in preparation for the reincorporation of the Netherlands into the Spanish Monarchy and the war with the United Provinces.[240] One of Bedmar's first tasks was to inform Spínola that after the archduke's death the civil and military government of the Southern Netherlands would not be separated. Thus, he would serve under Isabella as her lieutenant. This decision was inspired by Zúniga and Aliaga.[241] Finally, in 1620, don Luis de Velasco

[236] Esteban Estríngana, *Guerra y finanzas,* 120-121, 189 (as in note 34); Feros, *Kingship and Favoritism,* 210-211 (as in note 170).

[237] *CCE,* 1: 396-397 (as in note 6). In 1615 the newly appointed *veedor general* don Francisco Andía de Irarrazábal would come into conflict with Spínola on this matter. See Lefèvre, "Le Ministère Espagnol de l'Archiduc Albert," 215 (as in note 155).

[238] *CCE,* 1: 570 (as in note 5).

[239] *CCE,* 1: 512 (as in note 5).

[240] Lefèvre, "Les ambassadeurs d'Espagne à Bruxelles," 75-79 (as in note 234); Esteban Estríngana, "Los estados de Flandes" (as in note 2).

[241] Lefèvre, "Les ambassadeurs d'Espagne à Bruxelles," 78 (as in note 234); *CCE,* 1: 559 (as in note 5).

was appointed provisional commander in chief, in the eventuality of Spínola's incapacity or death, of the army that was to operate in the Palatinate; while don Iñigo de Borja became acting commander of chief of the Army of Flanders until the return of Velasco or Spínola.[242] In Madrid, as well as in Brussels, the defenders of a strong and military active monarchy had prevailed. The Spanish faction was clearly ready for the imminent reincorporation of the Southern Netherlands into the Spanish empire.

242 *CCE*, 1: 569-570 (as in note 5).

"*Vous estez les premiers vassaux que j'aye et que j'aime le plus.*" Burgundians in the Brussels courts of the widowed Isabella and of the Cardinal-Infant don Ferdinand (1621-1641)*

Birgit Houben

Introduction

The Spanish Monarchy was a composite state made up of various principalities and territories, each with its own languages, customs, economies and legal systems. The only thing that all these different lands had in common was the person of the ruler. Within the Monarchy, personal origins depended not only on one's place of birth, but also on the system of legal rules and privileges that defined that place. This makes the term 'nation' highly problematic, not only because the word had little exact definition at the time, but also because we now use it in a very different sense. A subject of the Spanish Monarchy might be Spanish, Italian, Portuguese or Netherlandish, but one could also speak of Castile and Aragon, or Brabant and Flanders, as distinct nations. Indeed, contemporaries sometimes went so far as to speak of the *naciones* of Seville, Lisbon and Florence. Somebody from Barcelona might, all at the same time, be of the Spanish, Aragonese, Catalan and Barcelonan nations.[1] The 'nation' to which a subject of the king of Spain belonged could be reducible to the most local unit of government. This makes it

* I would like to thank Karine Klein, conservator at the Bibliothèque Municipale de Besançon, Paul Delsalle, Peter De Cauwer and René Vermeir for their help and advice. Abbreviations: AGS: Archivo General de Simancas; AGR: Archives Générales du Royaume, Brussels; BMB: Bibliothèque municipale de Besançon; KB: Royal Library of Belgium, Brussels; RAH: Real Academia de Historia; *CC*: Collection Chifflet; *CSC*: Colección Salazar y Castro; *E*: estado; *GR*: Geheime Raad; *SSO*: Secretariat of State and War; ms: manuscript.

[1] Bernardo J. García García, "Presentación," in Antonio Alvarez-Ossorio Alvariño and Bernardo J. García García (eds.), *La Monarquía de las naciones: Patria, nación y naturaleza en la Monarquía de España* (Madrid, 2004), 19; Xavier Gil Pujol, "Un rey, una fe, muchas naciones: Patria y nación en la España de los siglos XVI y XVII," in *idem*, 39-76.

clear that in the territories of the king of Spain, the term 'nation' had layers of signification rather than a uniform meaning. At a local level, the people of the time undoubtedly felt their closest loyalty to be to their native province, giving the term a regional meaning. But in an international context, whether through contacts between the various realms within the Spanish Monarchy, or contacts with subjects of other monarchs, the geographical concept of the homeland broadened, so that a subject of the Spanish monarch would consider himself or herself primarily as a Spaniard, Southern Netherlander or Italian. For the purposes of the present study, this wider use of the term 'nation' seems most appropriate. We will be discussing Spaniards, Southern Netherlanders and Burgundians, although this last group was, again, a more regional designation. But as the Franche-Comté of Burgundy was comparatively isolated from all the other Spanish-Habsburg possessions, no broader geographical term can be applied to this province.[2]

The Franche-Comté or Free County of Burgundy, just to the east of the duchy of Burgundy, was one part of the Spanish-Habsburg composite state. The Franche-Comté had been among the dower lands of Margaret of Male (1350-1405), heiress of the count of Flanders, at her marriage to Philip the Bold, duke of Burgundy (1342-1404). This couple laid the basis for a brand new dynasty that systematically acquired considerable territory. After the death of duke Charles the Bold in 1477 his only child Mary of Burgundy inherited this complex of states. The lack of a male heir meant that Louis XI of France laid claim to the duchy of Burgundy. Philip the Bold had, after all, only been enfeoffed with the duchy in 1364 as an apanage from his father, France's king John the Good. Louis, however, not only occupied the duchy, but also invaded the Franche-Comté. The free county resisted this annexation and in 1493 France was forced to return it to Mary's son, Philip the Fair. Thus the Franche-Comté was to remain a possession of the Spanish-Habsburg heirs to the Burgundian inheritance until the Peace of Nijmegen in 1678. After the loss of the ancestral duchy of Burgundy – a fact from 1477, but only officially accepted at the Peace of Cambrai in 1529 – the title of Burgundy passed to the Franche-Comté, as "le plus antique patrimoine de la maison de Bourgogne," and henceforth 'Burgundians' meant the Franc-Comtois. In 1548 Charles

[2] John H. Elliott also takes the view that "loyalties were overwhelmingly reserved for the province of origin" but that "growing contacts with the outer world did something to give the natives of the peninsula a feeling of being Spaniards." See *Imperial Spain, 1469-1716* (London, 1965), 7.

V brought together his territories in the Low Countries, or *pays de par-deça*, and the Franche-Comté of Burgundy, or *pays de par-delà*, in a new unity, the Burgundian Circle of the Holy Roman Empire. But the Franche-Comté, a fifteen-day ride from Brussels and lying like an island in a sea of non-Habsburg territories, by no means felt united with the Low Countries. The Burgundian dukes had given the Comtois their own Parlement, university and administrative institutions, so that the Franche-Comté had little in common with the Netherlandish territories. The only tie, apart from the person of the prince, was the fact that from 1531 the Franche-Comté was to be ruled from Brussels. Charles V formally provided for Burgundians to be called to Brussels to advise on matters affecting the distant county. In the following decades, people from the Franche-Comté were prominent among those active in the central organs of government in Brussels. Figures such as Nicolas and Antoine Perrenot de Granvelle, Jean Richardot, Jean-Froissard de Broissia, and Nicolas Damant, a Southern Netherlander of Burgundian ancestry, had spectacular careers. The "plus antique patrimoine" enjoyed considerable autonomy through its involvement in central government, with the stipulation that the Privy Council in Brussels could only consider an *affaire comtoise* if it was allocated to a Burgundian councilor, and through the juridical sovereignty of the Franche-Comté, reflected in the powers of the Parlement of Dole, and the fact that this last institution, like all other administrative bodies within the Franche-Comté itself, was staffed entirely by Franc-Comtois. This autonomy was reinforced both by the remoteness of the Franche-Comté and by the absence of a court or other seat of central government in the county. Lucien Febvre was probably right in speaking of a "nationalisme naissant" in the 16th-century Franche-Comté. This was the period in which the first descriptions, maps and histories of the area were published.[3]

[3] See Jean-François Solnon, *Quand la Franche-Comté était espagnole* (Paris, 1983), 16-25 and endnote 218; Maurice Gresset and Jean-Marc Debard, "La Franche-Comté des Habsbourg," in Roland Fiétier and Claude I. Brelot (eds.), *Histoire de la Franche-Comté*, (Toulouse, 1977), 205-212; Marc Jacobs, *Parateksten, netwerken en conventies in de Spaanse Nederlanden en Franche-Comté (1621-1678): de familie Chifflet uit Besançon* (doctoral thesis, Vrije Universiteit Brussel, 1999), 252; Wim P. Blockmans, "De vorming van een politieke unie (veertiende-zestiende eeuw)," in Johan C.H. Blom and Emiel Lamberts (eds.), *Geschiedenis van de Nederlanden* (Baarn, 2004), 90-92; Lucien Febvre, *Philippe II et la Franche-Comté: Étude d'histoire politique, religieuse et sociale* (Paris, 1912), 93-119. Hugo De Schepper is of the opinion that the autonomy of the Franche-Comté was less extensive than that of the peripheral provinces of the Southern

The pronounced geographic diversity of the Spanish Monarchy was highly visible in, for instance, the administrative cadres and the army, where men of various backgrounds were employed. This diversity was equally apparent in the entourage of the sovereign. The court, and specifically the royal household, was, after all, one of the most important places in which the ruler could attempt to integrate the various territorial elites of his empire.[4] It is no surprise that the household was truly multinational.[5] A number of studies have shown that the same remarkable geographical diversity was also a characteristic of the courts of the governors-general of the Low Countries.[6] Furthermore, after the gradual *castellanización*[7] of the Madrid court under Philip II, the court policy of *naciones* probably became even more pronounced in Brussels. The geographical origins of members of the Brussels court, how these changed over time, the relative strength of the different groups, and the degree and types of interaction between them, are therefore important issues to study. There are a number of indications that these various groups brought their own norms and values with them, which could give rise to tensions.[8] We do have to ask ourselves in how far the elites of the disparate Spanish-Habsburg possessions were interchangeable, and whether they formed closed groups at the Brussels court or, on the contrary, forged trans-national alliances.

Netherlands, but I would suggest that the Franche-Comté was a far more important territory (as will be discussed later) than were such peripheral territories. See Hugo De Schepper, "La Franche-Comté, Besançon et les Pays-Bas à la fin du XVIe siècle: Un lien faible?" in Paul Delsalle and André Ferrer (eds.), *Les enclaves territoriales aux Temps Modernes (XVIe-XVIIIe siècles)*, Annales littéraires de l'Université de Franche-Comté 706 (Besançon, 2000), 328-329.

4 José Eloy Hortal, "La casa del archiduque Ernesto durante su gobierno en los Países Bajos (1593-1595)," in Alvarez-Ossorio Alvariño and García García [see n. 1], 193.

5 José Martínez Millán, "Las naciones en el servicio doméstico de los Austrias españoles (siglo XVI)," in Alvarez-Ossorio Alvariño and García García [see n. 1], 131-161; Santiago Fernández Conti and Félix Labrador Arroyo, "'Entre Madrid y Lisboa': El servicio de la nación portuguesa a través de la Casa Real, 1581-1598," in *idem*, 163-191.

6 Eloy Hortal, "La casa," 193-213; Diederik Lanoye, "Structure and Composition of the Household of the Archdukes," in Werner Thomas and Luc Duerloo (eds.), *Albert & Isabella, 1598-1621: Essays* (Turnhout, 1998), 107-119; Ellen Roegis, *Het hof van don Juan José de Austria, landvoogd in de Habsburgse Nederlanden (1656-1658)*, (Master's thesis, Ghent University, 2006), 79.

7 On this *castellanización*, see Martínez Millán, "Las naciones," 142-143.

8 See e.g. Eloy Hortal, "La casa", passim.

This article will attempt to clarify the position of the Burgundians in the successive Brussels courts of the widowed Isabella (1621-1633) and of the Cardinal-Infant don Ferdinand (1634-1641). This topic was not chosen at random. Examination of the sources relating to these two households shows that there was extremely close contact between the court office-holders from the Franche-Comté, and that despite their small numbers they played a leading role. This finding is in stark contrast to the assertions of other historians that the Burgundians at the Brussels court formed a tiny group of little importance, and simply count them as an adjunct to the Southern Netherlanders.[9] Are these assertions correct? Or should we go by the sources? In other words, did the Burgundian court dignitaries really play a prominent role in Brussels? And if so, how can this be explained? First we will give an overview of the court servants with Burgundian backgrounds, before studying their mutual relations and contacts. Could they count on one another to get ahead in this competitive environment, and if so, did this make them a close-knit group? Their relations with Isabella and with the Cardinal-Infant will then be illuminated, to see whether they had influence with their rulers, as will the relations between these Burgundians and their home base, the Franche-Comté. Were they able to turn their position at the Brussels court to the profit of their homeland, and did they become real power brokers who mediated between the central authorities and the regional and civic elites of the Franche-Comté? Finally, this case study will be used to provide an answer to the question of whether there was any kind of nationalities policy at court. This article seeks to contribute not just to the history of the Brussels court, but also to the history of the Free County, which Marc Jacobs has diagnosed as suffering undue neglect in the historical study of the Spanish Netherlands. He indicates, quite rightly, that the Franche-Comté needs to be given a higher profile in Belgian historical studies in order to emphasize that this apparent 'appendage' has to be taken into account in writing the history of the Southern Netherlands.[10]

[9] Lanoye, "Structure", 107; Roegis, *Het hof*, 79.

[10] Jacobs, *Parateksten*, 4.

The Burgundians in the households of Isabella and of the Cardinal-Infant: an introduction

Our subject here will be five Burgundian families who held high court office between 1621 and 1641. We will see that these families were very closely linked to one another, either through marriage or through patron-client relationships. It has to be emphasized that there were other Franc-Comtois serving in both households, but that they will not be considered here because they were among the lower office-holders of the court, such as the staff of the kitchens or the stables. It is not that these figures are of any less interest, but that the sources seldom go beyond their name and position. For many of the holders of lower places at court, the sources do not even provide evidence of their origins.[11]

The families d'Andelot, de Rye and de la Baume

Ferdinand le Blanc d'Andelot, Lord of Olans, Mignot and Myon, served as *mayordomo* in Brussels for at least thirty years. He is mentioned in this position at the court of the Archdukes as early as 1608. After the archduke Albert's death he continued to serve under Isabella – and later under her nephew Ferdinand – as *primer mayordomo*. He died in office in 1638.[12] He clearly belonged to a family with a strong record of service at Habsburg courts, for his father, Jean-Baptist, had been a *gentilhombre de la casa* to Philip II, and his grandfather *caballerizo mayor* to Charles V. One of Ferdinand's sons, Nicolas-Antoine, was a chaplain in the archducal oratory. Other members of the family also entered the service of the court. George d'Andelot, Ferdinand's uncle, had been a *kämmerer* to the emperor, and his grandson Adrien d'Andelot, Lord of Reusmes, became *gentilhombre de la boca* to the Archdukes. Ferdinand's other uncle, Gaspar, married Antoinette de Rye, and one of Ferdinand's daughters, Barbe, married Alexander, baron of Wiltz. Alexander's brother, Jean, *gentilhombre de la boca* to Albert, married first Madeleine

[11] It is often impossible to determine origins on the basis of surnames. French-sounding names could as easily be Southern Netherlandish as Burgundian, and much the same is true of Spanish-sounding names borne by Portuguese or Italians, as the sources (often written by Spaniards) tend to Hispanicize the names.

[12] Philippe Chifflet to Guidi di Bagno, Brussels, 8 January 1638, KBB, ms II 7277, fo. 537; Felix-Victor Goethals, *Dictionnaire généalogique et héraldique des familles nobles du royaume de Belgique* (Brussels, 1849), 1: 59; Jean Tiburce de Mesmay, *Dictionnaire historique, biographique et généalogique des anciennes familles de Franche-Comté* (Paris, 1958-1964), 1: 57.

de Rye and then her sister, Eléonore de Rye. Madeleine and Eléonore were Antoinette's nieces.[13]

Philibert de Rye, count of Varax, and Claudine de Tournon had at least six children, including the Antoinette already mentioned. Their second son, François de Rye, became *sumiller de cortina* of the Archdukes in 1606 and later their grand chaplain and grand almoner, positions he continued to hold under the widowed Isabella and under don Ferdinand.[14] His brother Claude de Rye, baron of Balançon, was appointed *gentilhombre de la cámara* to the Cardinal-Infant on 2 May 1635.[15] The sisters Madeleine and Eléonore, already mentioned above, were Claude's daughters. Eléonore was one of Isabella's ladies in waiting.[16] Alexandrine de Rye, sister of François and Claude, seems not to have held any position at court, but was a frequent visitor. She married Leonard II, count of Tassis, head of the famous Tassis postal service and a *kämmerer* of emperor Ferdinand II.[17] Yet another sister, Anne-Marguerite de Rye, was a lady in waiting to Isabella under the archducal regime and married Guillaume de Richardot, baron of Lembeek and later count of Galmaarden.[18] One of their sons became a chaplain of the oratory of the Cardinal-Infant on 1 January 1636.[19] Through a marriage with a de Rye, the Richardot family renewed their ties with their Burgundian roots.[20] This was another clan in which service at court seems to have run in the family. Gérard de Rye, Lord of

[13] Charles E.J. Poplimont, *La Belgique Héraldique* (Brussels, 1863), 1: 146-149; Goethals, *Dictionnaire*, 1: 57-62; Jules Mersch, "L'infante Isabelle," in *Biographie Nationale du pays de Luxembourg depuis ses origines jusqu'à nos jours*, 14: 537-538; J.-J. Chifflet to Guidi di Bagno, 19 October 1629 and 10 January 1630, and Ph. Chifflet to Guidi di Bagno, Brussels, 5 April 1630, in Bernard de Meester (ed.), *Lettres de Philippe et de Jean-Jacques Chifflet sur les affaires des Pays-Bas, 1627-1639* (Brussels, 1943), nos. 136, 149, 163; José Martínez Millán (ed.), *La Corte de Carlos V* (Madrid, 2000), 5: 30; José Martínez Millán and Santiago Fernández Conti (eds.), *La Monarquía de Felipe II: la casa del Rey* (Madrid, 2005), 2: 129.

[14] Jules Chifflet, *Traitté de la maison de Rye*, n.d., KB, ms. 1510, 21.

[15] Philippe Chifflet, *Diaire des choses arrivées à la cour de Bruxelles, depuis la fin de l'an 1633 aprés la mort de l'infante Isabel, jusques à l'an 1636*, BMB, *CC* 179, fo. 106r.

[16] Mersch, "L'infante", 538.

[17] Chifflet, *Traitté*, 24.

[18] Jürgen Vanhoutte, "Van robins tot très grands nobles: Carrièreplanning en huwelijksstrategie bij het geslacht Richardot in de Zuidelijke Nederlanden (1540-1701)," in Guido Marnef and René Vermeir (eds.), *Adel en macht: Politiek, cultuur, economie* (Maastricht, 2004), 45.

[19] Chifflet, *Diaire*, fo. 161r.

[20] Born in the Southern Netherlands, the Richardots after the famous Jean Richardot were no longer considered Burgundians.

Balançon, and his brother Joachim, Lord of Rye, the father and uncle (respectively) of Philibert, had both been *sumilleres de corps* to Charles V, one of the highest positions at court.[21]

Claude de Rye, baron of Balançon, married Claudine-Prospère de la Baume, sister of Jean-Baptiste de la Baume, marquis of Saint-Martin, who on 2 July 1636 became don Ferdinand's captain of the guard in succession to Christophe Gretsil, count of Emden, who had died a few months previously.[22] Jeanne, the sister of Guillaume de Richardot, married Antoine de la Baume, a son of the count of Saint-Amour, a relative of Jean-Baptist.[23]

The Perrenot de Granvelle-d'Oiselay family

Eugène-Léopold de Perrenot de Granvelle-d'Oiselay, margrave of the Holy Roman Empire and count of Cantecroix, became one of Isabella's *meninos* on 14 October 1630. He went on to become a chamberlain, councilor of state, and a favorite of emperor Ferdinand II, who knighted him in person. He was the son of François-Thomas d'Oiselay, who inherited the fortune and titles of his uncle, François Perrenot de Granvelle, grandson of the famous Nicolas Perrenot de Granvelle. François-Thomas was a knight of the Golden Fleece, *gentilhombre de la cámara* of the archduke Albert and ambassador to emperor Rudolf II in Prague. Rudolf II, Albert's brother, granted François-Thomas the titles of margrave of the Holy Roman Empire and count of Cantecroix. On 5 December 1607 he also gave him the hand of his legitimized daughter Carolina, marchioness of Austria. On 6 March 1635 their son, Eugène-Léopold, married the renowned Béatrix de Cusance, the baron of Belvoir's eldest daughter, in Brussels. Béatrix achieved notoriety after Eugène-Léopold's death through her second marriage, to Charles IV, duke of Lorraine, which caused scandal due to Charles still being married to his first wife, Nicole of Lorraine.[24]

[21] Chifflet, *Traitté*, 30; Martínez Millán, *La Corte*, 2:12.

[22] Aubert de la Chenaye-Desbois, *Dictionnaire de la Noblesse* (Paris, 1776), 11: 101; Chifflet, *Traitté*, 23; Chifflet, *Diaire*, fo. 183r-v.

[23] Vanhoutte, "Van robins", 40-42; Jacques S. De Herckenrode, *Nobiliaire des Pays-Bas et du Comté de Bourgogne par M. De Vegiano* (Ghent, 1865), 2: 1635.

[24] Philippe Chifflet, *Journal historique*, fo. 182v (BMB, *CC* 96); Herckenrode, 2:1546; Mesmay, *Dictionnaire historique*, 519; Ernest Gossart, *L'auberge des princes en exil: Anecdotes de la cour de Bruxelles au XVIIe siècle* (Brussels, 1905), 102-120.

The Chifflet family

The brothers Philippe and Jean-Jacques Chifflet, respectively chaplain of the oratory and physician of the body to both Isabella and the Cardinal-Infant, came from a respectable Bisontin family, in the lower reaches of the aristocracy.[25] Their father, Jean Chifflet, Lord of Palente, was physician to the city of Besançon and a member of the city council. His wife, Marguerite Pouthier, was the sister of a professor at the university in Dole, capital of the Franche-Comté. Jean-Jacques himself married Jeanne-Baptiste de Maubouhans, daughter of the mayor of Vesoul.[26] They had twelve children, eight of whom survived infancy.[27] Three of their offspring were to have careers at court. From 1648 Jules resided at the court in Madrid, where he had earlier been granted the titles of chancellor of the Golden Fleece and chaplain of the oratory of Philip IV. He returned to the Franche-Comté only in 1659, to take up the offices of abbot of Balerne and *conseiller-clerc* in the Parlement of Dole. Jean Chifflet was first appointed at the Brussels court as confessor to the governor-general, archduke Leopold-Wilhelm, and later as a chaplain of the oratory of Leopold-Wilhelm's successor, don Juan José. Henri-Thomas became almoner to queen Christina of Sweden.[28] Philippe and Jean-Jacques themselves continued to serve in the Brussels households of Leopold-Wilhelm and don Juan José after the Cardinal-Infant's death in 1641.[29] The Chifflets were a very scholarly family who produced

[25] The grandfather of Philippe and Jean-Jacques, Laurent Chifflet, was ennobled by Charles V on 5 November 1552, in recognition of his services. See Jacobs, *Parateksten*, 262.

[26] De Meester, *Lettres*, 1-2, 26-28; Emile Longin, "Jean Boyvin, président du parlement de Dole d'après ses lettres aux Chifflet (1625-1650)," *Mémoires de la Société d'Emulation du Doubs* (1911-1912): 394-395, 123-185; Albéric de Truchis de Varennes, *Les Chifflet à l'imprimerie plantinienne* (Besançon, 1909), 12; Auguste Castan, "Mathieu de Morgues et Philippe Chifflet," *Bulletins de l'Académie Royales des sciences, des lettres et des beaux-arts de Belgique*, 3rd ser., 10 (1885): 331; and the articles by Michel Prevost on various members of the Chifflet family, in Michel Prevost and Roman d'Amat (eds.), *Dictionnaire de Biographie Française*, (Paris, 1956), 43: 1142-1148; Jacobs, *Parateksten*, 542.

[27] Jacobs, *Parateksten*, 350-351.

[28] Prevost, *Dictionnaire*, 1145-1146; Roegis, *Het hof*, 70-71; Jules' appointment as chaplain of Philip IV, 13 June 1656, BMB, *CC* 25, unnumbered; De Meester, *Lettres*, 26-27.

[29] Appointment of Philippe as second almoner to Leopold-Wilhelm, 26 November 1649, and as second almoner to don Juan José, 16 May 1656, BMB, *CC* 30, fo. 252; Appointment of Jean-Jacques as physician of the body to Leopold-Wilhelm, 25 October 1650, BMB, *CC* 25, unnumbered.

a tremendous number of learned works, ranging from heraldry and genealogy to antiquarian researches and theological speculations. They were active citizens of the Republic of Letters, and corresponded with an enormous number of artists, scientists, prelates and members of the high nobility.[30]

The Burgundian network at the Brussels court

In the first half of 1621, Jean-Jacques Chifflet got in touch with his fellow Bisontin the count of Cantecroix, *gentilhombre de la cámara* to the archduke Albert, as well as with Cantecroix's wife, Carolina of Austria, and with Andreas Trevisius, archducal physician of the body, to try to bag an interesting position for his younger brother Philippe. Philippe had just graduated from the University of Leuven and had moved to Brussels. Jean-Jacques also contacted Aubertus Miraeus, chaplain of the oratory of Isabella, Pieter Peckius, Chancellor of the Council of Brabant, and Erycius Puteanus, a prominent professor at Leuven University. Puteanus in turn contacted Philip IV's ambassador in Brussels, Alonso de la Cueva, marquis of Bedmar, setting out the young cleric's qualifications for the post. So Puteanus, a friend of the Chifflet family, tried to use his influence on behalf of a former student, Philippe, to obtain an appointment as chaplain in Isabella's oratory. But ultimately it was François de Rye, grand almoner and grand chaplain to Isabella, who could fix things for Philippe, getting him appointed in May 1624.[31] It is more than likely that the Chifflets had called on the assistance of François' uncle, Ferdinand de Rye, archbishop of Besançon. When the archbishop died in 1636, François succeeded him and made Philippe his right-hand man by naming him his vicar

[30] The Republic of Letters can (very generally) be described as the ensemble of literati, scholars, or intellectuals active in science and learning in the Early Modern period. It arose in the 15th century, flourished, roughly speaking, between 1550 and 1750, and declined in the later 18th century. See Hans Bots and Françoise Waquet, *La République des Lettres*, Europe & Histoire (Paris and Brussels, 1997), 18, 29-34, 59-61. On the Chifflets as citizens of this Republic, see Jacobs, *Parateksten*.

[31] Puteanus to Alonso de la Cueva, Leuven, 6 September 1623, in Auguste Castan, "Les origines et la date du Saint-Ildefonse de Rubens," *Mémoires de la Société d'Emulation du Doubs*, 5th ser., 9 (1884): 79-81; Jacobs, *Parateksten*, 373, 382; François de Rye to Ph. Chifflet, Brussels, 12 May 1624, in Castan, "Les origines," 71-71.

general.[32] Jean-Jacques had to wait until October 1625 to obtain a place at court. He was appointed one of Isabella's physicians of the body. So François de Rye became a patron of the Chifflet brothers, having mediated for them to the infanta Isabella. The same was true of Ferdinand d'Andelot, the infanta's *primer mayordomo*. Andelot knew all about the affairs of the Chifflet family before they came to court, because his sister, Anne-Nicole d'Andelot, Madame de Chateaurouillard, a nun in the monastery of Salins, had been in frequent correspondence with the two brothers for some time. The *mayordomo* could also have been informed of the activities of the Chifflets by the Cantecroix-Austria couple. He was well acquainted with his compatriot the count of Cantecroix from when he had been *gentilhombre de la cámara* to Albert. After the archduke's death the couple retired to their residence in Besançon, but Carolina of Austria's letters to Jean-Jacques show that she knew very well who d'Andelot was.[33] Ferdinand d'Andelot not only gave the brothers his active support in the early 1620s, he also became Jean-Jacques' landlord, making a dwelling available near the palace.[34] At the head of Isabella's household, d'Andelot was able to arrange all sorts of matters for the Chifflets and kept them abreast of the latest gossip. In return, Jean-Jacques regularly provided medical assistance, or spoke to other influential people on behalf of the d'Andelot family. In June 1627, Philippe approached his other great patron, the papal nuncio Guidi di Bagno, for a dispensation for one of d'Andelot's sons, who wished to retain clerical benefices while taking up a commission as captain in the army of the king of Spain. When d'Andelot had a Latin inscription made for the altarpiece of the chapel of San Ildefonso in the church of St. James on the Coudenberg in Brussels, he wanted to have the text corrected by Puteanus, and asked the Chifflets to arrange this. Puteanus was glad to oblige. Together with Philippe the renowned Leuven professor also worked on the funerary inscriptions of d'Andelot's second wife and some of his sons. Not long after being appointed prior of Bellefontaine near Besançon, Philippe Chifflet began writing a book about the priory as a place of devotion, dedicating the work to Ferdinand d'Andelot and his family to reinforce the bonds between the

[32] François de Rye died before the appointment could be finalized, but the nomination was confirmed by his successor as archbishop, Claude d'Achey. See Jacobs, *Parateksten*, 634, 697.

[33] Various letters from Carolina of Austria to J.-J Chifflet in BMB, *CC* 24.

[34] Castan, "Les origines," 32, 74.

two Burgundian families. All in all, d'Andelot became one of the most important networkers for the Chifflet brothers.[35]

The brothers more than once made use of book dedications as a way of thanking friends, patrons or others who had supported their careers. When Philippe translated Herman Hugo's Latin account of the siege of Breda into French, he dedicated the translation to François de Rye, his patron and superior in the court chapel in Brussels. Furthermore, Philippe found an interesting link between the book itself and the dedication: the baron of Balançon, François' brother, had been one of the heroes of the siege. In the introduction Philippe praised his military achievements by quoting Spínola, who had reportedly said that "if the king had five or six servants with the same qualities as Balançon, he could conquer the whole world." Philippe sent a copy to the baron, who responded by pledging his future support to the Chifflet brothers.[36] This brought the baron of Balançon – who in 1635 became *gentilhombre de la cámara* to the Cardinal-Infant – into the Burgundian court network. Jules Chifflet, one of Jean-Jacques' sons, later honored the de Rye and d'Andelot families by compiling their genealogies.[37] Jules dedicated his *Traitté de la maison de Rye* to Alexandrine de Rye, the widow of the count of Tassis and the acting head of the famous post office during the minority of her son, Lamoral III. In the 1640s the Chifflets were also able to build up good relations with the house of Tassis. Jean-Jacques had found a powerful patron in Alexandrine, who wrote to Madrid on his behalf to get his royal pension paid, while her son Lamoral became the patron of Jules.[38] When Jean-Baptiste de la Baume – captain of the guard to don Ferdinand – became governor of the Franche-Comté in 1637, Jean-Jacques managed to establish friendly relations with him too. The physician offered him news from Brussels and information on the governor-general's state of health, while the marquis reciprocated

[35] Philippe Chifflet, *Histoire du prieuré Nostre Dame de Bellefontaine au comté de Bourgongne* (Antwerp: Balthasar Moretus, 1631). Jacobs, *Parateksten*, 416-417, 495-501; De Meester, *Lettres*, 8, 38-42, 54-65; Ph. Chifflet to Guidi di Bagno, Brussels, 18 June 1627, in De Meester, *Lettres*, no. 14; Ph. Chifflet to Guidi di Bagno, Brussels, 23 July 1627, KB, ms. II 7277, fo. 43.

[36] Herman Hugo, *Le siège de la ville de Breda*, translated by Philippe Chifflet (Antwerp: Balthasar Moretus, 1631). Claude de Rye, baron of Balançon, to Ph. Chifflet, Breda, 9 April 1631, BMB, *CC* 25, fo. 360; Jacobs, *Parateksten*, 545-548.

[37] Chifflet, *Traitté*; parts of the d'Andelot genealogy were published in Castan, "Les origines," 57-60.

[38] Jacobs, *Parateksten*, 753-759.

by reporting on the course of the war against France and the military strategies being pursued.[39]

Bonds of affection: Isabella and Burgundian servants at court

What made these Burgundians so remarkable is that they played prominent roles in the Brussels court. Isabella in particular seems to have been unusually fond of them, to judge by the favors and important missions she gave them, clear indications of trust. François de Rye, Ferdinand d'Andelot and Jean-Jacques Chifflet were each remembered by name in her will. This underlines the close bond they had with the infanta, especially considering that de Rye and d'Andelot received the two largest monetary bequests.[40]

Isabella showed her special bond with these Burgundians on numerous occasions. When François de Rye's uncle, the archbishop of Besançon, was getting on in life, he suggested his nephew as coadjutor with right of succession. Isabella seized the first opportunity to recommend her grand chaplain and grand almoner to the Pope, who a few weeks later acceded to her request that the appointment be made. When it became apparent that de Rye would have to pay a hefty fee to have the papal bulls issued that would confirm his appointment, the governess-general intervened to request a dispensation. She ordered Juan-Baptista Vives – her agent in Rome – to negotiate with the Pope. She also asked the nuncio in Brussels to support the cause, when it became evident that de Rye and Vives were not in sympathy with one another. The nuncio knew that obtaining such a dispensation was no easy matter, but in the event recommended to Rome that this favor be granted because de Rye "is much loved by the infanta, and nothing else could give her more pleasure."[41] On later occasions the governess-general again attested to a special relationship with de Rye, when he obtained the title of archbishop of Caesarea in 1626. The investiture took place in the court chapel, with Isabella and her full household in

[39] Various letters exchanged between them are in BMB, *CC* 107; Jacobs, 631.

[40] Charles Piot, "Le Testament et les codicilles de l'infante Isabelle," *Bulletin de la commission royale d'histoire*, 4th ser., 12 (1885): 14-15.

[41] Guidi di Bagno to Ludovisi, Brussels, 11 September 1621 and 24 June 1623, in Bernard De Meester, *Correspondance du nonce Giovanni-Francesco Guidi di Bagno, 1621-1627* (Brussels and Rome, 1938), nos. 93, 677; Louis Jadin, "Procès d'information pour la nomination des évêques et abbés des Pays-Bas, de Liège et de Franche-Comté," *Bulletin de l'institut historique belge de Rome*, 8 (1928): 170-173.

attendance. During the ceremony the infanta made him a gift of the miter that her deceased husband, archduke Albert, had received from his brother, emperor Rudolf II, on the occasion of his nomination to the archbishopric of Toledo. Isabella also ensured that François' brother, Claude, was well provided for. Albert had earlier rewarded him for his loyal service and courage on the battlefield by recommending him for a knighthood in the Order of Santiago, an honor that was bestowed by Philip III. In 1624-25 Balançon again proved his military skill during the siege of Breda. Isabella rewarded him by appointing him governor of the town on 21 June 1625.[42] During the siege of 's-Hertogenbosch in 1629 the infanta reinforced Claude's garrison at Breda with soldiers from the prince of Barbançon's units, something the prince was by no means pleased with. Balançon in any case rose rapidly: in 1630 Philip IV, at Isabella's recommendation, granted him the honorable title of councilor in the Madrid *Consejo de guerra*, and in 1631 he became general of the artillery in the Southern Netherlands. He declined Philip IV's offer in 1633 to appoint him governor of the Franche-Comté. He later became *gentilhombre de la cámara* to the Cardinal-Infant (1635), a member of the Brussels Council of State (1638), and governor of the province of Namur (1645).

Isabella was also close to d'Andelot. In 1629 she made him head of the prestigious fraternity of San Ildefonso, refounded in Brussels by the Archdukes in 1604. Together with Isabella he made plans for a magnificent altarpiece to adorn the fraternity's chapel in the church of St. James on the Coudenberg. As "l'inspirateur habituel des commandes artistiques de l'infante," d'Andelot was frequently in touch with influential artists who enjoyed the governess-general's approval.[43] So the *mayordomo* could recruit to his project another figure favored by Isabella, Peter-Paul Rubens, who a few years before had been appointed *gentilhombre de la casa* in the Brussels court.[44] When Isabella's *mayordomo mayor*, Ambrogio Spínola, left the Netherlands in 1628, his duties at court were temporarily undertaken by the most senior *mayordomo*, *primer mayordomo* d'Andelot. But when Spínola died in Italy, at Castelnuovo, in September 1630, one of the most important positions at the Brussels court fell vacant. Competition broke out between the

[42] Georges Baurin, *Les Gouverneurs du Comté de Namur, 1430-1794* (Namur, 1984), 194; Jacobs, *Parateksten*, 410.

[43] Castan, "Les origines," 23, 29, 33.

[44] Max Rooses and Charles Ruelens (eds.), *Correspondance de Rubens et documents épistolaires concernant sa vie et ses oeuvres* (Antwerp, 1904), 4:287.

marquis of Aytona, the marquis of Mirabel, the duke of Aarschot, and Ottavio Visconti, count of Gamalerio.[45] Here, again, Isabella showed a special affection for d'Andelot, defending his position at the Brussels court. A few months before Spínola's death, Philip IV had already written to his aunt to say that Aytona would be the best candidate to succeed him.[46] The governess-general, however, replied that "in the absence of the *mayordomo mayor*, the most senior *mayordomo* replaces him, and to act otherwise would be an insult." Naturally, this was not the only reason. Isabella feared that appointing Aytona – one of the most valued clients of the Count-Duke of Olivares – would give Madrid too much influence in her household; but nor would she appoint anyone else, leaving d'Andelot to do the honors. Although never officially given the title of *mayordomo mayor*, he in effect became so, with both contemporary and 18th-century writers naming him as such.[47] In the same year d'Andelot helped Isabella develop a plan to prevent the rich inheritance of the Burgundian baron of Ray from falling into French hands.[48] This again shows his closeness to the governess-general.

[45] Ph. Chifflet to Guidi di Bagno, Brussels, 18 October 1630, KB, ms. II 7277, fo. 383. Aytona was a confident of the Count-Duke Olivares in Brussels. After the death of Isabella he became governor-general ad interim. About Aytona, see René Vermeir, "Power elites and royal government in the Spanish Netherlands during the last phase of the Eighty Years' War (1621-1648)," in Ausma Cimdina (ed.), *Religion and political change in Europe: past and present* (Pisa, 2004) 87-103.

[46] Isabella to Philip IV, Brussels, 24 January 1630, AGR, *SSO* 202, fo. 56; Aytona to Philip IV, Brussels, 18 January 1630, KB, ms 16.149, fo. 7v.

[47] Isabella to Philip IV, Brussels, 24 January 1630, AGR, *SSO* 202, fo. 56; Diego de Aedo y Gallart, *El viaje del infante cardenal Don Fernando de Austria ...* (Antwerp, 1635), 162; Christophe Butkens, *Supplement aux Trophées tant sacrés que profanes du Duché de Brabant* (The Hague, 1726), 1:141; Testimony of Miguel de Olivares in the suit of Ana d'Oyenbrugghe against the executors of Isabella's will, 1641, AGR, *GR* layette R no. 16, unnumbered. With thanks to Michel Oosterbosch for his assistance with these trial bundles.

[48] The de Ray family was one of the oldest and wealthiest connections of the Franche-Comté. When Claude-François, baron of Ray, died in 1630, his seven-year-old daughter Marie was the sole heir to his fortune. Her mother Béatrix – a daughter of d'Andelot's second wife by an earlier marriage – retired to a convent in Dole, taking the religious name Maria-Victoria. The little baroness was entrusted to her godfather, Cleriadus de Vergy, count of Champlitte, the governor of the Franche-Comté. When he died, just a few months later, his wife, Madeleine de Bauffremont, acquired custody of the girl. This was a development of significant concern to d'Andelot, as Madeleine was very close to her sister-in-law, the marchioness of Sennecey, who resided at the court of Louis XIII and had two eligible sons. Isabella and d'Andelot insisted that the girl be brought to Brussels, where she could be raised among Isabella's *meninas*. Philippe Chifflet was sent to the Franche-Comté to make the necessary arrangements. In the event, Marie de Ray

The Chifflet brothers were also entrusted with delicate missions. In early April 1626 Jean-Jacques left for Madrid, at Isabella's request, to propose relocating the Parlement of Dole – the Franche-Comté's highest law court – to Besançon. This project was initially proposed by the magistrates and notables of Besançon, who wished to bring one of the most important institutions of the Franche-Comté to their city. As a true Bisontin, Jean-Jacques lobbied for the relocation and set his network of highly-placed figures in Brussels to work to convince the governess-general. Thanks to his good contacts with the governor of the Franche-Comté, the Cantecroix couple, Pieter Peckius, and Ferdinand de Boisschot, all of whom came out in favor of the project, Jean-Jacques was successful in the first phase of his mission. Ultimately the project failed, and the Parlement remained where it was, but for Jean-Jacques the journey to Madrid was fruitful in perhaps unforeseen ways. He met various influential men, and favorably impressed the most powerful of them all, the Count-Duke of Olivares, who was amazed at his diplomatic abilities and well-spokenness. At Olivares' suggestion, Jean-Jacques was appointed one of Philip IV's physicians of the body.[49] In October 1626 he was back in Brussels and had started work on a book the king himself had asked for: a history of the knights of the Golden Fleece.[50] Philippe was repeatedly honored by the infanta with important jobs, usually in the Franche-Comté. Besides his commission concerning Marie de Ray, in December 1628 he was given the task of reporting on a particular ceremony in the Franche-Comté. Philippe was able to combine it with his official installation as the new prior of Bellefontaine, a position he owed to the infanta's favor.[51] It was also Philippe who accompanied his sister-in-law and her children during their move from Besançon to Brussels in the winter of 1629-1630. In the mean time Isabella had arranged an annual pension and a chaplaincy in Besançon for Jean Chifflet, Jean-Jacques' second son. Isabella gave

was raised in the convent that her mother had joined, and in 1636 married the Southern Netherlander Albert de Mérode, marquis of Trelon. See Emile Longin, "Un marriage au dix-septième siècle: Marie de Ray," *Mémoires de la Société d'Emulation du Jura* 4 (1920): 3-50; Chifflet, *Journal historique*, BMB, *CC* 96, fo. 85.

[49] Isabella to Iñigo de Brizuela, Brussels, 18 October 1626, AGS, *E* 8344, unnumbered; Jacobs, *Parateksten*, 431-451; Castan, "Les origines," 75; Prevost, "Chifflet (Jean-Jacques)," in *Dictionnaire*, 43: 1145.

[50] Prevost, "Chifflet (Jean-Jacques)," in *Dictionnaire*, 43: 1146; Joseph-Jean De Smet, "Chifflet (Jean-Jacques)," in *Biographie nationale*, 4: 74; Jean-Jacques Chifflet, *Insignia gentilitia equitum ordinis Velleris Aurei* (Antwerp, 1632).

[51] Jacobs, *Parateksten*, 486-487.

her physician's wife and children a warm reception. She asked them for the details of their journey, but was particularly curious about Jeanne-Baptiste, Jean-Jacques' spouse, who was honored with a *tête-à-tête* with the governess-general in her private apartments. Within the year, Jeanne and Jacques were blessed with a new son. This child perfectly symbolized how tightly the Chifflet family was tied to the very center of the court. He was named Philippe-Eugène, after his godparents Philip IV and Isabella Clara Eugenia. At the christening, the godparents were represented by Ferdinand d'Andelot and by Anna-Maria Camudio, wife of the chancellor of Brabant.[52]

Changes under the Cardinal-Infant don Ferdinand

Under the governor-generalship of the Cardinal-Infant there appears to have been a discontinuity with the pattern of earlier years. The king's new representative did not share the infanta's special bond with the Franc-Comtois. This can be explained by the fact that as a young and inexperienced Spanish prince he had been invested with rule over a place he did not know. Don Ferdinand had not left the peninsula since his birth and had always been surrounded by Spanish noblemen. During his few years in the Southern Netherlands, this barely changed. It was due not only to don Ferdinand's personal preferences, but also to directives from Madrid, that the Brussels court took on a more Spanish look between 1634 and 1641. Towards the end of the sovereign reign of the Archdukes a tendency had already been apparent for vacant positions at court, formerly held by Spaniards, to pass to Southern Netherlanders. After her husband's death, Isabella firmly continued this policy as governess-general. Although the Southern Netherlands had reverted to Spain, the ministers in Madrid considered it prudent to maintain some continuity of regime and not to interfere with Isabella's appointments. This decision followed the advice of the Spanish ambassador in Brussels, Alonso de la Cueva, who warned that sending a crowd of Spanish ministers to Brussels would irritate the local nobility, needlessly complicating the reversion to Spain.[53] But after the

[52] Chifflet, *Journal historique*, BMB, *CC* 96, fos. 174-175, 183v; J.-J. Chifflet to Guidi di Bagno, Brussels, 2 May 1629, in De Meester, *Lettres*, no. 120; Jacobs, *Parateksten*, 522.
[53] Alonso de la Cueva, marquis of Bedmar, to Philip IV, Brussels, 23 July 1621, AGS, *E* 2035, unnumbered; Alicia Esteban Estríngana, *Madrid y Bruselas: Relaciones de gobierno en la etapa postarchiducal, 1621-1634* (Leuven, 2005), 28-32.

conspiracy of a number of South-Netherlandish aristocrats in 1632, and the infanta's death the following year, Philip IV decided to make a clean sweep of the gubernatorial household. Under the Cardinal-Infant there were not only more Spaniards appointed to the court than there had been under Isabella, there were also several new appointments hand-picked by Madrid for a clear record of loyal service to the Spanish crown. The marquises of Aytona, Este and Orani obtained, respectively, the three top positions at court of *mayordomo mayor*, *caballerizo mayor* and *sumiller de corps*. The key positions in the chapel went to Emanuel de Guzmán (grand almoner) and Fray Juan de San Agustín (confessor).

The Cardinal-Infant had received instructions, before leaving for the Netherlands, to treat Isabella's Burgundian former courtiers with all respect, as she had held them in high regard. During the brand new governor-general's first audience in Tervuren on 3 November 1634, he received many of Isabella's former servants who came to offer him their services. He told François de Rye that he need not kneel before him, and went on to say, "qu'il le cognoissait desia par rapport, et estait bien informé de luy et des biens services qu'il avait rendu, a son oncle et tante, et qu'il aurait toujours souvenance particulier de sa personne." Although de Rye declined to do so, the governor-general did him the signal honor of granting permission for him to remain covered in his presence.[54] At this first audience the Cardinal-Infant also made it clear to the Chifflet brothers that he had heard nothing but good of them.[55] He had met Jean-Jacques before, in Madrid, when the physician had been sent there by Isabella to negotiate the relocation of the Parlement of Dole.[56] The Chifflets were by this time past masters of the art of networking and were not adversely affected by the transition of power. They had already established good relations with the marquis of Aytona in 1630.[57] They were also able to make satisfactory contacts with the rest of the new power elite, by praising them in the introduction to

[54] Chifflet, *Diaire*, BMB, *CC* 179, fo. 46v. Although this gracious gesture by the Cardinal-Infant suggests the granting of a grandeeship – the highest honorific that a nobleman could receive from the king of Spain – it by no means went so far. The favor of being allowed to stand in the royal presence with one's head covered, could only be granted by the king and not by other members of the royal family. This fragment does, however, indicate that they could grant a somewhat comparable favor, which without doubt was also a great honor.

[55] Chifflet, *Diaire*, BMB, *CC* 179, fos. 38v, 44r.

[56] Jacobs, *Parateksten*, 451.

[57] Jacobs, *Parateksten*, 600.

a translation of a book by don Diego de Aedo.[58] The correspondence surviving in the Chifflet family archive shows that they were able to come to an understanding with the marquis of Este and with the marquis of Mirabel, Aytona's successor as *mayordomo mayor*.[59] The brothers also advanced their careers through good contacts with prince Thomas of Savoy (brother of the duke of Savoy and Aytona's successor as *gobernador de las armas* in the Southern Netherlands) and with Henriette of Lorraine (sister of duke Charles IV of Lorraine). These two princely figures became the godparents of Jean-Jacques' youngest son, Henri-Thomas.[60] Prince Thomas and Henriette went on to help Jean-Jacques' children's prospects by personally writing letters of recommendation to the king.[61] Don Ferdinand also declared to his brother that Jean-Jacques was the only non-Spanish physician in whom he had any confidence.[62] Ferdinand d'Andelot was the only Burgundian to suffer a serious reverse by the death of his powerful patroness, Isabella. As has already been mentioned, he unofficially held the position of *mayordomo mayor* in her household, a position that brought with it a beautiful apartment in the palace on the Coudenberg. When Aytona was named the Cardinal-Infant's *mayordomo mayor*, d'Andelot had to pack up and move out to a house beyond the palace gates. He was allowed to retain the rank of *primer mayordomo*, despite the maneuverings of his fellow *mayordomos* (see below), but was forced to share it with don Luis Lasso de la Vega, viscount of Puertollano, who was more frequently remarked in don Ferdinand's presence than was d'Andelot.[63] In 1635 the Cardinal-Infant appointed d'Andelot jailer of the abducted French-leaning Elector of Trier, Philip Christoph von Sötern, who was held in Ghent. This was a sign of how much confidence the ruler reposed in him, but it also kept him from attendance at court. He hated being away

[58] Don Diego de Aedo y Gallart traveled with don Ferdinand from Madrid to the Netherlands in the capacity of *ayuda de cámara*. He wrote a detailed report of the journey, published first in Antwerp in 1635 as *El viaje del infante cardenal don Fernando de Austria* ..., and subsequently in Madrid, in 1637, as *Viage, sucessos y guerras del infante cardenal don Fernando de Austria* ... . The work was translated by Jules Chifflet, Jean-Jacques' son, as *Le voyage du prince Don Fernande infant d'Espagne, cardinal* ... (Antwerp, 1635).

[59] Series of letters from the marquis of Mirabel, the marquis of Este, prince Thomas, and Henriette of Lorraine, BMB, *CC* 24.

[60] Chifflet, *Journal historique*, BMB, *CC* 96, fo. 104; Jacobs, *Parateksten*, 620-638.

[61] Henriette of Lorraine to Philip IV, Brussels, 14 June 1643, AGS, *E* 1059, unnumbered; Jacobs, *Parateksten*, 756.

[62] Cardinal-Infant to Philip IV, Arras, 10 October 1636, AGR, *SSO* 215, fos. 323-324.

[63] Chifflet, *Diaire*, BMB, *CC* 179, fos. 42-43.

from the center of power, where all important news was to be heard first, and lamented this isolation to his loyal client Philippe Chifflet.[64] Two Burgundian newcomers at the court of the Cardinal-Infant were Claude de Rye, baron of Balançon, and Jean-Baptiste de la Baume, marquis of Saint-Martin, both already referred to above. Balançon's career blossomed under don Ferdinand's governor-generalship. In 1635 Philip IV appointed him *gentilhombre de la cámara* of don Ferdinand and in a letter of 16 January 1638 the king informed his brother that he wanted to appoint Balançon as governor of Luxemburg. But this letter to Brussels crossed with one that don Ferdinand had written to Madrid on 2 January, strongly recommending Claude de Lannoy, count de la Motterie, for the same position, to which Ferdinand had already provisionally appointed him in expectation of a positive response from Madrid. The Cardinal-Infant took the view that Balançon "está ya bastantemente proveído." Philip IV was furious and demanded that Pieter Roose account for what had happened. The president of the Privy Council hedged, explaining that Lannoy's appointment was only provisional and would expire in March. In the end Balançon was not appointed, but was recompensed with a prestigious appointment as councilor of state. He ultimately became governor of the province of Namur in 1645.[65] We know little about the marquis of Saint-Martin, appointed captain of the Cardinal-Infant's guards in July 1636. He belonged to one of the oldest families in Bresse, became governor of Dole in 1633, and took up arms in the service of the king of Spain and the emperor. He saw service in Flanders, Italy, the Holy Roman Empire, and the Franche-Comté, and was imperial general of artillery. When the archbishop of Besançon died in 1636, Philip IV desperately needed a new provincial governor for the Franche-Comté. The county was going through a nadir of French plundering and hostilities (the so-called Ten Years' War, 1633-1644). Although Balançon was again the king's first choice, he turned the position down for a second time. Ultimately the governorship went to his brother-in-law, the marquis of Saint-Martin.[66]

[64] Ferdinand d'Andelot to Ph. Chifflet, Ghent, 20 November 1635, BMB, *CC* 25; Chifflet, *Diaire*, BMB, *CC* 179, fos. 42v-43v.

[65] Baurin, *Les Gouverneurs*, 186-187; Roose to Philip IV and Olivares, Brussels, 3 December 1637, AGR, *GR* 1500, fo. 195.

[66] Philip IV to the Cardinal-Infant, Madrid, 5 December 1639, RAH, *CSC* A 87, fo. 48; Xavier Brun, *La Franche-Comté sous les archiducs Albert et Isabelle, 1598-1634* (Lons-Le-Saunier, 1939), 30; Xavier Brun, *Histoire de la guerre de dix-ans en Franche-Comté, 1633-1644* (Lons-Le-Saunier, 1937), 8-9, 200; Chenaye-Desbois, *Dictionnaire*, 2: 101.

Although the Cardinal-Infant distanced himself from his aunt's Burgundian servants and preferred to surround himself with Spaniards, this did not result in any outward loss of prestige or career prospects for the Burgundian office-holders at court. It is clear from his first audience that don Ferdinand had been very thoroughly briefed in advance on the good and loyal service that Isabella's Burgundian courtiers had demonstrated, and that they were to be treated with all respect. The Cardinal-Infant was not close to them, as Isabella had been, but they received support from Madrid, as can be seen in the case of the baron of Balançon. The Franc-Comtois in Brussels were not to be treated cavalierly.

"Ceux de nostre nation": origins and envy

The previous sections indicate the prominence of Franc-Comtois at the Brussels court. The positions that they held were largely key posts that granted direct access, otherwise strictly controlled, to the person of the governess-general. In the 1630s Isabella made this access, if anything, more exclusive for men, it having come to her attention that "on se donnoit licence d'entrer dans la pièce voisine de sa chambre et de se mesler parmi les Dames, contre l'usage et les ordonnances de sa maison." Jean-Jacques Chifflet wrote to Guidi di Bagno that the new measures meant that in future the infanta's door would be closed to men while she was eating, with exceptions made for the *mayordomo mayor*, the *mayordomo* in waiting, and the physicians of the body. All others, even the *grandes* and knights of the Golden Fleece, were to wait in the antechamber.[67] Ferdinand d'Andelot, Jean-Jacques Chifflet and, naturally, the lady in waiting Eléonore de Rye – the baron of Balançon's daughter – were therefore all assured of access. Not much later an ordinance was issued stipulating "qu'auncun Menine dez l'age de douze ans n'eust a entrer dans la chambre de Son Altesse." Only one page was exempted from this restriction, the young Burgundian count of Cantecroix.[68] This will have been due to his mother having been related to Albert, rather than to his Burgundian patrimony, but the fact remains that it was a Franc-Comtois who was favored. As the

[67] J.-J. Chifflet to Guidi di Bagno, Brussels, 10 January 1630, KB, ms. II 7277, 296-297; Jacobs, *Parateksten*, 521.
[68] Chifflet, *Journal historique*, BMB, *CC* 96, fo. 200r.

head of the court chapel, François de Rye also had access to the infanta's presence.[69]

The envy with which these Burgundians were regarded by other courtiers shows how exceptional their good standing with the governess-general was. After Jean-Jacques' return from Spain, he repeatedly complained that he was still not treated with the same honours as Isabella's other physicians, and was considering retiring from court. According to his brother part of the fault lay with Spínola, "qu'il n'est pas grand amis de ceux de nostre nation."[70] But Philippe was convinced that Dr Andreas Trevisius, another of Isabella's physicians of the body, was working against his brother. A Florentine, Trevisius had gone from being one of the Chifflets' first contacts at court, a friend and patron, to being a jealous rival. Trevisius resented the affection that the governess-general showed Jean-Jacques, and tried to keep him away from her as much as possible. Trevisius even tried to prevent Philippe being awarded the priory of Bellefontaine. When Isabella heard of Trevisius' hostility towards the Chifflet brothers, "Son Altesse ne luy donne plus d'escoute et ne parle de luy que avec indignation." Trevisius fell from Isabella's favor and Jean-Jacques became one of the leading physicians in her chamber.[71] Furthermore, the Franc-Comtois resented Trevisius, an outsider, having been given control of the rich salt mines of Salins. When he died in June 1633, Carolina of Austria admitted to Jean-Jacques "que ie suis ayssé de ce que le docteur André est mort car il traversat toutjours aux affaires de Bourgogne."[72] That d'Andelot's position was also enviable is shown by the behavior of his Southern Netherlandish fellow *mayordomos*, the counts of Noyelles, Grimbergen and Roeulx, when the new governor-general, the Cardinal-Infant, arrived at Jülich in October 1634. On 22 October d'Andelot welcomed the new governor-general, but he returned to Brussels shortly afterwards. In his absence the other three *mayordomos* of the late infanta – the counts of Roeulx, Noyelles and Grimbergen – strove to get ahead of the

[69] The functions of the grand almoner and grand chaplain are explained in Alfred De Ridder, "Les Règlements de la cour de Charles-Quint," *Messager des sciences historiques ou archives des arts et de la bibliographie de Belgique*, 1893, 395-398; and Antonio Rodríguez Villa (ed.), *Etiquetas de la casa de Austria* (Madrid, 1913), 49.

[70] Ph. Chifflet to Guidi di Bagno, Brussels, 21 January 1628, KB, ms. II 7277, 121.

[71] Ph. Chifflet to Guidi di Bagno, Brussels, 24 March and 28 May1628, KB, ms. II 7277, 147-149 and 169-171; Jacobs, *Parateksten*, 476-477.

[72] Carolina of Austria to J.-J. Chifflet, Besançon, 26 August 1633, BMB, *CC* 24, fo. 309; Longin, "Jean Boyvin" (1912): 153.

more senior d'Andelot by being the first to be reappointed to their old posts at court.[73] These three former *mayordomos* of Isabella were indeed able to take up their positions again under don Ferdinand, but a few days later d'Andelot was also reinstated at his former rank of *primer mayordomo*. This did not, however, keep the Southern Netherlandish *mayordomos* from disputing d'Andelot's precedence.[74] Balançon's success also made him a hate figure for the South Netherlandish nobility, "pour avoir trop affecté les façons & recerché la faveur des Hespagnolz." The prince of Barbançon, as we have seen, was furious when Isabella added his men to the baron of Balançon's command during the siege of 's-Hertogenbosch.[75] During the Cardinal-Infant's governorship he again offended the Southern Netherlandish nobility in his new position as councilor of state. After Pieter Roose's fearsome efforts to remove the nobility from the Council of State by introducing new rules of precedence, there were by 1639 only three aristocrats left in the council. These were the count of Vertaing, who refused to recognize Roose's new rules, retired to Lille, and died there the same year; the duke of Aarschot, who had been imprisoned in Madrid in the aftermath of the 1632 conspiracy, so could not take part in council business; and the baron of Balançon. He too refused to attend, as a protest against Roose, but eventually did arrive at a session of the Council with the fig-leaf that "respeto de ser Borgoñon no podia la nobleza del pais quexarse de que se huviesse allando a lo que los demas nobles rehusavan."[76]

Envy and hostility towards Burgundians as such indicates that they were a recognizable group. It also demonstrates that descent, and being of a particular nation, came out more clearly in situations of conflict or competition. It was, and is, therefore impossible to lump the Franc-Comtois together with the Southern Netherlanders.

[73] Chifflet, *Diaire*, BMB, *CC* 179, fo. 42v.

[74] Chifflet, *Diaire*, BMB, *CC* 179, fo. 57r.

[75] Peter De Cauwer, *'Tranen van bloed:' Het beleg van 's-Hertogenbosch en de oorlog in de Nederlanden, 1629* (Amsterdam, 2008), 130. Daniel Heinsius, *Histoire du Siege de Bolduc...* (Leiden, 1631), 146-147.

[76] Cardinal-Infant to Philip IV, Dunkirk, 17 October 1639, AGR, *SSO* 223, fos. 312-313; René Vermeir, *In staat van oorlog: Filips IV en de Zuidelijke Nederlanden, 1629-1648* (Maastricht, 2001), 214.

The Burgundian courtiers as power brokers

In the introduction to *Princes, Patronage, and the Nobility*, Ronald Asch states that

> patronage could be a crucial instrument for the extension of the authority of central government in previously autonomous provinces and sections of society. For royal patronage the court was the great market-place where all kinds of grants, privileges, and offices were haggled over. For the many 'provincial brokers' of patronage the ministers and court nobility were the patrons upon whom they were dependent, whilst courtiers and office-holders themselves played the role of brokers in relation to the king.[77]

Nothing could be truer of the Franc-Comtois at the Brussels court in general, and of the Chifflet brothers in particular.

The Burgundians at the Brussels court were bombarded with requests for support and information by their co-nationals in the province. The count of Saint-Amour often contacted Jean-Jacques Chifflet to ask for his mediation on behalf of relatives seeking all sorts of appointments and promotions. The provincial governor of the Franche-Comté in the 1620s, the count of Champlitte, carried on a voluminous correspondence with Isabella's physician in which the count was continually asking for information about decisions being taken in Brussels. As has already been said, the Cantecroix couple also exchanged numerous letters with the brothers. Philippe was their contact on the Brussels art market, while Jean-Jacques was regarded as a privileged channel to the infanta herself. In 1628 the count of Cantecroix explained to the physician that his wife's half-brother, Charles, margrave of Austria, had died intestate in Vienna. He took the view that the inheritance should pass to his wife and that this could be arranged with the emperor, but that some help would be appreciated. The countess of Cantecroix had therefore written a letter to Isabella, asking her to mediate with the emperor. The countess wanted Jean-Jacques to deliver the letter to the infanta with his own hand, being confident that she would not refuse him. The countess also relied on Jean-Jacques in private matters, asking

[77] Ronald G. Asch, "Introduction: Court and Household from the Fifteenth to the Seventeenth Centuries," in Ronald G. Asch and Adolf M. Birke (eds.), *Princes, Patronage, and the Nobility: The Court at the Beginning of the Modern Age, c. 1450-1650*, (Oxford, 1991), 17.

him to write to Juan Oswaldo Brito, Secretary of the *Consejo Supremo de Flandes y Borgoña*, to find out whether she would be entitled to a pension after her husband's death. She even called on the help of the brothers to find a suitable wife for her son. And indeed, Jean-Jacques and Philippe brokered the marriage between her son and the famed Béatrix de Cusance in 1635. The brothers also helped obtain noble titles and ecclesiastical preferment for their compatriots. In 1637 Jean-Jacques recommended Claude d'Achey to prince Thomas for the vacant archiepiscopal see of Besançon. In return he asked that his brother, Philippe, be appointed vicar general. Claude d'Achey was consecrated on 12 December 1638. He kept his word, naming Philippe as his vicar general.[78]

Those seeking a place in the Parlement of Dole, the provincial council of the Franche-Comté, made sure to get in touch with their compatriots in Brussels. When Jean-Jacques and Philippe's father got married for a second time, to Isabelle Dard, this gave a connection to Antoine Brun, Isabelle's nephew. Antoine and Philippe became good friends, and lived together during their student days in Bourges. When Antoine's father, a councilor of the Parlement of Dole, died in 1621, Antoine got Philippe, already in Brussels, to pull strings for him. He asked his friend to recommend him for the vacant seat in the Parlement, but unfortunately for Antoine the appointment went to somebody else. In April 1630 the position of *premier maître* of Dole's Chamber of Accounts fell vacant, and again Antoine turned to his friends in Brussels. He asked them to get the backing of Isabella's intimate circle, among whom he counted Ferdinand d'Andelot. The campaign on Brun's behalf was again unsuccessful, this time because powerful patrons were supporting the ambitions of a certain Henri Mathot, whose goal was to be a councilor of the Parlement. By making councilor Grivel *premier maître*, an opening was created for Mathot. Towards the end of the year Antoine made yet another attempt, when councilor Berreur died. He asked Philippe to recommend a certain Menou for this position, so that Antoine himself could succeed to Menou's lucrative job as lieutenant-general of the bailiwick of Amont. But the Chifflets were backing Berreur's son, who obtained the position. Antoine finally became the Parlement's advocate-general.[79] He began angling for a seat on the Brussels Privy Council, but was thwarted by the fierce opposition of

[78] Jacobs, *Parateksten*, 473-474, 618-619, 772.

[79] Albéric de Truchis de Varennes, *Un diplomate franc-comtois au XVIIe siècle: Antoine Brun, 1599-1654* (Besançon, 1932), 11-13, 16, 43-44, 48-49; Jacobs, 531, 572-573.

Pieter Roose, who according to Jules Chifflet had "peu d'inclination ... pour la Bourgogne."[80] It is likely that Antonio Sarmiento, the count of Gondomar's son and a *gentilhombre de la cámara* of the Cardinal-Infant, also had something to do with Antoine's reverses. The two could not stand one another, and don Antonio had pull in Madrid as well as in Brussels. Antoine, however, found a new patron in the marquis of Saint-Martin, another opponent of don Antonio.[81] In 1640 the marquis insisted that Brun be given a seat on the Privy Council, but again Roose vetoed the appointment. In 1642, Antoine Brun did manage to acquire a seat on the *Consejo Supremo de Flandes y Borgoña* in Madrid.[82]

In Antoine Brun's case, the Chifflets seem to have been unable, or unwilling, to use their influence to good effect. Things were somewhat different when they recommended Jean Boyvin as president of the Parlement of Dole in 1631. Boyvin's most important supporters at the Brussels court were François de Rye and Jean-Jacques Chifflet. But this time the brothers were unable to mobilize d'Andelot, as he was supporting the candidacies of Jean-Baptist Gollut and Girardot Nozeroy. There was also yet another strong contender, Froissard-Broissia, who had the support of Olivares' cousin, the marquis of Leganés. Matters were further complicated when Roose expressed a lack of sympathy for Boyvin. The situation became so complex that an appointment was postponed indefinitely. Thanks to intensive lobbying by the Chifflets, however, Boyvin was finally appointed president of the Parlement in 1639.[83]

Purposefully placing Burgundians at court?

The allocation of positions at court was clearly carefully dosed to bring in figures from each of the various territories in the Spanish-Habsburg 'composite state.' That this was the result of deliberate policy is demonstrated by a letter from Philip IV to don Ferdinand, in which he advises his brother to appoint only "naturales del pays" as *gentilhombres de la cámara*, and that half of his *gentilhombres de la boca* should be

[80] Longin, "Jean Boyvin", 153-154.
[81] Truchis de Varennes, *Un diplomate*, 186-187, 223.
[82] Annelies Vanhaelst, *De Hoge Raad voor de Nederlanden en Bourgondië: Leden en bevoegdheden (1627-1665)*, (Master's thesis, Ghent University, 2002), 135-136.
[83] Longin, "Jean Boyvin," 414-421; Jacobs, *Parateksten*, 531-532.

Southern Netherlanders, the other half Spaniards and Italians.[84] Nor were the subjects unaware of this conscious sharing out of important positions between different nationalities. On 8 April 1639 the *Consejo de Estado* considered the request of the baron of Laubespin-Dramelay, a Burgundian, to be appointed *mayordomo* of the Cardinal-Infant in succession to the recently deceased d'Andelot, another *natural de la dicha provincia.*[85] We do not know whether he obtained the post, but in later years he is listed as *mayordomo* of two governors-general in turn, Leopold-Wilhelm and don Juan José de Austria.[86] By a careful distribution of the various nationalities at court, the central authorities encouraged the role of office-holders as power brokers, whose clientage networks with their homeland would reinforce the crown's authority and control over the far-flung territories of the Spanish Monarchy.[87]

The Burgundians were an essential part of such calculations because the Franche-Comté was important to the Spanish Habsburgs in three ways. It was, in the first place, the last remaining fragment of the ancestral homeland of the dukes of Burgundy, the territory to which the Spanish branch of the dynasty had the longest-standing title. This gave the county a tremendously important symbolic resonance as the mark of continuity with the dynasty's Burgundian forefathers.[88] Burgundian descent was important, among other reasons, because it underlay the claim to headship of the prestigious Order of the Golden Fleece. The sovereignty of the order passed by heredity to the head of the House of Burgundy – the duke of Burgundy – and not territorially with the Burgundian state. When, in 1529, Charles V definitively renounced his claim to the duchy of Burgundy in favor of the king of France, he retained the honorary title of duke of Burgundy, to safeguard his power over the order.[89] Philip IV and Charles II of Spain, in their turn,

[84] Philip IV to the Cardinal-Infant, Madrid, 25 March 1635, AGR, *SSO* 212, fos. 349-350.

[85] Petition of the baron of Laubespin, Madrid, 8 April 1639, AGS, *E* 2054, unnumbered.

[86] Roegis, *Het hof,* 84.

[87] On 'brokerage' by court office-holders as an instrument of political integration in France, see Sharon Kettering, "The Historical Development of Political Clientelism," *Journal of Interdisciplinary History*, 18, 3 (1988): 419-447.

[88] Jean-Marie Cauchies, "Philippe le Beau, comte de Bourgogne: une esquisse," in Paul Delsalle and Laurence Delobette (eds.), *La Franche-Comté à la charnière du Moyen Age et de la Renaissance, 1450-1550,* Annales littéraires de l'Université de Franche-Comté 759 (Besançon, 2003), 114.

[89] Vicky Noens, *Het standpunt van het Madrileense hof inzake de onafhankelijkheid van de aartshertogen met betrekking tot binnenlandse aangelegenheden,* (Master's thesis, Ghent University, 2006), 28.

continued to bear the title of duke of Burgundy. This important dynastic and symbolic tie can also be seen in the letters of the kings of Spain. Philip IV spoke of his Burgundian subjects as "vasallos mejores que yo más precie," or as "les premiers vassaux que j'aye et que j'aime le plus."[90] Secondly, the Franche-Comté had high strategic value, as the 'Spanish Road', the overland route for the movement of Spanish troops between Italy and the Netherlands, ran right through the province. When the Cardinal-Infant failed to eject the French forces of occupation from Lorraine in 1634, and when France declared war on Spain in May 1635, it meant the loss of this strategic overland connection with the Netherlands.[91] These events further isolated the already remote Franche-Comté still further from the rest of the Spanish Monarchy. As a result of Charles V's decision in 1531 that Burgundians were henceforth to advise in Brussels on matters touching the Franche-Comté, and of the already mentioned *castellanización* of Philip II's household and his definitive withdrawal to Madrid, where subsequent kings of Spain were to remain, the Burgundians at the Brussels court became the center's only link with their symbolically and strategically important county.[92] This explains in part why the Franche-Comté was so autonomous and relatively independent in internal matters, as already mentioned in the introduction, but also why the Burgundians played such a prominent role in Brussels. It was tremendously important that the Franc-Comtois be kept happy, so that they did not end up as part of a group of Spanish malcontents. France was very close and easily reached. Politically, the county was enormously important in the struggle against France, which is the third reason why this province was so important to the crown. It was also desirable to have reliable and loyal councilors, and who better than the "tan buenos y fieles vasallos" of *par-delà*? Brussels already had a strong *tradition pepinière*, attested by the successful careers of high-flying jurists and councilors from the Franche-Comté such as the two Granvelles, Jean Richardot, and Froissard-Broissia. Between 1621 and 1641 there were no really important Burgundians in the Brussels councils, but their prominence as courtiers shows that this

[90] Philip IV to Charles IV of Lorraine, Madrid, 31 March 1638, AGS, *E* 2245, unnumbered; Philip IV to the Parlement of Dole, Madrid, 1638, in Francisco Elías de Tejada, *La Franche-Comté hispanique* (Dole, 1977), 79.

[91] Geoffrey Parker, *The Army of Flanders and the Spanish Road, 1567-1659: The Logistics of Spanish Victory and Defeat in the Low Countries' Wars*, 2nd ed. (Cambridge, 2004), 51-52, 66-67, 72-78.

[92] Jacobs, *Parateksten*, 252; Febvre, *Philippe II*, 162-168.

tradition was maintained over the long term, albeit arguably at a lower rank.

It is noticeable that the Burgundians in the Brussels court all came from families with key positions in the Franche-Comté, making them perfect power brokers and network providers. It is therefore possible that the central authorities made this one of their criteria in selecting and appointing office-holders at court. The eldest brother of Claude and François de Rye, for example, was grand bailiff of Dole, and their uncle was archbishop of Besançon. Before they were appointed to the court, Ferdinand d'Andelot was colonel of the regiment of Amont and governor of Gray, while Jean-Baptiste de la Baume was governor of Dole.[93] Jean-Jacques and Philippe Chifflet's father was a member of Besançon's city council and a respected physician, their uncle was a professor at the University of Dole, and Jean-Jacques' father-in-law was mayor of Vesoul. Both brothers furthermore already had very good contacts with the Burgundian nobility and the Bisontin urban elite before they were appointed to Isabella's household. The Franc-Comtois Charles-Emmanuel de Gorrevod, marquis of Marnay, grand bailiff of Amont and a member of the Parlement of Dole, had been one of archduke Albert's *gentilhombres de la cámara*. He no longer held office at court under the infanta, but his Southern Netherlandish wife Isabelle de Bourgogne and her sister Marguerite were both among Isabella's *dueñas de honor*. When Charles-Emmanuel died in 1625, his eldest son succeeded him as grand bailiff and his second son was appointed *sumiller de cortina* of governors-general Leopold-Wilhelm and don Juan José de Austria. He also became archbishop of Besançon, in succession to Claude d'Achey.[94] A document from 1622 preserved in the archive of the *Audience* in the General State Archives, Brussels, mentions a certain Benito de Thomasin as a chaplain in Isabella's oratory. This individual is not mentioned in any of the other sources relevant to this study, nor has further information about him been found. But if this Benito can be identified as Benoit de Thomassin, then this chaplain of the oratory was also a perfect power broker, and furthermore an excellent choice to maintain contacts with the free county of Burgundy. For Benoit was

93 Brun, *La Franche-Comté*, 29-30; Goethals, *Dictionnaire*, 59; Chifflet, *Traitté*, 17-21.

94 Guidi di Bagno to F. Barberini, Brussels, 9 November 1624 and Guidi di Bagno to Spada, Ghent, 11 December 1625, in De Meester, *Correspondance*, nos. 1164, 1442; Chifflet, *Nobiliaire de Franche-Comté*, BMB, *CC* 185, fo. 71v; Brun, *La Franche-Comté*, 29; Herckenrode, *Nobiliaire*, 1:281-282; Roegis, *Het hof*, 67; Castan, "Les origines," 70.

the son of Adrien, President of the Parlement of Dole from 1605 to 1631.[95]

It has already been indicated that once appointed to the household, the career of these Franc-Comtois went from strength to strength. They received knighthoods in prestigious orders of chivalry, pensions, important positions in the army, in the Church or in one of the central organs of government, they were able to obtain remunerative positions for their children or to marry them into influential families. So we have to ask ourselves whether these favors were showered on them solely in recognition of services already rendered and because of their personal access to the king's deputy in Brussels, or because this also suited the purposes of the crown. When the position of court office-holders was boosted, this increased their value as power brokers, whose ability to grant access to the wellsprings of princely patronage guaranteed the loyalty and support of their province. The Burgundian court dignitaries helped to maintain and extend the authority of the central powers in out-of-the-way Franche-Comté. This is probably why, for example, Philippe Chifflet was named abbot of Balerne in 1639. It suited Philippe, but it also suited the central powers, as the abbacy put their creature in a position to make present or recommend candidates for important ecclesiastical benefices in the Franche-Comté.[96] Furthermore, because Philippe resided at the Brussels court and not in his Burgundian abbey, his decisions could be influenced. Philip IV's attempts to appoint the baron of Balançon as provincial governor of the Franche-Comté, and the ultimate appointment of his brother-in-law, the marquis of Saint-Martin, should probably be seen in the same light. Since the second half of the 16th century the governors of the Franche-Comté had barely left the province and had held no positions at court.[97] But when the governorship fell vacant at the death of Ferdinand de Rye in 1636, Philip IV was clearly looking for a replacement within his brother's household. After Balançon had declined the post at least twice, the king reluctantly appointed the marquis of Saint-Martin.[98] He could just as well have sought out a candidate he would have liked better and who lived in the province itself, as had been done in the past, but now

[95] Incomplete household list of Isabella, 1622, AGR, *Audience* 20, fo. 16v; Mesmay, *Dictionnaire*, 327; Brun, *La Franche-Comté*, 29.

[96] Jacobs, *Parateksten*, 634-637.

[97] Gresset and Debard, "La Franche-Comté", 209-210.

[98] Roose to Philip IV and Olivares, Brussels, 3 December 1637, AGR, *GR* 1500, fo. 195v.

that the loss of the Spanish Road had made the Franche-Comté even more inaccessible, somebody with connections to the Brussels court must have seemed a better choice. Furthermore, in 1640 Saint-Martin married Lambertine de Ligne, further ensuring contact between the Franche-Comté and the Southern Netherlands.[99]

Conclusion

The Burgundians at the Brussels court were clearly very aware of their origins and identity. They were closely connected by marriage and by patron-client relations. We can, without doubt, speak of a Burgundian network and of a Franc-Comtois nation at the Brussels court. To some extent this made them a closed group, but there was still room for friendly relations or alliances with other groups at court. There were a few marriages between Burgundians and Southern Netherlanders, and the Chifflets also had excellent contacts with people from outside the Franche-Comté. The Chifflet brothers not only had Burgundian patrons, but also obtained patronage from Thomas of Savoy, the Italian Guidi di Bagno, and the Portuguese marquis of Castel-Rodrigo. The Chifflets actively defended the interests of the Franche-Comté and intensively mediated between their compatriots and the Brussels court, but more than once they did the same for non-Burgundian friends and acquaintances, such as, for instance, the Moretus family.[100] In brief, there was a clear Franc-Comtois group at the Brussels court, but it was one that was open to non-Burgundian contacts and relationships. Only by studying this Burgundian group does it become clear that the allocation of positions at the Brussels court resulted from deliberate policy and careful planning. This allocation was dual: the central authorities consciously shared offices out between the different nations of the Spanish Monarchy, and at the same time, while only appointing those with a track record of loyal service, also had an eye to who was a potential power broker. This was a smart political move, as the monarchy was highly dependent on patronage as a crucial element in extending and maintaining control over its disparate territories. All the nations at court provided the central authorities with clients in their homeland, bringing these regions closer to the crown and furthering the political integration of the Spanish Monarchy. For this particular

[99] Chenaye-Desbois, *Dictionnaire*, 11: 101.
[100] See Jacobs, *Parateksten*, passim.

purpose the crown probably looked to Burgundian courtiers rather more than to others, because they were one of the few ties that still bound the distant and isolated Franche-Comté to the rest of the monarchy. This was not only a strategically and politically important province, but also of immense symbolic value, as the oldest territory of the Burgundian inheritance. For this reason the Burgundians played a highly significant role in the court, which could often provoke envy and mistrust. being appointed to a lucrative position at court generally went hand in hand with moving up the social ladder, which also increased an individual's value as a power broker. It is possible that the central authorities rewarded useful servants at court with offices and other favors precisely to increase their prestige and value as a patron. However that may be, between 1621 and 1641 the Brussels court was a significant locus for the integration of elites from the numerous Spanish-Habsburg territories, and a lively point of contact between the political center and the provincial and local notables.

Anne of Austria, founder of the Val-de-Grâce in Paris

Olivier Chaline
Université Paris IV – Sorbonne

It might be rather surprising to include an article concerning a Parisian abbey in a book on the Habsburg courts. I was nevertheless delighted to accept the invitation to contribute to this volume since it gives me the opportunity to re-place that singular royal foundation in a new and wider perspective, the *pietas austriaca*, than that of traditional French historiography. Apart from some concise and often misleading allusions to the Escorial, the historians who have been studying Anne of Austria or the Val-de-Grâce Abbey never tried to relate the former infanta's religious sensibility with that of her Spanish and Austrian relatives. They ignored the Styrian court of Graz as well as the convents of the *Descalzas Reales* and the *Encarnación* in Madrid. Consequently, the Val-de-Grâce, obviously one of the most outstanding 17th-century century Parisian buildings, remains quite neglected and misunderstood, in spite of very valuable studies by art historians.[1] It appears like a rather strange exception without any significant consequences on French classicism: an abbey founded by a devout queen who withdrew there in accordance with the piety of a foreign and often rival dynasty, a Roman-inspired church in a country supposed to have resisted the so-called "temptation of baroque architecture". A detailed study what Anne of Austria intended to do will certainly bring out a more accurate and renewed definition of the whole architectural enterprise of the Val-de-Grâce.

[1] Claude Mignot, *Le Val-de-Grâce. L'ermitage d'une reine* (Paris, 1994), 14-27, is the best study. The same author published too the estimates and contracts: Claude Mignot, "L'église du Val-de-Grâce, nouveaux documents," *Bulletin de la Société de l'histoire de l'art français*, 1975, 101-136. See also *Trésors d'art sacré à l'ombre du Val-de-Grâce*, ed. Jacques Charles (Paris, 1988), and Olivier Chaline, "Val-de-Grâce et Théatins,", in Rainer Babel, Guido Braun and Thomas Nicklas (eds.), *Bourbon und Wittelsbach* (Mûnster, 2010), 365-387. The two main sources are Jacques Ferraige, *La vie admirable et digne d'une fidèle imitation de la B. mère Marguerite d'Arbouze* (Paris, 1628) and Claude Fleury, *La vie de la vénérable mère Marguerite d'Arbouze, abbesse et réformatrice de l'abbaye royale du Val-de-Grâce* (Paris, 1684).

Why founding the Val-de-Grâce?

The encounter with Mother Marguerite

When in 1615 the infanta Anna left her father the Spanish king to become queen of France, he advised her to visit convents as she used to do before.[2] In France, too, kings' and queens' daughters would do it as a rule, like several devout ladies of the court. In 1616 or 1617, the queen met the Benedictine prioress of Notre-Dame de Grâce de la Ville-l'Evêque, near Paris, Marguerite de Veny d'Arbouze, whose religious name was Mother Marguerite de Sainte-Gertrude.[3] She spoke Spanish very well and the queen became friendly with her.[4] When the prioress was recalled to her abbey at Montmartre, Anne of Austria asked her royal husband to make her abbess somewhere. The king chose to appoint her to the Val-Profond Abbey at Bièvres, south of Paris, a religious place that in 1513 started to be known as the Val-de-Grâce de Notre-Dame de la Crèche ("Our Lady of Nativity's in the Vale of Grace"). On 21 March 1619, the queen attended the new abbess's investiture and her own coach took her to the abbey. At the queen's request, Louis XIII granted permission to the nuns to move from Bièvres to Paris, where they bought the house of the Petit-Bourbon in the southern suburbs (Faubourg Saint-Jacques) in front of the Carmelite nuns' house. On 4 March 1621, the queen announced that she would become the founder of the abbey, giving enough money to buy the new house, and, in September, while she was still busy with the king besieging the southern protestant town of Montauban, the nuns moved from Bièvres to Paris, near queen and court.

[2] Ruth Kleinman, *Anne of Austria, queen of France* (Columbus OH, 1985). See 3-16 "The Infanta Dona Anna," 53-54, visiting convents, moving to Paris, 186-187, building the church, 286, last will.

[3] Mignot, *Le Val-de-Grâce*, 14-17.

[4] A generation earlier, in Madrid, when the young queen Margaret arrived from Styria in 1599 without being fluent in Castilian, she could speak in German at the convent of the Descalzas Reales with empress Maria (widow of emperor Maximilian II) and her daughter sister Margaret of the Cross: Magdalena Sánchez, *The Empress, the Queen and the Nun. Women and Power at the Court of Philip III of Spain* (Baltimore and London, 1998), 141.

The queen's vow

In doing so, Anne of Austria felt individually protected.[5] She paid all the more visits to the Val-de-Grâce as her position at court became more difficult. After a miscarriage in 1622, the king deserted her and didn't trust her anymore. As a foreign woman unable to give a Dauphin to the kingdom, she found herself in a hopeless situation, the centre of court intrigues and constantly espied by the king's and Richelieu's creatures. In such conditions, Mother Marguerite's friendship and spiritual advice made the Val-de-Grâce especially attractive.

After Marguerite's death 1626, the queen gave Father Ferraige – the Val-de-Grâce chaplain – the responsibility of writing a life of Mother Marguerite, which was published 1628. Its frontispiece shows how strong the queen's attachment to the abbess was. Both are represented kneeling and praying, on either side of the *corpus Christi*, the queen with a globe and sceptre, the abbess with a crook and ruler. The Nativity is represented behind this radiant monstrance, and, on both sides, the Virgin Mary and the angel Gabriel, are reminiscent of the Annunciation. The engraving shows the angel's promise and its extraordinary fulfilment, and also conveys a dual feeling of suffering as well as hope: the lack of a Dauphin as well as the faith in God to whom nothing is impossible. The childless queen identifies with the Virgin and the angel's promise applies to her, too. Anne vowed to build a magnificent church if she were given a son.

Unfortunately, time went on without the queen producing any child, and the king declared war on Spain. Lonely, under close watch, the queen would often visit the Val-de-Grâce, whose abbess, Louise de Milley, the spiritual heiress of Mother Marguerite, was born in Franche-Comté, a Spanish territory. The abbey was used by the queen as a secrete letter-box for her correspondence with her brother the Cardinal-Infant, governor of the Low Countries, and his mayordomo mayor, the marquis of Mirabel. When it was discovered in August 1637, chancellor Séguier and the archbishop of Paris, Gondi, entered the Val-de-Grâce and searched the nuns' cells and the queen's own apartment. They found nothing there, but the abbess was deposed and exiled in a castle outside Paris, the queen herself interrogated about her letters and in the end proved guilty by Richelieu of corresponding with the enemy. The worse was still to come: she was forced to write and sign

[5] Claude Dulong, "Anne d'Autriche, la piété d'une reine, la piété d'une mère," in *Trésors d'art sacré à l'ombre du Val-de-Grâce* [see n. 1], 48-51.

a full confession she submitted to her husband. From then on, the king forbade her to enter any convent without his permission.[6]

Fulfilment

Still without a Dauphin and guilty of secret correspondence with the king's enemies, Anne of Austria was in grave danger of being repudiated and she was obliged to abandon her fate to Richelieu. But the cardinal was well aware that the kingdom without a Dauphin was on the road to destruction, and he urged the king to draw closer to his wife. In January 1638, it became clear that the queen had become pregnant and on 5th September she gave birth to Louis Dieudonné whose Christian name expresses how immensely relieved the new parents felt. Later, in 1640, Anne gave birth to another son, Philip, duke of Anjou. Louis XIII granted his wife permission to visit convents again, except the Val-de-Grâce whose access remained forbidden to her. She therefore refused to visit any convent as long as she could not visit her own foundation. However, her unexpected double motherhood greatly improved her situation at court. Richelieu died in 1642 and when Louis XIII died, too, in May 1643, she became queen-regent. As soon as her husband died, she sent for Louise de Milley. At few weeks later, on Whitsunday, she herself returned to the Val-de-Grâce.

Anne of Austria was very proud of her sons. She was now queen-mother and regent, unexpectedly leaning on cardinal Mazarin to govern France. The prayers of the barren and humbled queen were granted. It now remained for her to fulfil her vow and build a large and magnificent church. In April 1645, the still very young king, Louis XIV, laid the foundation stone. A gold medal, by Jean Varin, explains the importance of such a ceremony: on one side the queen and her son are represented, alluding to the prayers' fulfilment; on the other side, the church stand for the vow's fulfilment.[7]

The former infant of Spain is now the queen-regent of France at a time of war with Spain, and her main task is to preserve her son's royal inheritance and establish his power. She shows how grateful she is for being the king's mother. Three ceremonies can sum it up: 1624, the queen lays the foundation stone of the first abbey buildings; 1645, her son the king does the same for the church; and 1655, her younger son,

[6] Mignot, *Le Val-de-Grâce*, 26.
[7] Mignot, *Le Val-de-Grâce*, 33-34.

the duke of Anjou, attends the monastery's achievement.[8] Both Anne's sons were therefore associated to their mother's vow.

The queen's monastery

The original abbey

Moving 1621 to the *Faubourg Saint-Jacques*, the Benedictine nuns settled on the outskirts of the capital's not far away from other important convents, those of the Carmelite nuns, the Ursulines, the Feuillantines, etc., along the ancient road to Spain and Santiago de Compostella. We know little about the original abbey. It consisted of medieval buildings, the *Petit-Bourbon* (later destroyed) and of new ones, erected from 1624 onwards. The cloister remained unfinished.[9] Such a haphazard complex of buildings is typically reminiscent of the *Descalzas Reales* in Madrid, the former house of the *contador* Gutiérrez, which was used as residence by empress Isabella and later turned into a convent.[10] Empress Maria, Maximilian II's widow, when she returned to Spain, settled in her apartment near the closure and was therefore able to communicate with her daughter, *Sor Margarita de la Cruz,* the former archduchess Margarita.[11]

At the Val-de-Grâce, Anne of Austria, who first settled in the *Petit-Bourbon* – which, despite its name, was never a royal house –, hard an apartment fitted for her inside the abbey, on the first floor of the eastern wing overlooking the garden. This was the very place of the 1637 search. Unfortunately, we have no remaining drawing, not even a description, of the queen's apartment. We just know that it comprised a room for the ladies in attendance, a bedchamber, a study, a wardrobe and another room. However, a report written by Guillet de Saint-Georges about the painter Philippe de Champaigne (born in Brussels) tells us that he created

[8] Pierre Lemoine, "L'Abbaye royale de Notre-Dame du Val-de-Grâce," in *Trésors d'art sacré à l'ombre du Val-de-Grâce* [see n. 1], 76-83.
[9] Mignot, *Le Val-de-Grâce*, 17-24.
[10] Antonio Bonet Correa, *Monasterios reales del Patrimonio nacional* (Barcelona, 1988), 27-39.
[11] See Magdalena Sánchez, *The Empress, the Queen and the Nun* [see n. 4], especially chapter six, 137-155.

the decoration of two rooms.[12] For one, he painted a series of portraits of empresses and queens who died in odour of sanctity: it was said to feature no less than 5 empresses from Occident and 15 from Orient, 17 holy queens who became nuns, 23 queens nuns, 4 queens who were compelled to become nuns, 4 nuns who became queens and died in the world, 4 others who endured the same fate but died nevertheless in a convent, 21 daughters of Roman emperors, 8 of Byzantine emperors. None of these portraits survived to this day, but they could be compared to the series of Habsburg ones at the *Descalzas Reales*. The Bourbon family portraits were hung in the chapter's room until the Revolution. For the second room, Champaigne and his workshop painted 12 scenes of St. Benedictus' life, inspired from Sangrinus's *Speculum et exemplar christicolarum vita beatissimi patris Benedicti monarchor. Patriarchae sanctissimi*, published in Rome 1587.[13] Nowadays, 8 of them still exist: St. Benedict fed by friar Romanus (Brussels, Musée Royal des Beaux Arts); Poison avoided, or the poisoned jug (St. Petersburg, Ermitage); St. Benedict meets Placidus and Maurus (Menton, Musée); The axe fastered again to its handle (Brussels); Placidus pulled by Maurus out of the water (Brussels); Stone exercised (Brussels); Risen child (Brussels).

Lastly, thanks to a 1644 estimate, it's known that, in the queen's bedroom, the chimney piece was decorated with two sculptures of virtues and angels bearing her coat of arms. Another painting by Champaigne (now at Versailles) shows Anne of Austria, Louis XIV and the duke of Anjou presented by St. Benedict and St. Scholastica to the Holy Trinity. From her apartment, the queen could keep up with the advance of church's building from 1645 onwards.

Monastery-palace or hermitage?

In 1645, the church's architect F. Mansart submitted a very ambitious design for a monastery-palace. At that time, the possibility that the Val-de-Grâce could turn into some sort of Escorial was at its highest. A large church surmounted by a dome would be built between the abbey to the South and the palace of the queen-regent to the North. The nuns' choir

[12] Bernard Dorival, *Philippe de Champaigne 1602-1674* (Paris, 1976), 3 vol., especially I, 198-200. About this famous painter, see also Lorenzo Pericoloso, *Philippe de Champaigne* (Tournai, 2002) and the catalogue of the exhibition in Lille, *Philippe de Champaigne 1602-1674. Entre politique et devotion* (Lille, 2007).

[13] Dorival, *Philippe de Champaigne,* I, 48-49 and III (Catalogue), 61-63, nrs. 100-108 [see n. 12].

would have linked the church with the abbey, while St. Anne's chapel would have the same with the church and palace. The whole building complex would have been preceded by a large rectangular forecourt, closed by railings and flanked by two pavilions, resembling a castle's main forecourt.[14]

However, it never came to anything. It should have given Paris an absolutely unique building without any real precedent in French history. Mansart was dismissed as early as 1646 and the work entrusted to Lemercier, the architect of the Sorbonne chapel, although the endless war with Spain and the incoming Fronde hindered the project. St. Anne's chapel was built, but not the queen's palace. We don't know precisely if the abandonment of the project owes more to the overwhelming financial difficulties or to the queen's own decision. When Lemercier died in 1654, Le Muet succeeded him and there was no further reference to the projected palace of the queen-mother.[15] Louis XIV soon became of age.

Anne of Austria had an apartment fitted for herself in the North-east corner of the convent buildings now in the process of being enlarged.[16] Between 1654 and 1655, a corner pavilion facing both the dome and gardens was erected. On its pediment, under a pelican feeding its young and the initials "A and L", one can still read nowadays the following motto: "natos et nostra tuemur" (Let's protect our children and estates). The queen's apartment was then laid on two floors: a lower hall paved with black and white marble and decorated with 4 landscapes by Philippe de Champaigne, whose subjects are the lives of holy hermits and a ceiling painting of Mary Magdalen borne into heaven by angels; a bedroom with an alcove also decorated by Champaigne, and a small chapel.

The queen-mother had a true hermitage at her disposal, both within the closure and perfectly autonomous, for praying and meditating. But she never became a nun and remained the founding queen who left her imprint on the whole building.

[14] Mignot, *Le Val-de-Grâce*, 28-35.

[15] Mignot, *Le Val-de-Grâce*, 35-38 and 46-51.

[16] Mignot, *Le Val-de-Grâce*, 39-42 about the first apartment, and 51-53 about the second. I'd like to thank my colleague Krista De Jonge who turned my attention to the form of the pavilions without any equivalent elsewhere in France. They can be compared with the Spanish pavilions looking like towers at the Escorial or in the Cárcel de Corte in Madrid. The original model is nevertheless Flemish.

Royal magnificence

Despite the queen's admiration for Mother Marguerite, certain disagreements remained with the abbess because of her insistence on austerity. Mother Marguerite, and, later, Louise de Milley and Marie de Burges, were reforming abbesses who succeeded in strictly enforcing the Benedictine rule. Soon, Mother Marguerite persuaded the queen not to turn the abbey into a palace.[17] And when thirty years later, it was finally possible to resume work and complete the cloister, its buildings were as imposing as austere. The unique exception was precisely the queen's pavilion, perched on top of columns, and overlooking the dome.

But the queen imposed her will on the nuns as far as the church-building was concerned. She fulfilled her own vow. God had given her a Dauphin, now the Most Christian King of France. For such a favour, it was impossible for her not to express her deep gratitude through the magnificence of her scheme, as suited an infanta of Spain and queen of France. Le Muet completed a very Roman-looking church with the highest dome in Paris at that time, covered in gilt-coppered plates, as the Invalides dome, later modelled after it. Inside the church, deals were made with Mignard for the dome's fresco in 1663, and with Le Muet and Le Duc for the main altar. For it, the queen refused a design by Bernini. The queen's mark is everywhere. On the front both initials "A and L" give its meaning to the Latin inscription "Jesu nascenti Virginiq. Matri". Celebrating the Nativity, it's her own motherhood that the queen reminds everyone. Outside, as inside, *fleurs de lis* appear everywhere, like the intertwined initials and the arms of France and Spain. The sculptures on the nave's vault (medallions with figures of St. Zacharias and St Elizabeth, the Virgin and St. Joseph, St. Anne and St. Joachim) link the birth of the Dauphin with miracles: Elizabeth was too old to give birth to a child, and so was Anne, who lived apart from Joachim.

The dome expresses the political and religious dimension of the queen's vow: the coats of arms of France and Spain are figured on the dome's pendentives; the royal initials are repeated on several places; at the basis of the drum, the church's dedication reads: "Anna Austria D.G. Francorum regina regniq. Rectrix cui subjecit Deus omnes hostes ut conderet domum in nomine suo Ecc. A.M.D.C.L.".

The fresco represents the Trinity, Ecclesia triumphans and militans, and the queen herself presented to the Trinity by her saint patron, St.

[17] Mignot, *Le Val-de-Grâce*, 32-33.

Anne, and St Louis, giving her the sceptre and a model of the Val-de-Grâce.[18]

Just as king Louis XIII vowed to dedicate his kingdom to the Virgin if he were given a Dauphin, the queen vowed to do the same with the Val-de-Grâce.[19]

Anne's religion

There is no study of Anne's religion. For that reason, it remains difficult to distinguish what belongs to the *pietas austriaca*, what is in accordance with the gallican traditions and what originates in the queen's individual faith. Nevertheless, the Val-de-Grâce enables us to trace some of its major features.

Founder-queen

As a founder since 1621, the queen fits into a dual French and Habsburg tradition. Many French queens had founded abbeys or convents, but there were no recent examples. Nevertheless, Mary de Medici, Henry IV's queen, had supported the settlement of the Spanish Carmelite nuns in France. Anne of Austria, taking the Val-de-Grâce under her protection, paid for the new establishment in Paris and persuaded the king to abandon his right to appoint the abbess, re-establishing the triennal election system there.

But Anne of Austria went further and, in doing so, recalled two other Habsburg women who also founded convents: doña Juana of Austria, widow of don Juan Manuel of Portugal, who founded the *Descalzas Reales* (Royal Discalced Poor Clares) in Madrid in 1555, and Anne's mother herself, the archduchess Margarita, sister to the future emperor Ferdinand II and queen of Spain, also founded in 1610 in Madrid the *Encarnación* for Augustinian sisters.[20] She laid the foundation stone in

[18] Jean-Claude Boyer, "La fresque de Pierre Mignard," in *Trésors d'art sacré* [see n. 1], 152-156.

[19] René Laurentin, *Le Vœu de Louis XIII, passé ou avenir de la France* (Paris, 2004).

[20] Sánchez, *The Empress, the Queen and the Nun* [see n. 4], 140. The queen founded the convent as a thanksgiving act to God for expulsion of the Moriscos which began in 1609. It is worth noting that she designated as prioress her friend nun, Mariana de San José who she knew from Palencia near Valladolid. Quite the same story happened again with queen Anne and Marguerite d'Arbouze a few years later in Paris. Mother and daughter were founder and patroness.

July 1611 and died prematurely some months later. The convent stands near the Alcazar in Madrid and a secret passage links the palace and the convent.[21] Built very carefully, the *Encarnación* provided the pattern for several later buildings in Madrid. The same was true later in Paris with the Val-de-Grâce.

But I'd like to report a more significant similarity between mother and daughter. The devotion to Corpus Christi was a permanent feature of *pietas austriaca* insisting both on the incarnation and God's real presence in the consecrated host.[22] Margarita of Austria founded the *Encarnación* and her daughter the Val-de-Grâce de Notre-Dame de la Crèche, whose dedications are pretty similar. In both monasteries, the adoration of Corpus Christi was the most important element of the nuns' daily life with the holy Mass. We have also seen the frontispiece's engraving recalling Mother Marguerite's biography. There is even a possibility that Mother Marguerite, who spoke Spanish and whose name was Margaret, too, was like a spiritual mother to the young queen, although I am incapable of saying whether the appointment of Mother Marguerite as abbess of the Val-de-Grâce was rather the outcome of chance than that of the queen's request. It remains that from the beginning of her life in France, Anne of Austria took a keen interest in those Benedictine nuns.

A keen interest in the Benedictine nuns of the Val-de-Grâce

In supporting a Benedictine abbey, Anne of Austria had chosen an order that was not the most cherished one in her family. She was not deeply attached like other infantas to the Poor Clares and she did not choose the Augustinian sisters her mother loved so much. But she was no less resolute than her. Margarita of Austria, born at the Styrian court where the Jesuits knew a special favour, refused to accept a Franciscan confessor, as it was usual in Spain, but retained an Austrian Jesuit as her confessor.[23] Her daughter proved to be no less attached to Benedictines than her mother to the Jesuits and the Augustinian sisters. Her iconography expresses it very clearly: the twelve paintings about St. Benedict's life were in the queen's apartment, and another painting by Champaigne shows the queen and her sons being presented to the

[21] Bonet Correa, *Monasterios reales* [see n. 10], 48-55.

[22] Anna Coreth, *Pietas austriaca. Österreichische Frömmigkeit im Barock* (Vienna, 1980, 2nd ed.). We completely lack such a study for the French kings of the Modern Era.

[23] Sánchez, *The Empress, the Queen and the Nun* [see n. 4], 143.

Trinity by St Benedict and his sister St. Scholastica who thereby became the intercessors of the French royal family.[24]

Consequently, Anne of Austria, the young king and the duke of Anjou are at home there. But when the queen goes to the Val-de-Grâce, she is alone, not even in the king's company. Her apartment is distinct from the king's. Thus we can trace both similarities and differences with the Spanish tradition of royal monasteries: on the one hand, the queen's apartment is not a mere annexe, but really belongs to the abbey. Anne of Austria could take part in the monastic life as often as she wished, which can be compared with the royal housing in medieval Castilian monasteries. On the other hand, Anne of Austria never went to the abbey with her court. The Val-de-Grâce was not a royal palace and remained a place of retreat for the queen.

Retreat

Choosing the Val-de-Grâce as a place of retreat, the queen followed at least partly her own family tradition. The *Descalzas Reales* had successively welcome two widows: doña Juana and empress Maria. Both were born in that place. But Anne's position in 1643 France was completely different. Firstly, for both women, their husband's death signified the end of their public life, but for Anne it meant, on the contrary, becoming queen-regent. She spent several days of retreat went in the Val-de-Grâce, but never left power nor wordly life (although it was sometimes said that she intended to do so). Secondly, it is obvious when one looks at the queen's portrait as a widow in 1643 that she didn't follow the Spanish tradition established by empress Maria: she does not look like a nun. Finally, the queen had her own apartment inside the abbey, a simpler one than that of Louvre but very luxurious in comparison with the nuns' cells. She could stay with the nuns and walk in the gardens, whereas empress Maria lived outside the closure.

Except in the years 1637-1643, Anne of Austria went very frequently to the Val-de-Grâce. When Mother Marguerite was still alive, twice a week and each Friday she had lunch with the nuns. She attended all the feasts of the Virgin Mary and just before Christmas was in charge of laying the infant Jesus in the manger in the church's nativity piece. From 1643 to her death in January 1666, she went 537 times to the abbey

[24] Pericoloso, *Philippe de Champaigne* [see n. 12], 145, and *Philippe de Champaigne 1602-1674* [see n. 12], 220-225.

and spent 146 nights there. She took part in the liturgy and adoration of Corpus Christi. She spent time conversing with the abbess. In the first chapel she could pray on the grave of Mother Marguerite and often said: "If she obtains a child for me, I will made her a saint". Nevertheless, she didn't share her mother's passion for relics. She longed for solitude, as Mme de Motteville noted, which explains why her apartment was decorated with scenes from lives of hermits.[25]

There, at Christmas 1664, physicians informed her that she had cancer. She wanted to die near the nuns, like a widowed infanta, but the king, her son, ordered her to go back to the Louvre and die there in a palace, instead of a monastery.

Conclusion

The Val-de-Grâce is an exceptional foundation in France, mingling *pietas austriaca* and French monarchical traditions. The Escorial's pattern was quickly abandoned but the comparison is obvious with the *Descalzas Reales* and the *Encarnación*. Anne of Austria was the worthy daughter of Margarita and grand-daughter of Maria Anna of Bavaria, two somewhat unknown figures in France. The Val-de-Grâce was founded by a queen who became regent, and not by the king himself. The fact dismisses any comparison with the Escorial. Anna of Austria didn't build a monastery-palace, but an abbey with a place of retreat for herself, where she could find peace and energy to carry out her duty as a queen. The Val-de-Grâce, unlike the *Descalzas Reales*, never became a place of retreat for widows, unmarried or illegitimate kings' daughters. After Anne's death, no other queen occupied her apartment. Her niece and daughter-in-law, Maria Teresa of Austria, also founded in Paris a small Carmelite convent she often visited. Anne of Austria created another Bourbon necropolis in 1662 when she obtained from the king her dead grand-daughter's heart to be sent to the Val-de-Grâce. Her last will and testament also provided for her own heart to be buried there, in St. Anne's chapel.

[25] *Philippe de Champaigne 1602-1674* [see n. 12], 230-237.

Some reflections on the ceremonial and image of the kings and queens of the House of Habsburg in the sixteenth and seventeenth centuries[1]

Alejandro López Álvarez
Instituto Universitario "La Corte en Europa"
(Universidad Autónoma de Madrid)

Introduction: Stables, state vehicles and the modern courtier

One of the departments of the Spanish royal households that underwent the greatest transformation during the sixteenth century was the Stable (*Caballeriza*) incorporating changes that would be even more significant in the following century. This department was responsible for expressing the majesty of the sovereigns beyond the palace and presenting the

[1] The writing of this article was made possible by the financial support provided by a postdoctoral Herzog-Ernst-Stipendium from the Fritz Thyssen Stiftung which enabled the author to spend 2006 in the Forschungszentrum Gotha für kultur- und sozialwissenschaftliche Studien at Erfurt University. Abbreviations used: ACA (Archivo de la Corona de Aragón); AGS (Archivo General de Simancas), AGP (Archivo General de Palacio, Madrid); AHN (Archivo Histórico Nacional, Madrid); BA (Biblioteca de Ajuda, Lisbon); BAE (*Biblioteca de Autores Españoles*); BNE (Biblioteca Nacional de España); BNF (Bibliothèque Nationale de France); BNH (National Library, Budapest, Hungary); BNP (Bibliothèque Nationale de France, Paris); BPR (Biblioteca Palacio Real, Madrid); BSB (Bayerische Staatsbibliothek, Munich); CJH (Consejo y Juntas de Hacienda); CSR (Casas y Sitios Reales), E (Estado); COA (College of Arms, London); CODOIN (*Colección de Documentos Inéditos para la Historia de España*, Madrid, 1842–1895, 113 vols); FBG (Forschungsbibliothek, Gotha); IVDJ (Instituto Valencia de Don Juan, Madrid); KVC (Kunstsammlungen der Veste Coburg); LJG (Landesmuseum Johaneum, Graz); MCM (Museo de Carruajes de Madrid); ME (Monasterio de El Escorial); MDRM (Monasterio de las Descalzas Reales, Madrid); MNA (Museo Nacional de Arte de Cataluña, Barcelona); GNM (Germanisches Nationalmuseum, Nuremberg), RAH (Real Academia de la Historia, Madrid); RMEM (Real Monasterio de la Encarnación, Madrid); SCD (Sherborne Castle, Dorset); SFG (Stiftung Schloss Friedenstein Gotha, Schlossmuseum); SND (Schloss Neuburg an der Donau, Neuburg); UCM, Universidad Complutense de Madrid (PhD. diss.); USBK (Universität- und Stadtbibliothek, Cologne); ZKW (Zamek Królewski, Warsaw) and WLBS (Württembergisches Landesbibliothek, Stuttgart).

royal image and figure to their subjects and the rest of the world.[2] From the mid-sixteenth century, this area of the household increased in importance and significance in the court; gradual changes in the organization, structure, and functions of the Stables were designed to respond better to the needs of the royal service, and adjust to new socio-economic realities and the obligations of etiquette and formal ceremony which were being codified throughout this period. An analysis of this development reveals, amongst other things, the transformation of the medieval organizational model into a modern one, more suited to the baroque court. Various circumstances contributed to such a radical transformation of the Stable. The development of the royal household caused the Burgundian Stable to gradually assume pre-eminence over its Castilian counterpart, whilst the establishment of the court in Madrid brought in its wake the restructuring of certain ordinances of the royal household. There is no doubt that the Stable was subject to the most changes in this respect, being required to fulfil a different mission and acquire a set of competences it did not have when the court travelled about. Thirdly, the introduction and systematic use of state vehicles also changed the Stables in various ways: apart from increasing expenditure and the number of servants, it modified the protocols and ceremonial associated with the king and queen, as well as their public image. It is to these latter questions that we are going to devote our attention here, with illustrations drawn from a wide-ranging set of pictorial sources.[3]

[2] For the Stables in the medieval period, see Jaime Salazar y Acha, *La Casa del rey de Castilla y León en la Edad Media* (Madrid, 2000), 30, 33, 35, 114–115, 125 and 148–149; Álvaro Fernández de Cordova Miralles, *La Corte de Isabel I: Ritos y ceremonias de una reina, 1474–1504* (Madrid, 2002), 189–90. For the period covered here, see Alejandro López Álvarez, "Organización y evolución de la Caballeriza," in José Martínez Millán and Santiago Fernández Conti (eds.), *La Monarquía de Felipe II: La Casa del rey* (Madrid, 2005), 1: 293–310. Focussing on expenditure and the eighteenth century, Miguel Ángel Gacho Santamaría, *La Real Caballeriza en el siglo XVIII* (UCM, 2002). There are interesting contributions about the Stables of the European courts in Daniel Roche (ed.), *Les écuries royales du XVIe au XVIIIe siècle* (Paris, 1998); see also, John Christopher Sainty and Robert O. Bucholz (eds.), *Officials of the Royal Household 1660–1837: Part II: Departments of the Lord Steward and the Master of the Horse* (London, 1998), 58–68; and especially, Jaroslava Hausenblasová, *Der Hof Kaiser Rudolfs II* (Prague, 2002), 100–103, 136–137, 167–171, 178–179, 190–192 and 422–453. For analysis of the Stables from an architectural point of view, see Wolfgang Götz, *Deutsche Marställe des Barock* (Berlin, 1982); Dominique Massounie, *L'architecture de la Grande et de la Petite Écurie de Versailles* (Paris, 2003). Other works on the Stables of the Spanish queens are cited later.

[3] Spanish pictorial sources relating to our topic of interest are, unfortunately, rather scarce; for this reason and to underline, in passing, the broad geographical spread of the

When we speak of state vehicles, we are referring to a series of vehicles already in use by princes and lords in the medieval period, such as the litter, or introduced into the Stable in the course of the sixteenth century, such as sleighs, coaches, carriages and sedan chairs. The emblematic state vehicle of medieval times was, of course, the litter. This was a kind of box covered in decorative upholstery and hung on two poles and borne by two horses. Litters were mainly used by ladies of rank, although since before the mid-fifteen hundreds men had also begun to use them, as we know that Charles V[4] and Philip II[5] used them and that they were in

phenomena we are analysing, we will make use of more than a hundred images from French, German, Dutch, Flemish, English and Polish sources. The absence of paintings, drawings and engravings of state vehicles in Spain during this period contrasts with the intensity and duration of the debate sustained in the literature of the time. For this aspect, see Alejandro López Álvarez, *Poder, lujo y conflicto en la corte de los Austrias: coches, carrozas y sillas de mano, 1555–1700* (Madrid, 2007), 319–616.

[4] It was said of Charles V that he had used them when he was ill, and was carried about in them when he was "indisposed," *Historia del invencible emperador Carlos Quinto, rey de España, compuesta por su majestad cesárea*, in Manuel Fernández Álvarez (ed.), *Corpus documental de Carlos V* (Salamanca, 1979), 4: 519, 556. It is, in fact, emperor Charles V who is associated with the only litter in existence from before the eighteenth century, an example of the kind used for travelling and without much decoration (MCM 10008046), see Eduardo Galán Domingo, "De las Reales caballerizas a la colección de carruajes del Patrimonio Nacional," *Arbor* 665 (2001): 227. This is reproduced in Eduardo Galán Domingo (ed.), *Historia del carruaje en España* (Madrid, 2005), 87. The Madrid example is very similar to the one used by the emperor in an anonymous picture where he is shown taking his leave, in 1552, of John Frederick, the Magnanimous, elector of Saxony (SFG, Inv. 63/ SG/ 22), reproduced in the exhibition catalogue *Ernst der Fromme (1601–1675), Bauherr und Sammler* (Gotha, 2001), 53. There were some which were much more decorated. See the one used by the elector of Palatinate in 1556 for his entry into Heidelberg in the woodcut by Michael Ostendorfer in *Hollstein's German Engravings, Etchings and Woodcuts 1400–1700* (hereafter *Hollstein's German Engravings*), 30: 178–179. One copy of this woodcut has been recently acquired by the Government of Bavaria, SND (ND. G 14). For this item, see the exhibition catalogue *Von Kaiser Gnaden, 500 Jahre Pfalz-Neuburg* (Augsburg, 2005), 295-296.

[5] On his way to the Monastery of El Escorial in 1583, Friar Miguel de Alaejos, the prior, fell ill and Philip II ordered "that he should come to San Lorenzo in his litter lest he came to harm. This litter had belonged to the Emperor Charles V, and only these three had ever been in it, the Emperor, our Lord the King and the prior of San Lorenzo," see *Memorias de fray Juan de San Geronimo* in CODOIN, 7: 70. In another letter written at the time, Philip II comments: "this litter is one which belonged to my lord, the Emperor, may he be in glory, and is large, although no bigger than the average, and is good for such things, although I brought another small one that I left here because it did not seem as suitable," Fernando Bouza (ed.), *Cartas de Felipe II a sus hijas* (Madrid, 1998), 107, 109.

common use amongst courtiers.[6] The sleigh was a wooden, horse-drawn structure open to the elements, with seating for one or several people, which slid over the snow on two smooth runners. These also supported the passenger compartment, which tended to be rich and varied in its decoration. The sleigh was used for excursions and rides, rather than for travelling, and for games and masques, weather permitting. It was introduced into Castile in the time of Philip II, who attempted to make it a permanent feature of his Stable shortly after he had discovered it on his travels,[7] since it had been common in northern and central Europe for some time.[8] It was never quite as common as in the courts of central Europe, but was nonetheless kept in use for a long time, reflecting the mutual influence between the Habsburg households.[9]

Despite the importance of the litter, sleigh and sedan chair,[10] the vehicle that really changed the Stable, royal image and ceremonial was the coach. From the end of the thirteenth century, apart from the usual litter, ingenious wagon-like contrivances, mainly used by women and noted for their luxurious upholstery and cushions, began to be constructed in the French Burgundy area.[11] These wagons were technically improved

[6] See the comments by Gonzalo Fernández de Oviedo, *Libro de la Cámara Real del prínçipe don Juan e offiçios de su casa e serviçio ordinario* and *Adición o segunda parte de los oficios de la Casa Real*, 1547, published as *Libro de la Cámara real del príncipe don Juan* (Madrid, 1870), ix–xii, 163–164.

[7] Bouza, *Cartas de Felipe II*, 136, 149, 162. One, sent by Rudolph II arrived at the court in 1593, and must have been copied, Almudena Pérez de Tudela and Annemarie Jordan Gschwend, "Luxury Goods for Royal Collectors," in *Jahrbuch des Kunsthistoriches Museums Wien*, vol. 3 (2001), 79.

[8] Heinrich Kreisel, *Prunkwagen und Schlitten* (Leipzig, 1927), 129ff; also Fritz Fischer, *Dem Volk zur Schau: Prunkschlitten des Barock* (Munich, 2002), 13ff. The Renaissance mind considered the sleigh a luxury item and princes were often depicted in their sleighs, witness Breu's famous engraving in which Charles V appears with his sister Mary, king Ferdinand and his wife Anna, illustrated in *Hollstein's German Engravings*, 4: 198. For emperor Ferdinand I and his wife in a sleigh, see the engraving by Amberger, in *ibidem*, 2: 4. Other engraved images of gentlemen and ladies in sleighs by Beham, in *ibidem*, 3: 242.

[9] When the king, queen and royal children wanted to go for a sleigh ride in the winter of 1625, examples had to be brought from the royal Stable and the house of the German ambassador so that there would be time to get them ready, AGP, *Administrativa*, leg. 1046 (no pagination), and *Libro de noticias particulares, así de nacimientos de príncipes, como entrada de Reyes* (Madrid, 2005), 40. They still featured in Stable inventories at the end of the seventeenth century.

[10] For sedan chairs, see *infra*.

[11] Bernard H. Prost, *Inventaires mobiliers et extrait des comptes des ducs de Bourgogne de la Maison de Valois, 1363–1477* (Paris, 1908–1913), 2: 76, 93–94, 127, 168, 169–170, 183, 185, 189, 192, 198, 213, 296–297, 394, 524–525, 537, 556 and 623.

in the mid-fourteenth century in Hungary by adding a suspension system, consisting of leather straps or chains which made them much more comfortable when travelling, hence their name *chars branlants* or hanging coaches. Their use was widespread throughout the Habsburg Netherlands and the Empire, and particularly in Italy, the cradle of a good many court innovations. Further technical improvements modified these carriages, and they eventually came to be known as *kocsi*, or coaches, from the name of the Hungarian town Kocs where they originated.[12] These new vehicles began to be much sought after in the princely courts towards the middle of the sixteenth century. In Italy, there were quite a lot of them;[13] in the Imperial court, Ferdinand I delighted in using them and gave them away as state gifts, whilst his son-in-law, Albert V of Bavaria was accused by his counsellors of wanting to travel only by coach, neglecting the noble art of horsemanship in his attempts to imitate the emperor.[14] In 1540, Francis I, king of France received a coach as a gift from the duke of Mantua, and he was so thrilled with it that he decided to copy it in order to have others in his court.[15] Shortly afterwards, they started to be used in the Spanish court, giving rise to the first complaints concerning their use and requests to ban them in the *Cortes* held in 1555.[16]

[12] For the technical development of the coach see Kreisel, *Prunkwagen und Schlitten*, 3–101; Rudolf H. Wackernagel, "Zur Geschichte der Kutsche bis zum Ende des 17. Jahrhunderts," in Wilhelm Treue (ed.), *Achse, Rad und Wagen: Fünftausend Jahre Kultur- und Technikgeschichte* (Göttingen, 1986), 197–235; Rudolf H. Wackernagel, "Festwagen," in *Reallexikon zur Deutschen Kunstgeschichte* (Munich, 1987), 8: 407ff; Rudolf H. Wackernagel, *Der französische Krönungswagen von 1696–1825: Ein Beitrag zur Geschichte der repräsentativen Zeremonienswagen* (Berlin, 1966), 11ff; Rudolf H. Wackernagel (ed.), *Staats- und Galawagen der Wittelsbacher* (Stuttgart, 2002), 2: 9–19; Julian Munby, "Les origines du coche," in Daniel Roche (ed.), *Voitures, chevaux et attelages du XVIe au XIXe siècle* (Paris, 2000), 75–83. All have extensive bibliographies.

[13] Joseph Jobe, *Au temps des cochers* (Lausanne, 1976), 15–16.

[14] Monica Kurzel-Runtscheiner, "Fasto cortesano y sobriedad elegante: Los coches de la corte de Viena entre las edades barroca y contemporánea," in Galán, *Historia del carruaje*, 226; also *Mémoires de la vie de François de Scepeaux, sire de Vieilleville et comte de Durestal, Maréchal de France*, in *Nouvelle collection des mémoires pour servir à l'Histoire de France*, by Michaud and Poujoulat (Paris-Lyon, 1853), 9: 311.

[15] Carmelo Occhipinti, *Carteggio d'arte degli ambasciatori estensi in Francia, 1536–1553* (Pisa, 2001), 48; Monique Châtenet, *La cour de France au XVI siècle: Vie sociale et architecture* (Paris, 2002), 126.

[16] *Cortes de los antiguos reinos de León y de Castilla* (Madrid, 1883–1903), 5: 688–689.

The royal coaches

The appearance of coaches in Castile and their incorporation into the Royal Stable took place relatively late compared to other kingdoms but they were rapidly assimilated. Amongst other reasons, a series of changes were taking place in the Spanish Monarchy that paved the way for using the coach as an element to promote the distancing of the monarch. The coach was a means of creating hierarchy and marking social distinctions, an instrument of political integration and social control; in other words, a highly useful way of reinforcing and displaying the new conditions and power relations that were being forged at court. The changes can be appreciated from 1560 onwards, and are consolidated especially from 1585. After 1600, the image of the sovereign is indistinguishable from that of his vehicles, a process that culminates in the second half of the century when carriages form the stuff of royal propaganda and an indispensable element in enhancing the sacred mystery of the king.

The king in his coach: changes in ceremonial and etiquette

Although the stereotypical image of the sixteenth century noble was the man on horseback, the gradual use of the coach amongst princes influenced the development of new representations and royal images.[17] The coach harked back to a series of elements from Antiquity where the use of the chariot was associated with gods, heroes, and certain dignitaries. For that reason, when vehicles began to be used in princely courts, it was entirely consistent to attempt to link them to sacred and secular power. This explains why, by the time of Philip II, the monarch was represented in a chariot like the sun gods,[18] or the heroes of ancient

[17] For a more detailed analysis of the changes in the royal image occasioned by the coach, see López Álvarez, *Poder, lujo y conflicto,* 39–126.

[18] So, for example, Jacobo da Trezzo, in 1555, cast a bronze medal which associated Philip II with Apollo driving the sun chariot, an emblem with important precedents in classical medals and was repeated in what later became the impress par excellence of the king, the one designed by Ruscelli, which appeared in Venice in 1566. Virgilio Bermejo, "Princeps ut Apolo: Mitología y alegoría solar en los Austrias hispanos," in *Actas del I Simposio Internacional de Emblemática* (Teruel, 1994), 480ff; idem, "En torno a los resortes de la imaginería política en la Época Moderna: Numismática y medallística en la iconografía de Felipe II," in *Lecturas de historia del Arte,* 4 (1994), 230–242; Víctor M. Mínguez, "Los emblemas solares, la imagen del príncipe y los programas astrológicos en el arte efímero," *Actas del I Simposio Internacional de Emblemática*, 209–253. For Ruscelli's medal, see Andreu Galera i Pedrosa, "Un emblema solar para Felipe II," *ibidem*, 457–467.

Rome. Francisco de Guzmán presented the king in this way, being carried by ladies as he was being armed as a knight, in his *Triumphos morales* or *Moral Triumphs* (fig. 1), from which the following lines are taken:

After they had girded on his arms
The ladies taking him by the hand
Raised him onto a triumphal chariot
After the fashion of the Roman triumphs
And they sat him in the centre
In the manner of the Spaniards of old
When they went into battle in olden times
According to the stories told today.[19]

Fig. 1 – Philip II is armed as a knight by some ladies in this engraving as well as in the *Triumphos morales* by Francisco de Guzmán, 1565 (BNE R 6877 fol. 179).

From a more prosaic point of view, the use of the coach was a factor in the new ceremonial arrangements in the Stable. Shortly after becoming king, Philip II issued a series of instructions concerning the new ceremonial to be followed in this department. The first, drawn up in 1561

[19] Francisco de Guzmán, *Triumphos Morales*, 1565, BNE, R 6877, fol. 179. Some years earlier an engraving was made representing queen Isabella of Castile being driven in another triumphal chariot, accompanied by the following lines:

She will come in a triumphal chariot
And will bring for company
A number never seen before
Of Virtues, with tenacity
Being chief amongst her virtues,

Hernando de Acuña, *El caballero determinado*, 1553, BNE, R 10359, fol. 77r. This is reproduced in the exhibition catalogue, *Los Austrias: Grabados de la Biblioteca Nacional* (Madrid, 1993), 212–213. See also, somewhat later images of Elizabeth I of England mounted on other triumphal chariots, Roy C. Strong, *Portraits of Queen Elizabeth I* (Oxford, 1963), 103, 121. There is also the 1585 fresco depicting a solemn entry by the Polish king, Casimir Jagellon, in 1485; Teresa Zurawska, "Polnische Prunkwagen und Schlitten im 16.–18 Jahrhundert," in *Achse, Rad und Wagen, Beiträge zur Geschichte der Landfahrzeuge*, vol. 10 (2002), 32, fig. 3. For other later examples, see below.

or shortly afterwards, set out the order of ceremony to be followed by his officers when they accompanied the king's horse in public.[20] This plan became rather complicated, according to information from 1563, when other officers were included, such as the musicians or the master of the horse himself, in another rite of passage carried out when livery or mourning was issued to the servants.[21] The ceremonial for the king's outings by coach, very similar to those on horseback, and with a distinct Burgundian stamp, must also have been formulated during these years. This ceremony was carried out in the following way: when the king announced he was going out, the master of the horse would propose which coaches or horses were available and give orders to his subordinates to make them ready. The following day, the master of the horse would go to the stable and check that his orders had been carried out and then return to the palace, whence, at the appointed time for the king to leave, he would order the coach or horse to be brought to the palace in a procession following the protocols mentioned previously. When the horse or coach arrived, the king, surrounded by his guards, would come down to board it, followed, to his right, by the lord steward, with the master of the horse to the right of him, and the *sumiller de corps* to the monarch's left, whilst the captain of the Royal Bodyguard was to the right of the master of the horse. If the king was travelling by coach, the three senior officers entered the vehicle with him, although only the lord steward did so without being summoned, whilst the others waited for a sign from the king. If the king was going into the country, travelling, or setting off on a military campaign, it was the privilege of the master of the horse to attend upon him, whether serving him his food or dressing him.[22] This practice made it clear that the vehicle had become a space for courtly ritual and socializing, and

[20] *Memoria de la orden q se a de guardar en acompañar el cavallo que se llebare para Su mag.d el dia q sale en publico y los ofiçiales de la Cavalleriza que estan obligados a acompañarle desde que sale de ella y el lugar que a cada uno toca*, IVDJ *Envío 7* (II) fol. 57r.

[21] *La orden que se ha de tener en acompañar al Cavallerizo maior de su casa a Palacio el dia que se viste Librea o Luto General, es la sig.te*, RAH 9/683, fols. 191r–191v. The order was given on August 15, 1563, when livery was put on.

[22] *La forma que tenia y guardaba el rey Felipe II quando habia de salir en publico o en coche*, RAH, K-58, fols. 196–200v. This ceremony became rather more complex as the years wore on, as can be seen in the *Plantta de el acompañamiento que el día que sale a caballo en público lleba su magesttad, en Etiquetas de palacio ordenadas por el año de 1562 y reformadas el de 1617*, AHN, *Consejos*, lib. 1189, fols. 236r–237r.

that the master of the horse had become one of the three most senior servants, controlling all service to the monarch outside the palace. From then on the king made increasingly regular use of his vehicles,[23] gradually modifying his traditional image as a knight on horseback. One of the results of this was that pictorial representations of the royal coaches began to abound.[24]

However, it was in the 1580s when the use of state vehicles proved decisive in emphasizing the remoteness of the figure of the king, the result of the process of institutionalizing the Monarchy. From that time on, and in close parallel with changes in palace etiquette and the pragmatic sanction of 1578 which restricted carriages to those who could afford to have them drawn by four horses, with the aim of making them the particular preserve of courtiers the coach made a special contribution to the glorification and remote grandeur of the sovereign, a phenomenon that crystallized in 1585–1586; from then on, very few people had close access to Philip II.[25] It was precisely in 1585 that the Stable was given fresh instructions, the exact contents of which we are unaware, but which enable us to suppose that – in view of what happened in

[23] From 1560, the Stable and its coaches would be charged with providing for the increasing mobility of the king, who left the palace "so frequently and at such odd hours," as stated in *La orden que se ha de tener de aqui adelante*, IVDJ, *Envío 7* (II), fol. 48r. One traveller stated in 1577 that Philip II went "hunting by coach in the countryside three or four times a week," José García Mercadal, *Viajes de extranjeros por España y Portugal: Desde los tiempos más remotos hasta comienzos del siglo XX* (1st ed. 1948; Valladolid, 1999), 2: 403.

[24] Amongst the first images of state vehicles in Spain is the coach which appears in the portrait *Las infantas Isabel Clara Eugenia y Catalina Micaela*, painted around 1568–1569 by Sánchez Coello (MDRM 00612070). For French examples, see the 1569 engraving by Du Cerceau, in Wackernagel, *Der französische Krönungswagen*, fig. 2a; also the famous drawing by Antoine Caron, "La Cour de France quittant le château d'Anet" in the Louvre Museum, reproduced in Châtenet, *La cour de France au XV siècle*, 17. A tapestry based on this drawing, and made between approximately 1582 and 1585, is still preserved today in the Pitti Palace in Florence, see exhibition catalogue, *Les Trésors des Médicis: La Florence des Médicis une ville et une cour d'Europe* (Paris, 1999), 82–83. For Imperial images, see drawings by Jost Amman of Maximilian II's entry into Nuremberg in 1564, in Kreisel, *Prunkwagen und Schlitten*, figs. 4, 5, pp. 23, 28, 29. Although not directly related to the Holy Roman Emperor, see the carriage on the triumphal arch erected on the occasion of Maximilian's entry into Vienna in 1563, *Hollstein's German Engravings*, 22: 187.

[25] José Martínez Millán and Carlos Javier de Carlos Morales (eds.), *Felipe II (1527–1598). La configuración de la Monarquía hispana* (Valladolid, 1998), 245. For the pragmatic sanctions of 1578, see López Álvarez, *Poder, lujo y conflicto*, 152–156.

later years – coaches had to emphasize, more than ever before, royal distance and majesty. At about this time, the use of the vehicles by the king and royal children was systematically referred to in festive accounts; the coach became a state gift;[26] access to the palace entrance was controlled;[27] the coach was used in the ceremonial framework of meetings and farewells; it served to regulate the distance of the monarch; and was particularly used in entries into major cities.

In the latter cases, it can be clearly seen how the coach changed ceremonial practice and the image of the king. Philip II sought, like other sovereigns, to regulate his public appearances, by showing himself on each occasion as he thought most appropriate. This can be observed from the very beginning of his reign, when, wishing to be present at the ceremonial of the Spanish queens, he took part secretly, invisibly, yet nonetheless publicly, by means of rumour. This fact, which already had precedents, was evident at the entries of queens in 1560 and 1570. Sebastián de Orozco wrote of Isabella of Valois's entry into Toledo:

> And all this our Lord, the king saw and observed, disguised with other gentlemen, according to rumour, because I did not see him. At least, if I saw him I didn't recognize him. And this is to be believed, because it was not a thing to miss seeing.[28]

[26] Some examples of these gifts are found in AGS, E. leg. 403 fols. 138 and 140; García Mercadal, *Viajes*, 2: 537–538; *Relación del viaje de Conde de Lemos a Roma*, 1600, in Francisco Rafael de Uhagón (ed.), *Relaciones de los siglos XVI y XVII* (Madrid, 1896), 282; also Félix Labrador Arroyo (ed.), *Diario de Hans Khevenhüller, embajador imperial en la corte de Felipe II* (Madrid, 2001), 489.

[27] The possibility of the vehicle entering the palace was an indicator of the social status of its owner. To prevent access to the palace entrance there were eight gatekeepers. Entry of the coaches through the palace gateway was controlled with particular zeal from the middle of the 1590s, creating a few problems of protocol, BPR II/ 2149, doc. 111; José Ignacio Tellechea Idígoras, *El ocaso de un rey: Felipe II visto desde la Nunciatura de Madrid, 1594–1598* (Madrid, 2001), 196. For discussion of this, see BA 51-VI-37. In 1609, the same thing was repeated, *Orden que se dio a los Porteros de Cadena para la entrada de los Coches y Cavallos en el Zaguan de Palacio*, AGP, *Administrativa*, leg. 623 (no pagination). The limited access to the palace entrance was frequently questioned, in 1622 and 1664, for example, AHN, *Consejos*, leg. 7136 (no pagination). For the French case, see, Wackernagel, *Der französische Krönungswagen*, 22.

[28] *Relación y memoria de la entrada en esta cibdad de Toledo, del rey y reina nuestros señores don Felipe y doña Isabela y del recebimiento y fiestas y otras cosas, año de 1561* in Uhagón, *Relaciones históricas*, 193; at another time: "they say they have seen our Lord, the King, disguised and pretending to be someone else," *ibidem*, 200.

Equally, on the occasion of the entry of Anne of Austria into Segovia, Báez de Sepúlveda wrote that the king had been secretly watching:

> It is said, by the way, that His Majesty ambled in disguise across the fields on a white hackney, and that he arrived at the awning, where they say he saw our lady, the Queen, for the first time, and in the same disguise, saw her again in various parts of the city. Four or five other men in disguise accompanied His Majesty.[29]

However, in 1599, king Philip III no longer went on horseback to see his wife, but, after eating, the monarch left "secretly in a coach" to see the queen's entry.[30] As we have pointed out, these changes had become firmly established by approximately 1585, as various accounts of the time make clear. We know, for example, that in 1584, the prince left the palace on the day he took his oath, in an open carosse, sitting on his governess's lap.[31] Another account from the same year highlighted this ritual concealment of the king by commenting on his "leaving secretly in a coach," the royal princesses and the ladies in theirs, and the princesses flouting the rules by taking the vehicle round the outside of the town instead of through the expected streets.[32] The coach offered

[29] Jorge Báez de Sepúlveda, *Relación verdadera del recibimiento que hizo la ciudad de Segovia a la magestad de la reyna nuestra señora dona Anna de Austria, en su felicísimo casamiento que en la dicha ciudad se celebró*, 1570 (Segovia, 1998), 75.

[30] *Relacion de la entrada de sus magestades en Madrid, el domingo 26 de octubre de 1599*, RAH, 9/3764, fol. 13r. Going out in secrecy did not necessarily imply travelling incognito but the absence of company, as is indicated in another account which stated that after going to the palace from San Jerónimo "through another gate, his Majesty entered a coach, the Marquis of Denia with him and one of the Marquis de Velada's sons, a *menino*, and they rode through the streets, although with their faces covered [but] with the curtains of the coach drawn back, for everyone saw them without any other coach or servants except for two or three of the marquis's,"*Entrada de la Reyna en Madrid* in Jenaro Alenda y Mira (ed.), *Relaciones de solemnidades y fiestas públicas de España* (Madrid, 1903), 1: 130.

[31] Jerónimo de Sepúlveda, *Historia de varios sucesos y de las cosas notables que han acaecido en España y otras naciones desde el año de 1584 hasta el de 1603*, in Julián Zarco Cuevas (ed.), *Documentos para la historia del monasterio de San Lorenzo el Real de El Escorial* (Madrid, 1924), 4: 5.

[32] *Relacion del Juramento del Principe nuestro señor don felipe tercero de este nombre, en el su Real monesterio de san Jheronimo de la Villa de Madrid*, RAH, 9–426, fols. 181–182. In the Constable of Castile's 'obedience' to the pope in 1586, we learn of the frequent use of 'unmarked' coaches to travel to Rome in secret, to lodge in an ambassador's house, and so on, *Relación del viaje que hizo a Roma el Condestable de Castilla* in Uhagón, *Relaciones históricas*, 184–186, 192.

security and discretion which were impossible to achieve on horseback: being able to see without necessarily being seen was a great advantage for a king who wanted to be inaccessible without being invisible, and who adopted different measures to regulate his appearances in public. In this respect, the vehicles broadened the range of possibilities for the monarch's appearances in public, offering him specific new ways of showing himself, allowing himself to be seen, quite unlike the reserve supposedly typical of Spanish monarchs. On the other hand, as this information reveals, a careful political strategy was set in motion; the aim was to regulate the royal appearances, and this further heightened the mystery surrounding a monarch ever disposed to conceal himself or let himself be seen, depending on his inclination. This could be achieved, for example, by eliminating an escorting vehicle, or by concealment, using the curtains of the coach; the curtains made it easier than ever before, thanks to the technical advances popularized by the trapezoidal box over the semicircular one used until then, to ride with the curtains drawn, or open and allowing the occupants of the coach to be seen[33] (fig. 2).

From then on, in fact, the monarch showed himself quite regularly to his subjects in his coach with the curtains drawn back in order to be better appreciated, regulating his presence in public and to the extent to which he saw fit. In 1591, returning from the reception of the duke of Savoy, the king, the prince and the duke took the high street "with the coach constantly open to view." On his return from Aragon, the king and their highnesses entered Madrid and, after visiting the empress in the Convent of the Discalced Carmelites, they went to the palace "with the coach open to view, and the people lamenting at the sight of His Majesty, thin and old, much more so than when he had left Madrid." From that time on, as Cabrera de Córdoba would relate, the king drove

[33] Compare the close boxes of the hanging car, like the one belonging to Frederick III, constructed around 1451 (LJG, Inv. no. 248), or the one used by the prince elector of Saxony, John Frederick the Magnanimous, in his wedding to Sibylla of Cleves, in 1527 (in the Veste Coburg, but destroyed in 1945, reproduced in Kreisel, *Prunkwagen und Schlitten*, figs.1B, 2 and 4A), with the open carriages used at the weddings of John Casimir, duke of Saxe-Coburg, in 1586 and 1599 (KVC, Inv. no. 12, 2 and no. 12, 3, reproduced in Axel Gelbhaar, "Die Kobelwagen, Karossen und Kutschen im Besitz der Kunstsammlungen der Veste Coburg," in *Achse, Rad und Wagen: Beiträge*, 7 (1999), 78–84).

Fig. 2 – This drawing of the coach used at Maria of Portugal's wedding to Alessandro Farnese in 1565 shows the box typical of the earliest vehicles, a structure which prevented its occupants from being easily seen (Illustrated in G. Bertini, *Le nozze di Alessandro Farnese* (Milan, 1977), 53).

round Madrid in his coaches with his children to show his strength and spirit and to "demonstrate to his court and his enemies that he was not as finished as they said he was, which brought joy to his people, who loved them."[34] The prince followed the same custom, the novelty

[34] Luis Cabrera de Córdoba, *Historia de Felipe II, rey de España*, ed. José Martínez Millán and Carlos Javier de Carlos Morales (Salamanca, 1998), 3: 1395, 1440, 1626.

of it attracting his courtiers' attention.[35] His entry into court in 1598, by then as king, took place "in a coach with the curtains open."[36] The king, the infanta and their duennas left for Valencia the same way in 1599.[37] The public coach ride became the customary way for the king and queen to show themselves at court, to see and be seen and was used more frequently than the supposed invisibility of the monarch would lead us to believe, as numerous accounts bear witness.[38] From 1600, the sovereign even governed from one, as meetings and councils took place there.[39] The

[35] Shortly before Philip II died, the prince left on Midsummer's Eve by coach for the Prado of San Jerónimo with the marquises of Velada and Denia, and Cristóbal de Moura, "which he had never done before, and the coach was open until he returned at two in the morning." When he became king, the first news of his journeys always repeated the same thing: that Philip would leave by coach in the afternoon, accompanied by the same personages, on his daily visit to his sister, Tellechea, *El ocaso de un rey*, 256, 303.

[36] *Relacion de la entrada que hiço nuestro señor don felipe tercero deste nombre, en la villa de Madrid*, RAH, 9/425 (42), fol. 55r.

[37] *La jornada que el cardenal Arçobispo de Sevilla mi señor prosigue de Madrid a Valencia* in *Relaciones breves de actos públicos celebrados en Madrid de 1541 a 1650*, ed. J. Simón Díaz (Madrid, 1982), 40.

[38] T. Pinheiro da Veiga related the king's clandestine sorties by coach in Valladolid: "And so you will not be surprised that the king too might be seen in a coach, in disguise, alone and without a guard, just some nobles dressed as rustics, sprawled out as if in a ladies' coach; and since some had come on ahead saying they thought the king was on his way, that the coaches should be stopped as he approached, it was thought a joke and a thousand jibes were made: that they were a bunch of rogues, that the king of hearts would be riding in it, and about which, 'it's said, the king laughed heartily later with his queen, saying that they had offended him at his own feast," Narciso Alonso Cortés (ed.), *Fastiginia: Vida cotidiana en la Corte de Valladolid*, 1605 (Valladolid, 1973), 58. In the procession of San Isidro in 1620, the king left for the church of San Andrés by coach after eating at the palace, and went out again in it with his children "to see the Court and the Grandees that there were" at the altars set up in various parts of Madrid, Francisco Bravo, *Avisos de Madrid*, BNE, MSS. 18666/67–68, fol. 78r. In 1623, it was noted that the king had taken a coach ride to San Jerónimo, "with the curtains open and, taking unusual streets," or that he had passed by in his vehicle "with the curtains closed, and in secret, with two other coaches behind," *Relación del gran recibimiento que ... Felipe IV hizo al Príncipe de Gales* y *Entrada en público del Príncipe Carlos de Inglaterra en la Corte de Madrid*, in Simón Diaz, *Relaciones*, 200 and 201.

[39] F. Bermúdez de Pedraza said of the Councils of State and War, that they were superior to the others because they were presided over by the king himself, that "exalted by such a sovereign President, they follow the Royal figure like a shadow wherever he is for the future contingencies that normally occur whilst still on the road; and H.M. leads the Council of State in his coach," *El secretario del rey*, 1620, ed. Manuel Carrión Gutiérrez (facsimile edition, Madrid, 1973), fol. 1v.

vehicle ended up being used so frequently by the monarch that Gascón de Torquemada never ceased to comment on the fact that a few days after his arrival at the Portuguese court, Philip III had taken a ride on horseback, "giving everyone in Lisbon a good day, because from the time he had arrived, he had taken the coach each time and they were looking forward to seeing him on a horse."[40]

In any case, the most important manifestation in this process of distancing and exalting the monarch was the entry by coach, a practice that changed the traditional chivalric entry, on horseback and under a canopy, dating from the beginning of the fourteenth century. The ceremonial associated with the Royal Entry was fundamental to the political life of Castile, where communication with vassals was closer and more intense, and the king made his power manifest, receiving submission and fealty from his subjects.[41] The entry required considerable paraphernalia in the way of participants, decoration and rich finery to properly frame an event of such importance as a prince making contact with his vassals. It was a fundamental part of it that the entry should make it possible for the monarch to be seen at close quarters and on his horse, surrounded by important figures and guards, but relatively accessible nonetheless, and, above all, with his whole body visible. However, in the course of the modern age, this traditional dialogue, bordering on the theatrical, between governor and governed, was gradually reduced to an affirmation by the monarch and the submission of the citizens, in favour of a ceremony which was increasingly elitist and courtly and less populist.[42] The institutionalization of the Monarchy begun by Philip II was also reflected in this sphere, contributing, through the use of the coach, to the process of modifying the festival and underlining the sovereign power of the king.

[40] Gerónimo Gascón de Torquemada, *Gaçeta y nuevas de la Corte de España desde el año 1600 en adelante*, ed. Alfonso de Ceballos-Escalera y Gila (Madrid, 1991), 67.

[41] Rosana de Andrés Díaz, "Las 'entradas reales' castellanas en los siglos XIV y XV, según las crónicas de la época," *En la España Medieval* 1, no. 4 (1984), 47–62; José Manuel Nieto Soria (ed.), *Orígenes de la Monarquía hispánica: propaganda y legitimación, ca. 1400–1520* (Madrid, 1999), 51–56.

[42] It was precisely Philip IV's entry into Valencia in 1645 in a carriage that Rafael Narbona Vizcaíno indicated as the beginning of the process which dismantled the ceremonial developed between the fourteenth and seventeenth centuries, "Las fiestas reales en Valencia entre la Edad Media y la Edad Moderna (siglos XIV–XVII)," *Pedralbes* 2, no.13 (1993): 463–472, esp. pp. 465n, 472.

The coach had prevailed over the horse for travelling because it afforded greater comfort; although the king used to leave the court on a horse, it did not take him long to transfer to a coach for most of the journey and then mount his horse again for the entry into cities. This practice was maintained virtually without change until 1585 when the urban entry in a coach began to be frequent.[43] The first of the entries in a coach on that journey to Aragon took place in Guadalajara, where the bridge had to have a couple of stones removed so that the monarch's carriage could cross it,[44] but the most notorious was in Barcelona.[45] This practice became somewhat more common in later years. In 1592, on the journey to Tarazona, the king entered Segovia one Sunday night "with no public welcome," although festive lights were placed "in every street." The prince entered on horseback and the king and royal princess in their coach and they went as far as the Alcázar.[46] That same year, the monarch also entered Valladolid in a vehicle, and after receiving his vassals in an arbour, "he entered by the aforementioned Puerta del Campo, and crossed the Plaza Mayor and the Platería and went to lodge in his palace."[47] The use of the coach highlighted both the distance and the sacred quality of the king, a remoteness brought out in another account of the same entry in which the author, trying

[43] Entries into towns in coaches had already occurred before, such as in 1570 in Lora del Río, but at that stage, the process of distancing the king had not yet reached its definitive formulation and the political importance of a measure of this kind was not as great as it would be years later, José González Carballo, "Felipe II en Lora (28 de abril de 1570)," *http://es.geocities.com/loradelrio/felipe.htlm*.

[44] Francisco Layna Serrano, *Historia de Guadalajara y sus Mendozas en los siglos XV y XVI*, 2nd ed. (Guadalajara, 1995), 3: 274, 276, 463, 465.

[45] Enrique Cock, *Anales del año ochenta y cinco*, in Mercadal, *Viajes*, 2: 511. Cabrera de Córdoba did not mention the use of the coach but wrote that he entered at night "to avoid very ancient ceremonies held by the Catalans as sacred and immutable, but inappropriate to the greatness of the present monarchs and omitted so many times by their early lords," *Felipe II, rey de España*, 3: 1089. An account of the event gave the information that the king had entered Barcelona "in a coach and without a reception," *Relacion de la entrada de su magestad en Barcelona* in Alenda y Mira, *Relaciones*, vol. 1, no. 319.

[46] Enrique Cock, *La Jornada de Tarazona que su magestad hizo el año 1592 recopilada por Enrique Cock, arquero del rey nuestro Señor, Notario y Escribano apostólico* in Mercadal, *Viajes*, 2: 572. The king also entered Simancas by coach, where he arrived at sunset and "ordered the coach to be opened on all sides and he slowly climbed the hill which, once the bridge over the Pisuerga has been crossed, leads into the town," *ibidem*, 577.

[47] Cock, *La Jornada de Tarazona*, 578. Eyewitness accounts of the king's entry with the royal princess in a coach and the prince on horseback, in Tellechea, *El ocaso de un rey*, 17.

to make the opposite point, emphasized precisely the fact that, in order to be able to see the monarchs well, the king and the infanta entered Valladolid in an:

> open carosse so that everyone might easily see the Royal personages inside, because that was what His Majesty had wished, to give satisfaction and comfort to his beloved people who had so longed to see him; and for the same reason, His Majesty granted another special favour and mercy, which was to request that his Highness, the Prince, should enter on a horse beside the carriage, which certainly comforted all those who were watching him.[48]

This approach was underlined some time later, in Pamplona; after receiving the viceroy, the bishop, the clergy and the elders of the city in some tents, the king travelled by coach:

> as far as the city, and on entering the gate, where the canopy was set up, His Majesty drove under it as far as the main church or Cathedral... and there he alighted and went to pray, according to custom, and on his return, he went to the Viceroy's palace where he lodged.[49]

These entries, with the monarch riding in a carriage, question the alleged inflexibility and universal application of the rules of etiquette that prescribed entry into a city on horseback. In fact, it was observed that use of the coach gradually prevailed towards 1600[50] and two decades later it had become quite usual. So, in the entry into Trujillo in 1619, the king entered in "the richly brocaded coach, drawn by six

[48] *Relacion de un Sacerdote Ingles escrita a Flandes ... de la venida de su Magestad a Valladolid, y al Colegio de los Ingleses, y lo que alli se hizo en su recibimiento*; cf. Zarco Cuevas, *Documentos para la historia del monasterio*, 4: 137. Despite opening up the vehicles, the effect of the coach was to separate the king, make him distant, even when accounts indicated the opposite. Thus, for example, in 1600, the queen entered Segovia "in a coach dressed in bright red in full view of everyone and went straight to her palace," *Relacion de la entrada del Rey don Philipe terçero nuestro señor, en la çiudad de Segovia, el año de mil y seisçientos* in Alenda y Mira, *Relaciones,* no. 459.

[49] Cock, *La Jornada de Tarazona*, 595.

[50] Occasionally, the carriage was used for the queen's Entry, as described by Gilles du Faing, who travelled with Albert of Austria, Margaret of Austria and the infanta Isabella Clara Eugenia in 1599–1600. Arriving at Villarreal, the queen was to enter on a hack, but went by coach instead because of the wet weather, in Mercadal, *Viajes*, 2: 650 and 652. In Barcelona, the queen, infanta and ladies all entered a coach, see, ACA, *Consejo de Aragón*, leg. 1350.

Fig. 3 – The entry by coach of the archduchess Constance of Habsburg on the occasion of her wedding to king Sigismund III in Krakow in 1605, as depicted in what is known as the "Stockholm Scroll" or "Polish Scroll" (ZKW/1528).

white horses and with the coach open to view."[51] This trend continued with his son, Philip IV, who increasingly shrank from direct contact with the world from horseback; he preferred to make his entries by coach, as is clear from his trip to Andalusia in 1624 where it was the norm, as most of the royal entries were made in a coach.[52] This practice, seen in other

[51] *Relacion y Historia Verdadera que trata de la Jornada que hiço el Rey nuestro señor Don Phellipe Tercero Al Reyno de Portugal haçer Cortes a la Çiudad de Lisboa, y a jurar Al Principe Don Phellipe Quarto nuestro señor*, 1622, in Pedro Gan Jiménez, "La jornada de Felipe III a Portugal (1619)," *Chronica Nova*, no. 19 (1991), 411–412.

[52] The king entered Malaga in a coach "as in the other cities," in Gascón de Torquemada, *Gaçeta y nuevas*, 193. So that the monarch could enter Tarifa "on a straight path, and without the coaches twisting and turning, many houses at the entry [to the town] were

European courts, was also reflected in visual representations of the royal family[53] (fig. 3).[54]

The coach and the sacred character of kingship

The beginning of the seventeenth century, particularly from 1611 when use of the coach was institutionalized, gave impetus to the royal vehicle as one way of bringing out the sacred quality of the king. The pragmatic sanction of that year forbade anyone who had not obtained a licence from the Council of Castile from riding in a coach. These licences, which had been granted regularly throughout the reign of Philip III and the early years of Philip IV, led to the coach becoming the strict monopoly of the elites governing the Monarchy, that is to say, the aristocracy at court, the ministers and servants of the royal household, high-ranking ecclesiastics and anyone closely associated with them in the major cities, especially the chaplains of the cathedral chapters and municipal leaders. In this context of sumptuary competition, investing the royal vehicle with an aura of sacredness was accentuated even further, as we can see from several poems of those years, in which the monarch's coach ascended to the celestial court and was compared with the

purchased and demolished," Pedro Espinosa, *Bosque de Doña Ana*, 1624, in Francisco López Estrada (ed.), *Pedro Espinosa: Obra en prosa* (Malaga, 1991), 397.

[53] In France, entry on horseback was the rule until the mid-seventeenth century. Exceptions began to be made under Louis XIII, who, at the beginning of the 1620s, entered some cities in a carriage, Wackernagel, *Der französische Krönungswagen*, 21n. Reproductions of carriages for royal entries are, however, quite common from 1630 onwards, especially in the Empire. See, for example, engravings of the entry of Ferdinand III into Regensburg in 1652 and into Augsburg in 1653, John Roger Paas, *The German Political Broadsheet, 1600-1700* (Wiesbaden, 2005), 8: 117–118, 129. The engravings made to celebrate the triumphal entry of the exiled dukes of Mecklenburg into Güstrow in 1631 are previous to these, Paas, *German Political Broadsheet*, 5: 157–160. See also, those of the ceremonial entry of Gustavus Adolphus into Nuremberg in 1632, Paas, *German Political Broadsheet*, 6: 122. William III's entries by carriage into The Hague in 1691, in *Hollstein's Dutch and Flemish Etchings, Engravings and Woodcuts ca. 1450–1700* (hereafter, *Hollstein's Dutch and Flemish Etchings*), 36: 184–185.

[54] The second wife of king Sigismund III, archduchess Constance of Habsburg entered Krakow in a coach in 1605. The image is captured in what is known as the "Stockholm Scroll" or the "Polish Scroll," an anonymous painting fifteen metres long, kept in the Royal Castle of Krakow (ZKW/1528). See the exhibition catalogue, *The Eagle and the Three Crowns: Polish-Swedish Relations across the Baltic from the 16th to the 18th Century* (Wroclaw, 2002), 2: 26; also Zurawska, "Polnische Prunkwagen und Schlitten," 34 and 40.

Fig. 4 – In this image, engraved to commemorate the death of Rudolph II in 1612, the emperor can be seen being driven to the Sala d'Olimpo in a vehicle drawn by a lion and some eagles (FBG Biogr. fol. 593/1 (98)).

Eucharist.[55] It is significant that, on the death of emperor Rudolph II in 1612, an engraving should be made, depicting his ascent to heaven in a carriage, an illustration of the degree of interest in such topics in the courts at the time (fig. 4).[56] The sacred character of kingship

[55] Alonso de Ledesma compared a ride in the royal coach to the Ascension in *Tercera parte de conceptos espirituales*, 1612, BNE, R 16027, fol. 93. José de Valdivieso also emphasized the sacred nature of the king's coach comparing him with Christ in *Romancero espiritual*, 1612, ed. José María Aguirre (Madrid, 1984), 121–123.
[56] FBG, Biogr. fol 593/1 (98).

gathered more strength in later times, when the royal coach tended to be compared with a monstrance or tabernacle:

> *Long live the glorious monarch, the Lion of Spain!*
> *In a coach, to whom*
> *Phoebus may yield in lofty grandeur,*
> *Since he exceeds him in primacy,*
> *He is the colour of the goddess Flora, with fringe of gold*
> *And a blessed monstrance of priceless treasure.*[57]

New images were superimposed over this one, notably that of the vehicle as a metaphor for government. These are dealt with at length in collections of emblems,[58] the most outstanding of which is Romeyn de Hooghe's engraving of Charles II offering his state coach when he meets a priest carrying the viaticum, in 1685 (fig. 5).[59] This image highlights

[57] *Descripcion de la augusta felicissima venida a esta imperial villa de Madrid de los catolicos reyes D. Carlos II y Doña Maria Luisa de Borbon su digna Consorte*, 1679, BNE, VE 113-22, fols. 4r–v.

[58] See for example Phaeton in Alciato, *Emblemas*, ed. Manuel Montero Vallejo (Madrid, 1975), 120; Juan Pérez de Moya, *Philosofía secreta de la gentilidad*, 1585, ed. Carlos Clavería (Madrid, 1995), 244. Apart from references to Phaeton, political thinkers and moralists also liked the metaphor of the coachman and the chariot, see Hernando de Soto, *Emblemas moralizadas*, 1599, ed. Carmen Bravo-Villasante (facsimile edition, Madrid, 1983), fols. 61–63; Sebastián de Covarrubias Orozco, *Emblemas morales*, 1610, ed. Carmen Bravo-Villasante (Madrid, 1978), Centuria II, emblem 69; Saavedra Fajardo, *Idea de un príncipe político cristiano representada en cien empresas*, 1640, ed. Francisco Javier Díez de Revenga (Barcelona, 1988), 446–447. Father Nieremberg wrote in 1649 that the government of a republic "could not only be likened to a ship but also to a chariot, and it was in this way that Divine Providence and the government of the Hebrew people was revealed to the prophet Ezekiel, in that chariot of four mysterious beasts, covered with eyes, because those who pull the chariot of the republic along are the magistrates who have to be very attentive and alert," *Epistolario*, ed. Narciso Alonso Cortés (Madrid, 1957), 87.

[59] BNE, Est. 13987. For this image, see López Álvarez, *Poder, lujo y conflicto*, 117–126; Antonio Álvarez-Osorio Alvariño, "Virtud coronada: Carlos II y la piedad de la Casa de Austria," in Pablo Fernández Albadalejo, José Martínez Millán and Virgilio Pinto (eds.), *Política, religión e inquisición en la España Moderna* (Madrid, 1996), 27–57. In the context of the state coach as a metaphor for government, there is a curious precedent in the interesting motif painted by Mazo in 1666, in his portrait of queen Mariana, now in the National Gallery, London. In the middle ground the young prince can be seen with his governess and her daughter, and a little further back, a coach used by Charles round the palace, and whose construction in 1660 we believe we have identified, AGP, *Administrativa*, leg. 1046 (no pagination). It is probably the same one that appears in a 1674 inventory in which "three luxurious little coaches" are marked, one of which is noted as being "a small calash used by H.M in the Palace, of crimson and gold material, with golden wheels and four curtains, two large and two small, of bright

Fig. 5 – Charles II offering his carosse to the Eucharist, engraving by Romeyn de Hooghe, who celebrated the monarch meeting the viaticum, as it was being taken to a sick man, 1685 (BNE Est. 13987).

a complex set of circumstances in the court at that time. Giving way to the Eucharist formed part of the heritage of ancient traditions in the House of Austria that urgently needed reform at a particular moment in the history of Castile, in this case in an attempt to guarantee the continuity of the dynasty. Furthermore, what was being demonstrated was that the privilege of entering the royal coach was a prerogative of the King of Kings. Seen in the context of the metaphysical thought of the time, Charles II's offering to the viaticum revealed the subordination

red and gold, lined in 'cloth of gold' of the same colour," AGP, *Administrativa*, leg. 1079 (no pagination). Using the interpretation of the painting suggested by Mercedes Llorente "Imagen y autoridad en una regencia: los retratos de Mariana de Austria y los límites del poder," *Studia Historica* 28 (2006): 211–238, we believe that the coach in the background of the scene represents the government to which the future sovereign was destined after the regency of his mother. Otherwise, a representation of this kind is a special case, in the opinion of R.H.Wackernagel, with whom I discussed the painting in 2006. It is reproduced in López Álvarez, *Poder, lujo y conflicto*, fig. 32.

Fig. 6 – Allegory of emperor Leopold I in a triumphal chariot, 1685, (detail) BNH App. M. 222.

to religion advocated by the regime and, by interweaving the topos of the chariot or charioteer, Charles was handing over the reins of the kingdom to God. In addition, the king was also demonstrating that he was carrying out the pragmatic sanctions which prohibited the use of the French *grand carrosse* type of vehicle that had appeared in 1674 and 1684[60] and was showing himself in one which was characteristic of Castile, and considered at the time to be of the kind typically used by the emperor.[61] The coach, which had allegedly belonged to Charles V,

[60] *Pragmatica que su Magestad manda publicar sobre la reformacion en el excesso de Traxes, lacayos, y coches, y prohibicion del consumo de las mercadurias de Francia... y otras cosas*, 1674, BNE, R 23879 (18), fols. 5v–7r and AHN, *Consejos*, leg. 51438/1 and *Pragmatica que su magestad manda publicar para que se guarde, execute, y observe la que se publicó el año de 1674 sobre la reforma en el Excesso de Trages, Lacayos, y Coches, y otras cosas en esta contenidas*, 1684, BNE, R 23879 (23).

[61] Around the early 1680s, there was still a common belief, which had arisen about 1620, that the emperor had introduced the coach into Castile, see Condesa de Aulnoy, *Viaje por España en 1679 y 1680*, ed. Marta Corominas and Mercedes M. Villalta (Barcelona, 1962), 1: 166–167, 169, and 171–172; Juan de Bolea, *Medula literaria de noticias*, ca. 1693, BNE, MS. 9489, fols. 17r–v. This tradition was vindicated in the engraving by showing a coach considered to be contemporary whilst linking it with his figure; an "ecclesiophany" appears in the top half of the illustration, a break in the burst of Glory enabling an allegory of the Church to be seen whilst other figures hold up a

and the scene of piety were twin reminders of the Castilian stamp at that time in the court of Charles II. It is very tempting to relate this image to another one composed in the same year which, despite their thematic differences, clearly parallels it, since the emperor is shown riding in a triumphal chariot (fig. 6). The sacred nature of the king and his vehicle shows a clear parallel with the motif of the king in his triumphal chariot that had appeared in the mid-sixteenth century. It was quite common at the time, in all the courts of Europe, to represent the monarch in that way, surrounded by the more or less elaborate sacred symbolism used to celebrate good government or military triumphs,[62] dynastic union or the royal couple.[63]

medal representing an act of piety by Charles V; some angels are carrying a phylactery on which are visible the words "*Maiorum exemplo*".

[62] Amongst other royal images in a triumphal chariot, see that of Louis XIII, produced in 1625 by Lucas Vosterman, in which we can see the king being crowned as he drives a chariot drawn by four horses trampling over certain important figures on the ground, as they pass under a triumphal arch. Piety and Religion are allegorised to right and left of the vehicle, *Hollstein's Dutch and Flemish Etchings,* 43: 108, 110. Another example is Matheus Merian the Elder's 1638 engraving of Ferdinand III, in *Hollstein's German Engravings,* 26: 155. In one allegory of Maximilian II of Bavaria, engraved by Philipp Kilian, the prince can be seen on a medal, borne along by allegorical figures, which, in turn, are in a chariot drawn by lions, *ibidem*, 18: 81. In the glorification of William III of England engraved by Joachim von Sandrart, the monarch appears in a two-wheeled, horse-drawn chariot, *Hollstein's German Engravings*, 40: 169. Johannes Van Vliet represented the triumph of Frederick Henry, prince of Orange, who is in a triumphal chariot accompanied by the Virtues, and driving over Tyranny and Envy. This image is comparable to another very similar one, in which the prince is passing through a triumphal arch, *Hollstein's Dutch and Flemish Etchings,* 41: 213, and 24: 8–9. Another engraving from 1632, author unknown, shows Gustavus Adolphus in a two-wheeled vehicle, drawn by two eagles as he is crowned with a laurel wreath; a second one represents the sovereign riding in a chariot whilst being celebrated as the liberator of the Protestant religion in Germany, Paas, *German Political Broadsheet*, 6: 139, 141ff, 340. Other engravings were composed on the occasion of the peace in the middle of the century, in which triumphal chariots appeared. See the one of emperor Ferdinand III signing the Treaty of Westphalia in 1648, Paas, *German Political Broadsheet*, 7: 349 and those of the triumphal entry of John George I, Elector of Saxony, where he is portrayed in a chariot as guarantor of peace in the Empire in 1650, and also celebrating peace, Paas, *German Political Broadsheet*, 8: 95, 289–291. The same personage appears in another engraving, riding in a chariot just before passing under a triumphal arch, *German Engravings, Etchings and Woodcuts*, 19: 96.

[63] In the allegory of the reign of Ferdinand Maria and Henrietta Adelaide, the two monarchs are shown riding in a triumphal chariot, drawn by four horses, engraving by E. Hainzelmann, *Hollstein's German Engravings,*12a: 106–107. See also the engraving marking the wedding of the king of Poland, *Hollstein's German Engravings*, 52: 87.

The significance that state vehicles assumed in composing both the royal and courtly imaginary in the second half of the seventeenth century also led to the ambassadors' vehicles playing an important role in promoting the image of the monarch in courts abroad. Coaches, horses, and the Stable in general were the most favourable elements for the ambassador to project the power of the monarch he served, as well as his own status, given the fact that he was an impressive figure in the public sphere. At a reception, the ambassadors' coaches conveyed to the host the high political regard in which their lord was held, whilst the status of the envoy was also perceived in the use he was able to make of his own vehicles and those of the monarch. Moreover, depending on the power they represented and in accordance with their own economic means, this was how the ambassadors maintained their own Stables and their vehicles in them. In this way, the ambassador underlined the rites of passage of his sovereign and the extraordinary circumstances that had taken place in his court, seeking to leave the best opinion possible of his lord, even as he took part in the ceremonies of the court welcoming him, as well as those for the other envoys, showing the relations between the different Crowns. For these reasons, vehicle and Stable alike were at the centre of ritual confrontations in disputes over etiquette and the violent clashes occasioned by them. The most important act that an ambassador could perform was the public entry, an event that normally had considerable propagandistic repercussions. During this public act, the kind, number and deployment of the coaches not only testified to the wealth of the envoy and his monarch, but also made it possible to give expression to a programme of iconography relevant to the objective of the embassy or the image of the Crown.[64] Moreover, the ambassadors' parade with their coaches and servants not only had to remain in the memory of the spectators; the event had to be rounded off with some account of the event[65] and some engraving which showed,

[64] The most illustrative case is the iconographic programme used to decorate the carosses used by the marquis of Fontes in the embassy to Rome in 1716, José Calvet de Magalhâes, Elsa Garret Pinho and Silvana Bessone, *Embaixada do Marquês de Fontes ao Papa Clemente XI* (Lisbon, 1996). For the Spanish case, see the drawing of the back of a carosse commissioned, according to tradition, by the viceroy of Naples between 1650 and 1670, today in the Rensi Collection, Museum der Bildenden Künste, Leipzig, vol. 12: 30, reproduced in López Álvarez, *Poder, lujo y conflicto*, 514.

[65] For the role of the state vehicle in the accounts of Spanish embassies, see *Carta escrita de la corte de Francia a 24. de junio 1679. en que viene Relacion de la magnifica, y pompossima Entrada, que hizo en Paris el Excelentissimo señor Marques de los Balbases, Embajador Extraordinario de Su Magestad al Rey Christianissimo*, BPR, III/ 6527 (7);

in detail, the sumptuousness of the vehicles and the way the entourage was deployed.[66]

The Stable, state vehicles, and the queen

Just as in the king's household, so too the queen's Stable underwent significant changes from the second half of the sixteenth century. State vehicles were not exempt from these changes, since their use modified the ceremonial and image of the Catholic queen to a large extent. In the case of Isabella of Valois (1559–1568) and Anne of Austria (1569–1580), whose households, and therefore their Stables, were organized along Castilian lines, the role played by the litter and the coach can be followed in some detail in the decades between 1560 and 1580, along with the introduction of Burgundian elements into ceremonial, especially relating to arrangements made for the entries in 1570 and through the etiquette of 1575. The absence of a queen in the final two decades of the sixteenth century brought that process to a halt. However, from the reign of Margaret of Austria (1598–1611) onwards, the establishment of a new image of the queen becomes apparent, stemming in large part from the Stable and the coaches. Amongst the novelties of the period is the development of a new ceremonial involving the sedan chair.[67]

Descripcion de la pompossima entrada que a 14. de setiembre del presente año 1679. hizo el Excelentissimo señor Duque de Pastrana, y Francavilla, Principe de Melito, Conde de Saldaña... & Embajador Extraordinario de Su Magestad, al Señor Rey Christianissimo, BPR, III/ 6527 (3). For the embassy to Paris in 1700, *Relación de la entrada en París del Excelentisimo señor Condestable de Castilla, y Leon, Embaxador Extraordinario del Rey Catholico al Christianissimo, y su Audiencia en Versalles*, 1701, AHN, *Nobleza Frías*, Caja 62/44. The account, together with other documents, was published by the duke of Frías, "El cumplimiento del testamento de Carlos II: La embajada del Condestable de Castilla a Felipe V de España y Luis XIV de Francia," *Hispania* 97 and 98 (1964), 43–45 and 263–284 respectively.

66 This kind of pictorial document is scarce in Spain. The engraving made to mark the embassy sent to Rome, led by the duke of Segorbe, to Pope Clement X in 1676 can be consulted in BNE, Inv. 15478, reproduced in López Álvarez, *Poder, lujo y conflicto*, fig. 22. Among the most interesting specimens are the engravings by Gommarus Wouters of the entry of cardinal Francisco Maria de Medici into Rome in 1687 and that of prince Anton Florian of Liechtenstein in 1692, also into Rome; *Hollstein's Dutch and Flemish Etchings*, 54: 46–47, 50–51. See also the engraving by A. Schoonebeek of the arrival of the ambassadors at the palace of Rijswijk in 1697, *Hollstein's Dutch and Flemish Etchings*, 26: 26.

67 For the general evolution of the queens' Stables, Félix Labrador Arroyo and Alejandro

Litters and coaches: changes in the queen's ceremonial (1560–1580)

Until the mid-sixteenth century, the Stable of the Spanish queen had not played a significant role amongst the departments of her household, organized according to the Castilian model of queen Isabella the Catholic.[68] In it, horses and mules were the main means of transport and representation. Apart from these, the only vehicle used by the queens from medieval times had been the litter, a distinctive sign of her power and status.[69] By the mid-sixteenth century, a series of courtly scenarios and rituals of Burgundian and Italian influence, in which etiquette played a leading role, had been established in the Spanish court, promoting the ritual adoration of the prince. In addition, it became the order of the day for the various social groups in attendance to try to outdo each other in ostentatious luxury. Litters at that time were plainly at the peak of their vogue in Castile and the arrival of queen Isabella of Valois emphasized this process even further. Indeed, in France and Burgundy, litters were very common and had, for some time, been an indispensable item for queens, who used them for outings, rides, journeys and public entries. In fact, according to French ceremonial, until approximately 1600, queens mainly used the litter for their entries, whilst wheeled vehicles were reserved for ladies

López Álvarez, "Las caballerizas de las reinas en la Monarquía de los Austrias: cambios institucionales y evolución de las etiquetas, 1559–1611," *Studia Historica Historia Moderna* 28 (2006): 87–140.

[68] For some comments on this, see Labrador Arroyo and López Álvarez, "Las caballerizas de las reinas," 89–93.

[69] In 1462, queen Juana of Portugal, wife of Henry IV of Castile, went as far as Madrid in a litter but, before she entered the city, the king and other lords came out to meet her and "seeing that she had come in a litter, he ordered that she should be put on the crupper of her mule, so that she might enter Madrid as far as the Alcázar with greater honour and comfort"; cf. Rafael Domínguez Casas, *Arte y etiqueta de los Reyes Católicos: artistas, residencias, jardines y bosques* (Madrid, 1993), 321–322. For the litters of Isabella the Catholic, see Engracia A. de la Torre, "Viajes y transportes en tiempo de los Reyes Católicos," *Hispania* 14 (1954): 391–394. Diego de Velasco described the entry of princess Maria Manuela in October 1543 in these terms: "She arrived adorned so finely with pearls and gems, that I couldn't tell you about her mule, more about her person...she brought three litters, one with the most luxurious brocade I ever saw in my life," cf. José María March, *Niñez y juventud de Felipe II: documentos inéditos sobre su educación civil, literaria y religiosa y su iniciación en el gobierno, 1527–1547*, 2 vols. (Madrid, 1942), 2: 79.

of lower rank.[70] When Isabella of Valois came to Spain, she did so in a litter, as was the norm at the time[71] and used it, following French tradition, to carry out several of the ceremonies in which she took part, such as the entry into Rheims for the coronation of the king; the queen rode to this ceremony in her litter, under a canopy of white damask borne by four dignitaries, who took her to the church.[72] After the queen had entered Spain, the royal entourage continued to Pamplona; here, French protocol was followed once more, and Isabella, who claimed that it had been cold,[73] made her entry in a litter beneath a canopy carried by municipal leaders, whilst a troupe of children, dressed as men-at-arms, surrounded her vehicle and fired arquebus salvos[74] (fig. 7). There was no shortage of people who favourably compared the entry in an open litter with one on horseback, from which, undoubtedly, the personage would have been better viewed:

> … she made her entry in a litter, open at both sides, and it was no less beautiful to see, than if she had entered on a horse, they were followed in procession by her ladies and young women[75].

Once in Castile, entries reverted to customary usage, and unlike her entry into Pamplona, when she arrived at Toledo, the queen left her litter and mounted a white hackney in order to "ride freely, so that all the people, who wanted nothing less, could enjoy seeing her."[76] Nonetheless, there

[70] Théordore and Denys Godefroy, *Le ceremonial françois, ou description des ceremonies, rangs et seances, observees en France en divers Acts, & Assemblées solennelles*, 1649, FBG, H 2º 369, 1: 733, 745, 747, 793, 806, 850, 873, 959 and 964ff.

[71] Agustín González de Amezúa y Mayo, *Isabel de Valois, reina de España, 1546–1568*, 3 vols. (Madrid 1949), 1: 90, 99, 101 and 105; *Relación de la entrega de la Reina nuestra Señora*, BNE, MS. 5938 fol. 183v.

[72] Louis Paris, *Négotiations, lettres et pièces diverses relatives au règne de François II* (Paris, 1841), 115. This ceremony had taken place in September 1559. For comments about the entry into Bordeaux, see González de Amezúa y Mayo, *Isabel de Valois*, 3: 16.

[73] González de Amezúa y Mayo, *Isabel de Valois*, 1: 107; Paris, *Négotiations, lettres et pièces diverses*, 190, 191–192.

[74] Alphonse de Ruble, *Le traité de Cateau-Cambresis* (Paris, 1889), 263.

[75] Paris, *Négotiations, lettres et pièces diverses,* 184.

[76] Álvar Gómez de Castro, *Recebimiento que la Imperial ciudad de Toledo hizo a su Magestad de la Reyna nuestra señora doña Ysabel, hija del Rey Henrrico II de Francia: quando nuevamente entro en ella a celebrar las fiestas de sus felicissimas bodas, con el Rey don Philippe nuestro señor. II. deste nombre*, BNE, R 9385, fol. 10v. Something similar occurred in Alcalá in 1560, where we know that the queen had arrived in an "extremely luxurious litter," *El recebimiento que la Universidad de Alcalá de Henares hizo a los Reyes … cuando vinieron de Guadalajara tres días después de su felicísimo casamiento, in Relaciones de los reinados de Carlos V y Felipe II*, ed. Amalio Huarte, 2 vols (Madrid, 1941), 1: 157.

was close access to the vehicle when the queen, shortly before she arrived at the city: "found the children of the Christian Doctrine and others from this city, who, in good order and smartly groomed, went ahead of H.M., and she consented to let some of them enter the litter, and there she stroked them and delighted in touching such pretty hair."[77]

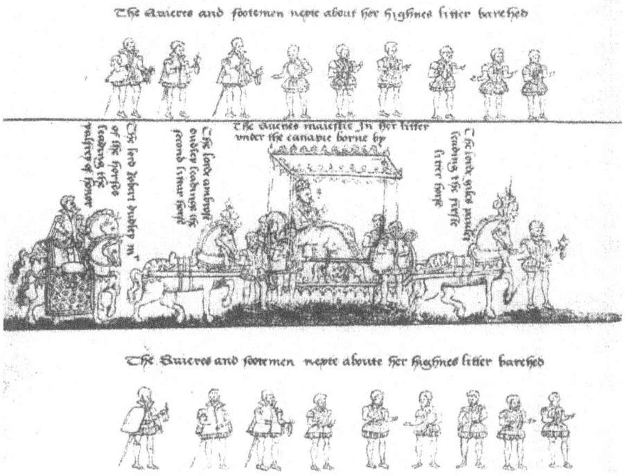

Fig. 7 – Illustrates the use of the litter in queens' entries into cities, representing that of Elizabeth I of England, in London, 1599 (COA MS 6 fol. 41).

From that time on, the queen began to be seen in her litter at various ceremonies: when the prince took his oath as heir, for example; in rides to the church; and even with the vehicle's curtains open, as when she visited a bullfight with princess Juana, accompanied by the king, the prince and don John of Austria. It is, in any case, highly significant

Similarly, before arriving at Guadalajara, the queen stepped down from the litter in order to take a hackney for the entry into the city, Ruble, *Traité de Cateau-Cambresis*, 265. The same thing happened in Bayonne in 1565, where she arrived in a state vehicle with her brothers and sisters, but then entered on horseback, González de Amezúa y Mayo, *Isabel de Valois*, 2: 231, 3: 315. Brantôme related, of this entry, that she was on a magnificently and richly harnessed hackney, completely embroidered with pearls belonging to the late empress when she made her entry into the cities, which was said to be worth more than a hundred thousand ecus, or even more, some said. She was very elegant on horseback, and she displayed herself well there; for she was so beautiful and pleasant that everyone was delighted with her, trans. *Des dames*, in *Oeuvres complètes*, 11 vols. ed. Ludovic Lalanne (Paris, 1866), 8: 12.

[77] G. de Ullera, *Entrada de la Serenísima Reyna nra Sra en Toledo*, BNE, MS. 5938 fol. 186.

that an act so typical of the Habsburgs as the bow or curtsy to the Christ in the Eucharist should be performed by the queen in her litter; it was related that, until her death, whenever her path crossed with the viaticum in the street, she would get down from the vehicle with her ladies and having knelt to worship it, she would accompany it on foot to the sick person's house, even escorting it later with her retinue to the church it had emerged from.[78]

Even so, it was the coach that was to take on the truly significant role in the changes made in the ceremonial of the Stable and the image of the queen, as had been the case for the king. This was not the first time that a queen had used a state vehicle of this kind in Castile, since it was recalled that, some time before, archduchess Margaret had brought with her various chariots, as they were called in these kingdoms, when she had arrived to marry prince John.[79] However, it was the first time they were used as a matter of course and when they began to give rise to changes that were crucial to the way the Stable was structured.[80]

From the beginning of the reign, and with increasing frequency, use of the coach came to be habitual in the queen's household. Isabella, who had brought her "charriots branlants" with her from France, and which added to the existing coaches in Philip II's Stable,[81] made good use of them during the time she stayed with princess Juana in Toledo between 1560 and 1561, when they often used a vehicle to make excursions

[78] *Relación y memoria de la entrada en esta cibdad de Toledo*, in Uhagón, *Relaciones históricas*, 72, 82, 84 and 90. Also González de Amezúa y Mayo, *Isabel de Valois*, 3: 107, 1: 316, who quotes a funeral eulogy written on the death of the queen by Monsignor Vigor, the royal preacher, 293–294.

[79] There are comments about Margaret's vehicles, "each one with four wheels and four horses" in Fernández de Oviedo, *Libro de la Cámara Real*, 163–164. Their existence in Spain is attested by the discovery that, amongst archduchess Margaret's belongings given by the Catholic Monarchs to the lords San Piqué and de Veere in September 1499, there were, in addition to litters, various samples of cloth suitable for a vehicle and the portable platform used to carry the litter, José Ferrandis, *Datos documentales para la historia del arte español* (Madrid, 1943), 3: 46, 47–48, 49–50. Fernández de Oviedo also pointed out that this kind of vehicle, not yet known as a coach, was used by the ladies of Germana de Foix in Margaret's entry into Toledo in 1526: "She entered in a litter covered with black woollen cloth, [...] and behind the litter, three or four aged duennas, and further behind, ten or twelve ladies, and following these a four-wheeled French vehicle with some more women," *Relación de lo sucedido en la prisión del rey Francisco I de Francia*, BNE, MS. 8756 fols. 36–39.

[80] For the introduction of new posts into the Stable of queen Isabella associated with the use of coaches, see Labrador Arroyo and López Álvarez, "Las caballerizas de las reinas," 93–109.

[81] Paris, *Négotiations, lettres et pièces diverses,* 196–199, 201–203.

into the surrounding area. According to the diary of one of her ladies, in the month of May, 1560, the queen and princess went for a ride in the coach to various places at least once a week. This became so customary that Catherine recommended to her daughter that, for the good of her health, she should not travel by coach or horse, but only in a litter or on foot.[82] In 1567, ambassador Fourquevaux communicated the news of Isabella's possible pregnancy to her mother, Catherine de Medici, asking her to write to the duchess of Alba, chief lady-in-waiting to the queen, to take care of the queen's health and try to make her take exercise, "because they think in the palace that the Queen can only travel by coach or litter," said the ambassador, as if walking were beneath the dignity of Her Royal Majesty.[83] By that time, the number of coaches had multiplied[84] (as had the coachmen to drive them), and they were no longer used only by the queen, who used them for travelling and for hunting, but also by her ladies.[85]

However, the most important thing, in our opinion, is that the coach served to project the queen and her ladies in a new light; it was transformed into a space for socializing and an instrument for establishing hierarchy amongst the courtiers.[86] We think that, by initially following French tradition, which was less rigid in this respect, queen Isabella showed that she was more accessible than she was later. An example of this is that Brantôme should tell how, in 1564, he had seen her leaving the palace and getting into her vehicle: "toujours à la portière, comme c'estoit sa place ordinaire: aussi telle beauté ne debvoit estre recluze au dedans, mais descouverte" [always sitting by the door as it was her usual place; also, such beauty should never be hidden away

[82] Paris, *Négotiations, lettres et pièces diverses,* 611–612.

[83] González de Amezúa y Mayo, *Isabel de Valois*, 2: 414.

[84] From the data we know of, the queen had at least seven vehicles during her reign, AGS, CSR, leg. 79, fols. 113, 128, 131, 146, 147 and 148. This figure is not insignificant, since Elizabeth I of England had eleven coaches available between 1564 and 1603, Julian Munby, "Queen Elizabeth's Coaches: the Wardrobe on Wheels," *The Antiquaries Journal,* 83 (2003), 311–367.

[85] González de Amezúa y Mayo, *Isabel de Valois*, 1: 189, 287 and Edmond Cabié, *Ambassade de Jean Ebrard seigneur de Saint-Sulpice de 1562 à 1565 et mission de ce diplomate dans le même pays en 1566* (Albi, 1903), 365, 368 and 386.

[86] The coach was a bone of contention between the servants of queen Isabella of Valois, such as Madame de Clermont and the countess of Ureña. The vehicle was also at the root of the complaints made by the duchess of Montpensier to Philip II concerning the treatment given to Alba de Liste's daughter, one of the queen's ladies, González de Amezúa y Mayo, *Isabel de Valois*, 1: 165, 166; Paris, *Négotiations et lettres*, 519–520.

inside, but be on view].[87] Similarly, when the queen visited Pamplona, after returning from Bayonne, "she rode through the city in her coach, to the general satisfaction of the townsfolk, and the people who went to see her."[88] The public appearances of the queen formed part of a rather ambivalent strategy, which aimed, on the one hand, to project the sovereign as a remote and sacred figure, whilst, at the same time, strengthening the bonds with her vassals.[89] The image of the queen, as had been the case with the king, was also associated with her state vehicles, transformed, additionally, into an element of courtly taste and distinction.[90]

The rules of etiquette drawn up for queen Anne of Austria in 1575 are further evidence of the growing importance of the use of vehicles in court: the protocol for receiving the queen's coach into the palace was accorded prime importance, giving the master of the horse a much more prominent role than he had had in the Castilian tradition. This was a question that had come to the fore again after 1560. We know that the procedure for receiving the queen's coach was similar to the one for receiving the king's coach: the order was given to the master of the horse to be at the palace to direct the reception of the animals or vehicles which would be used for the queen's journey. This regulation, following Burgundian practice, is quite clear about the status that the

[87] Brantôme, *Des dames*, 8: 82.

[88] Estebán de Garibay, *Compendio historial de las Crónicas y universal historia de todos los reynos de España*, 1571, BNE, R 823, p. 653.

[89] Joanna of Austria, daughter of emperor Ferdinand I and wife of the duke of Tuscany, commissioned a luxury coach through her brother, archduke Ferdinand II of Tyrol which she never got to enjoy because her husband neither approved of her independent attitude, nor did he wish her to ride through the streets of Florence in a vehicle, Hilda Lietzmann, "Der florentinische Wagen: Eine Kutsche für Giovanna d'Austria," *Münchner Jahrbuch der bildenden Kunst* 54, no. 3 (2003): 167.

[90] Probably the first pictorial representation of a state vehicle in Spain can be linked to Isabella of Valois. It is an architectural drawing, attributed to Diego de Siloé (which dates it no later than 1563), and shows scenery for the theatre, most probably for one of the works performed in the palace. The drawing can be found in MNA/GDG 107786/D, and is reproduced in the exhibition catalogue *Carolus* (Madrid, 2000), 372. In France, the coach had already provided the illustration which, in 1547, accompanied the poem by queen Margaret of Navarre "La Coche," reproduced in Wackernagel, *Der französische Krönungswagen*, 14. On the same topic in the Germanic field, see the woodcut by Nicolaus Solis to mark the wedding in 1568 of Renata of Lorraine and William V, duke of Bavaria, in which the bride's coach can be seen, reproduced in Kreisel, *Prunkwagen und Schlitten*, fig. 3 and pp. 23, 24, 28. Dated some time later, in 1579, is a drawing of the countess palatine Anna Maria's vehicle used at her wedding, reproduced in Wackernagel, *Staats-und Galawagen der Wittelsbacher*, 2: 16.

office had attained, since the master of the horse, now part of the palace inner circle, only served the queen directly on special occasions.[91] It was the equerries, whose number had increased in recent times, who were generally responsible for accompanying the retinue, which gained, as a result, in elegance and distinction. They would be on horseback if the queen went out in a vehicle and on foot if she was riding her hackney. The instructions were as follows:

> On those occasions when the Queen has to go out, and the abovementioned Princes are accompanying her, neither the Master of the Horse, nor the Princes' tutor are to go behind the Grandees, and the Master of the Horse must ensure that he goes to the palace to carry out his duties, and give the order for the coaches, litters, or hacks, together with any other necessities to accompany the coach, litter or horse that the Queen uses; and the equerries will go on horseback and other officers of the Stable on foot, so that no one is missing, not even the footmen, but if the Queen is to go on horseback, the equerries will go with her on foot.[92]

The moment when the animals and vehicles were handed over went to the very heart of the rules of etiquette; once more, another Burgundian element. This influence is also noticeable in the routine orders to be followed by the master of the horse whenever the queen went out, which aimed to ensure that the equerries carried out their functions; these were to exalt and set the queen apart by surrounding her, and so enhance the pomp and remoteness of the sovereign when she was out and about in the locality:

[91] For example, during queen Anne's entry into the city of Burgos, Philip II indicated the place that his wife's master of the horse should occupy: "then the queen will go under the canopy, which is to be carried for her by the municipal leaders, as is customary, and next to Her Majesty, to one side, whoever is serving her as master of the horse will walk under the canopy, so that he is at hand should she require anything," L. Pérez Bueno, "Del casamiento de Felipe II con su sobrina Ana de Austria," *Hispania* 28 (1947): 399. For the entry into Madrid, the master of the horse led the palfrey by the reins of the bridle, together with the other equerries, Jean Lhermite, *El pasatiempos de Jehan Lhermite: Memorias de un gentilhombre flamenco en la corte de Felipe II y Felipe III* (Madrid, 2005), 489, 511. For changes in the figure of the master of the horse serving the queen, see Labrador Arroyo and López Álvarez, "Las caballerizas de las reinas," 112–115.

[92] For the king's Stable, see López Álvarez, "Evolución de la Caballeriza," 296, 313–314. For the queen's etiquette, see *Etiquetas de la Casa de la reina Ana*, 1575, AGP, Sección Histórica, Caja 49, exp. 3. This citation here and the following ones.

> Whenever the Queen goes out to a Church, Monastery or Chapel, or to some festivity, or anywhere else in the place where she happens to be, the Equerries will accompany her on foot, with heads uncovered, and on either side of the hack, coach, or litter which the Queen might be using, maintaining the authority and respect due to her; they will not talk to her, except to answer if she asks them a question and the Master of the Horse will arrange this and for the other Officers to walk there, as appropriate.[93]

The importance of the Stable in the public representation of the queen, following the model of the king, was given a decisive impetus when, in 1570, several entries into Burgos, Valladolid and Segovia were organized for Anne of Austria in the Burgundian manner. These entries remained the model for later years and became part of the etiquette of the Spanish Monarchy.[94] Despite this, numerous elements of the first decades of the second half of the sixteenth century failed to develop as foreseen because of the early death of the queen and the subsequent absence of one for almost twenty years.

The image of the queen after 1598

During Philip III's reign, the court was institutionalized, the protocols and ordinances of the royal household were laid down and court ceremonial consolidated. It was in this context that the queen's household came to assume a hitherto unusually high profile, establishing itself as a model after a period when it had, in fact, been absent. Contrary to the often maintained position, it was queen Margaret herself who was to play a major role in bringing this about and in the image of the Crown communicated to the vassals. In this mission, her Stable was to acquire

[93] This regulation was repeated in the one issued to the equerries who were ordered to take great care that "whenever the Queen goes out, they should go to the palace, taking with them all the equipment of the Stable when the Queen goes out nearby, or to some Monastery, or Orchard, even if it is just to go outside. If it is not for a long journey, they must walk on both sides of the Queen's hack, litter or coach, and in this matter and everything else they are to obey the master of the horse and follow whatever instructions he gives them." From this regulation and the previous one, we gather that the equerries went on horseback on longer journeys.

[94] For an introduction to Burgundian ceremonial in the royal entries, see Félix Labrador Arroyo and Alejandro López Álvarez, "Lujo y representación en la Monarquía de los Austrias: la configuración del ceremonial de la caballeriza de la reina Margarita: 1598–1611," *Espacio, tiempo y forma. Serie IV, Historia Moderna*, 23 (2010), 19-39.

considerable influence as that section of the household responsible for representing the royal couple to the world.[95] From that moment, the ceremonies carried out with a state vehicle, the number used, and particularly their sumptuousness and luxury, frequently became the stuff of royal propaganda. From that time, the image of the queen was to display ostentatious wealth, much of it centred on the state vehicles, although the image had, simultaneously, to be brought into line with those which sought to project her as a Catholic queen and a model for the court. Therefore, in Ferrara, where she was to receive a highly luxurious carosse as a gift from the pope, when he invited her after her marriage by proxy on November 15, 1598:

> to take a short ride in her carosse around Ferrara, ... so that the people could see her, which they greatly desired, ... Her Majesty the Queen very wisely responded, as a good Christian should, that having taken Communion the very morning of her marriage, it was not appropriate to go out and see frivolous things in the streets, nor did she want to be seen, except in the churches and nunneries.[96]

The extreme wealth of the queen's Stable had been anticipated by the austere Philip II, who proposed an impressive escort of vehicles for Margaret, having a coach, a litter and twelve spare coaches built in Milan.[97] As we have already mentioned, the Holy Father had also

[95] In fact, in the etiquette and ceremonial of the royal household, compiled in definitive form in the middle of the seventeenth century, it is noticeable that when the queen showed herself in public, the Stable clearly played a prominent role. This was the case when they went to mass, with the king on horseback and the queen in a coach; for the festive entry into Madrid; and for excursions by coach or on horseback, see especially Christina Hofmann, *Das Spanische Hofzeremoniell von 1500–1700* (Frankfurt, 1985), 95–96, 160–161, and 174–175.

[96] Felipe de Gauna, *Relación de las fiestas celebradas en Valencia con motivo del casamiento de Felipe III*, 2 vols. (Valencia, 1926), 1: 37–38, 42, 65. However the chronicler indicated that on the following Monday she went to visit a church and a monastery in the company of her mother, the archduchess, and her principal ladies, "in their carosses, with archduke Albert and other Grandees of Spain, also accompanying them in other carosses every day that they went out."

[97] Philip II, in a written communication to the Constable of Castile on June 3, 1598, instructed him to have everything ready to receive archduchess Margaret, and that some Spanish clothing should be made ready for her. He sent 200,000 ducats to defray expenses, AGS, E. leg. 1285, no. 15. The king also wrote to ambassador San Clemente on the same day, mentioning that there was a shortage of the necessary coach horses for Milan, AGS, E. leg. 2450 (no pagination). More information about the preparations in AGS, E. leg. 182 (no pagination). The choice of Milan for coach building was not

presented the queen with an extraordinary vehicle in Ferrara. In the entry into this city, the sovereign, accompanied by the pope's legate cardinals, went up to:

> a sumptuous carosse of crimson velvet, completely harnessed in gold, with six beautiful horses adorned in the same way, two coachmen in matching livery and just two seats. And once Her Majesty had entered with her mother, the Archduchess, and both were seated inside the carosse, then the lord Cardinals and the legates climbed into a similarly sumptuous carosse.[98]

However, the height of luxury, as far as carosses are concerned, was attained in Milan, where the richness of the vehicles was completed with an impressive ceremonial. Furthermore, the entry, in this case, had a special significance since, after the death of Philip II, Margaret was no longer a princess, but the queen of the Catholic Monarchy and arrived in the city as a duchess in her own right. Furthermore, Milan was the first city on her journey towards the peninsula which was subject to the Spanish Crown.[99] So, as she made her entry into this major city, the queen was presented with an extremely sumptuous state vehicle, which Gauna describes as:

> a very expensive, sumptuous carosse, never seen before, because it was made to the following standards of luxury: instead of wood, the complete coach body, pillars, and roof, both inside and out, were made of wonderfully well-wrought solid silver, and upholstered in an exquisite brocade richly embroidered in relief, and with fine pearls, diamonds and rubies. The same brocade on the uppermost point of the ceiling was embroidered with the escutcheon and armorial bearings of the king, Philip III of Spain and duke of Milan, made from diamond points and pearls, and with many emeralds of inestimable value; and on the back of the same carosse was another escutcheon and armorial bearings, embroidered like the ones above, belonging

coincidental, if we bear in mind the excellence of the textiles produced in the city, Paola Venturelli, "La produzione tessile dall'etá sforzesca al Settecento," in Valerio Terraroli (ed.), *Le arti decorative in Lombardia nella'etá moderna 1480–1780* (Milan, 2000), 55–79. Information about the abundance of coaches in Milan can be found in Lhermite, *Pasatiempos de Jehan Lhermite*, 66–67.

[98] Gauna, *Relación de las fiestas celebradas en Valencia*, 1: 37–38, 39, 40.

[99] Giovanni Altoviti, *Essequie della Sacra Católica e Real Maestà di Marguerita d'Austria Regina di Spagna, celebrate dal Serenísimo don Cosimo II, Gran Duca di Toscana III descrite da Giovanni Altoviti* (Florence, 1612), BNE, R 22299, p. 20.

> to the queen and duchess of Milan. The four wheels of the said carosse and all the rest of it were made of incorruptible wood, gilded over and wonderfully carved, drawn by twelve horses of the same strange colour with their blankets and harness of black velvet and all embroidered in fine gold and silver thread. Each of the horses had a sash of gold and silver cloth, all of them studded with pearls and priceless jewels; each had a garland on its head and a head piece of solid silver, even down to the engraving. They were driven by six coachmen in costumes of different brocade, covered with pearls and variously coloured feathers.[100]

It is highly significant, according to testimony, that the queen made her entry into Milan in this vehicle, showing her communion with the dukedom, a fact which was ritually underlined by the salvoes that accompanied the queen as she entered her coach, passed through the city walls, and alighted from her carosse in a sophisticated ceremonial that surprised all those who took part in it. The very entry by state vehicle expressed the queen's power over her city, and recalled the triumphal entries of the victorious Roman generals:

> In that same luxurious carosse, Her Majesty the Queen entered, together with the Archduchess, her mother, after having alighted from the litters in which they came on horseback [sic] and behind this carosse followed six carosses belonging to the principal ladies of the Queen and the Archduchess, and, all the abovementioned nobles entered in order along the street, the Milanese interspersed with the Spanish: except that Archduke Albert and His Eminence Cardinal Aldobrandino both went

[100] Gauna, *Relación de las fiestas celebradas en Valencia*, 1: 70. This Milan coach should be included in the *Brautwagen* series, that is bridal coaches, common from the Middle Ages, some of which were very famous, for example, those of Catherine of Austria, wife of Charles I of Baden-Baden (1447), Leonor of Portugal who married emperor Frederick III (ca. 1451), Beatrice of Anjou, second wife of the Hungarian king, Matthias Corvinus (1476), or Isabella Gonzaga who married in Mantua (1490), and so on. See further, Herbert Haupt, "'Der goldene Wagen' der österreichischen Herzogin Katharina (1420–1493)," in *Livrustkammaren: Journal of the Royal Armoury Stockholm* 14 (1976–1978): 173–194. However, the carosse decoration, with the escutcheons of the royal couple and pearl embroidery is quite similar to other later examples, such as that of the vehicle used by the duchess Maria Anna of Bavaria to make her entry into Graz in 1600, see also idem, "Der Brautwagen der Königin Anna vom Jahre 1611: Ein Beitrag zur Geschichte des Festswagens und seiner Funktion im Hochzeitszeremoniell der frühen Neuzeit," in *Achse, Rad und Wagen: Beiträge zur Geschichte der Landfahrzeuge*, vol. 1 (1991): 21–25. The state vehicles of Renata of Lorraine and the countess palatine mentioned above were of the same kind.

> together in front of the abovementioned carosse of Her Majesty the Queen.

At the same time, the entry by state vehicle was a metaphor for entry into the urban space of the city, underlined by a tremendous salvo at that precise instant, and again on the entry into the city itself:

> There was great joy in the castle of Milan when Her Majesty the Queen set foot in the abovementioned carosse in order to enter the city which was expressed by firing more than four hundred pieces of artillery and swivel-guns, not to mention all the other arquebuses which also fired a salvo, and as she entered through the city gate, the same artillery and arquebuses fired yet another salvo, which was really something to see and hear.

The same thing was repeated on their arrival at the palace as the queen was leaving the coach:

> It being more than ten o'clock at night, when, with their abovementioned accompanying escort, they all arrived at the royal palace; here, in the courtyard, Her Majesty the Queen followed by her mother, the Archduchess, stepped down from the luxurious coach in which they had arrived, with the help of his Eminence, Cardinal Aldobrandino and Archduke Albert accompanying them, and at that precise moment and hour, the complete artillery of the Castle of Milan fired another salvo, ..., and, together with the arquebusier infantry, with great joy and in harmony with the sound of the fifes and drums of war, leaving Her Majesty the Queen and everyone in her entourage astounded at the roar of the artillery and the cries of the people, making it seem as if the entire city was falling to the ground.[101]

[101] Gauna, *Relación de las fiestas celebradas en Valencia*, 1: 70, 73–74. The queen's Entry was carried out on horseback and under a canopy, according to other sources, Paola Venturelli, "La solemne entrada en Milán de Margarita de Austria, esposa de Felipe III (1598)," in María Luisa Lobato and Bernardo J. García García (eds.), *La fiesta cortesana en la época de los Austrias* (Valladolid, 2003), 240. Amongst the paintings produced for the queen's funeral rites in Florence in 1612, her entry into Milan was recreated, in which the queen appeared on horseback and under a canopy. See the exhibition catalogue *Glorias efímeras: Las exequias florentinas de Felipe II y Margarita de Austria* (Madrid, 1999), 250–251. If the entry really took place in this way – on horseback and under a canopy – Gauna's account is all the more interesting, putting forward a richer, more complex image of the queen in symbolic terms, in which, as previously noted, the state vehicle is regarded as a metaphor for government.

From the time of her arrival in Spain, the queen went about in similar sumptuous style. One reflection of this is the fact that the luxury of the vehicles used by the queen and her retinue never ceased to be commented on in festive narratives. Luxury of this kind in the Stable, particularly the state vehicles, was identified from this point onwards with the image of Margaret and her ladies,[102] something which is readily understandable, considering the army of servants in that institution responsible for maintaining it; the state vehicles of the queen, in fact, were constantly being renovated, partly because they rapidly lost their newness, but also because of the need to be fashionable and to have the most luxurious and sophisticated Stable possible, as was the case every time a journey to Portugal was planned.[103] The queen brought out new vehicles for every new ceremony, in lavish displays of luxury.[104] One such occasion was the mass given in honour of the prince in San Llorente in Valladolid, although there were others.

This process showed no signs of slackening, not even on the death of the queen; on the contrary, from 1611, and following the pace set by the institutional use of the coach, it acquired fresh impetus, as was demonstrated in the exchange of princesses in 1615. Through this exchange, the infanta Anne of Austria went to France as the wife of Louis XIII and princess Isabella of Bourbon was welcomed into Spain as the wife of the crown prince, the future Philip IV, in a context of renewed ritual confrontation between the two courts. The display of the catholic court in Burgos, where the weddings were to be celebrated by proxy, was already largely based on the wealth and luxury of the Stable of the king and the courtiers of greatest influence.[105] In fact, the focal point of the retinue that went to the cathedral where the proxy marriage ceremony took place was the future queen's state vehicle, the royal coach,

[102] The ladies hardly ever went out on horseback anymore, as Pinheiro da Veiga commented on the entry of the royal couple into the consistory in Valladolid, which had been "a very pleasant sight since it was unusual to see the ladies entering on horseback, with so much harmony and majesty" in *Fastiginia*, 125–126.

[103] The preparations for the visit to Portugal naturally included the construction of new coaches, about which Cabrera de Córdoba duly provided information in January 1602 and October and November 1604, *Relaciones*, 127, 164, 228 and 229. Expenses for the queen's vehicles, in AGS, CJH, leg. 444, fajo 15, and leg. 489, fajo 15, nos. 30–31.

[104] Pinheiro, *Fastiginia*, 100–101.

[105] Pedro Mantuano, *Casamientos de España y Francia, y viage del Duque de Lerma llevando la Reyna Christianissima Doña Ana de Austria al paso de Beobia, y trayendo la princesa de Asturias nuestra señora*, 1618, BNE, R 11.067, pp. 123–125, 152–155 and 156–166.

with prince Philip, his sister, Anna, queen of France, and the other royal children inside. According to one account, this coach was:

> very luxuriously upholstered inside, embroidered outside with large precious stones, studs and wheels, and all the woodwork inside and out richly decorated, and drawn by six very large Neapolitan sorrels with richly embroidered crimson velvet trappings: this coach was driven by two coachmen and two coach boys, clad in crimson velvet with full ceremonial gold embroidery.[106]

It was precisely the state vehicles at the moment of the exchange that provided the contrast between the Catholic and the French courts. It was said of the gifts that the duke of Uceda had left on a flat stretch of ground by the river that there were:

> three very opulent items so that our Lady, the Princess, when travelling to Spain could ride in them. They were a large carosse, a litter and a sedan chair, all studded with gold, with brocade curtains, silver wheels, six horses, and two famous mules, and richly dressed footmen carrying the sedan chair.

The contrast with the vehicles on the French side was stark:

> The French had, on their side of the river, for the queen, a litter with crimson velvet and silver handrails and a good coach, and, for the other ladies, two coaches and no litter, and when they had left for France, they sorely missed what they had left behind in Spain.

The ceremony and etiquette which awaited the future queen of France displayed the inferiority of that court, as was seen at the critical moment when the princesses took their leave:

> there were lots of tears on the part of the ladies who were moving to France, as well there might be considering what awaited them, because as they were completing the move, they all found themselves in the fields not knowing in which coaches or litters they were supposed to travel, nor who was to look after them.[107]

[106] *Relacion del desposorio que se celebró en la Cyudad de Burgos entre la serenissima Infanta de España Doña Ana y el Christianissimo Principe Luys de Francia*, 1615, BNE, MS. 2348, fol. 193r.

[107] *Relacion de la Jornada de las entregas de las Serenissimas Señoras Doña Ana Reyna de Françia, y Doña Isabel Prinçesa de España, hechas en los meses de Otubre y Noviembre de*

The images of the king and queen were inseparably linked to those of their Stables and coaches, and, from time to time, became essential instruments in the war of propaganda between the two courts. Proof of all this is that Pieter van der Meulen was commissioned to paint a picture of the occasion, and in which the vehicles ranged on each side of the river where the exchange took place appear in some detail.[108] Although it was produced at a later date and in a different context, the image of the queen of France's carosse is reminiscent of a 1651 engraving representing the occasion of the king on his way to the *parlement* in Paris to declare his coming of age (fig. 8).[109] There are countless other examples of princely European courts in which the queens' coaches played a major role, whether at their weddings, entries into cities[110] or for other reasons.[111]

este año de 1615, BNE, MS. 2348, fols. 226r, 227r and 228r. This account indicated that an accompanying retinue of some three thousand people took part in the queen of France's departure from Burgos, "so many litters, carosses, carts, horses and mules hired and mules presented as gifts, that to tell it all would need several large books," *ibidem*, fol. 219.

[108] This is a reference to *El intercambio de princesas en el río Bidasoa* (RMEM 00621531). It is reproduced in Galán, *Historia del carruaje*, 111.

[109] N. Cochin, *Marche du Roi allant au Parlement pour la déclaration de sa majorité*, 1651, BNF, Qb 1–1651 (September 7). Less detailed, but nonetheless interesting in this connection and closer in time, is the 1610 engraving by Crispijn de Passe de Oude representing queen Maria de Medici, *Hollstein's Dutch and Flemish Etchings*, 15: 258. Also worthy of mention is one of his engravings made in 1638 in which the queen's state vehicle can be seen, with the queen inside it, *Hollstein's Dutch and Flemish Etchings*, 14: 173.

[110] See the engravings made in 1614 by W-P. Zimmermann to mark the wedding of the duke of Bavaria, reproduced in the exhibition catalogue, *Wittelsbach und Bayern: Um Glauben und Reich. Kürfurst Maximilian I*, 2 vols. (Munich, 1980), 2: 145–147. Also the wedding vehicle used by Friedrich Ulrich, duke of Braunschweig-Wolfenbüttel at his wedding to Anna Sophia, marchioness of Brandenburg in 1614, Paas, *German Political Broadsheet*, 1: 313. One of the engravings made for the occasion of Ferdinand II's entry into Regensburg in 1622 showed, in detail, the state vehicles of the empress and her ladies, Paas, *German Political Broadsheet*, 4: 112. See also, the engraving of the entry into Munich of Adelaide, princess of Savoy in 1652, Paas, *German Political Broadsheet*, 8: 111. Among the most famous cases is the coach in the engraving of the entry into Paris of Louis XIV and his queen consort, Marie-Thérèse in 1660, Paas, *German Political Broadsheet*, 357. See also the drawing, in Wackernagel, *Der französische Krönungswagen*, fig. 3b.

[111] In Spain, it is worth remembering the image of Isabella of Bourbon sitting comfortably in her coach during a royal hunt, in the picture of 1636–1639 by Velázquez and Mazo, "La montería del Hoyo (La tela real)," whose English title is "Philip IV Hunting Wild Boar (The Royal Enclosure)," in the National Gallery, London (cat. no. 179), copy in the Prado, illustrated in Galán, *Historia del carruaje*, 140. See also, the

Fig. 8 – This engraving is a fine example of the interest shown in exhibiting the splendour of royal vehicles in the European courts of the mid-seventeenth century, N. Cochin, *Marche du Roi allant au Parlement pour la déclaration de sa majorité*, 1651 (detail), (BNF Qb 1–1651 (September 7)).

Ceremonial use of the Sedan chair

The list of modifications to the queen's Stable in terms of state vehicles would be incomplete without reference to the sedan chair. Until now, this has been considered as a simple artefact of no great significance, particularly when compared with the coach, carosse and litter;[112] however, we believe that its use deserves special consideration. Although we do not know much about its typological development,[113] nor exactly how it originated, the earliest pictorial evidence that we are aware of shows a sort of box, more or less close and of no great size, supported on poles and transported by servants.[114] But, beyond its formal appearance, a series of very significant elements replete with symbolic meaning came

paintings by Adam Frans van der Meulen, showing the coach of the queen consort, Marie-Thérèse before her entry into Arras in 1677, illustrated in ibidem, 113 or those by the same painter, illustrated in Wackernagel, *Der französische Krönungswagen*, figs. 5d, 6a, b and c.

[112] The occasionally found assertion that the sedan chair was a device of inferior category compared with the coach cannot be sustained, S. Bessone, "El camino hacia el carruaje," in Galán, *Historia del carruaje*, 107.

[113] When categorizing them, we have sometimes regarded them as a development of the litter, A. López Álvarez, "Silla de manos," in *Gran Enciclopedia Cervantina*, ed. C. Alvar (forthcoming).

[114] See WLBS, Cod. Hist. qt 148b, fol. 5, and Pietro Bertelli, *Diversarum nationum habitus*, 1594, BNE, ER 3567, nos. 31A and 31B.

together in these portable chairs.[115] In the beginning, they brought to mind *andas*, a structure made of horizontal parallel poles, and used in religious processions to carry sacred images.[116] However, these *andas* harked back to similar items already used in Antiquity and well known at the time,[117] as well as to the equally famous objects used by kings and local chiefs in Spanish American culture, particularly among the Mexicans and Incas.[118] In addition, we should not forget that the *sedia gestatoria,* or portable papal throne, on which the pope had long been carried about by an assigned corps of footmen, was in fact a form of *andas.*[119] Its use was described in some considerable detail in compilations on Roman ceremonial, as well as in the Capella ritual[120]

[115] There are interesting reflections in Sergio Bertelli, *Il corpo del re: Sacralità del potere nell'Europa medievale e moderna*, 2nd ed. (Florence, 1995), 132ff.

[116] *Andas* was the name used from medieval times to refer to the litter in Castile. In brief, it was a sort of close box used for transporting people.

[117] Alonso Carranza, for example, wrote of the Roman litters that they were carried "on the shoulders, as they are by hand today," and that they cost much more [then] than in his time, "because of their wonderful structure, with windows on all sides, and so capacious that there were beds and seats in them, and the Romans brought along their writing tablets and writing desks, and on the way, they read, wrote and carried out their business, surrounded by countless servants, and borne on the shoulders of six or eight," *Señor, la prematica del Rey don Felipe III*, 1622, BNE, VE 28-12, fol. 4r. All in all, the most interesting reflections on the classical precursors to the sedan chair are those of the eighteenth century. Chronologically speaking, the first approach is that of Johan Alstorph, *De lecticis veterum diatribe*, 1704, WLBS, altern. Oct. 29. In the same vein, but much briefer, is the minor treatise by Johan Heinrich Blank, *De lectulis et lecticis romanorum lucubratoriis dissertatio antiquaria*, 1758, BSB, 4 Exeg. 323 u. However, the most interesting for its breadth and systematic treatment is Carl Christian Schramm, *Abhandlung der Porte-Chaises oder Trage-Sänfften durch Menschen oder Thiere, in allen Vier Theilen der Welt, nach der Critic, Mechanic, Histoire, dem Recht, wie auch Cammer- und Policey-Wese ausgeführet und erläutert, Nuremberg*, Nuremberg, 1737, USBK, WCV93. We are preparing a study on this topic to be published shortly.

[118] See the study by Fr. Martín de Murua, *Historia general del Perú, origen y descendencia de los incas*, ed. Manuel Ballesteros-Gaibrois (Madrid, 1987), *passim*, as well as that written by Francisco López de Gómara, *La conquista de México*, 1552, ed. José Luis de Rojas (Madrid, 1987), passim.

[119] For information about the antiquity of the papal brotherhoods of the *Palafrenieri* and *Sediari*, see Matizia Maroni Lumbroso and Antonio Martini, *Le confraternite romane nelle loro chiese* (Rome, 1963), 47–50.

[120] The Capella ceremony involved organizing a procession in which the cardinal deacons, priests and bishops followed the various principal figures, see Francesco Sestini de Bibbiena, *Il Maestro di camera*, 1689, FBG, Geog. 8º 2735/2, (2), p. 35.

when the new pope took office,[121] just as it was the object of frequent artistic representations from the last third of the sixteenth century,[122] becoming a common sight in later papal iconography[123] (fig. 9).[124] In addition, travelling by sedan chair became a notable privilege in the Vatican. The cardinals could ride in them, although special permission from the pope was required to enter the papal palace and consistory.[125]

All these precedents undoubtedly influenced the proliferation of similar instruments in the princely courts of Europe from the middle of the sixteenth century. Together with a process clearly designed to affirm the sacred quality of kingship in such important circumstances, it is also likely that purely physical necessities contributed to their development, since in increasingly sedentary courts, the mobility of

[121] When the new pope took office, the ceremonial for the occasion included a cavalcade of great pomp, and with the largest number of people ever to take place in Rome, to the Basilica of St. John Lateran, "non restando Ambasciadore, Prencipe, o Signore, che non serva in questa occasione Sua Santità." The pope left with a great entourage: "hà delle bande il uso Maestro di Camera, e coppiere, e d'attorno numero grandissimo do Paggi, e Palafrenieri, e gli altri cardini. Cavalcano dopo S. Santità." As he entered the church, the pope, "portato in sedia sotto il Baldachino, quiu i scende, e si pone in ginocchioni," Sestini, *Il Maestro di camera*, 60–62.

[122] See the papal throne in the entry procession to St. John Lateran to open the holy door in the year 1575, FBG, Opp Gr 2º 1106/1 (9). It is reproduced in the exhibition catalogue, *Barock im Vatikan: Kunst und Kultur im Rom der Päpste, 1572–1676* (Leipzig, 2005), 91. Identification of the pope with the portable throne can equally be seen in the diatribes directed against him from the Protestant ranks; see the first in Luther, *Passional Christi und Antichristi*, 1521, BSB, Res/4 H. eccl. 870, 9 fol. 13. Rather later is that of a certain Totentanz, or Dance of Death, published in 1588, in which the pope was being carried on his throne, accompanied by his cardinals and soldiers represented by skeletons, whilst Death condemned the pontiff: "Wie g'fallen Euch Bapst die ding/ Ihr tantzen auch an diesem Ring:/ Sie dreyfach Bron mußt Ihr mir lon/ Und ewers Sessels rühwig stobn," in *Hollstein's German Engravings*, 59: 152–156.

[123] See *La cavalcatura con le sue ceremonie dun Pontefice nuovo quando piglia possesso a Santo Giovanni Laterano*, FBG, Opp Gr 2º 1106/1 (168). In an engraving representing the floor of the conclave set up for the vacant see of Gregory XV in 1623, the new pope can also be seen being borne in public to St. Peter's in a sedan chair and under a canopy, FBG, Opp. Gr 2º 1106/1 (20). Another example from 1656 is in Bertelli, *Il corpo del re*, 135, fig. 37. Also of great interest is the famous painting by Giovanni Maria Morandi, "Pope Alexander VII in the Corpus Domini Procession," kept in the Musée des Beaux-Arts in Nancy. It is reproduced in *Barock im Vatikan*, 315.

[124] An engraving from approximately 1591, in which Innocence IX can be seen in his sedan chair, being carried on the shoulders of footmen and surrounded by the Guard, FBG, Opp Gr 2º 1106/1 (22).

[125] Girolamo Lunadoro, *Relatione della Corte di Roma*, 1642, FBG, Geogr. 8º 2735/1, pp. 85–86.

Fig. 9 – The proliferation of sedan chairs among princes was undoubtedly due to the example set by the pope's *sedia gestatoria*. This 1591 engraving represents Innocence IX in his chair being carried on the shoulders of his *palafrenieri* [footmen] and surrounded by his guard (FBG Opp Gr 2° 1106/1 (22)).

the sovereign in the palace or relatively reduced urban spaces, seems to have increased. If the litter had been the most effective means of transport for moving about inside and outside the city until the mid-sixteenth century, it seems that, from that time onwards, some items of a more domestic nature began to be fashionable, serving as a throne, a seat, and a means of transport. There is abundant testimony of great interest concerning this kind of vehicle in the Italian courts prior to the seventeenth century,[126] and structures similar to *andas* were also used in the English court of Elizabeth I.[127] We find, some time later in the Imperial court, something like a chair placed on poles, which combined the need to carry the monarch about with the ritual worship of him. One was used in the ceremonials for the coronation of Mathias in 1612 (fig. 10).[128] Although this image is exceptional for its time, when it was the norm to represent the emperor on horseback and under a canopy,[129] or walking beneath a canopy,[130] it was not unique; the use of this chair can be seen in another engraving from 1636 depicting the coronation of Ferdinand III.[131]

[126] Heinrich Schickhardt, *Beschreibung einer Reiß / Welche der Durchleuchtig Hochgeborne Fürst und Herr / Herr Friderich Herzog zu Würtemberg unnd Teck / Grave zu Mümpelgart / Herr zu Heidenheim / Ritter beeder Königlicher Orden in Frankreich unnd Engelland / u. Im jahr 1599. Selb neundt / aus dem Landt zu Würtemberg in* Italiam *gethan*, 1602, modern edition *Voyage en Italie*, ed. André Bouvard (Montbéliard, 2002), 337.

[127] Queen Elizabeth I of England can be seen being carried on some kind of chair on the shoulders of her courtiers and under a canopy in the interesting "Procession Portrait of Queen Elizabeth I," SCD, catalogue no. 14, reproduced in Strong, *Portraits of Queen Elizabeth I*, fig. 19. Some comments about the portrait, its authorship and the significance of the chair, also in Roy C. Strong, *The Cult of Elizabeth* (London, 1977), 17–55, and *idem*, *Gloriana: The Portraits of Queen Elizabeth I* (London, 1987), 153–155.

[128] For the occasion of the coronation of Mathias in 1612, Wilhelm Peter Zimmermann engraved a plate where the emperor appeared under a canopy and on a chair placed on *andas*, being carried by some dignitaries GNM, Inv. HB 129, Kapsel 1255. It must certainly have been a series since there is another by the same author, entitled "Krönungsfeierlichkeiten auf dem Römerberg in Frankfurt," GNM, Inv. HB 17570, Kapsel 1255. It is significant that the first news of sedan chair porters in the Imperial court (Sänftenknechte) appears in 1615, when four of them are mentioned in a list of servants of emperor Mathias. This information was kindly provided by Dr. J. Hausenblasová, February, 2008.

[129] FBG, Biogr. fol. 593/1 (111).

[130] FBG, Pol. 8º 1393/1 (3), fig. E. For the coronation of the emperor Maximilian in Frankfurt in 1562, FBG, Hist. 8º 1160/2 (no pagination).

[131] At the moment of leaving for the banquet, to be exact, *Hollstein's German Engravings*, 46: 51.

Fig. 10 – During the celebrations marking the coronation of Mathias in 1612, the emperor was transported in a kind of chair on *andas* and carried beneath a canopy, engraving by Wilhelm Peter Zimmermann (GNM, Inv. HB 129, Kapsel 1255).

The phenomenon of the sedan chair, whether in the form of more or less close boxes or of *andas* supplied with seats, was introduced into Castile quite early on. Amongst the first references to them in the Spanish court are those belonging to Isabella of Valois and Anne of Austria.[132] Some time later, they appear to have attained some degree of importance in Philip II's household, probably when the health problems which prevented him from moving about freely on his own coincided with his interest in attributing symbolic significance to himself. At that time, various

[132] The first reference we have is a record of the existence of a "chair to be carried on the shoulders and in which they carried the Queen," AGS, CSR, leg. 79, fol. 128. As for Anne of Austria, we know that during her first pregnancy, the order from Philip II in El Escorial was that: "if the queen wants to leave the palace, remind her to go in a chair so that she doesn't have another fall," Henry Kamen, *Philip of Spain* (New Haven-London, 1997), 206.

devices were built for the purpose of transporting the monarch from place to place. The most famous of these, now reconstructed, is the so-called gout chair, designed to alleviate the monarch's gout pains.[133] This chair was not, however, the only special device that enabled the king to be carried. In the course of time, others, which we know something about, were constructed. For the journey which was to be his last, in June 1598, Philip was so weak "that he simply could not abide being shaken about in the coach," and was "carried in the arms of several men in a chair specially constructed for that purpose, in the form of a small litter and with almost all the comforts of the gout chair."[134] Significantly, the pope's nuncio also provided information about similar objects.[135] It

[133] The articulated chair, kept in El Escorial (ME 10014120), was drawn and described by Lhermite, *Pasatiempos de Jehan Lhermite*, 639, plate 9. See also the exhibition catalogue, *Felipe II un monarca y su época: Un príncipe del Renacimiento* (Madrid, 1998), 456 and 547–548. Lhermite said of it: "This special chair for gout was one of the best pieces of furniture to be found and the most comfortable that H.M. could have, not for its value in terms of material or luxury, but because of the immense comfort it afforded him in all his illnesses, and although it was only made of wood, leather and ordinary pieces of iron, it was worth ten times more than its weight in gold or silver. What more admirable object could a Prince and great monarch have than the goods and wealth that the good Lord has provided for his ease and comfort, principally during those times in his old age when he is burdened with major illnesses like those that afflicted this good king? He used this chair, then, to rest and relax all the limbs of his body when he left his sick bed, since he could remain seated in it from the morning, when he got up, till night when he lay down to sleep, when the king dressed in the most lightweight clothes, ..., he lay there as if he was in his own bed, since the seat was roomy and wide, measuring more than two and a half feet across, and its back could recline or fold forward by pulling the small handles which are marked HHHH in the figure. It was more than seven feet long and a small mattress made of crimson taffeta and stuffed with horsehair, which was certainly soft and cool, was placed behind his back, and brought the king great comfort," *Pasatiempos de Jehan Lhermite*, 251–252. This piece of furniture already existed in 1595, since we know that the king received the prince of Orange while reclining on it, *ibidem*, 258.

[134] He was transported in it by two men chosen from among his footmen who carried him, not without considerable effort. In his chair, he visited San Lorenzo, both inside and out, Lhermite, *Pasatiempos de Jehan Lhermite*, 398, 399–400.

[135] He related how, shortly before he died, the king had ordered "a kind of stretcher to go about in" to be made "with docile horses to pull it along." He also related how he went out in a sort of chair used to carry him round the palace, "carried by four footmen, one at each corner, and he didn't seem to use the small litter he had had made; and because he came out of the inns at four or five in the afternoon, one went at the front with an awning or large parasol to shade him and cover the chair to protect him from the sun; and eighteen or twenty people accompanied him on foot," Tellechea, *El ocaso de un rey*, 177, 253 and 255.

is worth remarking that the gout chair was not only of practical use but was used on state occasions, as can be deduced from some of the comments made about the preparations for the wedding of Philip and Margaret:

> When this is finished, His Majesty will be able to go and dine making his way through the festivities in the very same gout chair until he reaches the top of the stairs, where he will be able to change chair with the passageway covered by drapes, and if he no longer feels like attending part of the evening, he can then leave at any time by the same exit.[136]

In this context, briefly outlined here, the use of sedan chairs by Margaret of Austria seems to take on a deeper significance than is apparent at first glance. Apart from using them on her journey to Spain,[137] once she was in Madrid, she began to travel about in a sedan chair in 1601, when she was six months pregnant, using them "for pleasure" and "for greater safety" to visit monasteries or make other visits. However, the remote and sacred character of the queen's image being promoted also led to this vehicle being used for entries, as was the case in January 1602, when the queen went to the reception in Leon in a chair, with the king beside her on a horse, both under a canopy, perhaps due once more to a possible pregnancy. The same thing happened in Zamora and Toro, and the following year in the entry into Burgos.[138] This new practice brought with it a sharp rise in the number of sedan chair porters to carry the sovereign about. They were attached to the Stable and it is precisely in 1602 when their entry into service is first detected.[139]

In the complex political situation of those years, due in large measure to the negotiations over the *millones*,[140] the urban entries of the queen

[136] AGS, E. leg. 182 (no pagination).

[137] Ambassador San Clemente was sent some sedan chairs from Florence, see the exhibition catalogue, *Glorias efímeras*, 74.

[138] Cabrera de Córdoba, *Relaciones*, 74–75, 102, 107, 129–130, 134–135 and 182.

[139] Those responsible for carrying the queen's chair were the porters. In Margaret's household they began to serve in 1602 with the entry of two servants, increasing in 1603 to ten, then twelve, and remaining Stable at this number throughout the queen's lifetime. We do not know who carried out this function before that date. We have a report that, on some special occasions like the baptism of prince Philip, other servants, such as bedmakers also served, Cabrera de Córdoba, *Relaciones*, 246.

[140] Cabrera de Córdoba, *Relaciones*, 332, 341–342 and 374; María José del Río Barredo, *Madrid, Urbs Regia: La capital ceremonial de la Monarquía Católica* (Madrid, 2000), 88–92.

in a chair under a canopy and with the monarch riding beside her seem to us to suggest a subtler argument, of greater importance than mere precaution concerning her pregnancies. As with the coach, the queen's entries in a chair set her at some distance from the onlookers, enhancing her sacred character; however, at the same time, and unlike the coach, the chair gave easier access to her for those members of the urban elite who had to escort the queen at close quarters in the entry procession.[141] Furthermore, contemplating the queen in a kind of monstrance or tabernacle, or on a throne, an appropriate place from which she could be revered, drew a parallel with the same behaviour of the monarchs when they travelled, which Diego de Guzmán described some time later:

> Then their Majesties left for the city of Leon and Zamora, where they were welcomed under a canopy, since it was the first time.... Their Majesties gave many demonstrations of their piety and religion in these places, viewing, worshipping, and very gently and devoutly kissing the many beautiful relics there are in these cities in rich gold and silver chests, putting their Royal heads inside them.[142]

The image of the queen in a sedan chair recalled a series of sacred images of the monstrance and the throne.[143] Indeed, the funeral rites

[141] For outstanding figures to accompany the queen on foot was a sophisticated way of showing authority. M. Lisón y Biedma recalled some time later "that it is not such a remote memory, when it was a sign of increased importance to have ten or twelve old men in front of the chair and the most senior of them to offer his arm to the queen," *El Tapaboca que azotan. Respuesta del bachiller ignorante, al Chiton de las taravillas, que hizieron los Licenciados Todo se sabe, y Todo lo sabe*, 1630, in *La vida turbulenta de Quevedo*, Luis Astrana Marín (Madrid, 1945), 603–604. For the accompaniment of queen Margaret in her entries into Venice, Mantua and Lodi in a litter, see Giovanni Battista Grillo, *Breve tratatto di quanto sucesse alla maestà della regina d. Margherita d'Austria ... fino alla cittè di Genova*, 1604, BNE, 2/12869, pp. 8, 33 and 60.

[142] Diego de Guzmán, *Reyna catolica: Vida y muerte de D. Margarita de Austria Reyna de Espanna*, 1617, BNE, R 25370ff. 131r–132r.

[143] Father Flórez told how, on the day of his baptism in 1629, prince Balthasar Charles had been transported in a chair made of quartz which aroused the admiration of those attending, as it was an "anticipation of the diaphanous eternal throne which that baptismal ceremony began to make him worthy of," cf. Ana Martínez Arancón, *Geografía de la eternidad* (Madrid, 1987), 217. One account of the baptism described the chair used: "from the seat upwards, everything was made of quartz crystal so fine that hardly any flaws could be spotted, and adorned in silver, with four crows of the same metal, and on top of the aforementioned chair, there was a *cimborrio*, or tower-like dome, a span high, made of solid silver and covered in gold. The Lady Countess of Olivares was in the chair holding a fan, and ... the new-born prince was in her arms ...

Fig. 11 – Queen Margaret of Austria is transported in a sedan chair. Engraving by R. Schaminossi, in Giovanni Altoviti, *Essequie della Sacra Cattolica e Real Maestà di Margherita d'Austria* (Biblioteca Nacional de España, Madrid).

on her death in Florence in 1612, where the leitmotif of the funeral decoration represented the spiritual virtues over Death, and the practice of them as the only means of attaining Christian bliss and eternal fame,[144] significantly showed the queen being carried in a sedan chair (fig. 11).[145] Along with this, various factors affected the importance granted to the sedan chair as a means of representing the queen. One

She went by showing him off on all sides, because she was being carried slowly, as four valets and four grooms of the closet were carrying her along at the side wearing bright red sashes and golden lace trimming," Anonymous, *Segunda y mas verdadera relacion del Bautismo del Príncipe de España nuestro Señor, Baltasar Carlos Domingo, con todos los nombres de los Caballeros, y titulos que yvan en el acompañamiento*, in Simón Díaz, *Relaciones*, 382.

[144] Exhibition catalogue, *Glorias efímeras*, 219.

[145] Engraving by R. Schaminossi, in Giovanni Altoviti, *Essequie della Sacra Cattolica e Real Maestà di Margherita d'Austria* (Florence 1612), fig. 4. See also Benedetto Veli's painting of the funeral on which the engraving is based, *Margarita de Austria, reina de España, es recibida en Bussolengo por los embajadores de la República de Venecia*, reproduced in Glorias efímeras, 238–239.

of these, characterizing it as the proper vehicle for women, began precisely in Margaret's time. By then, sedan chairs had been common for some time in a number of European courts, and indeed were in quite general use, as for example in Castile[146] and some places in Italy, such as Genoa and Naples.[147] In Castile the use of sedan chairs was considered inappropriate for men, except for the old and infirm,[148] so an attempt was made to consolidate the restriction of their use to women by institutionalizing them; this was effected by a process that banned men from riding in them unless they had a licence from the Council of Castile.[149] In addition, the use of the sedan chair was controlled so

[146] Although there are earlier testimonies to its use, the first complaints about the proliferation of sedan chairs came from the Madrid *Cortes* of 1583–1585, where they were criticised because of the multiplication of their numbers after the obligatory increase in horses per coach due to the pragmatic sanction of 1578, as well as being considered an excessive expense and unnecessary novelty: "Removing coaches if they do not have four horses has provided a reason for women to go about in sedan chairs with curtains, and apart from it being a breach of authority, even if some (women) can afford to do so, they provide an excuse for those who cannot so readily, they do it, all the more so since the point about curtains in the streets is that they are reserved for images. We beseech His Majesty to prohibit and ban them," *Actas de las Cortes de Castilla* (Madrid, 1861–2006), 7: 834. §LXV. The monarch responded that "we shall look into it and make provision for what is best."

[147] See the comments made in 1593 by the nuncio Camilo Borguese about the use made in Madrid of objects similar to the "covered chair in the Genoese style," Mercadal, *Viajes*, 2: 625.

[148] It was the general opinion that the chair ought to be for women and only those men who were old and sick should use it. Thus it was said of the bishop of Barbastro that he visited his diocese, "his virtue and zeal overcoming as many difficulties as the extreme ruggedness of the terrain in some areas could offer him, to the point where he even had to be carried in a chair over the places which were impassable or unsuitable for travelling on horseback," Saturninno López Novoa, *Historia de la muy Noble y muy Leal ciudad de Barbastro y descripción geográfico-histórica de su diócesis*, Barcelona, 1861 (facsimile edition, Zaragoza, 1981), 1: 181. In Februrary 1599, Cabrera de Córdoba told how the duke of Terranova, "prevented by his gout," approached to kiss the hands of the monarch "in the chair in which he had been carried." In 1601, when peace was sworn with France, he mentions repeatedly that the Constable went to church in a chair because he did not feel well. Similarly, when in January 1606 the position of lord steward to the queen was given to don Juan de Borja, uncle of the duke of Lerma, he indicated that although suffering with his feet through extreme gout, he went to church in a chair, without missing the councils of State and Portugal. Finally, in 1608, the count of Miranda went "discreetly" to Alcalá in a sedan chair because he was ailing, Cabrera de Córdoba, *Relaciones*, 6, 102, 269 and 332.

[149] Pragmatic sanction in *Nueva Recopilación, Libro VII, Titulo XII, ley VIII*. The reasoning put forward by the councillors, which does not appear in the *Recopilación,* was to justify the ban on the grounds that, apart from "other drawbacks" which might

that, in certain places, those without the requisite social status should not have access to them. Thus, on June 23, 1609, the municipal leaders ordered that all sedan chair porters should only be present in the Plazuela de Herradores, not in the Plaza de Santa Cruz, or other areas. The elimination of the Plaza de Santa Cruz must have created problems of access for those who lived in the San Jerónimo, San Sebastián and Lavapiés neighbourhoods. These areas, particularly the latter, were full of actors and prostitutes.[150]

The power of these objects in the ritual glorification of the queen led to the creation of a new ceremonial which we think must have been drawn up in 1623.[151] In that year, some festivities were organized for the reception of the Prince of Wales in which, as Enríque Flórez said: "the attention devoted to lavishing magnificence and majesty was recognized." So it was that, at the first bullfight spectacle, queen Elisabeth of Bourbon arrived in a coach with the infanta, but:

> later discovering herself to be pregnant again, she went in a chair, accompanied on foot by the Gentlemen, Equerries and Stewards from the King's Household as well as from the Queen's, and that of the Cardinal-Infante Don Ferdinand. To the right went the Count of Benavente, her Lord Steward; to the left, the Marquis of Almazán, Master of the Horse. The Infanta Doña Maria went in the coach near to the Chair of the Queen with her brothers and sisters.[152]

follow, they had seen "the excess and disorder of men of all ages using the sedan chair needlessly and without any justification whatsoever except that of comfort and pleasure, that it had been introduced only a few years before this report and, being such an indecent thing, the praiseworthy and necessary exercise of horses is being forgotten," BNE, VE 40-75.

[150] San Sebastián was one of the neighbourhoods where people went in search of pleasure and actors and ladies of the court lived nearby. Lavapiés was not a neighbourhood where the wealthy lived; it was partly an area of houses of ill-repute. It should not be forgotten that prohibitions concerning prostitutes using coaches and chairs were issued a little later, in 1611, López Álvarez, *Poder, lujo y conflicto*, 568–573.

[151] In 1622, the queen suspecting that "she was pregnant when she had to move to Aranjuez, made the journey in a sedan chair, taking five days to cover the seven leagues. But the precaution only served to ease her concern since the desired effect that her suspicions had promised did not come to fruition," Enrique Flórez, *Memorias de las reinas Católicas*, 1761 (facsimile edition, Valladolid, 2002), 2: 925.

[152] Flórez, *Memorias de las reinas católicas*, 2: 926.

This order, which must have extended to other moments of the queen's life and which forced the horsemen to go on foot, caused a few complaints, such as this rather indignant assertion, made some time during the 1620s by Francisco of Portugal about gallants accompanying the ladies beside the coach step:

> Escorting the Queen's chair brought the degradation of their privileges in its wake, for the respect of the favourites broke this jurisdiction quite unnecessarily, for only courtesy dismounts the gallants, as that region is beyond the reach of power.[153]

Certain orders issued in 1638, regarding the placing of the equerry in charge of the hacks in the procession, show that accompanying the chair was consolidated into the ceremony in later years.[154] Alonso Carrillo also reported this ceremonial, asserting that the grandees normally accompanied the king and queen on foot and on horseback: "but paying more specific and due obligation to the queens, walking in front of their Majesties whenever they are pregnant and carrying them in a chair for greater safety in childbirth and the comfort of their health." He glossed this statement as follows:

> I should not omit to say that if the King and Queen are in the Buen Retiro and the Queen is pregnant, when Her Majesty enters Madrid (since that palace is at some distance, though not a great one from the town), the Grandees accompany Her Majesty on horseback, riding behind the sedan chair, with no change in the foot escort with respect to other Nobles and Officers of the Royal Household, but when they reach the inhabited part of the City (which is in the part of Madrid facing the Retiro near the well-known Capuchin Convent) the Grandees dismount from their horses and join the escort, taking up their position immediately in front of the chair.[155]

[153] Francisco de Portugal, *Arte de galantería*, 1670, BNE, R 4593, pp. 51–52. The work was written some time before since the author frequented the court of Philip IV and died in 1632.

[154] *Sobre el lugar que devia ocupar el Cavallerizo de los Quartagos en el acompañamiento de la Reina qdº. S. M. fuese sola*, AGP, Sección Histórica, Caja 49, exp. 13.

[155] Alonso Carrillo, *Origen y dignidad de Grande de Castilla*, 1657, BNE, R 313152/2, fol. 32r.

With the passage of time, flirting in the chair[156] and escorting those of high rank gradually spread throughout the court.[157] Finally, all that remains to be said is that the importance of the ceremonial of the chair can be seen in the fact that it was actually renewed at the beginning of the eighteenth century, a time when, thanks to certain technical improvements – basically the construction of sturdier and more compact wooden boxes – the sedan chair enjoyed an extraordinary resurgence.[158]

[156] In 1658, Barrionuevo related that almost every day that the countess of Niebla spent at the house of her father, the court favourite, her husband, the count, "walks beside the chair throwing out compliments; so that she drives him wild just with this refinement, and great things and courtesies are expected of him," *Avisos*, BAE, 222, p. 153.

[157] When the countess of Salvatierra, wife of the former viceroy of Peru, left for Spain following the death of her husband "she left in a sedan chair, carried by two Spanish footmen; and one of the sides of the chair was held by the lord viceroy Count of Alba de Aliste, and the other by Don Juan Enrique, her son. And accompanying them to the landing stage were the lord Archbishop, Don Pedro de Villagómez, all the judges of the Royal Assizes and all the noble gentlemen of this city," in Josephe de Mugaburu, *Diario de Lima: 1640–1694* (Lima, 1935), 35.

[158] In 1707, an ordinance was issued concerning the way the queen should go about Madrid in a chair, *Reglamento que dio el Sr. Rey Don Felipe Quinto para la salida de la Reyna en silla desde Palacio a visitar a Nra Señora de Atocha convocando a todos los Caballerizos, oficiales maiores y menores de la Cavalleriza de la Reyna: Orden que deven guardar en el acompañamiento los Gefes, coches de la Persona y uso de silla, solo para la camarera Maior*, BPR, II/2893, fols. 271r–275v. For some changes in the court at that time, see Carlos Gómez-Centurión Jiménez, "Etiqueta y ceremonial palatino durante el reinado de Felipe V: el reglamento de entradas de 1709 y el acceso a la persona del rey," *Hispania* 56/3, no. 194 (1996): 965–1005.

From Graz to Vienna: structures and careers in the *Frauenzimmer* between 1570 and 1657

Katrin Keller
University of Vienna

In August 1571, the wedding of archduke Charles, the youngest brother of emperor Maximilian II, and princess Maria Anna of Bavaria was celebrated in Vienna. The festivities lasted several weeks and were among the most magnificent of the second half of the sixteenth century.[1] The reputation of their splendour was such that features of the celebrations were replicated for the wedding of emperor Franz Joseph I and princess Elisabeth of Bavaria. The marriage of the archduke to his cousin stood at the end of a whole series of failed marital plans that had been hatched for Charles.[2] The union demonstrated and renewed the political and religious alliance between the two remaining great catholic dynasties of the Holy Roman Empire, the Habsburgs and the Bavarian Wittelsbach.

At the same time the marriage was an important step in the development of the town of Graz into an archducal residence. The estates of Styria, Carinthia and Carniola had already recognized archduke Charles as their future ruler during the lifetime of his father, emperor Ferdinand I. In accordance with the emperor's will, these three territories and some minor possessions on the coasts of the Adriatic became the archduchy of Inner Austria in 1564. The young archduke established his residence in Graz, where he immediately began creating the necessary governmental institutions and a representative court. His two foremost political goals were to organize on effective defence against the Turks and to stem the rise of protestantism among the members

[1] Karl Vocelka, *Habsburgische Hochzeiten 1550-1600. Kulturgeschichtliche Studien zum manieristischen Repräsentationsfest* (Vienna, Cologne and Graz, 1976); Katrin Keller, *Erzherzogin Maria von Innerösterreich (1551-1608). Zwischen Habsburg und Wittelsbach* (Vienna, Cologne and Weimar, 2012), 24-36.

[2] Peter Wiesflecker, "Adel und Residenz," in Walter Brunner (ed.), *Geschichte der Stadt Graz, Bd. 2: Wirtschaft – Gesellschaft – Alltag* (Graz, 2003), 599; about Charles: Georg Heilingsetzer, "Karl II.," in Brigitte Hamann (ed.), *Die Habsburger. Ein biographisches Lexikon* (Vienna-Munich, 1988), 203-206.

of the estates of Inner Austria.[3] The wedding of 1571 offered the opportunity to expand and complete the existing structures of the court of Inner Austria with a *Frauenzimmer*, or household for the archduchess. The creation of households for the couple's children followed soon thereafter. The marriage proved harmonious and produced 15 children, 12 of which survived their father. First as a spouse and subsequently as a regent during the minority of her eldest son Ferdinand, archduchess Maria Anna wielded considerable influence in political matters and played a determining role in the matrimonial alliances of her children.[4]

So far little is known about the life at court in the residence of Graz. The questions concerning the defence against the Turks and the beginnings of the Counter Reformation in Styria have until now dominated historical research.[5] Older studies nevertheless suggest three principal characteristics determining the format of courtly culture in Graz. First of all, there was the continuation of the archducal collections, for which the emperors Frederick III and Maximilian I had laid the foundations in the fifteenth century. In frequent exchanges with Munich, but also in contact with Rudolf II's court of the muses in Prague, the archducal couple acquired mainly precious arms and paintings, thereby gathering an extensive *Kunstkammer*.[6] Secondly, between 1564 and 1619 the court could boast a court chapel that was

[3] Alexander Novotny and Berthold Sutter (eds.), *Innerösterreich 1564-1619* (Graz, 1967); Helmut J. Mezler-Andelberg, "Die Steiermark als Zentralland des habsburgischen Teilstaates Innerösterreich 1564-1619," in Othmar Pickl (ed.), *800 Jahre Steiermark und Österreich 1192-1992. Der Beitrag der Steiermark zu Österreichs Größe* (Graz, 1992), 223-242.

[4] Wiesflecker, "Adel und Residenz," 598-601; about archduchess Maria: Keller, *Maria von Innerösterreich*, 95-150, 171-196; Magdalena S. Sánchez, "A woman's influence. Archduchess Maria of Bavaria and the Spanish Habsburgs", in Conrad Kent (ed.), *The lion and the eagle. Interdisciplinary essays on German-Spanish relations over the centuries* (New York and Oxford, 2000), 91–107.

[5] Novotny and Sutter, *Innerösterreich*; Gerhard Pferschy (ed.), *Die Steiermark, Brücke und Bollwerk* (Graz, 1986); France M. Dolinar e. a. (eds.), *Katholische Reform und Gegenreformation in Innerösterreich, 1564–1628 [Katoliška prenova in protireformacija v notranjeavstrijskihj deželah 1564–1628, Riforme cattolica e controriforma nell'Austria Interna 1564–1628]* (Klagenfurt, Hermagoras and Graz, 1994); Regina Pörtner, *The Counter-Reformation in Central Europe. Styria 1580-1630* (Oxford, 2001).

[6] Josef Wastler, *Das Kunstleben am Hofe zu Graz unter den Herzogen von Steiermark, den Erzherzogen Karl und Ferdinand* (Graz, 1897), 34f., 38f., 107f., 164; Johann Stefan Stolzer, *Die Grazer Schatz-, Kunst- und Rüstkammer unter Kaiser Ferdinand III. und den Erzherzögen Karl II. und Ferdinand II.* Diss. masch. (Graz, 2002); Keller, *Maria von Innerösterreich*, 70-77.

strongly influenced by Venetian musical styles and counted Orlandus Lassus among its composers. As such, the court chapel played an important role in spreading Italian musical forms north of the Alps.[7] Italian influences and the activities of the Jesuits moreover helped to foster a lively theatrical culture at court.[8] Thirdly and finally, archduke Charles and his son Ferdinand engaged themselves in numerous building projects and showed a clear predilection for Italian architects and artists. The transformation of the castle of Graz to a worthy residence, the implementation of the programme of the Counter Reformation into the interiors of the churches of the capital and the elaboration of dynastic monuments were at the core of these activities. The last two aspects determined the construction of the archducal mausoleum in Seckau from 1587 onwards as well as Ferdinand's tomb in the cathedral of Graz from 1614.[9]

Even less research has up to now been completed on the court of Graz as the centre of politics and administration of the newly constituted archduchy. Some older studies elucidate the structures of government.[10] None of the questions of modern court studies, however, have been researched for the court of Graz. There are no systematic studies of the way in which the court integrated the nobilities of the different regions of Inner Austria, of the problems of patronage and client networks as elements of courtly politics, nor of the careers of dignitaries of the

[7] Hellmut Federhofer, *Musikpflege und Musiker am Grazer Habsburgerhof der Erzherzöge Karl und Ferdinand von Innerösterreich (1564-1619)* (Mainz, 1967); Rudolf Flotzinger, "Der Grazer Hof – Umschlagplatz europäischer Musik," in Gerhard Pferschy (ed.), *Die Steiermark, Brücke und Bollwerk* (Graz, 1986), 273-276; Barbara Marx, "Italianità und frühneuzeitliche Hofkultur: Dresden im Kontext," in Barbara Marx (ed.), Elbflorenz. Italienische Präsenz in Dresden 16.-19. Jahrhundert (Amsterdam-Dresden, 2000), 26f.; Elisabeth Hilscher, *Mit Leier und Schwert. Die Habsburger und die Musik* (Graz, Vienna and Cologne, 2000), 97-102; Hanna Schäffer, "Maria von Bayern und die Musik. Musikmäzenatentum am bayrischen und am innerösterreichischen Hof," in *Zeitschrift des Historischen Vereins für Steiermark* 83 (1992), 205-272.

[8] Wastler, *Das Kunstleben*, 136-139; Reiner Puschnig, "Theaterleben in Graz, europäisches Theater am Hof," in Pferschy (ed.), *Die Steiermark*, 271f.

[9] Wastler, *Das Kunstleben*, 53-61, 157-162; Reiner Puschnig, *Die Grazer Burg* (Graz, 1985); Reiner Puschnig, Bildende Kunst am Grazer Hof, in Pferschy (ed.), *Die Steiermark*, 269f.

[10] Viktor Thiel, *Die innerösterreichische Zentralverwaltung 1564-1749, Teil 1: Die Hof- und Zentralbehörden Innerösterreichs 1564-1625, Teil 2: Die Zentralbehörden Innerösterreichs 1625-1749* (Vienna, 1916, 1930).

court.[11] This lack is not only to be regretted from the point of view of the court in Graz. The eldest son of the archducal couple would eventually succeed his cousins Rudolf II and Matthias as head of the House of Habsburg and as emperor Ferdinand II. In the wake of the transfer of the court of Graz to Vienna, followed the transfer of many structures and institutions that had progressed through their proper evolution between 1565 and 1619.

In 1991 Volker Press already argued that many of the roots of the seventeenth-century Imperial court were to be located in Graz.[12] This argument is for instance clear in bureaucratic structures and in the influence that the Jesuits – who were invited to Graz and supported by archduke Charles, his wife and his son Ferdinand – had on the religious and political life of the residence.[13] This has lately also been demonstrated for other elements of courtly life, not least of all for large sections of the written regulations of the Imperial court after 1619. Another such instance was the demise of the so called *Diener von Adel*, noble lords who did not hold a specific office and were a common feature in the households of the court of Vienna in the sixteenth century, but disappeared after the accession of the line of Inner Austria.[14] Further research into the influence of the household of Graz on the court of Vienna is certainly needed.[15]

We cannot fully address this question here, but wish to concentrate on two aspects that have a bearing on the relationship between the courts of Graz and Vienna and at the same time shed light on a part of the courtly structures that has until now received little attention,

[11] A few exceptions are: Hans Sturmberger, *Adam Graf Herberstorff. Herrschaft und Freiheit im konfessionellen Zeitalter* (Vienna, 1976); Walther Ernst Heydendorff, *Die Fürsten und Freiherren zu Eggenberg und ihre Vorfahren* (Graz, Vienna, Cologne, 1965).

[12] Volker Press, "The Imperial Court of the Habsburgs: from Maximilian I. to Ferdinand III. (1493-1657)," in Ronald G. Asch and Adolf M. Birke (eds.), *Princes, Patronage and the Nobility: The Court at the Beginning of the Modern Age 1450-1650* (London-New York, 1991), 307f.

[13] Theodor Graff, "Grazer Jesuitenuniversität und landesfürstliche Dynastie," in *Jahrbuch der Stadt Graz* 11/12 (1979/80), 37-65; Keller, *Erzherzogin Maria*, 136-138; Katrin Keller, "Habsburgerinnen in Graz, Krakau und Madrid und ihre Beichtväter," will be published in: Ulrike Gleixner, Martin H. Jung and Matthias Meinhardt (eds.), *Religion Macht Politik. Hofgeistlichkeit im Europa der Frühen Neuzeit 1500 – 1800* (Wolfenbütteler Forschungen) (Wiesbaden, 2014).

[14] Thiel, *Die innerösterreichische Zentralverwaltung*, 22; Mark Hengerer, *Kaiserhof und Adel in der Mitte des 17. Jahrhunderts. Eine Kommunikationsgeschichte der Macht in der Vormoderne* (Konstanz, 2004), 42, 280.

[15] An exception is: Hilscher, *Mit Leier und Schwert*, 101f.

namely the female household. A first part will analyse the structures of the *Frauenzimmer*, in other words the composition of the entourage of the archduchess or empress. Thereafter the continuity between Graz and Vienna in terms of female office holders will be addressed.

Studying the archduchess' or empress' household proves an appropriate instrument for gauging the relevance of the court of Graz for the Imperial court in the seventeenth century: since emperor Rudolf II never married, there was no *Frauenzimmer* in either Vienna or Prague between 1576 and 1611. Furthermore, there was no immediate continuity between the household of empress Anna, the wife of emperor Matthias between 1611 and 1618, and that of empress Eleonora Gonzaga (the Elder), who was the second wife of emperor Ferdinand II and as such resided in Vienna between 1622 and 1655. The influence of the traditions of the court of Graz on the organization of the female household of the young empress in 1622 can be detected in three aspects: the structure of offices for noblemen and –women, the fact that appointments to these offices were reserved for either spinsters or widows and lastly and most convincingly in the reuse and further elaboration of instructions for female members of the household.

The structure of offices and the size of the female household in Graz were for the first time codified in 1573 by an ordinance of the archduke for his spouse.[16] It listed the *Obersthofmeister*, the only male noble officer of the archduchess' household, the *Obersthofmeisterin*, the head of the female entourage, the *Unterhofmeisterin*, who was in charge of the noble *Hoffräulein* or ladies-in-waiting, and the six ladies-in-waiting themselves. All of these noble office holders received a salary. With the exception of the *Obersthofmeister* and the *Obersthofmeisterin*, they were also entitled to one ceremonial dress every year. The ordinance furthermore enumerates a *Kammerfrau* or lady of the bedchamber, three chambermaids, three servants for the *Kammerfrau*, the *Unterhofmeisterin* and the ladies-in-waiting, a washerwoman for the archduchess and one for the noble ladies, a nurse for the children, a washerwoman for the children and a female cook. The lower male staff consisted of two chamber servants, a doorkeeper, an apothecary, a surgeon and his servant, a doorkeeper for the *Frauenzimmer*, a table servant, a servant in charge of the fires and two boys. All told the household of the archduchess consisted of 20 women and 11 men.

[16] Thiel, *Die innerösterreichische Zentralverwaltung*, 187-190.

A comparison can be made on the basis of a list of the household of empress Eleonora that is dated 1629.[17] It names the following staff: *Obersthofmeister*, *Obersthofmeisterin*, *Frauenzimmerhofmeisterin* and 13 ladies-in-waiting, together with three ladies of the bedchamber and seven servants, a *Kreserin* (a woman who deals with the collars and the laces of women's wear) a female cook and two helpers, two fools of the bedchamber, two maids and seven servants for the ladies-in-waiting, a nurse for the children, a nurse for the sick with her helper, three female dwarfs, eight servants for certain women of the household and a dishwasher. On the male side, there were three chaplains, a secretary, a guardian of the wardrobe, a dancing master, a servant in charge of the fires and his boy, a doorkeeper and his boy, a servant of the table, together with two assistants and a boy, a doorkeeper of the hall, a doorkeeper of the *Frauenzimmer* and his boy, two *Kammertrabanten*, a gold embroiderer with his boy, as well as five servants, another servant of the table with his assistants and boy, two tailors for the ladies-in-waiting, a boy to care for the dogs and six additional valets. As such the household of the empress counted 55 women and 39 men, which made it considerably larger than that of the archduchess. The determining point, however, is the distribution of offices between noblemen and –women. In both cases there was only one male officeholder, namely the *Obersthofmeister*, while there were two positions of *Hofmeisterin* for noble widows and a greater or smaller number of ladies-in-waiting, who were by definition unmarried noblewomen.

Two examples will illustrate the difference of this court to the Imperial court of the sixteenth century. The only known list of the household of empress Maria of Austria dates from 1560.[18] It limits itself to the offices reserved for the nobility, which in itself marks a certain difference. There were no less than four positions for noblemen: the *Obersthofmeister*, the *Oberststallmeister*, and two *mayordomos*, alongside the *Oberstkämmerin*, two *Ehrenjungfrauen* and 11 ladies-in-waiting and a further three ladies of the bedchamber. An overview of the members of the household of queen Anna, the wife of emperor Ferdinand I, gives a similar picture.[19] Next to the *Obersthofmeister*, there were the *Oberststallmeister*, a *Fürschneider* and a secretary, whereby the latter office was at least for some time held by a royal counselor. Noble

[17] Österreichische Nationalbibliothek, *Handschriftensammlung* MS 10.100, f. 61r-73v.
[18] Österreichisches Staatsarchiv (ÖStA), *Abt. Haus-, Hof- und Staatsarchiv, OMeA/SR 182*, Nr. 40.
[19] ÖStA, *Abt. Allgemeines Verwaltungsarchiv, Familienarchiv Harrach* HS 115.

ladies held the offices of *Obersthofmeisterin* and *Unterhofmeisterin* or served as one of the ten noble ladies. At the time of the queen's death in 1547, two unmarried noble ladies moreover served as *Leibwärterin* for the archduchesses Eleonora and Magdalena, while four married noblewomen were reckoned to belong to the *Frauenzimmer*.

The two sets of lists demonstrate that the decrease of male officeholders in the household of the ruler's consort – that also manifested itself in other courts in the Holy Roman Empire[20] – was in the case of the courts of the Austrian Habsburgs linked to the accession of the line of Graz. The court of Graz led the way in reducing the number of male officers to one as well as in the exclusion of married noblewomen, two important characteristics of the *Frauenzimmer* in Vienna in the seventeenth and eighteenth centuries.

It is interesting to note that Graz not only served as an example for the court of Vienna, but also for the court of Munich. Thus duchess Anna of Bavaria, who was an archduchess of Austria by birth and became the mother of the future archduchess Maria Anna, introduced the office of *Unterhofmeisterin* when she joined the court of Munich.[21] Her son, duke William of Bavaria, entertained a lively correspondence with his sister Maria Anna, asking her to send him orders of precedence and instructions pertaining to the court of Graz. A list of the household of the archduchess was preserved in the archives of Munich.[22] It is therefore hardly surprising that the household of the duchess of Bavaria bears the same characteristics in terms of structure and nominations as that of the archduchess or empress. Apart from the *Hofmeister* and *Hofmeisterin*, the latter a widowed noblewoman, it consisted of a (likewise widowed) *Jungfrauenhofmeisterin*, five to seven ladies-in-waiting and an additional 19 female and five male servants.[23]

Whereas the evidence regarding the influence of Graz on the female household in Vienna was only indirect as far as structures and office holding were concerned, Graz's impact on the instructions for female

[20] Katrin Keller, *Hofdamen. Amtsträgerinnen im Wiener Hofstaat des 17. Jahrhunderts* (Vienna, Cologne and Weimar, 2005), 26f.; Britta Kägler, *Frauen am Münchener Hof (1651-1756)* (Münchener Historische Studien 18) (Kallmünz, 2011), 71-75.

[21] Bayrisches Hauptstaatsarchiv, *Abt. Geheimes Hausarchiv, Hofhaushaltsakten* Nr. 227, unpag., c. 1595.

[22] Bayrisches Hauptstaatsarchiv, *Abt. Geheimes Hausarchiv, Hofhaushaltsakten* Nr. 45, 181, 195, 197, 452.

[23] Bayrisches Hauptstaatsarchiv, *Abt. Geheimes Hausarchiv, Hofhaushaltsakten* Nr. 232, unpag., 1586; Nr. 276, unpag., 1580.

officers of the court of Vienna was straightforward and significant.[24] From the reign of archduke Charles and archduchess Maria Anna instructions have been preserved for the archduchess's *Obersthofmeister* and the *Obersthofmeisterin* dating from 1571 and for the *Unter-* or *Fräuleinmeisterin* from 1589.[25] No comparable instruction for the *Oberstmeisterin* is known for the court of Vienna, but there are instructions for the empress's *Obersthofmeister* from the years 1616, 1631, 1652 and 1655.[26] An even greater number of instructions survived for the *Frauleinhofmeisterin*, namely for the years 1627, 1648 and 1651, 1670, 1671, 1675 and 1740.[27]

A formal comparison between the instructions that have been preserved makes clear how important the instructions from Graz were for the *Fräuleinhofmeisterin*. In content as well as in form the instructions of 1589 set a pattern for those made for the successive empresses, even up to the point that the instructions of 1627, 1648 and 1651, 1670, 1671, 1675 and 1740 repeat almost verbatim passages from those of 1589. Some of the points remain unaltered up until the very last instructions. This consistency concerned above all the first items regarding the relationship with the *Obersthofmeister* (and after 1648 also the *Obersthofmeisterin*), confessional conformity and the attendance at mass:

1589/2 "Secondly, as we want to be cautious that in the *Frauenzimmer* of our dearest only Catholic persons will be accepted, so will the *Unterhofmeisterin* give particular attention und orders that neither the ladies-in-waiting nor others that belong in whatever way to the *Frauenzimmer* will be allowed to bring new sectarian tracts und writings, whether printed or otherwise, to the *Frauenzimmer* or engage in some oral disputation in matters of faith or religion, but that such things shall at all times be prevented and forbidden".[28]

[24] See the general remark by Hengerer, *Kaiserhof*, 280.

[25] ÖStA, *Abt. Haus-, Hof- und Staatsarchiv, Hofverwaltungen* Bd. 1, 166-170v, 1571; ibidem, *Familienakten* Karton 99, 1589.

[26] ÖStA, *Abt. Allgemeines Verwaltungsarchiv, Familienarchiv Trauttmansdorff* Karton 118, [1616]; *Abt. Haus-, Hof- und Staatsarchiv*, OMeA SR 76, 3 a), 11.04.1631; ibidem, OMeA SR 72, Teil 4, 9.09.1652 esp. 24.09.1655.

[27] ÖStA, *Abt. Haus-, Hof- und Staatsarchiv, Ältere Zeremonialakten* Karton 2/11, 7.10.1627; ibidem, OMeA SR 73, 4 da), [1648] and 8.05.1651; *ibidem, Ältere Zeremonialakten* Karton 8, 24.09.1670; *ibidem, Familienakten* 101, 1.01.1671 and 3.01.1675; *ibidem*, OMeA SR 73, Nr. 4h, 1740.

[28] "Zum anndern, wie wir darauf bedacht sein wellen, das in irer Lieb frawenzimer, lauther catholische personnen angenomen, also solle auch die underhofmaisterin ir

1740/2 "Secondly, as we ourselves want to be cautious that in our *Frauenzimmer* only catholic persons will be accepted, so will the *Hofmeisterin* give particular attention und orders that the ladies, spinsters and others belonging to the *Frauenzimmer*, whoever they might be, will not be allowed to bring sectarian tracts und writings, whether in German or otherwise, to the *Frauenzimmer* nor to engage in some oral disputation in matters of faith or religion, but that such things shall at all times be prevented and forbidden with all severity and diligence and that the honour and fear of God will prevail".[29]

Similar continuities can be observed for the overall supervision by the *Fräuleinhofmeisterin*, when her custody of the keys of the *Frauenzimmer* and her direction of the care for sick ladies-in-waiting and servants are concerned.

1589/12 "Twelfth, the aforementioned *Unterhofmeisterin* will with diligence and in person lock the *Frauenzimmer* every night at the appropriate time, hold the key with her all night and unlock it in the morning at the appropriate time".[30]

1657/7 "Seventh, the aforementioned *Hofmeisterin* will have the *Frauenzimmer* locked every night at the appropriate time, hold the key with her during the night and have it unlocked in the morning at the appropriate time".[31]

vleissigs aufmerkhen haben, vnnd bestellen, das den jungfrawen, noch anndern des frawenzimers verwandten, wer die seyen, nit zuegesehen oder gestattet werde, newe sectische tractätlein und schrifften, so im drukh oder sonsten außgehen, ins frawenzimer zu bringen, noch auch ainicher mündlichen disputation, in glaubens und religions sachen, sich zu gebrauchen, sonnder es solle solches alles yederzeit mit allem ernst und vleiß fürkhommen und verhüetet werden."

[29] "Zum anderten, wie wir selbst darauf bedacht seyn wollen, dass in unseren frauenzimmer allein catholische persohnen angenohmen werden, alß solle auch die hoffmeisterin ihr fleissiges aufmerckhen darauf haben, dass denen freylein, jungfrauen, und anderen des frauenzimmers verwandten, wer sie seynd, nicht zu gesehen, oder gestattet werde sectische tractätlein, und schrifften, so in teütsch- oder sonsten außgehen, ins frauenzimmer zu bringen, noch auch einiger mündlichen disputation in glaubens- und religions-sachen sich zu gebrauchen, sondern solches alles jederzeit mit allen ernst, und fleiß verhütten, und vor allen die ehr, und forcht Gottes einführen."

[30] "Zum zwölfften, soll mergedachte underhofmaisterin alle nacht, das frawenzimer, zu gueter zeit fleissig und selbst spören, den schlüssel über nacht bey ir behalten, und am morgens zu gelegener zeit widerumb aufspören."

[31] "Zum siebenten solle mehrgedachte hofmeisterin alle nacht das frauenzimmer zu rechter zeit fleißig sperren lassen, die schlüssel über nacht bey sich behalten, und morgens zur bestimmten zeit solches wider eröffnen lassen."

Finally, the same held true for the essential rules regarding the ladies-in-waiting such as their fidelity to catholicism, their respect for the empress, fitting behaviour when they attended to her person in church or regarding the discipline at table and the cordial relations between them. The rules for going into the city, for visits by relatives to the *Frauenzimmer* or for contacts with artisans and tradesmen were likewise copied from the instructions of 1589 until the end of the seventeenth century.

1589/9 "Ninth, the *Unterhofmeisterin* will not allow noble ladies, without the gracious permission of our beloved spouse, to go from the court into the city, but will always ask our dearest, as will the ladies-in-waiting, whether they want to go to the garden, to the young princess or to any such place at court, and will always inform the *Unterhofmeisterin* beforehand".[32]

1675/10 "Tenth, the *Hofmeisterin* will not allow ladies, without our gracious permission, to go from the court into the city; and when one or other lady goes, with our gracious consent and permission, in the abovementioned way, to visit a woman in the city and if that woman wants to take her further to churches, gardens or other company, it will not take place without us and the *Hofmeisterin* knowing of it beforehand, but we and our *Hofmeisterin* will always be asked in advance, unless it concerns the mother; so that one can always know where one or the other lady is and that every time she goes from the court to the city or elsewhere, she returns at the appointed time, particularly when there are public services at the court".[33]

[32] "Zum neündten, soll die underhofmaisterin khainer jungfrawen vom adl, ausser unnserer geliebten gmahel gnedigisten bewilligung, von hof in die statt zu gehen, erlauben, sonnder alzeit ir Lieb darumb fragen, wie dann auch die jungfrawen, do sy etwo in garten, zu den jungen fürstin, oder an dergleichen orth zu hof gehen wellen, solchs allzeit mit der underhofmaisterin vorwissen thuen sollen."

[33] "Zum zehnten solle sie hofmeisterin keiner fräulen, außer unserer gnädigsten bewilligung, von hof in die stadt zu gehen erlauben, auch da eine oder die andere fräule dergestalt mit unserm gnädigsten willen und erlaubnuß zu einer frau auf die weis, wie oben vermeldet, in die stadt fahren thäte, dieselbe frau aber sie anderwärts in die kirchen, garten, oder andere gesellschaft weiters führen wollte, solches solle ohne unser und der hofmeisterin vorwissen, nicht beschehen, sondern wir und unsere hofmeisterin allezeit darum befragt werden, welche es ohne unser vorwissen nur allein den müttern zu erlauben haben wird, damit man allezeit wissen möge, wo ein oder die andere sey; zumahlen aber jedes mals, sonderlich, da sie etwa außer hofs in der stadt, oder anderwärts wären, sich wiederum zu rechter zeit, bevorab wann offentliche dienste seynd, bey hof einfinden."

These instructions thereby illustrate in the clearest possible way that with the migration of the line of Inner Austria to Vienna many of the regulations of the daily activities at court were transferred from Graz to Vienna. No such close relationships in form or content can, on the contrary, be discerned in the three instructions for the *Obersthofmeister*, while the versions of 1652 and 1655 are almost identical. Interestingly enough, the draft for the instructions of the *Obersthofmeister* from 1616 relies heavily in its first three chapters on the instructions of the *Hofmeisterin* of 1589, with the items 1 to 3 being almost verbal copies. This relationship lacks in the following instructions of 1631, 1652 and 1655, nor is it present in those of 1571 either.

By and large, the *Fräuleinhofmeisterin* and the *Obersthofmeisterin* held considerable power in the female household. Their close contacts with the ruler's consort and their station within the courtly representation gave them an important position in the hierarchy at court. However, the *Obersthofmeister* was their superior in precedence as well as in competence. The division of tasks between these offices stipulated that the *Obersthofmeister* could not direct the female members of the household, while the *Obersthofmeisterin* could not give orders to the male members.[34] There was every indication that the areas where the attributions of the two offices overlapped were dwindling.[35] In 1571 there were still 10 out of 17 points in the instructions of the *Obersthofmeister*, where the two officers shared duties. By 1616 these were reduced to 5 out of 10. In the longer run the *Obersthofmeister* saw his tasks reduced to controlling the finances of the empress, organizing audiences and in more general terms proffering advice. The direct intervention of the *Obersthofmeisterin* on the other hand, was by 1631 reduced to keeping and controlling the inventory of the *Frauenzimmer* and to exercising the general surveillance of the ladies-in-waiting. The instructions of 1652 and 1655 merely mention an overall task of surveillance. More concrete attributions towards the empress or the household were no longer mentioned.

Upon comparison with the previous instructions – in particular with those of 1631 – a final and clear evolution concerned the much more explicit definition of the empress's or queen's power to issue regulations. In 1652, on the other hand, the *Obersthofmeister* is designated as the keeper of ceremonial traditions concerning the empress.[36] Apart from

[34] ÖStA, *Abt. Haus-, Hof- und Staatsarchiv, Hofverwaltungen* Bd. 1, f. 166v.

[35] For the instructions, see n. 25 and 26.

[36] ÖStA, *Abt. Haus-, Hof- und Staatsarchiv*, OMeA SR 72, Teil 4, 1652 resp. 1655/16.

the overall surveillance, the instructions specify the duties of the *Obersthofmeister* as ensuring that the empress and her ladies-in-waiting were treated with respect, being present during audiences accorded by the empress, regulating the entrance to the antechamber and accompanying the empress when she left the palace or undertook a journey. It was also his task to coordinate travel arrangements with the *Obersthofmeister* and the *Oberststallmeister* of the emperor and to swear in new members of the empress's household, two functions that were still exercised jointly with the *Obersthofmeisterin* in 1571.[37] Furthermore, he had to control the accounts of the treasurer of the empress and to pass on orders to the kitchen of the court. Finally, he needed to ensure that the empress's outgoing mail respected all conventions of protocol and propriety.[38] What was in any case lacking from the seventeenth-century instructions was an explicit ruling on the duty of the empress's *Obersthofmeister* to attend to the meetings of the Aulic Council or to the presentation of accounts by other leading officers at court.[39]

As regards to the duties of the *Obersthofmeister* a clear evolution could therefore be discerned between 1571 and the middle of the seventeenth century, an evolution that was detrimental to the tasks and competence of the *Obersthofmeisterin*. The principal attributions of the office of the *Fräuleinhofmeisterin*, however, remained unaltered during the entire seventeenth century and as such reflected the clearest continuity between Graz and Vienna.

When turning to the continuity between Graz and Vienna in terms of female office holders, it is important to take into account the hardly surprising fact that the area of recruitment for ladies-in-waiting and *Hofmeisterinnen* differed greatly between the two courts. In Graz women from families of Styria shared positions in the household with women from Carinthia, Carniola and Gorizia, but also with some from Tyrol.[40] In Vienna on the other hand, Tyrol played little if any part after the transfer from Inner Austria. Whereas the same could be said for Carinthia, Carniola and Goriza, Styria gained in importance as compared to the sixteenth century. Upper and Lower Austria as well

[37] ÖStA, *Abt. Haus-, Hof- und Staatsarchiv, Hofverwaltungen* Bd. 1, f. 166v, 167.

[38] For the duties, see Hengerer, *Kaiserhof*, f. 267f.

[39] ÖStA, *Abt. Haus-, Hof- und Staatsarchiv, Hofverwaltungen* Bd. 1, f. 167.

[40] The basis of this statement is a provisional analysis from ÖStA, *Abt. Finanz- und Hofkammerarchiv, Niederösterreichische Herrschaftsakten* W 61/A/9-B, Bl. 665v-666v; W 61/A/36-B, Bl. 702r-861r.

as Bohemia and Moravia were in any case more important for the recruitment of noblewomen for the court.[41]

Ladies from the Styrian nobility were of lasting importance among the *Hofmeisterinnen* in Vienna until at least the 1650s, well beyond the move from Graz to Vienna. Above all they were prominent among the *Fräuleinhofmeisterinnen* and the *Hofmeisterinnen* of the imperial children. Of the 31 *Hofmeisterinnen* in office between 1611 and 1657, 14 or almost 50 % belonged to families hailing from Styria or Gorizia.[42] The importance of women of the Styrian nobility has not yet received a satisfactory explanation, but may be a survival of the longstanding relations between the imperial house and the Styrian nobility. The appointment of widowed ladies from these families was an act of regal grace, supporting the families and strengthening their ties to the Imperial court. At the same time there was little continuity on a personal level before and after 1619 as regards to *Hofmeisterinnen* from Inner Austria, a marked difference with the male officers of the household.[43] At the time of the transfer from Graz to Vienna, emperor Ferdinand II was a widower and the households of his daughters, the archduchesses Maria Anna and Cecilia Renata, and their *Hofmeisterinnen* did not move permanently to Vienna until 1624.[44] A certain measure of continuity could, however, be noted among the *Hofmeisterinnen* of the 1620s and 1630s who had often served as ladies-in-waiting in Graz before they married and returned to take up office at the court of Vienna after they became widows.

[41] Katrin Keller, "Das Frauenzimmer. Zur integrativen Wirkung des Wiener Hofes am Beispiel der Hofstaate von Kaiserinnen und Erzherzoginnen zwischen 1611 und 1657," in Thomas Winkelbauer and Petr Mat'a (eds.), *Die Habsburgermonarchie 1620 bis 1740. Leistungen und Grenzen des Absolutismusparadigmas* (Stuttgart, 2006), 149f.

[42] Short biographies in Keller, *Hofdamen*, for: Susanna Elisabeth von Althann, Maria Salome von Ernau, Margarita von Herberstein, Margarethe von Mörsberg, Franziska Quiroga von Paar, Katharina Eleonora von Paar, Anna Barbara von Stübich, Maria Sidonia Stürgkh von Planckenwarth, Anna Maria Barbara von Urschenbeck, Maria Elisabeth von Wagensperg, Maria Katharina von Wangen; Ursula von Attems, Anna Maria Formentini, Anna Julia Valmarana.

[43] Johann Andritsch, "Landesfürstliche Berater am Grazer Hof (1564-1619)," in Alexander Novotny and Berthold Sutter (eds.), *Innerösterreich 1564-1619* (Graz 1967), 85-87.

[44] Renate Schreiber, "*Ein galeria nach meinem humor*". *Erzherzog Leopold Wilhelm* (Vienna, 2004), 14.

The case of Anna Maria Formentini (died 1629) offers an example of such a career.[45] She was first appointed *Frauleinhofmeisterin* of empress Eleonora Gonzaga the Elder in 1622, but exchanged that position for the office of *Obersthofmeisterin* in the household of the archduchesses in 1624. Anna Maria Formentini was born a von Rohrbach and had entered the household of archduchess Maria of Inner Austria as a lady-in-waiting in 1600. There she married Carl Formentini in September 1602, an archducal chamberlain and counselor, who served in the army of Ferdinand II and would later become Captain of Gradisca. He descended of a noble family from Gorizia. Lady Formentini was probably already a widow when she was appointed *Fräuleinhofmeisterin* in 1622. The following year she, her brother-in-law Caspar Formentini and her surviving children Ludwig, Aurora and Elisabeth were granted letters patent raising them to baronial rank with the honorific suffix *zu Tulmein*. At festivities at court she would often appear as an actress. She died in office in 1629 and the empress had her corpse embalmed and sent to Gorizia at her expense. In turn, the two daughters Aurora and Elisabeth Formentini became ladies-in-waiting, serving from 1627 to 1632 and from 1627 to 1634 respectively, the former in the entourage of the empress, the latter in that of the archduchesses. Their brother Ludwig Formentini (1604-1650) was an imperial chamberlain.

Another example is the career of Margarita von Herberstein (1580-1644), who was from 1630 until 1637 the *Obersthofmeisterin* of the archduchesses and from then until her death the *Obersthofmeisterin* of the empress-widow Eleonora Gonzaga the Elder.[46] Margarita was born countess Valmarana and descended from a leading family of Vicenza that had contacts with the Habsburgs since the sixteenth century. In 1596 she became a lady-in-waiting of the sisters of Ferdinand II in Graz, where her brother Ascanio Valmarana (1576-1623) was also serving in the household and would marry a lady-in-waiting. Two years later, Margarita married baron Bernhardin von Herberstein (1566-1624). He had served at the Bavarian court, before becoming the *Oberststallmeister* of archduke Ferdinand II in 1595 and would exercise that office until 1622. Due to his obligations, Margarita von Herberstein would have

[45] Keller, *Hofdamen*, 64, 73, 108, 161, 192, 275f.; see also Katrin Keller, "Ladies-in-Waiting at the Imperial Court of Vienna from 1550 to 1700: Structures, Responsibilities and Career Patterns," in Nadine Akkerman and Birgit Houben (eds.), *The Politics of the Female Household. Ladies-in-Waiting across Early Modern Europe* (Rulers & Elites 4) (Leiden-Boston, 2013), 84-97.

[46] Keller, *Hofdamen*, 59, 70, 82, 163, 179, 191f., 281f.

come to the court of Graz more or less regularly. After her husband's death, she made an agreement with her four sons that allowed her to continue the administration of the family estate for the next three years. Her eldest son was Johann Maximilian (1601-1680), the future member of the Privy Council and *Landeshauptmann* of Styria, who was at that stage a gentleman carver of Ferdinand II. The deed furthermore called Johann Georg (died 1641), who would become commander of Triest and *Oberstsilberkämmerer* of the empress-widow, a seneschal in Vienna and his brother Johann Bernhard (died 1630) a canon of the cathedral chapters of Salzburg and Olomouc. Hans Ferdinand and Hans Karl were still minors. Out of the previous marriage of Bernhardin with a countess Fugger, she moreover had a stepson Johann Wilhelm, who was an imperial chamberlain at the time.

The agreement over the administration of the estate enabled the eldest son to finish his education and prepare for a career as an officeholder. After the agreement had run its course, Margarita von Herberstein returned to court in 1630 as the *Obersthofmeisterin* of the archduchesses Maria Anna and Cecilia Renata. Her services must have been appreciated, because she was promoted to *Obersthofmeisterin* of the empress-widow when Ursula von Attems (1568-1641) resigned from that office in 1637. When the empress-widow resided in Graz for a few months in the summer of the same year, Margarita's eldest son was appointed her *Hofmeister*, a title that he would continue to bear even though he stopped exercising the office once the empress left the town. This and other cases make it clear that Margarita von Herberstein used her office and her access to the empress to the benefit of her family. She was explicitly mentioned in the letters patent raising the family von Herberstein to the rank of Austrian counts in 1644, yet another sign that successful holding of office by women served the interests of a family. That her only daughter, Maria Elisabeth – by marriage – von Wagensperg (1599/1600-1681) became the *Obersthofmeisterin* of the third spouse of emperor Ferdinand III in 1651, further demonstrates the enduring influence of her mother's tenure of office and at the same time highlights another lady from the nobility of Styria holding an important office at the court of Vienna.

The often neglected example of the female households provides a number of interesting answers to the rarely studied question of the influence of the court of Graz on the life of the court of Vienna in the seventeenth and eighteenth centuries. After the children of emperor Ferdinand II left Graz in 1624, the town would only rarely serve as a residence. It did so for some time during the stay of the empress-widow Eleonora Gonzaga the Elder in 1637 and again in 1645, when the children of the emperor were brought to safety from the advancing Swedish troops. In all, the town hosted a Habsburg court for just a few decades in the early modern period.[47] Due to dynastic developments that led the line of Inner Austria to occupy the imperial throne and settle in Vienna, these decades nevertheless had a profound influence on the structures and the representation of the imperial court. The Habsburg imperial court reconstituted itself after 1619, combining elements taken from the Rudolfine court of Prague, the Inner Austrian court of Graz and certain contemporary innovations.

As far as the female household was concerned, the time in Graz concluded the development from a medieval peripatetic to an early modern residential court. When the court was still moving around frequently, the ruler and his spouse were often apart for longer periods of time. As it had to be self-supporting, the household of the empress was larger and had a number of men holding offices. Parallel with the emergence of the fixed residence, the relationship between the male and the female household began to shift at the end of the fifteenth century.[48] The stable common residence of the ruler and his spouse resulted in a closer connection between their households, which was internally accompanied by a compartmentalization. On the one hand the female household became part of the overall imperial household. This was codified when the testament of Ferdinand II of 1621 stipulated that the unity of the House of Habsburg entailed the unity of the dynasty's households, meaning that the head of the dynasty – in other words the ruling archduke or emperor – would hold supreme authority over all dependant households of the members of the dynasty.[49] At the same time the household of the archduchess and later of the empress was increasingly set apart, resulting in stricter controls on who gained entry to the *Frauenzimmer* and in measures to ensure the moral and honourable conduct of the ladies attached to it. The latter has to be interpreted in a more general evolution of noble norms of behaviour to courtly standards. Both developments were clearly reflected in the instructions of 1589 for the *Fräuleinhofmeisterin* of the court of

[47] Wiesflecker, "Adel und Residenz," 595-598.
[48] Keller, *Hofdamen*, 25.
[49] Istvan von Žolger, *Der Hofstaat des Hauses Österreich* (Vienna-Leipzig, 1917), 171, 192f. That the court consisted of several households of members of the dynasty, was also the rule in France, Italy and Spain.

Graz. These would later be partially copied word by word or otherwise quarried for the instructions governing the female household of the court of Vienna.

A third avenue of influence from the court of Graz to that of Vienna sprung from continuity in personnel. It can be detected among the officers of the household of the empress as well as in the entourage of the emperor, where, it should be said, it was clearer still. Taken together our findings will hopefully inspire the growing number of studies concerning the court of Vienna to consider its links with the court of Graz more systematically.

The Innsbruck court in the 17th century: identity and ceremonial of a court in flux

Astrid von Schlachta

Ceremonial issues, orders of precedence and rank, and various forms of representation are of increasing interest to researchers into Early Modern court history. The new Cultural History has, in particular, provided influences and impetus for attempts to interpret ceremony as a system of rules and norms that assigned symbolic meaning to specific acts.[1] Ceremonial is given the character of a system of social signification; it enacted social order and was among the public actions of the ruler. Ceremonial acts might be addressed to a specific recipient, but were performed before an audience of courtiers and others who could be expected to interpret the acts they saw performed and respond accordingly.[2] Furthermore, rulership found its legitimization and its legitimating expression in ceremonial. This interpretation of Early Modern court ceremonies has gained further relevance in the wake of the new research on Absolutism that indicates that during the period of full-blown Absolutism, or its early stages, rulership was by no means

[1] For an overview, see Roger Chartier, "New Cultural History," in Joachim Eibach and Günther Lottes (eds.), *Kompass der Geschichtswissenschaft,* UTB für Wissenschaft 2271 (Göttingen, 2002), 193-205.

[2] Irmgard Pangerl, Martin Scheutz and Thomas Winkelbauer, "Zeremoniell und zeremonielles Handeln am Wiener Hof: Eine Skizze," in Irmgard Pangerl, Martin Scheutz and Thomas Winkelbauer (eds.), *Der Wiener Hof im Spiegel der Zeremonialprotokolle, 1652-1800: Eine Annäherung*, Forschungen und Beiträge zur Wiener Stadtgeschichte 47 (Innsbruck, 2007), 7-14, esp. 10; Barbara Stollberg-Rilinger, "Zeremoniell als politisches Verfahren: Rangordnung und Rangstreit als Strukturmerkmal des frühneuzeitlichen Reichstags," in Johannes Kunisch (ed.), *Neue Studien zur frühneuzeitlichen Reichsgeschichte*, Zeitschrift für historische Forschung, Beiheft 19 (Berlin, 1997), 91-132, esp. 94f; Peter-Michael Hahn and Ulrich Schütte, "Thesen zur Rekonstruktion höfischer Zeichensysteme in der Frühen Neuzeit," *Mitteilungen der Residenzen-Kommission der Akademie der Wissenschaften zur Göttingen* 13, no. 2 (2003), 19-47. For an examination of intercultural symbolic communication and the importance of signs and signals at the Court of Muscovy, see Claudia Garnier, "Wer meinen Herrn ehrt, den ehre ich billig auch: Symbolische Kommunikationsformen bei Gesandtenempfängen am Moskauer Hof im 16. und 17. Jahrhundert," *Jahrbuch für Kommunikationsgeschichte* 7 (2005), 27-51.

self-evident and thus needed to be represented to the outer world.[3] This was a fact already alluded to by Julius Bernhard von Rohr (1688-1742) in his *Einleitung zur Ceremoniel-Wissenschaft*.[4]

In what follows we will examine the court of Innsbruck in the first half of the 17th century from the perspective of ceremonial structures, representation and the transfer of power. The question necessarily arises of whether ceremonial was given added importance in legitimizing rule by the fact that the person exercising power, and the manner in which they did so, changed several times over these decades. Innsbruck was a court in flux, and the sources show that with each new ruler, as different lines within the Habsburg family succeeded one another in the Upper Austrian lands, ceremonial and representation had to be altered or adjusted anew.

By looking at the Innsbruck court in the first half of the 17th century we are confronted with an Early Modern court which lay at the periphery of the Habsburg lands and which furthermore had lost the importance that it had held in the 16th century. Up to 1595 Innsbruck was the home to a Tyrolean branch of the Habsburgs – represented by Charles V's brother, archduke Ferdinand I, and later by his son archduke Ferdinand II – whose vigorous court life took place in both the Hofburg and in Ambras Castle.[5] The situation changed

[3] Heinz Duchhardt and Ronald G. Asch (eds.), *Der Absolutismus — ein Mythos? Strukturwandel monarchischer Herrschaft in West- und Mitteleuropa, ca. 1550-1700*, Münsterische Historische Forschungen 9 (Cologne, 1996); for the Habsburg Countries, see Petr Mat'a and Thomas Winkelbauer (eds.), *Die Habsburgermonarchie 1620 bis 1740: Leistungen und Grenzen des Absolutismus-Paradigmas* (Stuttgart, 2006); see also Barbara Stollberg-Rilinger, "Die zeremonielle Inszenierung des Reiches, oder: Was leistet der kulturalistische Ansatz für die Reichsverfassungsgeschichte?" in Matthias Schnettger (ed.), *Imperium Romanum – irregulare corpus – Teutscher Reichs-Staat: Das Alte Reich im Verständnis der Zeitgenossen und der Historiographie*, Veröffentlichungen des Instituts für Europäische Geschichte 57 (Mainz, 2002), 233-246.

[4] For an analysis, see Kerstin Heldt, *Der vollkommene Regent: Studien zur panegyrischen Casuallyrik am Beispiel des Dresdner Hofes Augusts des Starken, 1670-1733*, Frühe Neuzeit 34 (Tübingen, 1997), 13.

[5] Josef Hirn, *Erzherzog Ferdinand II. von Tirol: Geschichte seiner Regierung und seiner Länder*, 2 vols. (Innsbruck, 1885-1888) – now somewhat dated but still fundamental. See too Veronika Sandbichler, "Festkultur am Hof Erzherzog Ferdinands II.," in Heinz Noflatscher and Jan Paul Niederkorn (eds.), *Der Innsbrucker Hof: Residenz und höfischer Gesellschaft in Tirol vom 15. bis 19. Jahrhundert*, Archiv für österreichische Geschichte 138 (Vienna, 2005), 159-174; Václav Bůžek, "Der böhmische und mährische Adel am Hof Ferdinands II. von Tirol in Innsbruck und Ambras," in *idem*, 425-438; also Volker Press, "The Habsburg Court as Center of the Imperial Government," *Journal of Modern History* 58 (1986), 23-45, esp. 26f, 32f.

after Ferdinand II's death in 1595. Due to his morganatic union with Philippine Welser, daughter of a burgher of Augsburg, his two sons, Andreas and Karl, were not legitimate heirs. His second marriage, to Anna Catherina Gonzaga, had 'only' brought forth three daughters, among them the later empress Anna, wife of emperor Matthias.

This dynastic rupture was the starting point for the decades with which we will be concerned. The break in the continuity of rulership at the Innsbruck court was to lead to the existence of three differently structured courts which can be characterized as follows: the court of a 'spiritual' governor exercising power on behalf of an absent sovereign, the court of a sovereign ruler with gradually growing competences culminating in the foundation of a new line of sovereignty, and at last the court of a noble widow exercising power on behalf of her under-aged son. The new line of sovereignty which started with archduke Leopold V and culminated in the hereditary transmission of the Upper Austrian lands in 1630, lasted only for two generations. In 1665 it came to an end when the last sovereign, archduke Sigismund Franz, a son of Leopold V and Claudia de'Medici, died without heirs. Upper Austria reverted to emperor Leopold I.

We will consider this versatile court from two angles: that of sovereign power, law and governance, and that of representation. The underlying themes include the relationship between Innsbruck and Vienna, and the integration of the Innsbruck court and the Upper Austrian lands into the whole edifice of Habsburg power.

The sovereign power and governance

Taking 1595 as our starting point, we are confronted with the unsettled succession after archduke Ferdinand II's death, leaving behind two sons, neither of them a legitimate successor, three daughters from his second marriage, and a widow. The years up to 1602 were characterized by negotiations about the general structure of the Habsburg lands and the succession in Upper and Outer Austria. In these years of interregnum, as well as in the ensuing period of rule by archduke Maximilian, the dependence of the Innsbruck court upon Vienna was pronounced. This was true not only with regard to the Innsbruck court's ability to set a political agenda, but also in taking initiatives in representation and self-portrayal, as exemplified in the building program, where what little was done had a heavily spiritual emphasis.

The epoch of interregnum was marked by negotiations between the line of the emperor, the brothers Rudolf, Matthias, Maximilian, Ernst and Albrecht, who wanted to keep the territories undivided, and the Styrian line, represented by Charles of Styria's widow, archduchess Maria, who pushed for a division between Tyrol and Vorlande.[6] Increasingly, from the beginning of 1596 onwards, the dividing line seems to have been more between the brothers Matthias, Maximilian and their sister-in-law Maria on the one side, and emperor Rudolf on the other. One of the main concerns was the formula to be followed for the act of homage in the Upper Austrian lands.[7] Finally, in August 1596, Matthias, acting as Rudolf's delegate, accepted the act of hereditary homage from the Tyrolean Estates; and, as was the tradition, the Estates put forward their request for the confirmation of their privileges combined with the request of indivisibility of the country.[8] Passing over the details, it finally took until 1630 before the Upper and Outer Austrian Lands were fully reunited under the sovereignty of an archduke who again had the power and the right to bequeath these countries to his own heir.

After much discussion between the cousins concerning the Upper and Outer Austrian Lands, the transfer of the various shares to Rudolf (*Erbvergleichung*), and the finalization of the form of government,[9] the emperor issued the *Prager Rezeß* (Prague Disposition) on February 5, 1602, empowering his brother Maximilian to govern the lands of Upper and Outer Austria.[10] Interestingly, in the course of these discussions a deputy of the Styrian line, Karl Schurff, who became a privy councilor under Maximilian III, suggested that archduchess Maria of Inner Austria should send her daughter Eleonore into the Haller Damenstift in order to keep and increase her influence in Tyrol.[11] This

[6] On the case made by the Styrian line, see Josef Hirn, "Tirols Erbtheilung und Zwischenreich 1595-1602," *Archiv für österreichische Geschichte* 29 (1903), 271-361, esp. 316f. Also his *Die ersten Versuche Kaiser Rudolfs II. um in den Alleinbesitz der Grafschaft Tirol zu gelangen* (Vienna, 1898).

[7] See Hirn, "Tirols Erbtheilung und Zwischenreich," 287-289.

[8] Josef Hirn, *Erzherzog Maximilian der Deutschmeister: Regent von Tirol*, (Innsbruck, 1915), 1:11f.

[9] See the corresponding documents in Tiroler Landesarchiv Innsbruck, Sammelakten, Reihe B, Abt. I, Lage 5; regarding the negotiations and the allocation of the territory, see also Hirn, "Tirols Erbtheilung und Zwischenreich," 324-338; Hirn, *Erzherzog Maximilian der Deutschmeister*, 1:16-20.

[10] See Hirn, "Tirols Erbtheilung und Zwischenreich," 349-351.

[11] Compare Hirn, "Tirols Erbtheilung und Zwischenreich," 351f. On Karl Schurff, see Viktoria Putz, "Beamtenschematismus der drei oberösterreichischen Wesen in den Jahren 1602-1619" (doctoral thesis, Innsbruck, 1973), 45f.

female influence was not immediately sought – it was only some time later that Eleonore entered the Damenstift – but a special regulation, reflecting the compromise with the Styrian line, was included in the treaty, stipulating that the lands at issue should pass to them after Maximilian's death. This finally took place in 1619, when the reign of Leopold V began.[12] On May 31, 1602, an instruction was sent to Tyrol which repeated the most important details of the Prager Rezeß. The reason it gave for the transfer of territory was that it would serve the countries "zu mehrern trost und sicherheit" should an "ansehenlich fürstlich haubt" live within the country and preside over it as governor.[13] Maximilian, already in possession of "andere Landt mehr nuzlich vnd wolgeregiert," should reign in these lands as "vollkhomenlicher Regent vnd Gubernator [., v.S.] das Ihrige was ainen Regierenden herren vnd Landtfürsten zuthuen gebürt vnd sowohl gemeinen Interessenten zu nuz und wolfart, als auch den gehorsamen landen vnd leuthen zu trost und rettung, schutz, schirm und aufnehmben." The time frame for the duration of Maximilian's rule was expressed very vaguely as until "wir uns aines andern einhellig miteinander vergleichen." The competences of the new governor were outlined and defined with great precision. Maximilian was, for instance, not allowed to summon or hold a Diet without Rudolf's approval, nor could he allocate fiefs or make appointments to high office without consulting Rudolf.[14]

During Maximilian's rule his powers were twice considerably altered by two incisive regulations. In the wake of the Treaty of Lieben, Matthias as new sovereign in the archduchy of Austria and in the kingdom of Hungary transferred his distributive share of Tyrol and the Outer Austrian lands to Rudolf II.[15] And in 1612, after Rudolf II's death, a notable enlargement of Maximilian's power took place. Although he

[12] For an overview, see Sabine Weiss, "Erzherzog Leopold V. – Ritter des Ordens vom Goldenen Vlies: Biographische Notizen zu Karriere und Lebenswelt eines frühbarocken Tiroler Landesfürsten," *Tiroler Heimat* 66 (2002): 29-80.

[13] 31 May 1602, Tiroler Landesarchiv Innsbruck, Sammelakten, Reihe B, Abt. I, Lage 5, Dokument Prag, [1v]; regarding the Prager Rezeß, see also Hirn, *Erzherzog Maximilian*, 1:19.

[14] 31 May 1602, [2r-3r]. See too Brigitte Steiger, "Erzherzog Leopold V. als Gubernator und Landesfürst von Tirol" (doctoral thesis, Innsbruck, 1970), 11; regarding the competences that were defined in the "Prager Rezeß," see Hirn, "Tirols Erbhteilung und Zwischenreich," esp. 350f.

[15] 25 June 1608, Tiroler Landesarchiv Innsbruck, Sammelakten, Reihe B, Abt. I, Lage 5, Dokument vom 25. Juni 1608, [1v]. See Hirn, *Erzherzog Maximilian*, 1: 128.

did not gain the rank of an independent ruler in Innsbruck, Maximilian nevertheless dropped the title *Gubernator* and enjoyed much wider competences than formerly.[16]

The rulers in Innsbruck – an overview

Maximilian III, the *Deutschmeister*, was born in 1558 as the fourth son of emperor Maximilian II and the Spanish infanta Maria. He spent his childhood and youth at the humanistically oriented and confessionally diverse court of his father.[17] After Maximilian II's death, Rudolf II took over the duty of providing for his brothers as befitted their rank; very soon it became clear that Maximilian was being steered towards an ecclesiastical career. After negotiations in various directions, he entered the Teutonic Order and was in time appointed to the office of Coadjutor of the Order with right of succession.[18] From 1593 to 1595 Maximilian was governor of Inner Austria as guardian to the under-aged children of archduke Charles. At the same time, he was active as commander in chief during the Turkish Wars.[19] Despite the wide range and geographical scope of his activities, Maximilian's central residence remained in Mergentheim, the administrative centre of the Teutonic Knights. In 1602 Maximilian finally took up the government of Tyrol, in the circumstances already described.

After Maximilian's death in 1618, archduke Leopold, of the Inner Austrian line of the family, took over the governance of Tyrol – a step that fulfilled the arrangements of the Prager Rezeß. He, too, had first held ecclesiastical office, as bishop of Passau and Regensburg. His residence was in Zabern, where he had established his court and his

[16] Hirn, *Erzherzog Maximilian*, 1: 149.

[17] Ursula Stampfer, "Die Hofbibliothek Erzherzog Maximilians III. (1558-1618): Analyse und Rezeption," *Mitteilungen der Gesellschaft für Buchforschung in Österreich*, 2004, 2:14; compare Heinz Noflatscher, "Erzherzog Maximilian Hoch- und Deutschmeister, 1585/90-1918: Das Haus Habsburg, der Deutsche Orden und das konfessionelle Zeitalter" (doctoral thesis, Innsbruck, 1980), 46-50.

[18] Regarding Maximilian's time as Coadjutor, see Noflatscher, "Erzherzog Maximilian," 64-111.

[19] His engagement in the Turkish war and his interest in warfare might explain his endeavours to reorganize the Tyrolean military system by issuing a new "Zuzugsordnung" in 1605. Compare Josef Egger, *Geschichte Tirols von den ältesten Zeiten bis in die Neuzeit* (Innsbruck, 1872), 2: 287f.

household.[20] After having received the *Gubernament* of Tyrol, Leopold very soon endeavored to extend his power in the Upper Austrian lands – he too had been restrained in his competences and depended on the emperor in many political duties.[21] A first success of his attempts dates from the year 1625, when a contract of inheritance between the brothers Ferdinand, Leopold and Charles settled that Leopold would get two thirds of the group of lands in Upper and Outer Austrian – not including Breisgau, Sundgau and Alsace, the four "Waldstädte am Rhein" (Rheinfelden, Säckingen, Laufenburg and Waldshut) and the *Landvogteien* Hagenau and Ortenau, where Leopold only held the office of a *Statthalter* (Lord Lieutenant).[22] In the regions assigned to Leopold, the act of homage was done in May 1626. It was only in 1630 that Leopold V also became hereditary sovereign of the remaining third.[23]

When Leopold V died in 1632, his wife Claudia de'Medici – together with the emperor – took up the reins of government as guardian for her still under-aged son Ferdinand Karl; she ruled until 1646. Her regency fell in the politically difficult time of the Thirty Years War.[24] Although the Upper Austrian lands were spared direct devastation, they were of major importance for emperor Ferdinand II as the western outpost of the Habsburg Monarchy, and therefore indirectly involved in the war.

The guardianship of Claudia de'Medici was regulated by Leopold V's testament, which contained exact specifications about the distribution of power after his death. Leopold bequeathed to emperor Ferdinand II, his brother, the "vollmächtigen Gewalttragen" as "Vormundten, vnd

[20] Karl Mussak, "Hofleben und Kulturpflege in Tirol unter Erzherzog Leopold V." (doctoral thesis, Innsbruck, 1962), 24.

[21] See Steiger, "Erzherzog Leopold V.," 11, 29-32.

[22] Steiger, "Erzherzog Leopold V.," 31; Weiss, "Erzherzog Leopold V.," 58; regarding the documents, see: Victor v. Renner, "Die Erbteilung Kaiser Ferdinands II. mit seinen Brüdern," *Zeitschrift des Ferdinandeums für Tirol und Vorarlberg* 18 (1873), 199-248.

[23] Steiger, "Erzherzog Leopold V.," 32f.

[24] On female guardianship in the courtly context in general terms, see Heide Wunder (ed.), *Dynastie und Herrschaftssicherung in der Frühen Neuzeit: Geschlechter und Geschlecht*, Zeitschrift für historische Forschung 28 (Berlin, 2002); Martina Schattkowsky (ed.), *Witwenschaft in der Frühen Neuzeit: Fürstliche und adelige Witwen zwischen Selbst- und Fremdbestimmung*, Schriften zur Sächsischen Geschichte und Volkskunde 6 (Leipzig, 2003); with regard to Claudia de'Medici, see Sabine Weiss, *Claudia de'Medici: Eine italienische Prinzessin als Landesfürstin von Tirol, 1604-1648* (Innsbruck, 2004); Hans Brugger, "Die Regierungszeit der Erzherzogin Claudia in Tirol" (doctoral thesis, Graz, 1952); Sigrid Philadelphy, "Die Geschichte der Stadt Innsbruck unter Claudia v. Medici" (doctoral thesis, Innsbruck, 1964).

Gerhaben mitt angelegenen vleiß und sonderem hohen Verthrauen,"[25] while Claudia was named *Mitgerhabin*.[26] Ferdinand II accepted these arrangements, and since he was too pressingly engaged elsewhere to give Tyrol his attention, he entrusted Claudia de'Medici both with the exercise of sovereignty in the Upper Austrian lands, and with guardianship of the heir to the throne, Ferdinand Karl. In March 1633, during the first Diet under the new regent, Claudia de'Medici's power was confirmed and announced to all authorities. Furthermore, an imperial "Creditiu schreiben" was sent to all authorities, decreeing that Claudia's instructions and commands were to be obeyed because she was authorized to rule on behalf of the emperor.[27] This defined Claudia's installation as acting sovereign and the structure of her power as Ferdinand II's "Mit Vormundin vnnd contutricin" (co-guardian and co-tutrix).[28]

In subsequent years, however, Ferdinand II did not take a passive role as co-tutor. From the beginning he clearly emphasized his claim to Tyrol and his supremacy in local and dynastic politics. The sources show that he took a clear interest in the education of the heir to the throne – with the aim of raising a ruler for the western parts of his Hereditary Lands who would govern in his spirit and would adhere to his political aims.[29] At the same time, it proved no disadvantage for Claudia de'Medici to have the backing of the emperor as guardian of her son. The emperor proved to be a strong ally who also guaranteed protection, a thing of no minor importance during the crises and conflicts of the Thirty Years War.

[25] Ferdinand II. and Claudia de'Medici, in: Tiroler Landesarchiv Innsbruck, Hs. 1097, 1r.

[26] According to Grimm's *Wörterbuch*, "Gerhabe" means "Vormund"; see *Deutsches Wörterbuch von Jacob und Wilhelm Grimm* (Munich, 1984; reprint of Leipzig, 1897), 5: 2552f.

[27] Tiroler Landesarchiv Innsbruck, Landschaftliches Archiv, Verhandlungen der Landschaft, Bd. 18, 1633-1639, 56r-v.

[28] Tiroler Landesarchiv Innsbruck, Landschaftliches Archiv, Verhandlungen der Landschaft, Bd. 18, 1633-1639, 58r.

[29] For further detail, see Astrid von Schlachta, "Herrschen und vorbereiten: Claudia de'Medici und ihre europäischen verwitweten 'Kolleginnen'," *Tiroler Heimat* 69 (2005), 33f.

Ceremonial, representation and court life

As already mentioned in the introduction, ceremonial and the diverse forms of representation at the court not only represented sovereignty but were also a major element of Early Modern political communication.[30]

In considering these forms of political communication at the Innsbruck court, it is first necessary to bear in mind that in the times of Maximilian III the institution was marked by three different courtly households whose relations to one another were not always harmonious: the household of the governor, the household of the last sovereign's widow, Anna Catherina Gonzaga,[31] and the household of Karl von Burgau, son of Ferdinand II by Philippine Welser. Anna Catherina, the widow of Ferdinand II, initially lived in the summer palace Ruhelust, which was surrounded by large gardens of the same name. Court life in her residence seems to have continued to be very lively; for the year 1595 the sources record a household of 61 persons. This is roughly half the size of the household of empress Maria Anna in early 17th-century Vienna.[32] But in subsequent years the court probably stagnated, in numbers as well as in importance. The same conclusion is suggested by the development of court music. From the first decade of the 17th century we know that the court musicians had to fulfill other duties besides their occupation in the Court *Kapelle*; for instance, the chapel singer Johann Kopp doubled as language tutor to Anna Catherina's oldest daughter Maria and as Pfennigmeister. In 1612 Anna Catherina, together with her oldest daughter Maria, joined

[30] For a theoretical foundation see Ute Frevert, "Neue Politikgeschichte," in Joachim Eibach and Günther Lottes (eds.), *Kompass der Geschichtswissenschaft*, UTB für Wissenschaft 2271 (Göttingen, 2002), 152-164; Luise Schorn-Schütte, *Historische Politikforschung: Eine Einführung* (Munich, 2006), 85-116; Barbara Stollberg-Rilinger, "Was heißt Kulturgeschichte des Politischen?" in *Was heißt Kulturgeschichte des Politischen?*, Zeitschrift für historische Forschung 35 (Berlin, 2005), 9-24.

[31] Regarding her life, see Elena Taddei, "Anna Caterin Gonzaga und ihre Zeit: der italienische Einfluss am Innsbrucker Hof," in *Der Innsbrucker Hof* [see n. 5], 213-240; Monika E. Wallas, *Anna Catherina Gonzaga: Leben und Wirken der zweiten Gemahlin Erzherzog Ferdinands II.* (Innsbruck, n.d.); Ellinor Forster, "Streit um das Erbe der Stifterin: Ein Kräftemessen zwischen Serviten und Regelfrauen in Innsbruck, 1621-1672," in Die vierte Tagung des Arbeitskreises für interdisziplinäre Männer- und Geschlechterforschung (2.-4. Februar 2006), downloaded at http://www.ruendal.de/aim/tagung06/pdfs/forster.pdf (last consulted 28 December 2007).

[32] In 1612 approximately 110 persons belonged to Maria Anna's household. See Katrin Keller, *Hofdamen: Amtsträgerinnen im Wiener Hofstaat* (Vienna, 2005), 23; Taddei, "Anna Caterina," 235, 239.

the Damenstift Regelhaus that she herself had founded. Twelve court ladies accompanied the former sovereign, as well as the courtly Kapelle, which was now again enlarged and also assumed musical duties in the new convent church.[33]

Besides the household of Maximilian III, which will be described below, and that of Anna Catherina, a third parallel household existed in Innsbruck. Karl von Burgau, son of Ferdinand II and his first wife Philippine Welser, had inherited Ambras Castle from his mother and established a household there, at least from time to time up to the year 1613. Furthermore, he possessed a palace in the town, the former armory (today the provincial parliament, or *Landhaus*).[34] The sources reveal some tensions between the various courts, with the political contacts between Maximilian and Karl von Burgau in particular being marked by issues arising from the dispersed constellation of land distribution. These show the scattered distribution of power in the area surrounding Innsbruck, and the difficulties of enforcing rulership downward. Karl von Burgau was not only entitled to Ambras Castle, but from the inheritance of his mother he also held the dominions of Petersberg, Sterzing, Stubai, Rottenburg and Hörtenberg.[35]

The relations between Maximilian and Anna Catherina, in contrast, seem not to have gone beyond regular visits. In this context there is a highly significant phrase in one of the letters that Maximilian sent to his sister, Margarete, in 1603: "Dennoch, unangesehen ichs nunmehr schier entwohnt und ohnedas nit sonders dazu geneigt, muß ich mich doch immer (wieder) einmal dem Frauenzimmer dahier, weil ich ihnen so nahend geraten, und sonderlich zu dieser Zeit mit Kurzweil erzeigen."[36]

[33] Walter Senn, *Musik und Theater am Hof zu Innsbruck: Geschichte der Hofkapelle vom 15. Jahrhundert bis zu deren Auflösung im Jahre 1748* (Innsbruck, 1954), 198f; Kurt Drexel, "Klöster und Stifte als Musikzentren: Stams, Marienberg, Neustift, Serviten und 'Versperrtes Kloster' in Innsbruck, Damenstift Hall," in Kurt Drexel and Monika Fink (eds.), *Musikgeschichte Tirols*, Schlern-Schriften 322 (Innsbruck, 2004), 2:153-157; see too Theophil Antonicek, "Die höfische Musik von Maximilian III. bis zur Auflösung der Hofkapelle," in *Musikgeschichte Tirols*, 2:41f; Taddei, "Anna Caterina," 235, 239.

[34] See Hirn, *Erzherzog Maximilian*, 2:275-308; Franz C. Zoller, *Geschichte und Denkwürdigkeiten der Stadt Innsbruck und der umliegenden Umgebung* (Innsbruck, 1816), 1: 289.

[35] Hirn, *Erzherzog Maximilian*, 1:96 (esp. footnote 2); see also: Zoller, *Geschichte und Denkwürdigkeiten*, 1:289f; Hirn, *Erzherzog Maximilian*, 2: 288f.

[36] Quoted from Hirn, *Erzherzog Maximilian*, 1: 95.

Turning now to the household of the ruler, the issue to be placed first and foremost is that under Maximilian III, representation at the Innsbruck court has to be seen as embedded in the spiritual sphere, largely as a result of his position. Representation was strongly marked by spiritual symbolism and the display of piety. On the one side this reflects Maximilian's ecclesiastical office and career, on the other side his limited competences as governor might also have shifted his priorities into the spiritual sphere.[37] Interestingly, the emperor ensured that he too was represented in Tyrol, for instance on newly created coins. From 1602 the Tyrolean thaler bore on its face the portrait of emperor Rudolf and the inscription "Rvdolphvus II. Dei Gratia Romanorvm Imperator Semper Avgvstvs Ac Germaniae Hyngariae Bohemiae Rex." On the reverse were the Habsburg coat of arms with the chain of the Golden Fleece and the archducal crown, and an inscription reading "Necnon Archidvces Avstriae Dvces Bvrgvndiae Comites Tyrolis."[38]

If one follows Volker Bauer's ideal typology, the Innsbruck court under Maximilian III could be characterized as a "householderly" court, rather than one that emphasized "princely glory." The household of the sovereign was more to the foreground as well as the "gute zucht, tugend, gottesfurcht und erbarkeit."[39] Maximilian built up his image of a "pious monarch"; *repraesentatio* was showing piety and displaying it by the corresponding attributes and signs. Examining his inventory of assets, it becomes obvious that the Hofburg was filled with items of devotion, altars, pictures of saints, statues of Mary and other pious objects.[40] This spiritual representation can also be traced in several illustrations that show Maximilian as Deutschmeister. Only in his later years was Maximilian portrayed with the insignia of temporal power, including the archducal crown[41]

[37] See also the description in Egger, *Geschichte Tirols* 2: 296f, 314f.

[38] See Heinz Moser and Heinz Tursky, *Die Münzen Kaiser Rudolfs II. aus der Münzstätte Hall in Tirol, 1602-1612*, Corpus Nummorum Tirolensium (Innsbruck, 1986), 80-84.

[39] Volker Bauer, *Die höfische Gesellschaft in Deutschland von der Mitte des 17. bis zum Ausgang des 18. Jahrhunderts*, Frühe Neuzeit 12 (Tübingen, 1993), 66f.

[40] Beda Dudik, "Des Hoch- und Deutschmeisters Erzherzog's Maximilian I. Testament und Verlassenschaft vom J. 1619," *Archiv für Kunde österreichischer Geschichts-Quellen* 33 (1865): 233-352; Noflatscher, "Erzherzog Maximilian," 317f.

[41] See Heinz Noflatscher, *Glaube, Reich und Dynastie: Maximilian der Deutschmeister, 1558-1618*, Quellen und Studien zur Geschichte des Deutschen Ordens 11 (Hamburg, 1987), ill. 17.

Despite the elevation of his rank in 1612, and a slight change in representation, Maximilian's spiritual office as Hochmeister of the Teutonic Knights continued to define his self-representation. This can be seen by, among other examples, his tomb, the design of which was planned by Maximilian as early as 1614. In his testament from that year he determined the exact location of the tomb in the parish church of Sankt Jakob in Innsbruck, as well as the symbols and signs that should adorn his final resting place. The gravestone was to be decorated only with the Prussian Cross of the Teutonic Order and an image of St George slaying the dragon. That Maximilian invested some energy in creating a representative tomb can also be seen in the fact that he was successful in getting the Dutch sculptor Hubert Gerhaert to execute his plans for the monument – a success that was not granted to his brother Albert, who also tried to bring Gerhaert to his court in Brussels.[42]

The sources show various pious foundations made by archduke Maximilian, underlying his piety. Substantial letters of foundation bear witness to the extent of the donor's engagement with these institutions and his desire to provide exact regulations and requirements for the foundations.[43] One of these foundations, for example, commemorated Maximilian's majordomo Gregor Sobietzki, a convert from Russian Orthodoxy to Catholicism. His grave was located in front of the large Lady Altar in the parish church, very near to the gravesite that Maximilian chose for himself. Sobietzki's sister, Potentiana, was also buried near her brother's and later Maximilian's grave.[44] The financial arrangements for this foundation are revealing, for the endowment was deposited with the city of Innsbruck and not with the bishop of Brixen – a manner of proceeding that brought a protest from the bishop. The foundation seems to reflect the distance between the rulers of Tyrol and the bishopric, a distance that grew up in the last part of the 16th century due to disagreements concerning the political integration of the imperially immediate territories of Brixen and Trent into the Tyrolean Diet, and the financial duties this entailed. A controversy with Brixen

[42] Dudik, "Erzherzog's Maximilian I. Testament," 245; Thomas DaCosta Kaufmann, "Archduke Albrecht as an Austrian Habsburg and Prince of the Empire," in Werner Thomas and Luc Duerloo (eds.), *Albert and Isabella, 1598-1621: Essays* (Turnhout, 1998), 22.

[43] Among other works, see Dudik, "Erzherzog's Maximilian I. Testament," 243ff.

[44] Compare Hirn, *Erzherzog Maximilian*, 2: v316; Nolfatscher, Glaube, Reich und Dynastie, 230.

concerning the local subjects' act of homage also dates from the first half of the 17th century.[45]

The representation of Maximilian III as a "pious monarch" in the style of early Baroque Catholicism is interestingly at odds with the relaxed confessional atmosphere of his court in Innsbruck, as well as with his generally conciliatory attitude towards Protestants.[46] He was not only conciliatory, but pursued an active policy of non-discrimination against Protestants. Almost thirty years after the Council of Trent, a quite pronounced confessional openness prevailed in Maximilian's household. Already in Mergentheim, Maximilian had Protestant nobles at his court, albeit mainly in minor functions rather than exercising high office. In 1602, when Maximilian took up the governance of Tyrol, Rudolf II advised him to dismiss all the Protestant servants from his household, as non-Catholic confessions were not tolerated in Tyrol. This advice was rather more than a mere suggestion, since the emperor had quite an extensive right to a say in the composition of the households of family members.[47] But it is an advice that Maximilian appears not to have taken, for in Tyrol too, non-Catholics were among his closest counselors, including the aforementioned Gregor Sobietzki even before his conversion to Catholicism, as well as the "Reichspfennigmeister" Zacharias Geizkofler and the "Hofpfennigmeister" Ferdinand Grabner, both of whom were Protestants.[48] Of major significance in this context seems to be a visitation report from the year 1610 in which it is

[45] See Jürgen Bücking, *Frühabsolutismus und Kirchenreform in Tirol, 1565-1665: Ein Beitrag zum Ringen zwischen "Staat" und "Kirche" in der frühen Neuzeit* (Wiesbaden, 1972), 47-55, 106-115; Iganz Egger, "Die Stellung des Fürstentums Brixen zum Tiroler Landtag von 1620-65" (doctoral thesis, Innsbruck, 1971); Hirn, *Erzherzog Maximilian*, 2: 316f, esp. footnote 2.

[46] Noflatscher, *Glaube, Reich und Dynastie*, 226-229; see also Maximilian's cautious approach in the case of Bobenhausen, described in Noflatscher, *Maximilian der Deutschmeister*, 234-238. Maximilian's tolerance is also underlined by the fact that he employed a Hutterite (i.e. an Anabaptist) as personal physician. See Hirn, *Erzherzog Maximilian*, 1: 246.

[47] See Keller, *Hofdamen*, 36; regarding the confessional orientation of Rudolf's court see also: Noflatscher, "Rudolf II.," in Werner Paravicini, Jan Hirschbiegel and Jörg Wettlaufer (eds.), *Höfe und Residenzen im spätmittelalterlichen Reich: Ein Handbuch*, (Ostfildern, 2003), 388-397; Volker Press, "The Imperial Court of the Habsburgs from Maximilian I to Ferdinand III, 1493-1657," in Ronald G. Asch and Adolf M. Birke (eds.), *Princes, Patronage and the Nobility: The Court at the Beginning of the Modern Age, c.1450-1650*, Studies of the German Historical Institute London (London, 1991), 302.

[48] Noflatscher, *Maximilian der Deutschmeister*, 227, 229; Hirn, *Erzherzog Maximilian*, 1: 213 f.

mentioned that Geizkofler's whole household and all his servants were suspect in terms of their faith.[49]

This tolerance or confessional openness is not only represented in Maximilian's library, which contained a wide range of confessional and scientific titles,[50] but can also be substantiated from the confessional politics in Tyrol, which around 1600 still involved the question of tolerating or expelling Protestants. On this issue the ruler came into conflict with the archbishops of Salzburg, in particular, who were given to demanding that Protestants be expelled from those areas of Tyrol that were parts of the archdiocese of Salzburg.[51] Maximilian III's tolerant and friendly disposition towards Protestants can be illustrated in the case of the Rosenberg family, a Protestant family that had mining rights in the Kitzbühel area. In the 1620s – by which time Leopold V was ruling – the Rosenbergs came under confessional pressure, with mandates requiring their expulsion. In a petition to Leopold V, the Rosenbergs pleaded for the right to stay, with an especially illuminating line of argument: they praise the "Religions tolleranz" that prevailed under Maximilian III. He had assured the family of their right to stay without molestation on religious grounds.[52] Nevertheless, the petition was unsuccessful and the Rosenbergs were forced to leave Tyrol. Thus we get a picture of a pronouncedly pious court that at the same time showed tolerance and a willingness to integrate confessional dissenters, apparently sometimes going against the head of the family to do so.

Alongside, and perhaps in part because of, the spiritual emphasis of courtly representations, court life in Innsbruck under Maximilian III was rather quiet. The household contained only 163 persons, a fraction of the size of the imperial household in Vienna, which until the second half of the 17th century numbered around 1,200 persons,

[49] Albert Forer, "Die nachtridentinischen kirchlichen Verhältnisse der Diözese Brixen von 1570-1613 im Spiegel der Visitationsprotokolle" (doctoral thesis, Innsbruck, 1970), 86.

[50] For an analysis, see Ursula Stampfer, "Die Hofbibliothek Erzherzog Maximilians III. von Österreich (1558-1618)" (doctoral thesis, Innsbruck, 2008).

[51] Karl Kirchmair, "Die religiöse Lage Tirols während der Regierungszeit Erzherzog Leopolds V." (doctoral thesis, Innsbruck, 1950), 122.

[52] Rosenberger petition, 19 January 1621, Tiroler Landesarchiv Innsbruck, Sammelakten, Reihe B, Abt. XV, Lage 3, No. 4; Astrid von Schlachta, "Wie geheim war der Protestantismus in Tirol? Protestantische Strömungen zwischen bäuerlicher Gesellschft und staatlich-kirchlichem Konformitätsdruck," in Georg Jäger and Ulrich Pfister (eds.), *Konfessionalisierung und Konfessionskonflikt in Graubünden, 16.-18. Jahrhundert* (Zürich, 2006), 79-109.

or the household of the Medici in Florence, which around the year 1600 comprised 500 souls.[53] It is recorded that the court music attained some renown, especially under Hofkapellmeister Johann Stadlmeyer. Regarding festivities, only one major event is recorded, moreover one that focused on the neighboring city of Hall and was also connected to the spiritual sphere. The archduchesses Maria Christina and Eleanor, daughters of Karl of Inner Austria, finally entered the Damenstift in Hall in 1607.[54]

Major architectural changes in Innsbruck are not recorded from the times of Maximilian III, or rather the impetus for them did not come from him.[55] Some changes in the appearance of the Innsbruck court go back to decisions taken by the former ruler, Anna Catherina Gonzaga. In 1607, she founded the cloister ensemble of the Versperrte Kloster and the Regelhaus. These architectonic changes were only marginal compared to the whole Hofburg complex, which suggests that archduke Maximilian had sparse ambitions to represent his power in buildings. Highly significant in this context is also the perception of the Hofburg itself, which was the central residence of the sovereign. The building was perceived as dark and depressing, gloomy and full of melancholy. A letter sent from Innsbruck to Vienna on December 12, 1619, describes the Hofburg as follows: "So gibt doch der augenschein mit sich, daß selbige gemach sonderß schwöchmüettig vnd kheines wehgs zurathen sein werde Jetziger Kay: Junge Herrschafft dahin zu

[53] See Hirn, *Erzherzog Maximilian*, 2:314; Martin Scheutz and Jacob Wührer, "Dienst, Pflicht, Ordnung und 'Gute Policey': Instruktionsbücher am Wiener Hof im 17. und 18. Jahrhundert," in *Der Wiener Hof* [see n. 2], 21; Jeroen Duindam, "The Court of the Austrian Habsburgs, *c.*1500-1750," in John Adamson (ed.), *The Princely Courts of Europe: Ritual, Politics and Culture under the Ancien Régime, 1500-1750* (London, 1998), 168; Mark Hengerer, *Kaiserhof und Adel in der Mitte des 17. Jahrhunderts: Eine Kommunikationsgeschichte der Macht in der Vormoderne*, Historische Kulturwissenschaft 3 (Constance, 2004), 35-63; Marcello Fantoni, "The Courts of the Medici, 1532-1737," in *The Princely Courts of Europe*, 262.

[54] Theophil Antonicek, "Die höfische Musik von Maximilian III. bis zur Auflösung der Hofkapelle," in *Musikgeschichte Tirols* [see n. 33], 2: 40f; Zoller, *Geschichte und Denkwürdigkeiten*, 1: 292.

[55] Regarding dynastic programs in Early Modern Court architecture, see Peter-Michael Hahn, "Das Residenzschloss der Frühen Neuzeit: Dynastisches Monument und Instrument fürstlicher Herrschaft," in Werner Paravicini (ed.), *Das Gehäuse der Macht: Der Raum der Herrschaft im interkulturellen Vergleich; Antike, Mittelalter, Frühe Neuzeit*, Mitteilungen der Residenzen-Kommission der Akademie der Wissenschaften zu Göttingen, Sonderheft 7 (Kiel, 2005), 55-74.

hofieren, ..."[56] Still in 1628, Philipp Hainhofer writes of the Hofburg: "Die Alte Burg ist ain sehr weitleuffes gebew von villem vnderkommen, aber gar melancholisch und altfränckhisch erbawet."[57] In contrast, the gardens of the Ruhelust, with the associated summer residence, were perceived as friendly and warm.[58]

Organization and structure

Regarding the organization and form of his government, Maximilian fell back upon structures that had been passed down from the times of Ferdinand II and earlier. The two key administrative bodies were the *Regiment* and the *Kammer*, above them was the *Hofrat* as highest authority or tribunal of appeal. The Hofrat assembled the highest *Hofchargen* and gave advice to the sovereign on important matters. After Ferdinand II's death a break within the administration occurred due to the interregnum. The Hofrat was liquidated and the positions of Hofchargen dissolved, with only the Hofkanzler remaining in office, and a new authority, the *Tirolische Departement* in Prague, was brought into being to replace it.[59] After 1602, in line with the stipulations of the Prager Rezeß, an assistant council (*Assistenzrat*) was established for Maximilian III, consisting of two delegates from the imperial line and two from the Styrian line. The Assistenzrat was to advise him on important political matters. One of the councilors was Hofkanzler

[56] 12 December 1619, Tiroler Landesarchiv Innsbruck, Kunstsachen, I, 994.

[57] Oscar Doering, *Des Augsburger Patriciers Philipp Hainhofer Reisen nach Innsbruck und Dresden*, Quellenschriften für Kunstgschichte und Kunsttechnik des Mittelalters und der Neuzeit, N.F., 10 (Vienna, 1901), 39; see also the description of the Hofburg in Vienna from the 18th century and the conservative imperial program which is expressed in the Hofburg. The emperor symbolized the conservation of his power by keeping the Hofburg in the old style. See Andreas Pečar, "Symbolische Politik: Handlungsspielräume im politischen Umgang mit zeremoniellen Normen; Brandenburg-Preußen und der Kaiserhof im Vergleich (1700-1740)," in Jürgen Luh (ed.), *Preußen, Deutschland und Europa, 1701-2001*, Baltic Studies 8 (Groningen, 2003), 284.

[58] Regarding the Ruhelust see the newly published Huberta Weigl, "Der 'Neue Palast' in Innsbruck: Ein erdbebensicherer Residenzbau von Christoph Gumpp," in Martin Engel and others (eds.), *Barock in Mitteleuropa: Werke, Phänomene, Analysen*, Wiener Jahrbuch für Kunstgeschichte 55/56 (Vienna, 2006/2007), 111-129; also Johanna Felmayr, "Ruhelust," in Johanna Felmayr and others (eds.), *Die Kunstdenkmäler der Stadt Innsbruck: Die Hofbauten*, Österreichische Kunsttopographie 47 (Vienna, 1986), 626-639.

[59] Regarding these developments, see: Hirn, *Erzherzog Maximilian*, 1:1.

Friedrich Altstätter, who had already been *Regimentsrat* since 1578 in the Upper Austrian government; this provided some continuity of personnel in high office between the last court under archduke Ferdinand II and the new court. Soon, the *Assistenzrat* developed into the *Geheime Rat*, which again became the highest court authority and stood above the Regiment and the Kammer.

The internal organization of the courtly offices and of courtly representation fell back upon precedents that had been collected and summarized in a memorial by Carl von Wolkenstein, who had served as *Regimentspräsident* since 1591. The memorial compiled by Wolkenstein on December 24, 1602, shows the efforts to equip the single units with written instructions.[60] It thus lay in the competence of the Regimentspräsident to elaborate on the responsibilities of the different offices at the court and to prepare the definition of limits and authoritative power. To fulfill his duty Wolkenstein – another repository of memories of the last court of Ferdinand II – went back to the instructions of the *Regiment* and the *Kammerräte* – "eltere, vnd neue" – "alles fleiß ersehen, berathschlaget," so that in the "Räthen alls Canzleyen, allenthalben guete bestendige ordnung gepflanzet vnd erhalten werden mechte."[61] The memorial also provides information about how a new *Instruktion* developed. First of all, all former Instruktionen from the time of emperor Ferdinand I (1536) up to those of archduke Ferdinand II – the last one from 1566 was only valid for the duration of the archduke's expedition against the Turks – were read word for word. Then the compilers considered the old Instruktionen and deliberated on the new one and the current circumstances to which it should be adapted.

A phase of transition marks the time between the death of Maximilian in 1618 and Leopold's definitive move to Innsbruck in 1621. Three committees installed by the emperor saw to the inventory of Maximilian's possessions – the committees were staffed by members from each archducal line on equal terms. Delegates to these committees were dispatched by the emperor, by archduke Albert, and, as the new

[60] Regarding "Instruktionen" in general, see Mark Hengerer, "Die Zeremonialprotokolle und weitere Quellen zum Zeremoniell des Kaiserhofes im Wiener Haus-, Hof- und Staatsarchiv," in Josef Pauser, Martin Scheutz and Thomas Winkelbauer (eds.), *Quellenkunde der Habsburgermonarchie (16.-18. Jahrhundert),* Mitteilungen des Instituts für Österreichische Geschichtsforschung, Ergänzungsband 44 (Munich, 2004), 76-93.

[61] Tiroler Landesarchiv Innsbruck, O.Ö. Geheimer Rat, Ferdinandea, Pos. 55-56, Karton 50, hier Pos. 55, 1r (own pagination).

Grand Master of the Teutonic Order, by archduke Charles.[62] A letter from archduke Albert to Leopold V, written from Brussels on January 4, 1619, proves that the work of the committee was by no means free of conflict, and that the cousins had strong and divergent interests in the matter. Albert, ruler of the Habsburg Netherlands,[63] thanks Leopold in the letter that he had "vertreülich communiciert" regarding the imperial *Kammerdiener* Joseph Preschel who had some – possibly not legitimate or rightful – involvement in the committee that was to inventorize Maximilian's movables. Leopold's expression of opposition to the *Kammerdiener* met with Albert's approval. He assured Leopold of their ongoing "gesambten Intereses" regarding the matter and asks his cousin to continue to report to him "vertreülich" in future.[64]

Thus, the Innsbruck court saw a short intermezzo without a ruler after Maximilian III's death in 1618. Though Leopold was appointed governor in January 1619, he decided that Innsbruck would not be his sole residence, and continued to keep his court in Zabern. In October 1619, after the death of Markus Sittikus von Hohenems, archbishop of Salzburg, he made attempts to gain the archiepiscopal throne – an attempt that ultimately failed.[65]

In 1621 the Estates of Tyrol asked emperor Ferdinand II to urge his brother to relocate his residence to Innsbruck, as Leopold continued to reside at Zabern. He did, however, name the Tyrolean *Landeshauptmann* Jakob Andrä von Brandis – a Tyrolean subject – as *Geheimer Rat*; at the same time he confirmed the privileges of the city of Innsbruck.[66] The request of the Tyrolean Estates to choose Innsbruck as sole residence shows that Leopold was still maintaining a double residence and household. Leopold kept a traveling household for the first years of his reign, as is shown by, among others, the court musicians. In 1619 his accession to power had led to the dismissal of most of Maximilian III's musicians.[67] The musicians in the traveling household were

[62] Dudik, "Erzherzog's Maximilians I. Testament," 239f; on the conflicts between the Teutonic Order and the House Habsburg concerning the assets of Maximilian, see Noflatscher, "Erzherzog Maximilian," 321 f.

[63] See in general: Dudik, "Erzherzog's Maximilian I. Testament".

[64] Albert to Leopold V, Brussels, 4 January 1619, Tiroler Landesarchiv Innsbruck, O.Ö. Geheimer Rat, Ferdinandea, Karton 221, Pos. 249-256, Pos. 253, [1r]. On Albert, see Thomas and Duerloo, *Albert and Isabella*.

[65] See Weiss, "Erzherzog Leopold V.," 53-55.

[66] Steiger, "Erzherzog Leopold V.," 16.

[67] Senn, *Musik und Theater am Hof zu Innsbruck*, 205, 207.

supplemented with musicians from Hall and Innsbruck.[68] Not until his wedding with Claudia de'Medici did Leopold dissolve his household in Zabern; in January 1626 he was released from the clerical state and the bishoprics of Passau and Strasburg fell vacant.[69]

The sources reveal that in the first half of the 17th century, the Innsbruck court was in a state of flux, with neither ceremonial nor rank securely fixed. This gave rise to a number of problems that required solution, precedence being one of the thorniest issues in Early Modern court life.[70] Especially in the first years of Leopold's reign, particular care had to be taken to organize the court, its procedures and ceremonial – to create order. At issue was which predecessor court would serve as exemplar for the reorganization. The sources make clear that the court of Ferdinand II was the main model for the new guidelines. There are documents from the 1620s that testify how backwards-looking the new order was, and how the court took its lead from "alten Herkommen," from instructions inherited from the late 16th century, from historical traditions regarding ceremonial, rank and general procedures. The eruption of disputes over rank and precedence, which in Early Modern court life amounted to "symbolic, or rather cultural, capital,"[71] made it clear that regulations and instructions regarding rank were needed, and especially concerning "precedence and subsequence."[72]

There are some clues about the discussion in a few documents surviving from the early years of court life under Leopold V. The anonymous writer of a document of May 14, 1622, refers to a decree, recently issued by Leopold, concerning the question of the relative precedence of the *Hofkanzler* and the *Kammerherren*. During Maximilian's reign, the *Hofkanzler* was the head of the *Hofkanzlei* and belonged to the *Geheime Rat* as one of the four *Geheime Räte*. For the whole period from 1602 to 1619 the post was held by Friedrich Altstätter, who had been Regimentsrat since 1578.[73] Leopold's 1622 decree now determined that the *Hofkanzler* precede the Kammerherren in *Actibus publicis*. Nevertheless, at Leopold's court the rank seems not to have been fixed

[68] Mussak, "Hofleben und Kulturpflege," 25.

[69] Steiger, "Erzherzog Leopold V.," 41; Weiss, "Erzherzog Leopold V.," 68.

[70] See among others: Scheutz/Wührer, Dienst, Pflicht, Ordnung, esp. 35.

[71] Stollberg-Rilinger, "Zeremoniell als politisches Verfahren," 107; also: Hahn/Schütte, Thesen zur Rekonstruktion, 22.

[72] Tiroler Landesarchiv Innsbruck, Hofregistratur, Kanzlei Erzherzog Leopold, Sonderpositionen, 27-26, Karton 61, no. 34; on the importance of rank, see: Stollberg-Rilinger, "Zeremoniell als politisches Verfahren," 103-108.

[73] See Putz, "Beamtenschematismus," 36-39.

and the decree caused some turmoil. The writer of the document of May 1622 states on the one hand that he understands that special honor was due to the *Hofkanzler*, as the "fürnembst vnd lebendig Archivum eines Botentaten," and that he had a special reputation to maintain, but on the other hand he mentions an earlier discussion about the competences of *Hofkanzler* Hans Ulrich Hemmerle – a discussion that must have taken place in Outer Austria, where Hemmerle had been *Hofkanzler* in Ensisheim before 1620. At that time the dispute had been decided in favor of the *Kammerherren*.[74] The writer is afraid that Leopold's new decision would upset the longer-serving *Kammerherren*, who upon returning from the current wars would unload their vexation upon the writer. He therefore requested that Leopold issue regulations that would fully clarify the situation.

The Tyrolean court can here be seen looking back to developments in Outer Austria, where Hemmerle had been *Hofkanzler*, and the writer of the document of May 1622 includes Hemmerle's letter of appointment as *Hofkanzler*, dated February 2, 1616. According to that letter, Hans Ulrich Hemmerle had started his career under cardinal Andreas, then took service with Rudolf II, and finally went to Passau in 1613, where he served archduke Leopold as *Camer Praesident*. A short time later Hemmerle moved to Ensisheim and became a member of Leopold's household as *Hofkanzler* and *Geheimer Rat*. He therefore held an intermediate position between Leopold and the *Geheime Rat*, and he became one of Leopold's closest confidants.[75] Hemmerle was also occupied with restructuring the finances, a weighty task insofar as Leopold had run into debt after his attempt on Jülich and the levying of an army that had failed to seize Prague in 1611.[76] Later, Hemmerle's experience in financial matters enabled him to encourage reforms of the coinage in Tyrol.[77]

The changes in the ceremonial regulation of precedence and subsequence, and the right of precedence of the *Kammerherren* over the *Hofkanzler*, reveal the lack of consistency of ceremonial structures at the court in Innsbruck and the need for regulations. Looking at the

[74] Tiroler Landesarchiv Innsbruck, Hofregistratur, Kanzlei Erzherzog Leopold, Sonderpositionen, 27-26, Karton 61.

[75] Archduke Leopold V., 16 February 1616, Tiroler Landesarchiv Innsbruck, Hofregistratur, Kanzlei Erzherzog Leopold, Sonderpositionen, 27-26, Karton 61, [1v].

[76] Weiss, "Erzherzog Leopold V.," 43-45.

[77] Raimund Tasser, "Beamtenschematismus der drei oberösterreichischen Wesen in den Jahren 1619-1632" (doctoral thesis, Innsbruck, 1973), 213f.

developments in Innsbruck alongside those at the court in Vienna, we can see that the ceremonial of the imperial court had also not yet taken a fixed form in the first half of the 17th century. The first order of precedence dates only from 1637, and the allocation of rank that it provided was not accepted by all groups at the imperial court until the reigns of Joseph I and Charles VI.[78] Andreas Pečar furthermore emphasizes the primacy of the courtly office-holders over the hereditary nobility. Thus, at least in the late 17th century, the *Kämmerer* and the *Geheime Räte* at the imperial court were more privileged ceremonially than the hereditary noble ranks.[79]

The document just discussed concerning precedence and degree possibly also fits into another discussion that dates from the latter period of Maximilian III's reign.[80] An "Extract" about how in the times of the deceased Ferdinand II "mit dero hochen Officiern unnd Räthen, des Vorgangs halber vngeuehrlich gehalten worden," passes down the practices of the "Vorgehen" of the times of Ferdinand II, as well as for the times before and after 1612.[81] The significant changes concern the *Geheime Räte*, who after 1612 collectively had the first place after Maximilian. Then followed the *Kammerherren*, and then the *Regierung* and *Kammer*. Under Ferdinand II and before 1612, the *Obrist-Hofmeister* and the *Obrist-Kämmerer* had the first place, immediately behind the sovereign; then followed the *Hofkanzler*, and behind him the *Regimentspräsident* of Upper Austria and the *Kanzler* of Tyrol. In 1602 the order changed somewhat, since Carl von Wolkenstein, *Regimentspräsident* of Upper Austria, had to cede precedence to the *Obrist-Hofmeister* and was followed by the *Hofkanzler*.

[78] Irmgard Pangerl, "'Höfische Öffentlichkeit': Fragen des Kammerzutritts und der räumlichen Repräsentation am Wiener Hof," in *Der Wiener Hof im Spiegel der Zeremonialprotokolle* [see n. 2], 257; Andreas Pečar, "Das Hofzeremoniell als Herrschaftstechnik? Kritische Einwände und methodische Überlegungen am Beispiel des Kaiserhofes in Wien (1660-1740)," in Ronald G. Asch and Dagmar Freist (eds.), *Staatsbildung als kultureller Prozess* (Cologne, 2005), 392; regarding the Court in Vienna, see too Jeroen Duindam, *Vienna and Versailles: The Courts of Europe's Dynastic Rivals* (Cambridge, 2003); Press, "The Imperial Court of the Habsburgs," 289-312.

[79] Pečar, "Das Hofzeremoniell als Herrschaftstechnik?," 391.

[80] As Maximilian is not referred to as "the late" but the changes of 1612 are mentioned, it must be from the final phase of Maximilian's reign.

[81] Tiroler Landesarchiv Innsbruck, Hofregistratur, Kanzlei Erzherzog Leopold, Sonderpositionen, 27-36, Karton 61.

Important for all questions of rank and ceremonial at the court were those, such as Carl von Wolkenstein (mentioned above), who could provide a living witness to how things had been done at the court of Ferdinand II. Another figure consulted early on in Leopold's reign was *Schatzregistrator* Hans Finck, who had held this post since 1589.[82] Although he could not recall exactly how Ferdinand II had handled *Vorgehen* and *Nachgehen* in the case of the government, the *Statthalter*, and the *Präsident*, he did send a list with the names of those *Statthalter* who presided over the government from 1557 to 1589 – the last name given being that of Carl von Wolkenstein.[83] For details regarding precedence and subsequence, Finck indicated that the information sought should be available from the old *Hofkanzlei*. As sources for the information about the *Obristkämmerer, Küchenmeister* and *Hofmarschalck*, Finck mentions the "gewesten Hoffpfennigmaister Ambts Schrifften und Raittungen." In his written reply Finck includes another list from 1577 that records the money disbursed to the *Hofchargen* when Ferdinand II received imperial fiefs from emperor Maximilian II.

Outlook and summary

Finally, a short view of court life under Leopold V and Claudia de'Medici will illustrate the on-going changes of the court in Innsbruck up to the middle of the 17th century. Regarding representation and its general bias, from 1619 onwards, and especially after Leopold and Claudia's marriage, the court completely changed its image – a fairly lively court life returned to Innsbruck, and a small Baroque court developed. From the beginning, Leopold tried to legitimize and consolidate the power of his line – attempts that seem to be symptomatic for the beginning of new lines of succession. The household of Leopold and Claudia encompassed about 300 persons, some residing in the Hofburg and some in the nearby Castle Ruhelust.[84]

[82] See Tasser, "Beamtenschematismus," 167f.
[83] Tiroler Landesarchiv Innsbruck, Hofregistratur, Kanzlei Erzherzog Leopold, Sonderpositionen, 27-26, Karton 61.
[84] Steiger, "Erzherzog Leopold V.," 42f.

We have records of several festivities that were extensively celebrated and which were characterized by significant Italian influences.[85] Not only the opera flourished, but also other festivities; the *Roßballett*, for example, was danced in the Florentine style and apparently reached Vienna from Innsbruck.[86] The sovereign also initiated some significant architectural changes to Innsbruck's urban aspect. Endeavors to express the presence and the power of the sovereign were more ambitious than any undertaken by Maximilian III. In 1619 the foundation stone of the new Jesuit church was laid; the church was consecrated in 1646, and became the mausoleum for the territory's new line of rulers, the burial place of Leopold, Claudia, and their children. Furthermore, Leopold built the Court Theatre, and replaced the summer palace Ruhelust, which had burnt down in 1636, with the newly built Neue Residenz.[87] Under Leopold and Claudia there was also a flowering of courtly panegyric, reflecting the desire for a greater public profile and the social importance of events at court.[88]

As we have seen, in contrast to other Habsburg courts, and especially relative to Vienna, the Innsbruck court passed through considerable changes during the first half of the 17th century, in its representation, ceremonial and household. Tyrol's political-strategic significance, on the other hand, was largely derived from its geographical location in the system of the Habsburg lands, and was predicated with great consistency. In the 16th century the country already played an important defensive role as the western outpost of the Habsburg hereditary lands. Thus, Maximilian I had called the country a "heart of the Roman Empire" and "a bridge into Italy," and Charles V is quoted by the Tyrolean estates as having said, "that if Tyrol were lost, the hereditary lands in Germany could no longer be maintained," but as long as Tyrol was among the hereditary lands, it would be hard for enemies to "conquer the rest." Up to the 18th century the Tyrolean Estates used these statements to

[85] Sabine Weiss, "Der Innsbrucker Hof unter Leopold V. und Claudia de'Medici," in *Der Innsbrucker Hof* [see n. 5], 241-348; Oscar Doering, "Hofstaat, Hofsitte und Hoffestlichkeiten unter Erzherzog Leopold dem Frommen zu Innsbruck," *Neue Zeitschrift des Ferdinandeums für Tirol und Vorarlberg* 2 (1836), 17-57.

[86] Sabine Weiss, "Eine italienische Prinzessin als Landesfürstin von Tirol: Claudia de'Medici und ihre Rolle in der Tiroler Geschichte," *Tiroler Heimat* 69 (2005), 44f.

[87] Huberta Weigl, "Der 'Neue Palast' in Innsbruck," 111-129.

[88] Stefan Tilg, "Claudia de'Medici und ihre Innsbrucker Familie in der höfischen lateinischen Panegyrik," *Tiroler Heimat* 69 (2005), 17-25; for a general discussion, see Heldt, *Der vollkommene Regent.*

bolster their case for the importance of their territory.[89] An interesting antithesis, though, is a remark made by archduchess Maria of Styria in a letter written to Rudolf II in 1595, setting out her views on Tyrol and on the political situation in the land. She perceived Tyrol as being different from the other Habsburg territories. Maria's remark originates from the discussion after Ferdinand II's death concerning the future form of governance in Tyrol, and thus has to be contextualized. The archduchess positions her Inner Austrian opinion by saying that Tyrol would not need an independent sovereign, as the territory would not be threatened by outer enemies and the country furthermore was not troubled by religious conflicts.[90] Although the remark clearly has Maria's political agenda behind it regarding governance and the installation of a governor, it nevertheless shows a view different from the Upper Austrian perspective as put forward, for example, by the Estates.

One can conclude from the aforementioned facts that the installation of a governor or sovereign in Tyrol was by no means insignificant, but dependent on weighty strategic considerations. It was also important to the imperial line that the branch of the family ruling in Tyrol would not become too independent, but be committed to the wider interests of the House of Habsburg. The Viennese influences can be seen in the example of the guardianship of Claudia de'Medici after the death of Leopold V, when the emperor intervened decisively in the upbringing of Ferdinand Karl in order to avoid any possibility that the heir develop "alienations of sympathy from His Imperial Majesty."[91]

To sum up, one has to say that the Innsbruck court in the first half of the 17th century was marked by political constellations that showed it only slightly independent from Vienna and closely related to wider

[89] See Astrid von Schlachta, "Identität und Selbstverständnis: Die Landstände in Tirol in der ersten Hälfte des 18. Jahrhunderts im Vergleich mit Ostfriesland," in Gerhard Ammerer and others (eds.), *Bündnispartner und Konkurrenten der Landesfürsten? Die Stände in der Habsburgermonarchie*, Veröffentlichungen des Instituts für Österreichische Geschichtsforschung 49 (Vienna, 2007), 394-419; with regard to these arguments, see also Martin Schennach, "Der wehrhafte Tiroler: Zu Entstehung, Wandlung und Funktion eines Mythos," *Geschichte und Region / Storia e Regione* 14, no. 2 (2005), 85f. He remarks that the statements about the importance of Tyrol were only made to remind the Tyroleans to pay the requested taxes.

[90] Quoted after: Hirn, "Tirols Erbtheilung," 283.

[91] See the *Instruktion* "Puncta. So mit Hl. Volmär angehen Erzherzoglichen Hofkanzler, vor seiner abreis, in Ihrer Kayl: MayL. Namen, alhir zu conferiren und abzureden seindt," 24 October 1650, Haus-, Hof- und Staatsarchiv, Familienarchiv, A. Familienakten, II, 8. Testamente und Verlassenschaften, Kart. 76, 61r-69v, esp. 62r; see also von Schlachta, "Herrschen und vorbereiten," 34f.

Habsburg politics. This was especially the case under Maximilian III, who focused on conveying an image of piety and showed very few signs of initiative in representation and self-portrayal. The building program of court architecture in Innsbruck was, if anything, a spiritual program. With regard to the role of the Innsbruck residence and its household, research has shown that for Maximilian his residence in Mergentheim, where he was a sovereign in his own right, continued to play an important role throughout his reign. The court of the Teutonic Order was in large part staffed by nobles from the Habsburg lands. Heinz Noflatscher has pointed out that during his time in Innsbruck, Maximilian's "imperial range of action" unfolded through Mergentheim, his network into the Empire established mostly via the Teutonic Order.[92]

Under Leopold V, the Innsbruck court became somewhat more independent of Vienna, but this development was reversed under Claudia de'Medici. The fact that when Leopold's court was established in Innsbruck his court officials had to go back to the times of Ferdinand II to find models on which to order ceremonial and political structures shows the extent to which Maximilian's period of rule had represented a gap in the development of the Innsbruck court. In the early days of Leopold's sovereignty, court life was focused on his residence in Zabern, but it moved to Innsbruck only a few years later. Thereafter we can discern the development and expansion of an institution that could be classified as a "ceremonial court."[93] The evolution of a new line of sovereignty was legitimized and anchored by representation and memorial, by ceremonial acts and written specification. Thus, *Hofstaatsverzeichnisse* and ceremonial protocols emerged that gave norms for the life of the court and which were modeled on those of late 16th-century Innsbruck. This underpinned the rise of the new line and enabled the growth of their households, both Leopold's and Claudia de'Medici's. Nevertheless, this 'revival' came to an end when Sigismund Franz died in 1665 and the Upper Austrian countries came to be governed from Vienna in full.

[92] Noflatscher, *Maximilian der Deutschmeister*, 231; Stampfer, "Die Hofbibliothek Erzherzog Maximilians III. (1558-1618)," 15.

[93] Bauer, *Die höfische Gesellschaft*, 57-63; also Steiger, "Erzherzog Leopold V.," 43.

Quo vadis: present and potential approaches to the relations between the courts and households of the Habsburg dynasty in the Early Modern period

At present, there is an unprecedented level of enthusiasm for studies on the relationships within the House of Austria[1]. In very general terms, there are three main approaches being taken.

First is the cultural transfer approach that was developed in the 1980s by Michel Espagne and Michael Werner[2], which has since risen to prominence in the field of cultural history. This model aims to delineate the dynamic process involved in the transfer or exchange of cultural elements. This process, characterized by reciprocity and multipolarity, has three interconnecting fundamental components: the society of departure, the instance of mediation and the receiving society. This model has been adapted to analyse the exchange of diplomatic gifts between different courts, which in turn has led to the investigation of the decision making processes surrounding the selection of gifts, the intermediaries involved in the transfer, and the rituals associated with their delivery.

When investigating such gifts[3], the study of 'material culture' is also a useful approach – that is to say, the examination of all visible and concrete aspects of a culture, and in this particular case the relationship between people and the objects produced by a society. The materiality of such gifts was attributed considerable value by all those involved in diplomatic exchanges, and this was understood not only as the actual cost of materials and objects, but the perception of their physical presence as well[4]. The exchange of these goods (which were not always entirely

[1] Many thanks to Rubén González Cuerva for his advice regarding the current state of affairs.

[2] Michel Espagne and Michael Werner (eds.), *Transferts. Les relations interculturelles dans l'espace franco-allemand (XVIIIe-XIXe siècles)* (Paris, 1988).

[3] In particular, Bartolomé Clavero, *Antídora. Antropología católica de la economía moderna* (Milan, 1991).

[4] Marieke von Bernstorff, Sybille Ebert-Schifferer and Susanne Kubersky-Piredda (eds.), *L'arte del dono. Scambi artistici e diplomazia tra Italia e Spagna 1550–1650* (Milan, 2013), 8.

gifts) ranged from horses, jewellery and paintings to Mediterranean fruit seeds. In this field of study, we find the work of Diana Carrió-Invernizzi as applied to Habsburg Italy[5], as well as those looking at exchanges within the House of Austria, including Pablo Jiménez Díaz[6], Milena Hajná[7], Ferrán Escrivá Llorca[8], Almudena Pérez de Tudela[9], Annemarie Jordan[10] or Vanessa de Cruz's recent project conducted under the aegis of the 'Villa I Tatti' research institute at Harvard University's Center for Italian Renaissance Studies[11].

With regards to a second, seemingly more traditional political approach, two main lines of inquiry are being explored. First, adapting the classical field of biography to new research questions. Instead of simply writing about a particular historical personage, the current goal is to examine the life of a political actor, and to use it as a framework for analysing complex historical processes in detail. The ideal case is that of ambassadors or other dynastic agents, such as Luc Duerloo's research on

[5] In particular her *El gobierno de las imágenes. Ceremonial y mecenazgo en la Italia española de la segunda mitad del siglo XVII* (Madrid-Frankfurt am Main, 2008).

[6] His *El coleccionismo manierista de los Austrias entre Felipe II y Rodolfo II* (Madrid, 2001) is a pioneering work on the artistic exchanges among the aristocracy of Bohemia and the Spanish Monarchy at the end of the sixteenth century.

[7] For her research regarding the imposition of Spanish fashions at the imperial court, among others, see "Moda al servicio del poder. La vestimenta en la sociedad noble de la Europa Central en la Edad Moderna y las influencias de España," in Miguel Cabañas Bravo, Amelia López-Yarto Elizalde and Wifredo Rincón García (eds.), *Arte, poder y sociedad en la España de los siglos XV a XX* (Madrid, 2008), 71-82 o "*Premáticas de los vestidos* aneb Královská nařízení o odívání a módě v renesančním Španělsku," ["*Premáticas de los vestidos* or Royal Regulations on Clothing and Fashion in Renaissance Spain"] *Miscellanea Oddělení rukopisů a starých tisků Národní knihovny České republiky*, 16 (1999-2000), 189-208.

[8] In his study of the influence of Spanish court music at the court of Rudolph II via the works of Mateo Flecha (https://upv.academia.edu/FerranEscriv%C3%A0Llorca).

[9] Through her studies regarding exchanges with Bavaria: "Relaciones artísticas de los duques de Baviera con España en el reinado de Felipe II," in José Martínez Millán and Rubén González Cuerva (eds.), *La dinastía de los Austria: las relaciones entre la Monarquía Católica y el Imperio* (Madrid, 2011, III, 1769-1836), or with Anna of Austria: "La reina Anna de Austria (1549-1580), su imagen y su colección artística," in José Martínez Millán and María Paula Marçal Lourenço (eds.), *Las relaciones discretas entre las Monarquías Hispana y Portuguesa: Las Casas de las Reinas (siglos XV-XIX)* (Madrid, 2009), III, 1563-1616.

[10] With her work regarding Maria of Portugal and Joanna of Austria as collectors, "Dotes reales. Las colecciones de tapices de María de Portugal y Juana de Austria (1543-1573)," in Fernando Checa Cremades and Bernardo José García García (eds.), *Los Triunfos de Aracne. Tapices flamencos de los Austrias en el Renacimiento* (Madrid, 2011), 295-348.

[11] http://itatti.harvard.edu/appointees/vanessa-de-cruz-medina-0.

archduke Albert of Austria[12], Vojtech Krouzil's work on Juan de Borja y Castro[13], Rubén González Cuerva's on Baltasar de Zúñiga[14], or Tibor Martí on cardinal Pázmány[15]. Such individual case studies are useful in exploring some of the most common questions regarding dynastic relations: how an agent created and maintained a clientele in another court, the limits of service and conflicts over concurrent loyalties to several members of a dynasty, the ability to influence or pressure other ruling members of a dynasty, and the representation of the House of Austria via its members and servants to other powers.

The other political approach comes at the crossroads with social history, and involves the analysis of networks. Biographical research is not abandoned, but the analysis is primarily prosopographical in nature. This method attempts to give a global, comprehensive picture of the relational dynamics between the various dynastic courts, while emphasizing that such contacts and interactions were possible thanks to the existence of a large group of individuals willing to engage in mediation out of a mixture of self-interest and obligation. Friedrich Edelmayer explicitly takes this approach in his 2002 analysis of the client relations established by Philip II in the Holy Roman Empire by examining the profiles of the pensioners and mercenaries, which he identified with courtiers and soldiers[16]. More recently, Pavel Marek has focused his latest work on Spain's embassy in the Empire between the mid-sixteenth and seventeenth centuries, a centre of power he used to elucidate the client relations that the Catholic King tried to develop in the imperial court in order to advance his interests[17]. Meanwhile, new research by Étienne Bourdeu on the same period has expanded our view of the relations between the dynasty's courts, showing the complexity of contacts established between the Spanish monarchy and the Electorate

[12] *Dynasty and Piety. Archduke Albert (1598-1621) and Habsburg Political Culture in an Age of Religious Wars* (Farnham, 2012).

[13] *Diplomatické mise dvou větví habsburské dynastie 1577-1583* [*Diplomatic missions by the two branches of the Habsburg dynasty, 1577-1583*] (Prague, 2011).

[14] *Baltasar de Zúñiga. Una encrucijada de la Monarquía Hispana* (Madrid, 2012).

[15] He has dealt with the subject in several articles, including: "Pázmány diplomáciai hatása (A spanyol kapcsolat)," ["The importance of the diplomatic activity of Cardinal Péter Pázmány: the Spanish contacts"] *Jubileumi emlékkönyv Pázmány Péter egyetemalapításának 375. évfordulója tiszteletére. Szerk. Maczák Ibolya,* PPKE, 2010, 202-211.

[16] *Söldner und Pensionäre: das Netzwerk Philipps II im Heiligen Römischen Reich* (Vienna-Munich, 2002).

[17] Pavel Marek, *La embajada española en la corte imperial (1558-1641). Figuras de los embajadores y estrategias clientelares* (Prague, 2013).

of Mainz, a relationship mediated from within the imperial court and in which patronage strategies also played an important role[18].

Finally, the third approach consists of developing an intra-court analysis. This is being carried out via a project meant to elucidate the relationship between the two main branches of the House of Austria, centred on Madrid and Vienna, via the notion of 'the Spanish faction'. That is, to address the imperial court's power dynamics and its factional stratagems taking into account the long-term: the Catholic King's systematic patronage of a selection of the emperor's servants, who then had to find a way to reconcile at least two different loyalties. This project, directed by Rubén González Cuerva and Pavel Marek[19], aims to unite researchers engaged in the analysis of dynastic relations in order to further our understanding of concepts such as loyalty and service, power clique and faction, and to study these informal groups in order to flesh out the internal relations of the House of Austria.

As we have seen, new research into the relationships between the various branches of the Habsburgs in the Early Modern era are definitely moving away from old paradigms of international relations, and are increasingly making use of approaches that conceive of the relations between the two entities from a dynastic point of view, rather than that of the state. In this fashion, interdisciplinarity is also becoming prevalent, and the research on the subject is expanding. This book aimed to shed more light on these various approaches by demonstrating how joint investigations can overcome the traditional barriers that have, until recently, separated the various Habsburg branches during the Early Modern period.

José Eloy Hortal Muñoz, Dries Raeymaekers and René Vermeir

[18] Étienne Bourdeu, "*Le premier prince de l'Empire, le vote le plus sûr dont dispose Votre Majesté et sa Maison Royale*". *Les archevêques de Mayence et la projection espagnole dans le Saint Empire (milieu du XVIe siècle – milieu du XVIIe siècle),* (unpublished doctoral thesis, Paris, EHESS, 2012).

[19] The project's website can be consulted at http://faccion.hypotheses.org/.

Appendix: Principal offices of the court of the Spanish Habsburg kings[1]

Casa de Borgoña (Household of Burgundy)

1. Capilla (Royal Chapel)

- Capellán mayor (high chaplain, dean of the chapel)
- Limosnero mayor (lord almoner)
- Patriarca de las Indias (Patriarch of the Indies)[2]
- Teniente de limosnero mayor (assistant-lord almoner)
- Sumiller de cortina y oratorio (usher of the curtain and oratory)
- Confesor (confessor)
- Maestro de capilla (chapel master)
- Teniente del maestro de capilla (assistant-master of the chapel)
- Maestro de ceremonias (master of ceremonies)
- Capellán de altar (altar chaplain)
- Capellán de banco (chaplain of the bench)
- Capellanes de honor (honorary chaplains): capellán de Castilla, capellán de Aragón, capellanes de las Órdenes Militares (Santiago, Alcántara, Calatrava, Montesa, San Juan), capellán de la Corona de Italia (Nápoles, Sicilia y Milán)
- Musical offices: cantor (cantor), afinador de órgano (organ tuner), afinador de clavicordio (clavichord tuner), músico de vihuela (vihuela player), músico de violón (violone player), músico de corneta (cornett player), músico de bajón (dulcian player), músico del arpa (harp player)...

[1] The composition of the offices of the different courts of the Spanish Habsburg kings varied from one reign to another. As such, we have decided to use the list of the offices in the households of Burgundy and Castile during the reign of Philip IV because it is the most complete and the research is the most up to date. The offices in this list appear in singular, but some of them were held by more than one person at a time.
[2] Usually the offices of high chaplain, lord almoner and Patriarch of the Indies were held by the same person.

- Casa de los cantorcicos (Household of the choirboys): rector de la Casa (principal of the household), maestro de gramática (grammarian), cantorcicos (choirboys)
- Minor offices: cura de palacio (palace priest), ayuda de oratorio (oratory assistant), mozo de capilla y oratorio (groom of the chapel), sacristán (sacristan) ...

2. Oficios de la Casa (Household offices)

- Mayordomo mayor (lord steward or high steward)
- Mayordomo (steward)
- Gentilhombre de la boca (gentleman of the king's table)
- Gentilhombre de la casa (gentleman of the household)
- Contralor (comptroller)
- Grefier (greffier)
- Varlet servant (valet)
- Costiller (coustiller)
- Offices in the panetería (bakehouse), frutería (fruitery), cava, schançonerie (cellar), cocina (kitchen), sausería, salsería (salsery), guardamangier (larder), cerería (chandlery), botica (pharmacy), tapicería (tapestry works)
- Furriera (lodging masters): aposentador de palacio (palace harbinger), aposentador (harbinger), aposentador de Casa y Corte (gentleman harbinger), ayuda de la furriera yeoman of the harbingers), Sotayuda de la furriera o mozo de retrete (groom of the closet), Correo mayor (master of the post)
- Physicians: médico de familia (physician of the household), cirujano (surgeon), algebrista (algebraist), oculista (oculist), sangrador (phlebotomist), barbero (barber) ...
- Cleaning offices: alguacil de la limpieza de palacio (constable of palace cleaning), barrendero (sweeper) ...
- Portero de saleta (doorkeeper of the antechamber)
- Portero de palacio, ujier de la maison (doorkeeper of the palace)
- Artistic offices: pintor del rey (painter of the king), escultor (sculptor) ...
- Estados (estates): estado de la cámara (estate of the chamber) and estado de la boca (estate of the table), with steward, grooms and laundress

3. Oficios de la Cámara (Chamber offices)

- Camarero mayor (lord chamberlain)
- Sumiller de Corps (groom of the stool or stole, first gentleman of the bedchamber)
- Gentilhombre de la cámara (gentleman of the chamber)
- Maestro de la cámara (treasurer of the chamber)
- Secretario de cámara (secretary of the chamber)
- Escribano de cámara (notary of the chamber)
- Ayuda de cámara (valet of the chamber)
- Ujier de cámara (usher of the chamber)
- Jewelry: guardajoyas (master of the jewels), ayuda de guardajoyas (yeoman of the jewels), mozo del guardajoyas (groom of the jewels)
- Wardrobe: guardarropa (master of the great wardrobe), ayuda del guardarropa (yeoman of the great wardrobe), mozo del guardarropa (groom of the great wardrobe)
- Pintor de cámara (painter of the chamber)
- Músico de cámara (musician of the chamber)
- Entertainers: enano (dwarf), hombre de placer (jester), bufón (clown), loco (fool), negro (black African)
- Physicians: médico de cámara (physician of the chamber), barbero de Corps (king's barber)...
- Laundresses: lavanderas de Corps (royal laundress), lavandera de cámara (laundress of the chamber)...
- Craft offices of the chamber: sastre (tailor), calcetero (hosier) ...

4. Oficios de Caballerizas (Stable offices)

- Caballerizo mayor (master of the horse or high marshal)
- Primer caballerizo (first equerry)
- Caballerizo (equerry)
- Veedor y contador (clerk of the counting house and surveyor)
- Secretario de la caballeriza (secretary of the stables)
- Picador (lancer)
- Palafrenero mayor (serjeant palfreyman)
- Sobrestante de coches o cochero mayor (head coachman)
- Guardanés (harness keeper)
- Furrier (furrier)
- Correo (courier)
- Librador (avener)

- Varlet de Corps (valet)
- Craft offices: guarnicionero (harness maker), sillero (saddler), cabestrero (halter-maker)...
- Ceremonial offices: macero (macebearer), Rey de Armas (King of Arms)
- Offices related to carriages and wagons: cochero (coachman), literero (litter maker), lacayo (footman) ...
- Armory: armero mayor (chief armourer), armero (armourer), guarnicionero de espadas, espadero (swordmaker), arcabucero (arquebusier) ...
- Household of the pages: headed by the ayo de los pajes (preceptor of pages), pajes (pages), and 18 offices of teachers, cleaners, cooks, ... to educate the pages in being courtiers
- Mule stable: acemilero mayor (chief muleteer), veterinarios (veterinarians), carreteros (carters) ...

5. Guardas reales (Royal guards)

Guarda de archeros de corps (Archers of the king's guard)

- Capitán (captain)
- Teniente (lieutenant)
- Furrier (fourrier)
- Capellán (chaplain)
- Archeros (*Hartschiere*, halberdiers)
- Minor offices such as asesor (assesor), trompeta (trumpeter), herrador (farrier)...

Guarda española (Spanish guard)

- Capitán (captain)
- Teniente (lieutenant)
- Alférez (ensign)
- Secretario (secretary)
- Furrier (fourrier)
- Guarda amarilla (Yellow guard)
    - Sargento (sergeant)
    - Cabo de escuadra (corporal)
    - Capellán (chaplain)
    - Alabardero (halberdier)
    - Tambor (drummer)
    - Pífaro (fifer)

- Guarda vieja (Veterans guard)
  - Sargento (sergeant)
  - Cabo de escuadra (corporal)
  - Alabardero (halberdier)
  - Tambor (drummer)
- Guarda a caballo (Horse guard)
  - Cabo de escuadra (corporal)
  - Capellán (chaplain)
  - Escudero (squire)
  - Sillero (saddler)
  - Herrador (farrier)
  - Trompeta (trumpeter)

Guarda alemana o tudesca (German guard)

- Capitán (captain)
- Teniente (lieutenant)
- Alférez (ensign)
- Sargento (sergeant)
- Furrier (fourrier)
- Cabo de escuadra (corporal)
- Capellán (chaplain)
- Escribano (notary)
- Alabardero (halberdier)
- Tambor (drummer)
- Pífaro (fifer)

6. Caza (Hunting - from the Household of Castile)

Caza de volatería (Falconry)

- Cazador mayor (master of the foxhounds)
- Teniente de cazador mayor (assistant-master of the foxhounds)
- Capellán (chaplain)
- Secretario (secretary)
- Alguacil (constable)
- Escribano (notary)
- Cazador (huntsman)
- Cazador del búho (huntsman of the owl)
- Minor offices, as guantero (glover), halconero (hawker), trompeta (trumpeter)...

Caza de montería (Hunting)

- Montero mayor (master of the huntsmen)
- Sotamontero (assistant-master of the huntsmen)
- Secretario (sercretary)
- Pagador (paymaster)
- Capellán (chaplain)
- Montero de traílla a pie (huntsman on foot)
- Montero de traílla a caballo (mounted huntsman)
- Montero de lebreles (huntsman with sighthounds)
- Montero de ventores (huntsman with scenthounds)
- Minor offices: ayuda de montero (assistant-huntsman), criador de los sabuesos y lebreles (breeder of the hounds), cirujano y barbero de la montería (surgeon and barber of the hunt) ...

Casa de Castilla (Household of Castile)

Capilla (Chapel)

- Capellán mayor de la Casa de Castilla, arzobispo de Santiago (High chaplain, archbishop of Santiago)
- Predicador (preacher)
- Capellán de altar (altar chaplain)
- Musicians offices: cantor (cantor), organista o músico de tecla (organist), maestro de los ministriles (minstrels instructor), examinador de los ministriles (examiner of the minstrels), ministril de la capilla (minstrel of the chapel)
- Portuguese chapel offices: maestro capellán cantor de la capilla portuguesa (chief cantor of the Portuguese chapel), músico de cámara por la Corona de Portugal (chamber musician for the Crown of Portugal), cantor por la Corona de Portugal (cantor for the Crown of Portugal)

Offices

- Mayordomo (steward)
- Teniente de mayordomo mayor (assistant-lord steward)
- Veedor y contador (clerk of the counting house and surveyor)
- Despensero mayor y pagador (quartermaster and paymaster)

- Escribano (notary)
- Aposentador mayor (chief harbinger)
- Aposentador (harbinger)
- Médico (physician)
- Minor offices: corrier (corrier), bibliotecario de San Lorenzo de El Escorial (librarian of the Monastery of San Lorenzo), tesorero del Alcázar de Segovia (treasurer of the Alcázar of San Lorenzo), contino (contino) ...
- Musicians offices of the stables: ministril de la caballeriza (minstrel of the stables), trompetas italianas y españolas (Spanish and Italian trumpeters), atabalero (drummer)
- Montero de Espinosa o de Guarda (guard huntsman of Espinosa)
- Porteros de cámara (doorkeepers of the chamber): Madrid, Chancillería de Valladolid (Chancery of Valladolid), Chancillería de Granada (Chancery of Granada)
- Portero de cadena (chain keeper)
- Escuderos de a pie (foot squires)

Index

D

G

H

I

T

www.ingramcontent.com/pod-product-compliance
Ingram Content Group UK Ltd.
Pitfield, Milton Keynes, MK11 3LW, UK
UKHW051919100926
8556IPUK00021B/1269

9 789058 679901